PERFECT WORLD

4   Rie Aruga

Research Help:
Kazuo Abe (Abe Kensetsu Inc.)

contents

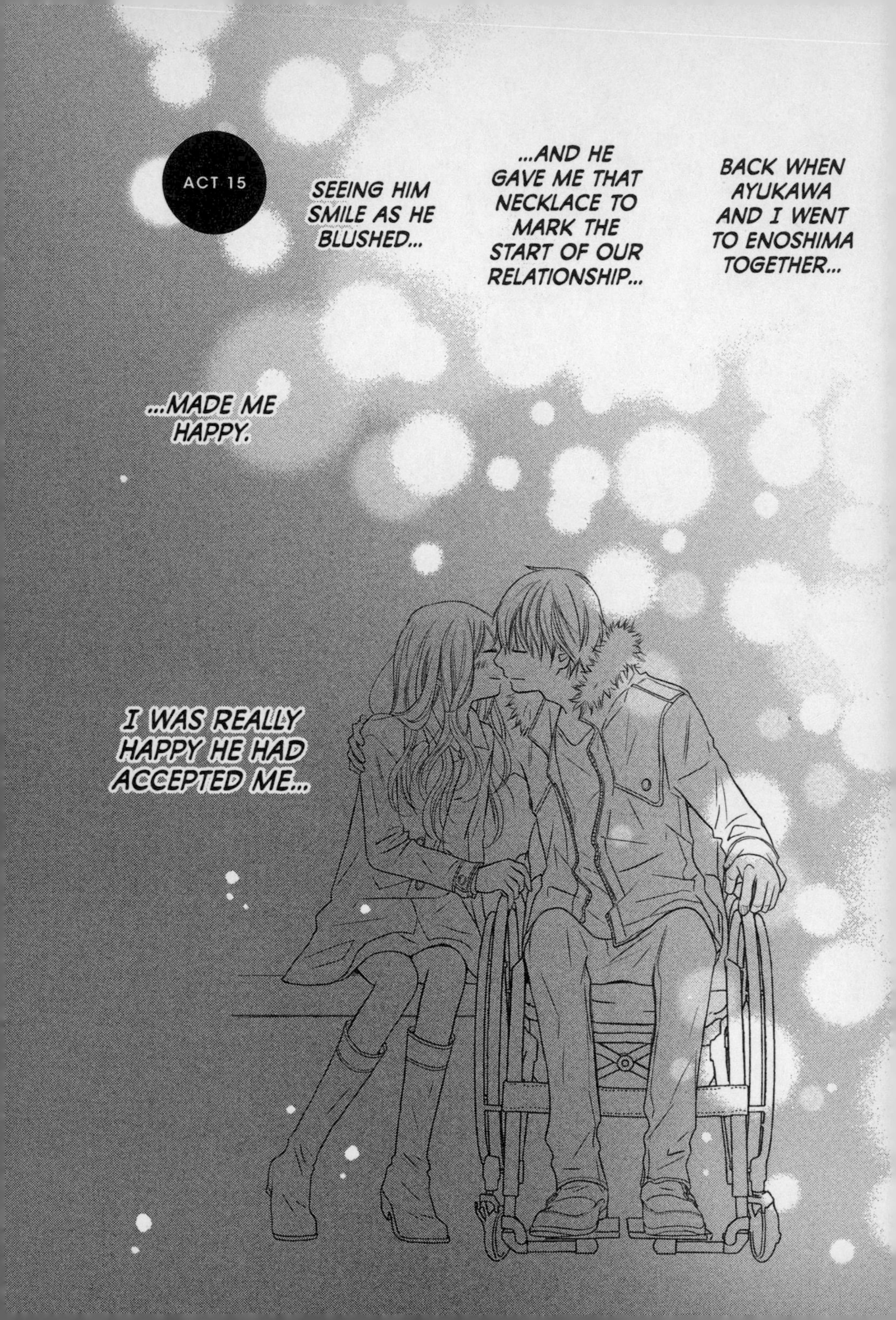
ACT 15
BACK WHEN AYUKAWA AND I WENT TO ENOSHIMA TOGETHER...
...AND HE GAVE ME THAT NECKLACE TO MARK THE START OF OUR RELATIONSHIP...
SEEING HIM SMILE AS HE BLUSHED...
...MADE ME HAPPY.
I WAS REALLY HAPPY HE HAD ACCEPTED ME...

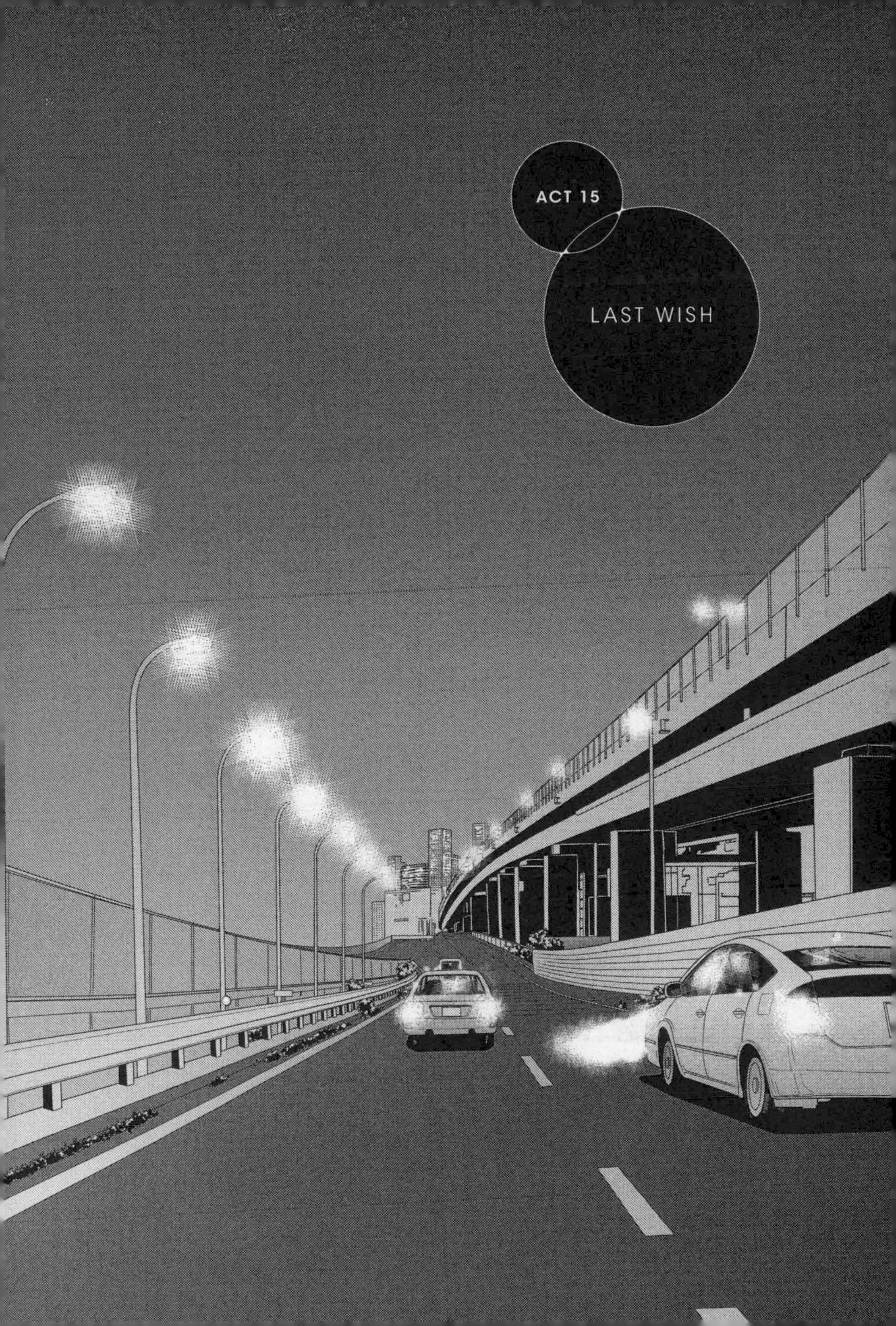
ACT 15
LAST WISH

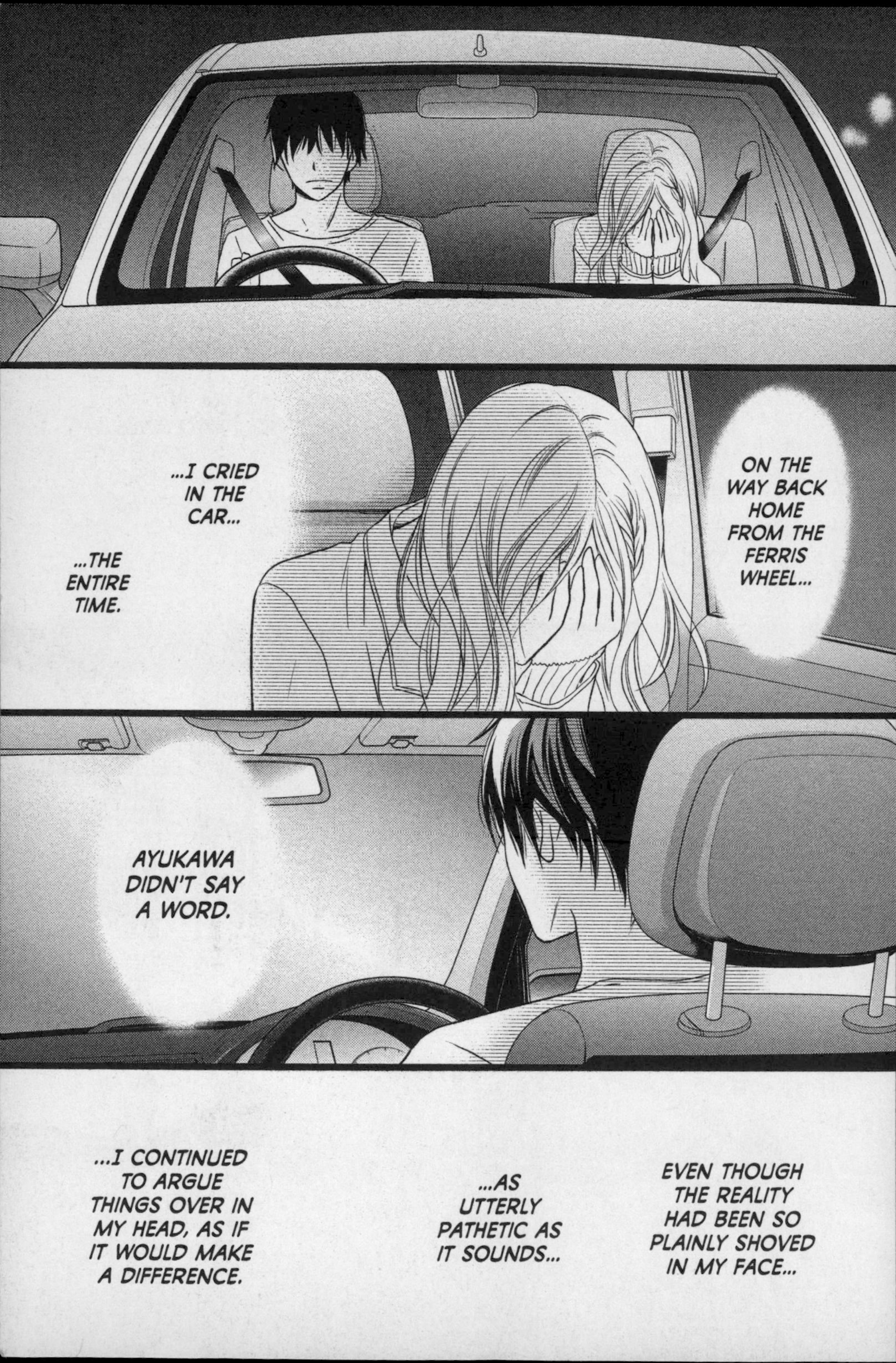
ON THE WAY BACK HOME FROM THE FERRIS WHEEL...
...I CRIED IN THE CAR...
...THE ENTIRE TIME.
AYUKAWA DIDN'T SAY A WORD.
EVEN THOUGH THE REALITY HAD BEEN SO PLAINLY SHOVED IN MY FACE...
...AS UTTERLY PATHETIC AS IT SOUNDS...
...I CONTINUED TO ARGUE THINGS OVER IN MY HEAD, AS IF IT WOULD MAKE A DIFFERENCE.

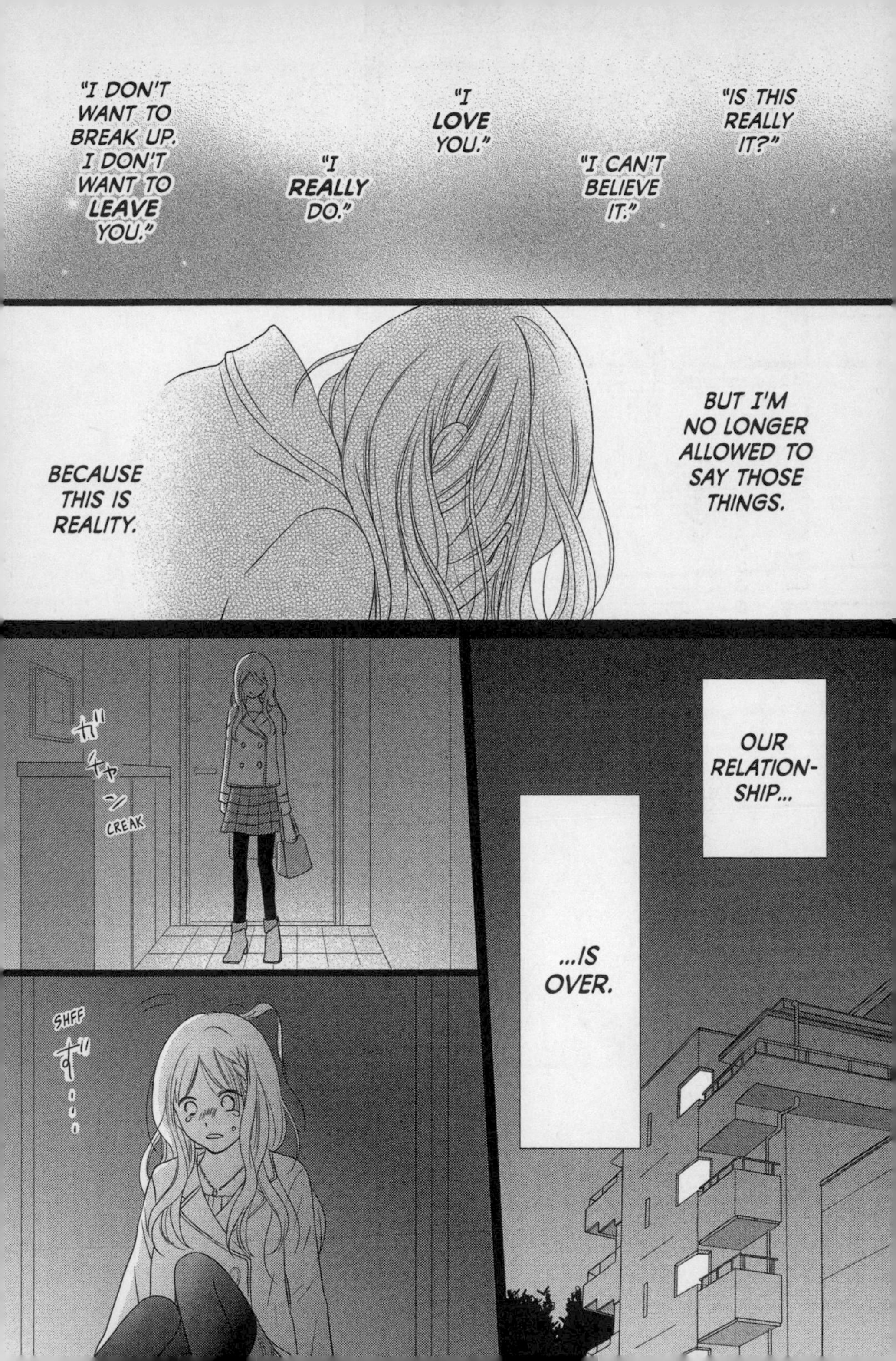
"IS THIS REALLY IT?"
"I CAN'T BELIEVE IT."
"I LOVE YOU."
"I REALLY DO."
"I DON'T WANT TO BREAK UP. I DON'T WANT TO LEAVE YOU."
BUT I'M NO LONGER ALLOWED TO SAY THOSE THINGS.
BECAUSE THIS IS REALITY.
OUR RELATIONSHIP...
...IS OVER.
ガチャン
CREAK
SHFF

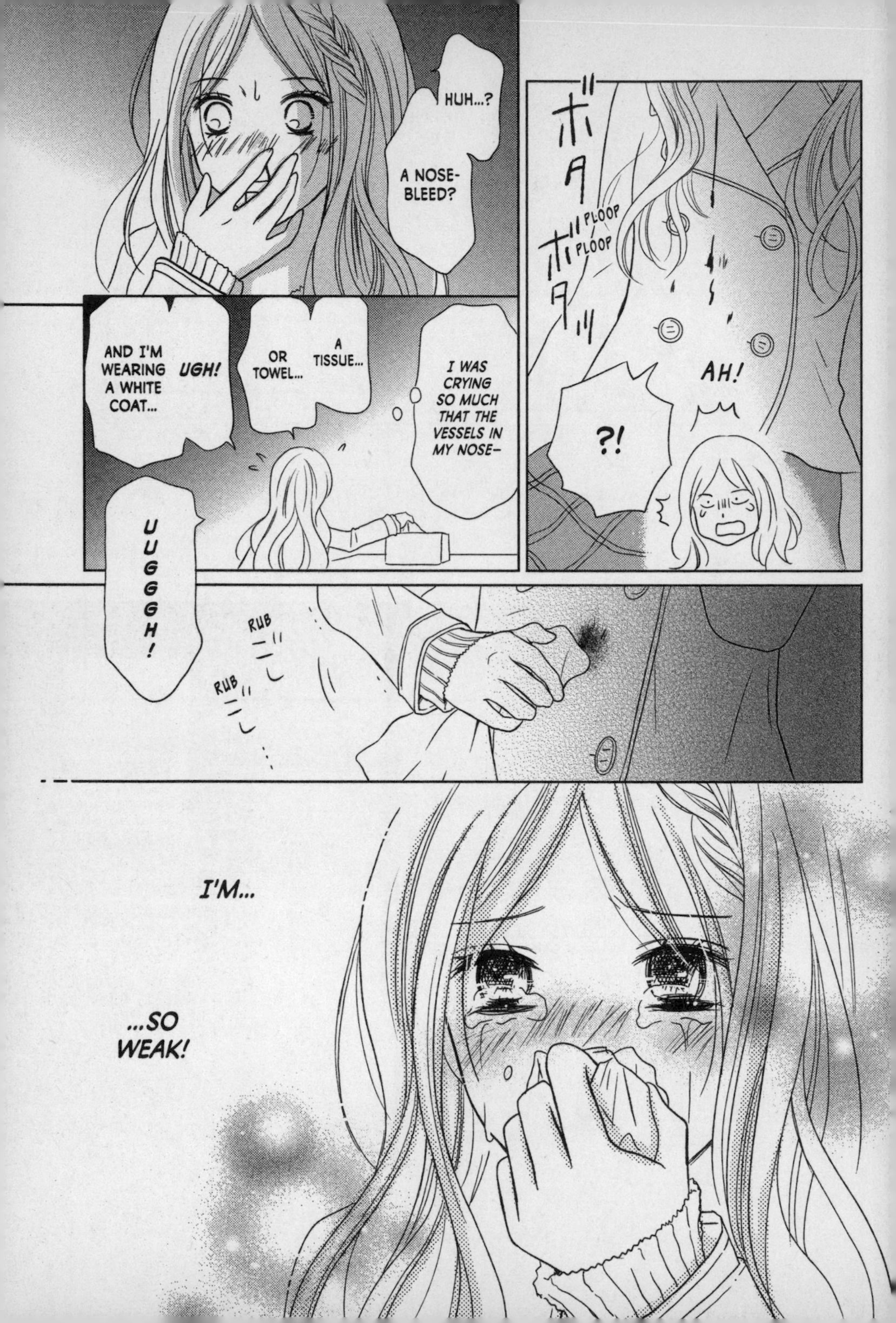
ボタ
ボタッ
PLOOP PLOOP
AH!
?!
HUH...?
A NOSE-BLEED?
I WAS CRYING SO MUCH THAT THE VESSELS IN MY NOSE–
A TISSUE...
OR TOWEL...
UGH!
AND I'M WEARING A WHITE COAT...
UUGGGH!
RUB
RUB
I'M...
...SO WEAK!

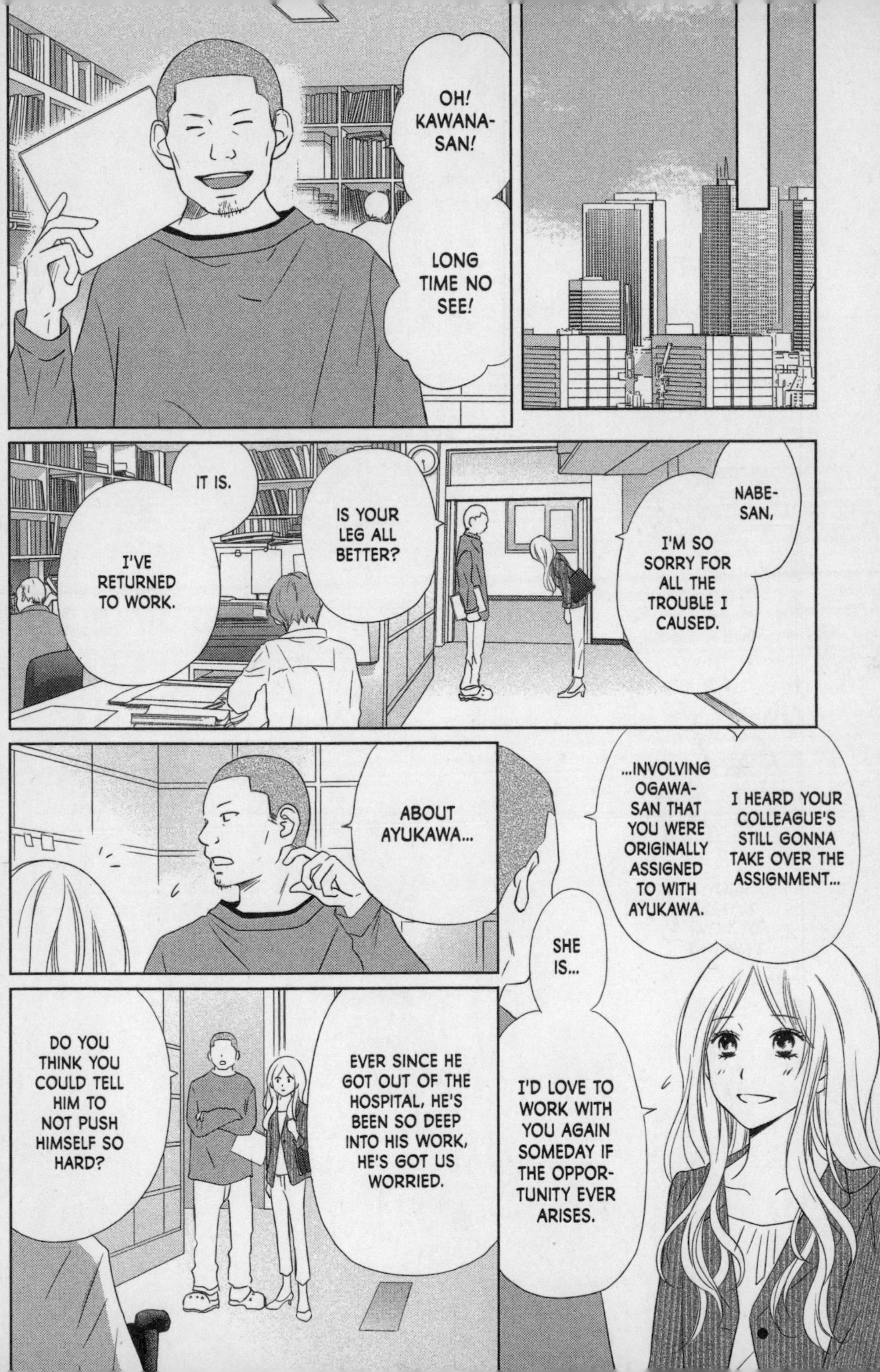
OH! KAWANA-SAN!
LONG TIME NO SEE!
NABE-SAN,
I'M SO SORRY FOR ALL THE TROUBLE I CAUSED.
IS YOUR LEG ALL BETTER?
IT IS.
I'VE RETURNED TO WORK.
I HEARD YOUR COLLEAGUE'S STILL GONNA TAKE OVER THE ASSIGNMENT...
...INVOLVING OGAWA-SAN THAT YOU WERE ORIGINALLY ASSIGNED TO WITH AYUKAWA.
SHE IS...
I'D LOVE TO WORK WITH YOU AGAIN SOMEDAY IF THE OPPORTUNITY EVER ARISES.
ABOUT AYUKAWA...
EVER SINCE HE GOT OUT OF THE HOSPITAL, HE'S BEEN SO DEEP INTO HIS WORK, HE'S GOT US WORRIED.
DO YOU THINK YOU COULD TELL HIM TO NOT PUSH HIMSELF SO HARD?

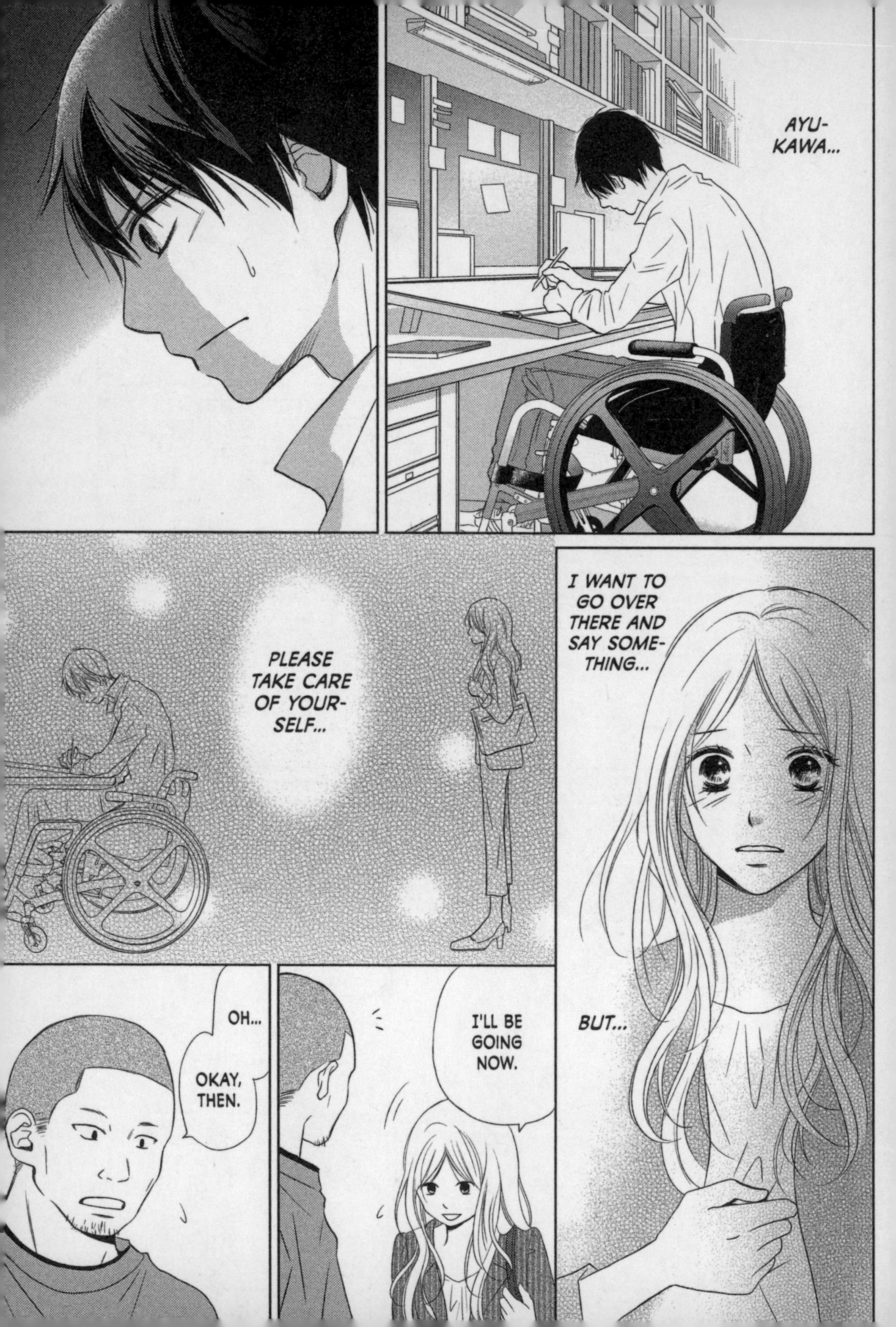
AYU-KAWA...
I WANT TO GO OVER THERE AND SAY SOME-THING...
BUT...
PLEASE TAKE CARE OF YOUR-SELF...
I'LL BE GOING NOW.
OH...
OKAY, THEN.

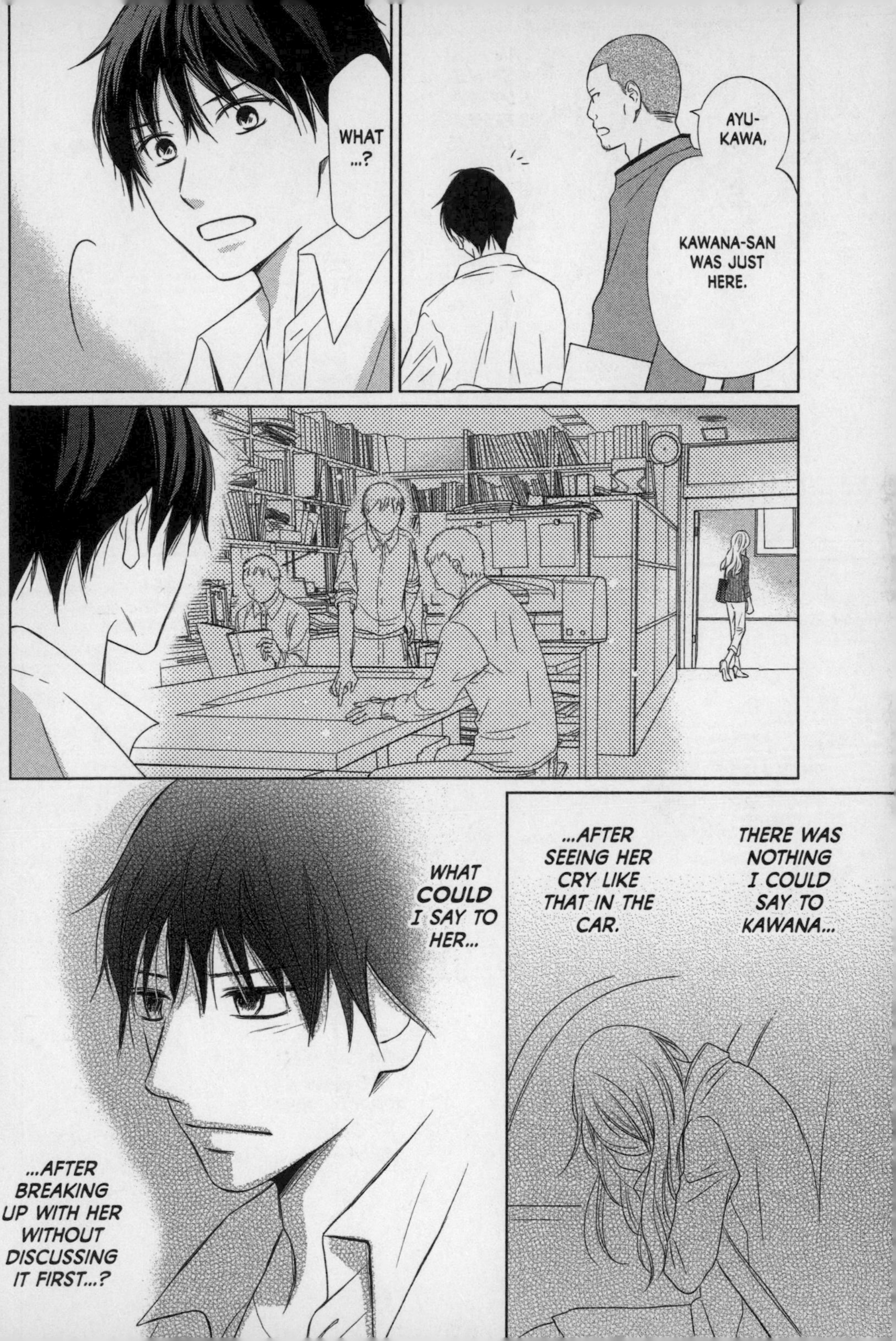
AYU-KAWA,
KAWANA-SAN WAS JUST HERE.
WHAT ...?
THERE WAS NOTHING I COULD SAY TO KAWANA...
...AFTER SEEING HER CRY LIKE THAT IN THE CAR.
WHAT COULD I SAY TO HER...
...AFTER BREAKING UP WITH HER WITHOUT DISCUSSING IT FIRST...?

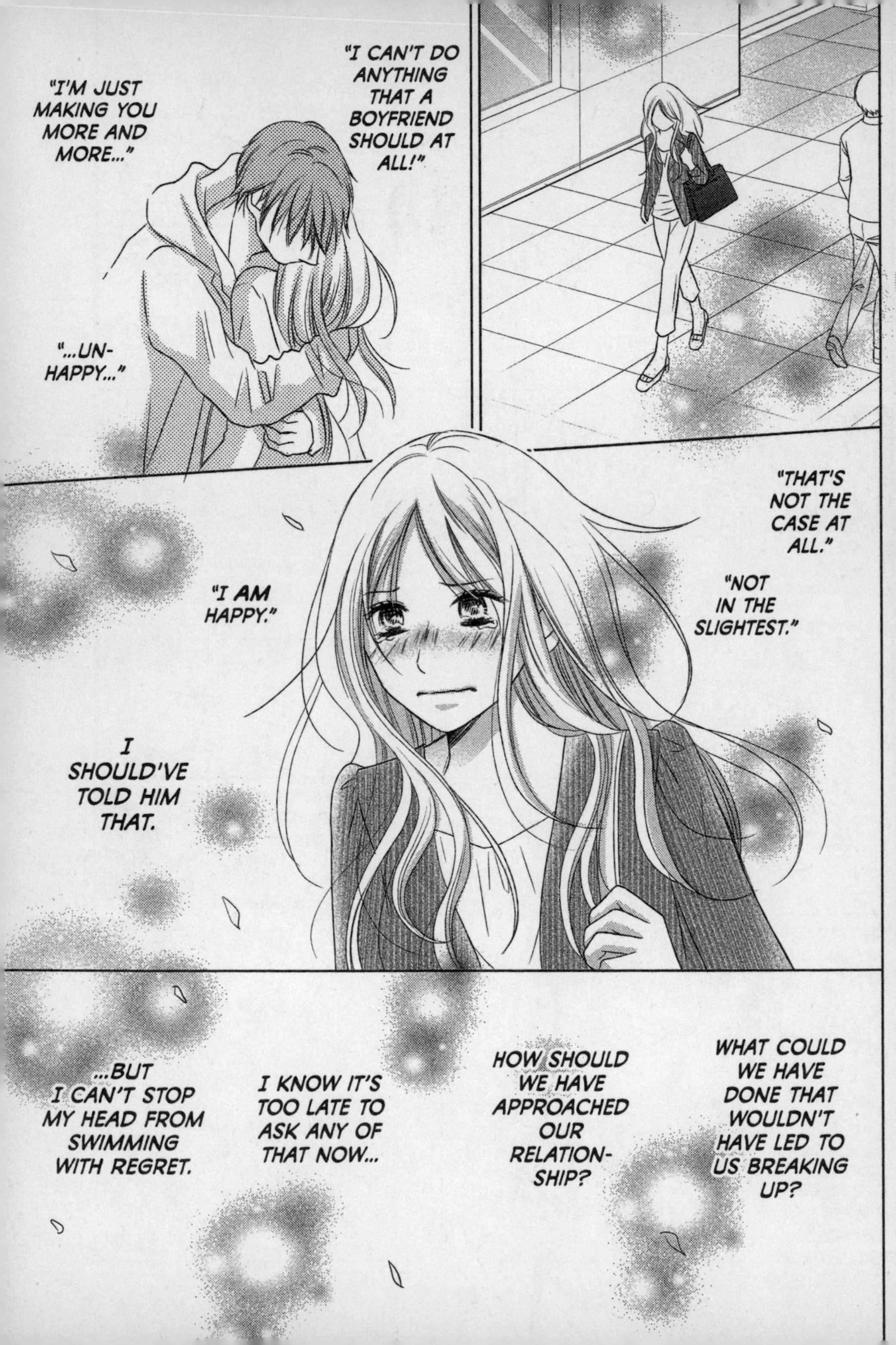

"I CAN'T DO ANYTHING THAT A BOYFRIEND SHOULD AT ALL!"
"I'M JUST MAKING YOU MORE AND MORE..."
"...UN-HAPPY..."
"THAT'S NOT THE CASE AT ALL."
"NOT IN THE SLIGHTEST."
"I AM HAPPY."
I SHOULD'VE TOLD HIM THAT.
WHAT COULD WE HAVE DONE THAT WOULDN'T HAVE LED TO US BREAKING UP?
HOW SHOULD WE HAVE APPROACHED OUR RELATION-SHIP?
I KNOW IT'S TOO LATE TO ASK ANY OF THAT NOW...
...BUT I CAN'T STOP MY HEAD FROM SWIMMING WITH REGRET.

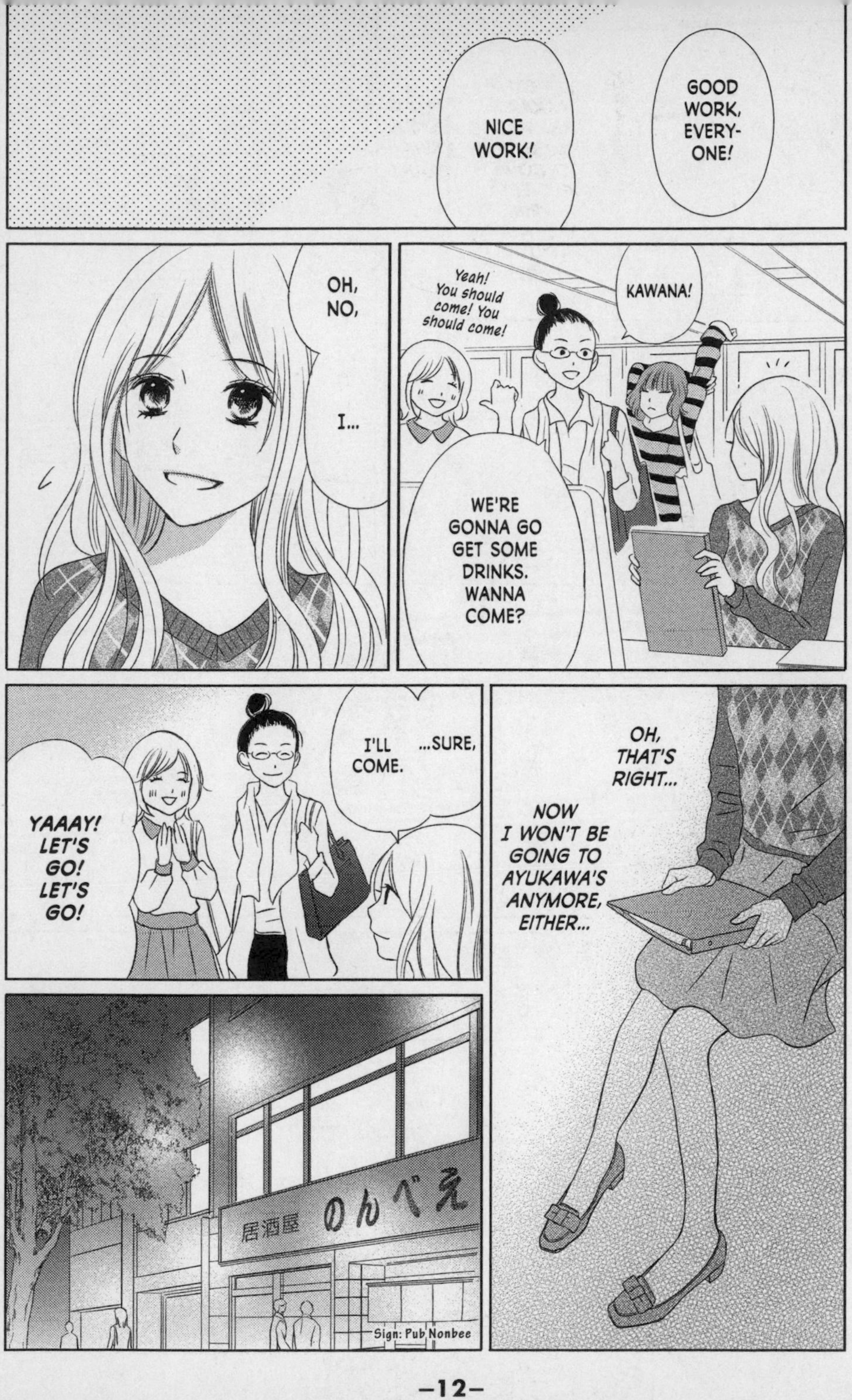
GOOD WORK, EVERY-ONE!
NICE WORK!
KAWANA!
Yeah! You should come! You should come!
WE'RE GONNA GO GET SOME DRINKS. WANNA COME?
OH, NO,
I...
OH, THAT'S RIGHT...
NOW I WON'T BE GOING TO AYUKAWA'S ANYMORE, EITHER...
...SURE,
I'LL COME.
YAAAY! LET'S GO! LET'S GO!
居酒屋 のんべえ
Sign: Pub Nonbee

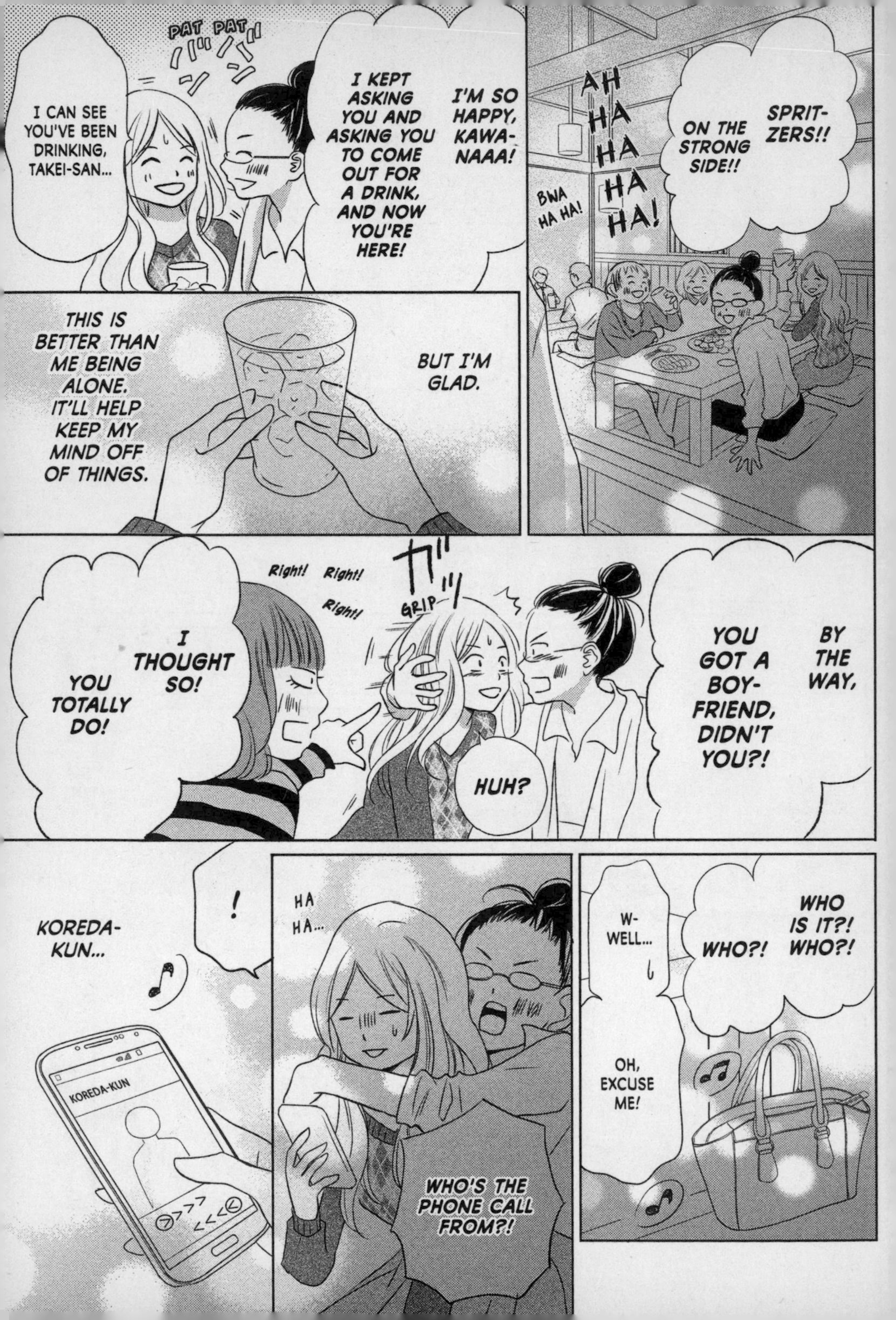
SPRIT-ZERS!!
ON THE STRONG SIDE!!
AH HA HA HA HA!
BWA HA HA!
I'M SO HAPPY, KAWA-NAAA!
I KEPT ASKING YOU AND ASKING YOU TO COME OUT FOR A DRINK, AND NOW YOU'RE HERE!
PAT PAT
I CAN SEE YOU'VE BEEN DRINKING, TAKEI-SAN...
BUT I'M GLAD.
THIS IS BETTER THAN ME BEING ALONE. IT'LL HELP KEEP MY MIND OFF OF THINGS.
BY THE WAY,
YOU GOT A BOY-FRIEND, DIDN'T YOU?!
HUH?
GRIP
Right! Right!
Right!
I THOUGHT SO!
YOU TOTALLY DO!
WHO IS IT?! WHO?!
WHO?!
W-WELL...
OH, EXCUSE ME!
HA HA...
WHO'S THE PHONE CALL FROM?!
!
KOREDA-KUN...
KOREDA-KUN

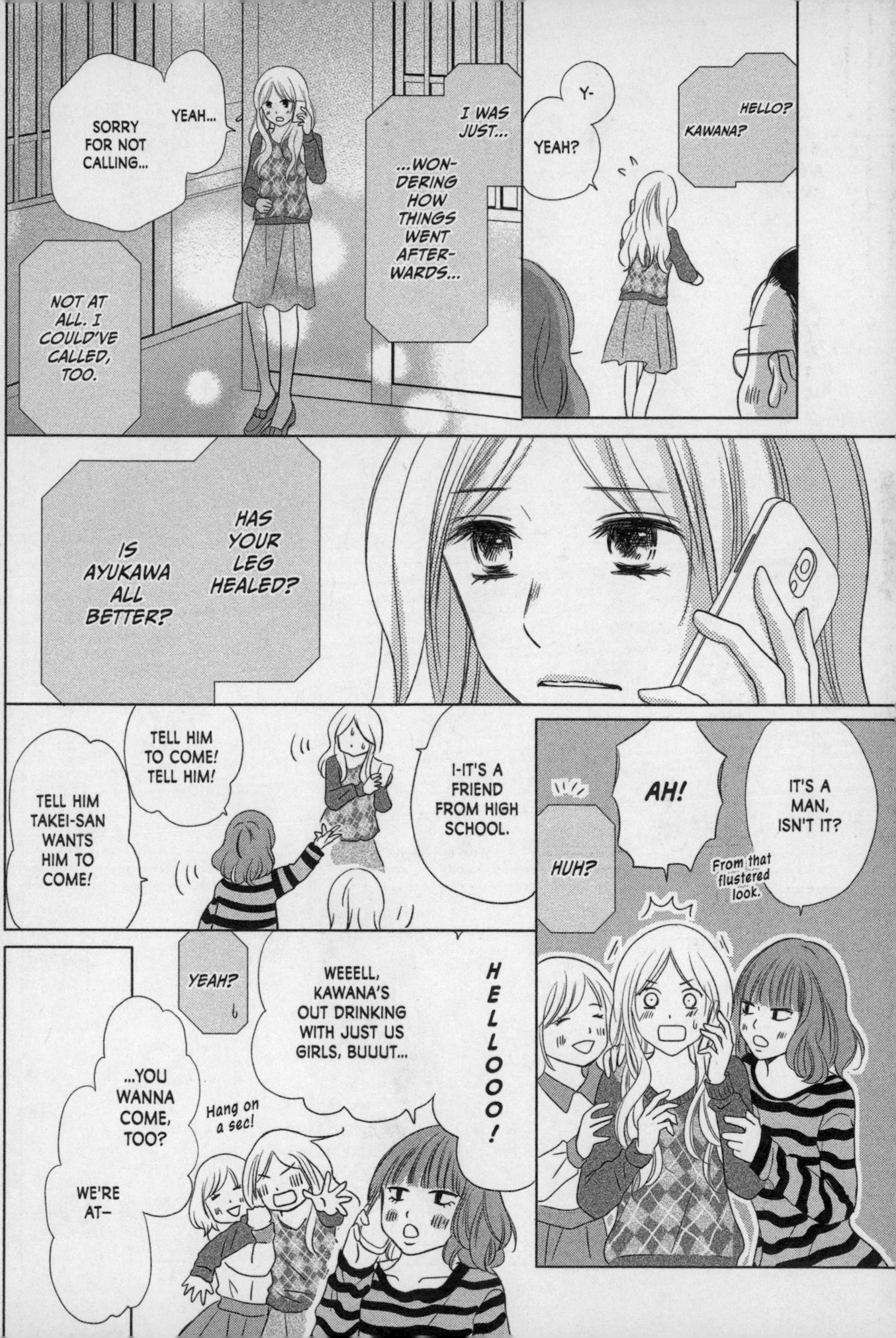
HELLO?
KAWANA?
Y-
YEAH?
I WAS JUST...
...WON-DERING HOW THINGS WENT AFTER-WARDS...
YEAH...
SORRY FOR NOT CALLING...
NOT AT ALL. I COULD'VE CALLED, TOO.
HAS YOUR LEG HEALED?
IS AYUKAWA ALL BETTER?
IT'S A MAN, ISN'T IT?
From that flustered look.
AH!
HUH?
I-IT'S A FRIEND FROM HIGH SCHOOL.
TELL HIM TO COME! TELL HIM!
TELL HIM TAKEI-SAN WANTS HIM TO COME!
HELLOOOO!
WEEELL, KAWANA'S OUT DRINKING WITH JUST US GIRLS, BUUUT...
YEAH?
...YOU WANNA COME, TOO?
Hang on a sec!
WE'RE AT–

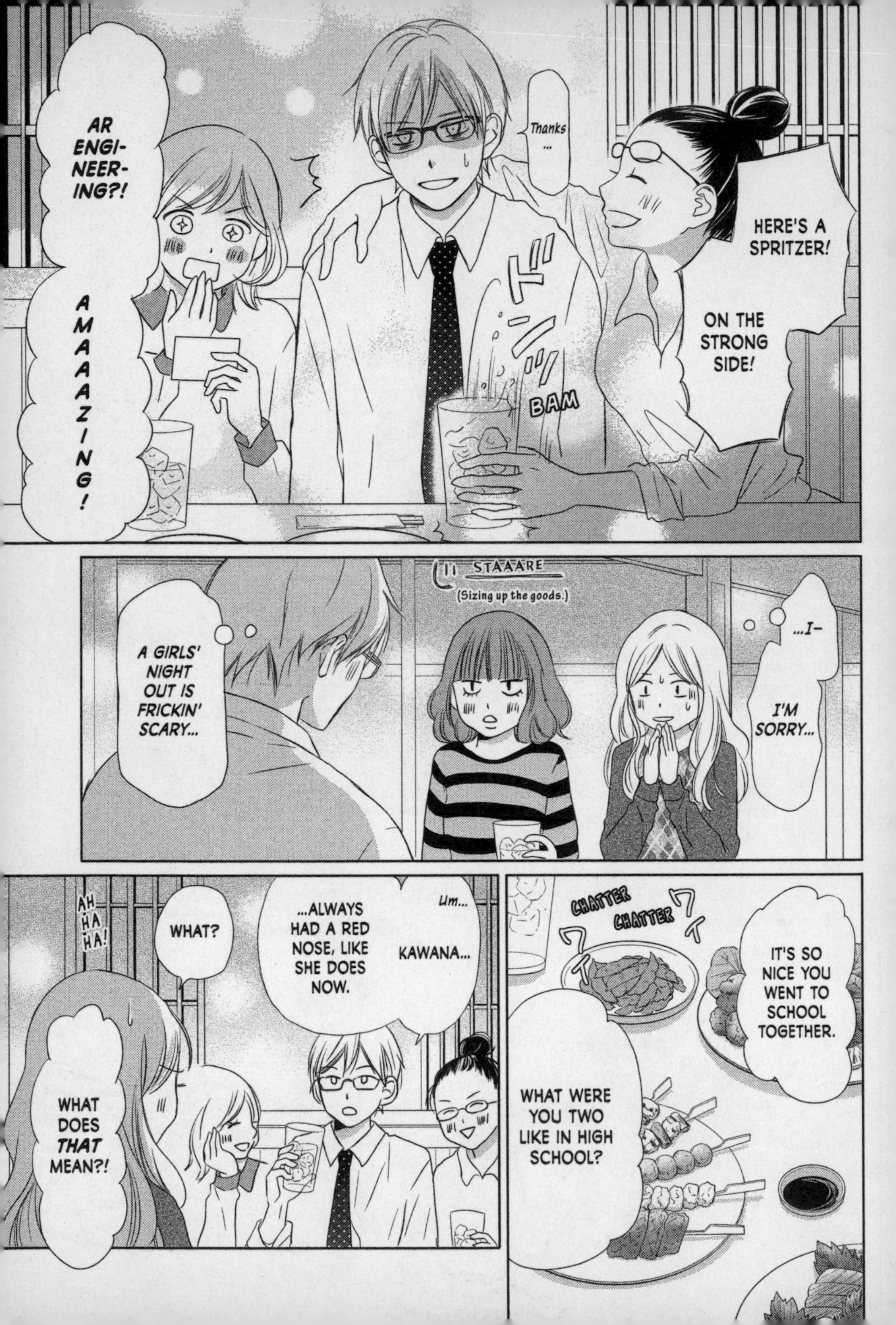
HERE'S A SPRITZER!
ON THE STRONG SIDE!
BAM
Thanks ...
AR ENGINEERING?!
AMAAAAZING!
STAAARE
(Sizing up the goods.)
...I-
I'M SORRY...
A GIRLS' NIGHT OUT IS FRICKIN' SCARY...
CHATTER CHATTER
IT'S SO NICE YOU WENT TO SCHOOL TOGETHER.
WHAT WERE YOU TWO LIKE IN HIGH SCHOOL?
Um...
KAWANA...
...ALWAYS HAD A RED NOSE, LIKE SHE DOES NOW.
WHAT?
AH HA HA!
WHAT DOES THAT MEAN?!

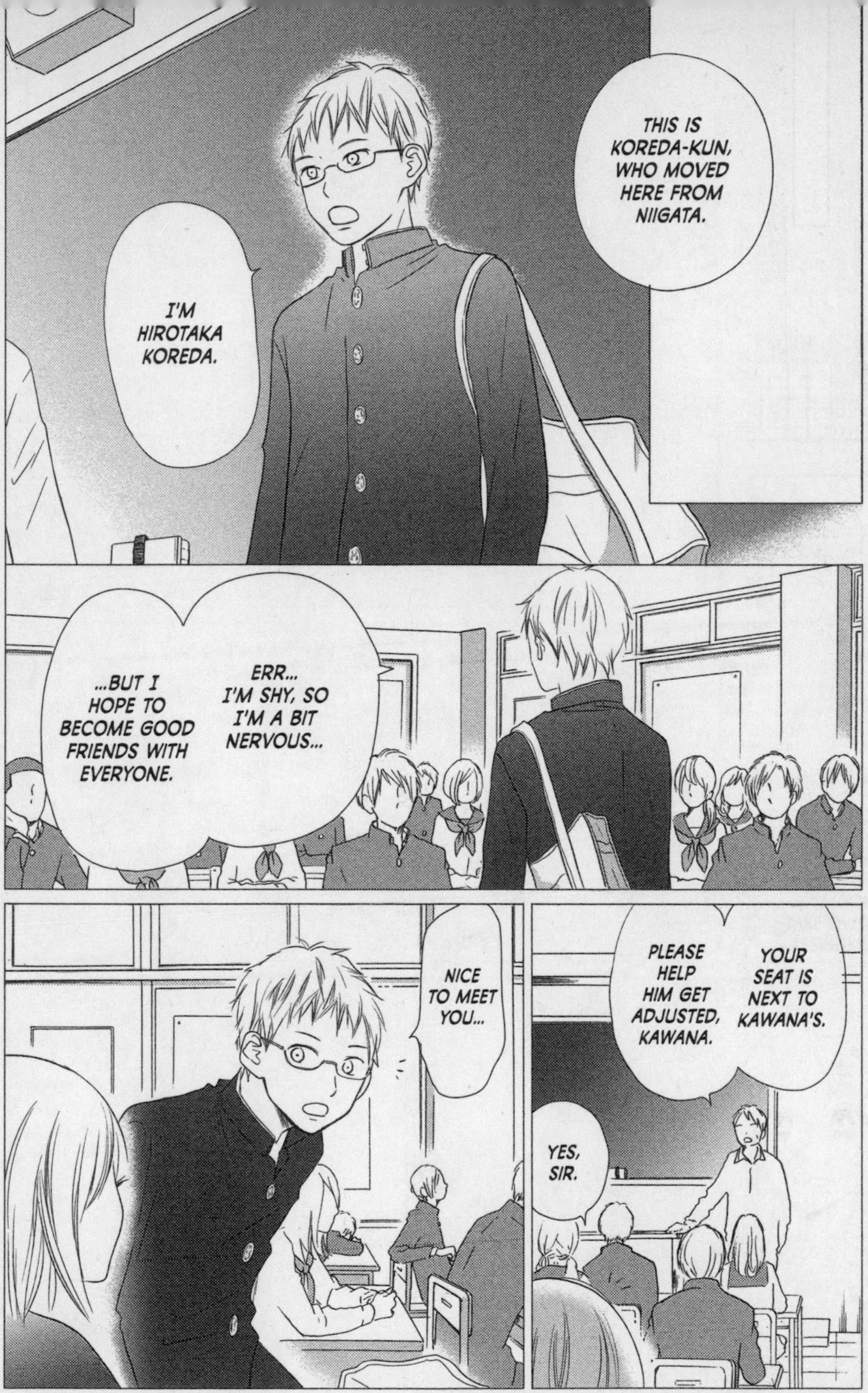
THIS IS KOREDA-KUN, WHO MOVED HERE FROM NIIGATA.
I'M HIROTAKA KOREDA.
ERR... I'M SHY, SO I'M A BIT NERVOUS...
...BUT I HOPE TO BECOME GOOD FRIENDS WITH EVERYONE.
YOUR SEAT IS NEXT TO KAWANA'S.
PLEASE HELP HIM GET ADJUSTED, KAWANA.
YES, SIR.
NICE TO MEET YOU...

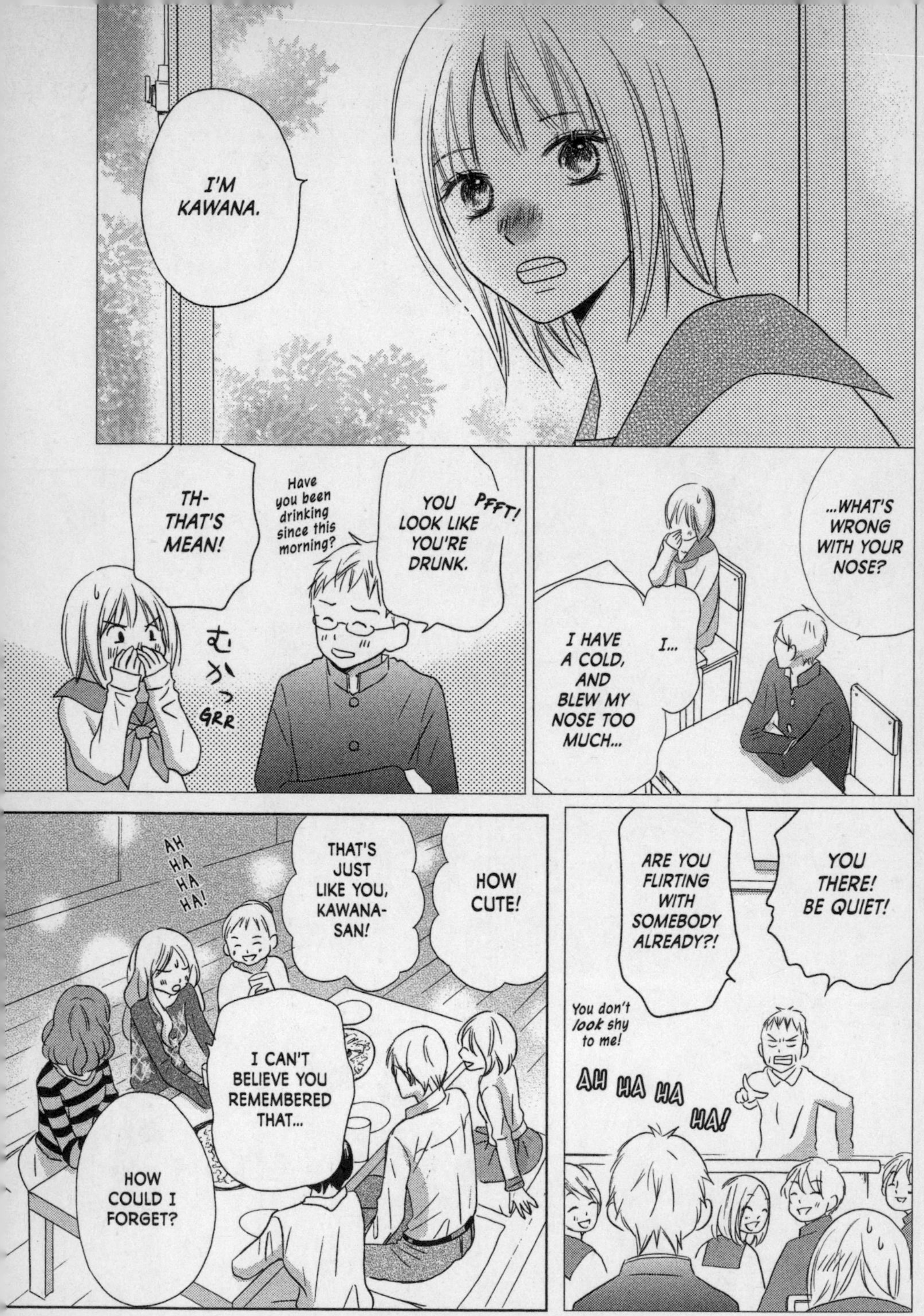
I'M KAWANA.
...WHAT'S WRONG WITH YOUR NOSE?
I...
I HAVE A COLD, AND BLEW MY NOSE TOO MUCH...
YOU LOOK LIKE YOU'RE DRUNK.
PFFT!
Have you been drinking since this morning?
TH-THAT'S MEAN!
むかっ
GRR
YOU THERE! BE QUIET!
ARE YOU FLIRTING WITH SOMEBODY ALREADY?!
You don't *look* shy to me!
AH HA HA HA!
HOW CUTE!
THAT'S JUST LIKE YOU, KAWANA-SAN!
AH HA HA HA!
I CAN'T BELIEVE YOU REMEMBERED THAT...
HOW COULD I FORGET?

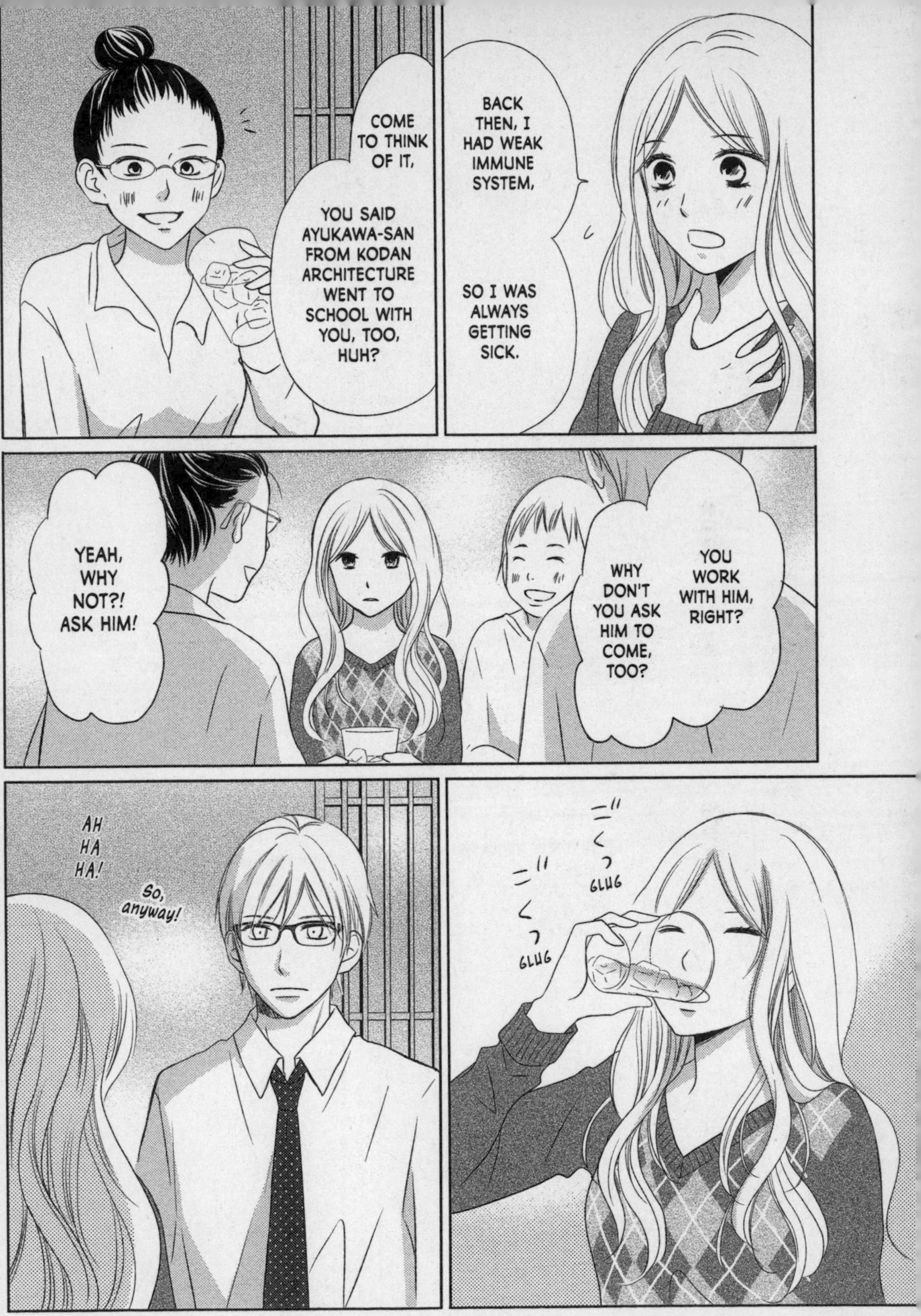
BACK THEN, I HAD WEAK IMMUNE SYSTEM,
SO I WAS ALWAYS GETTING SICK.
COME TO THINK OF IT,
YOU SAID AYUKAWA-SAN FROM KODAN ARCHITECTURE WENT TO SCHOOL WITH YOU, TOO, HUH?
YOU WORK WITH HIM, RIGHT?
WHY DON'T YOU ASK HIM TO COME, TOO?
YEAH, WHY NOT?! ASK HIM!
ゴくっ
GLUG
ゴくっ
GLUG
AH HA HA!
So, anyway!

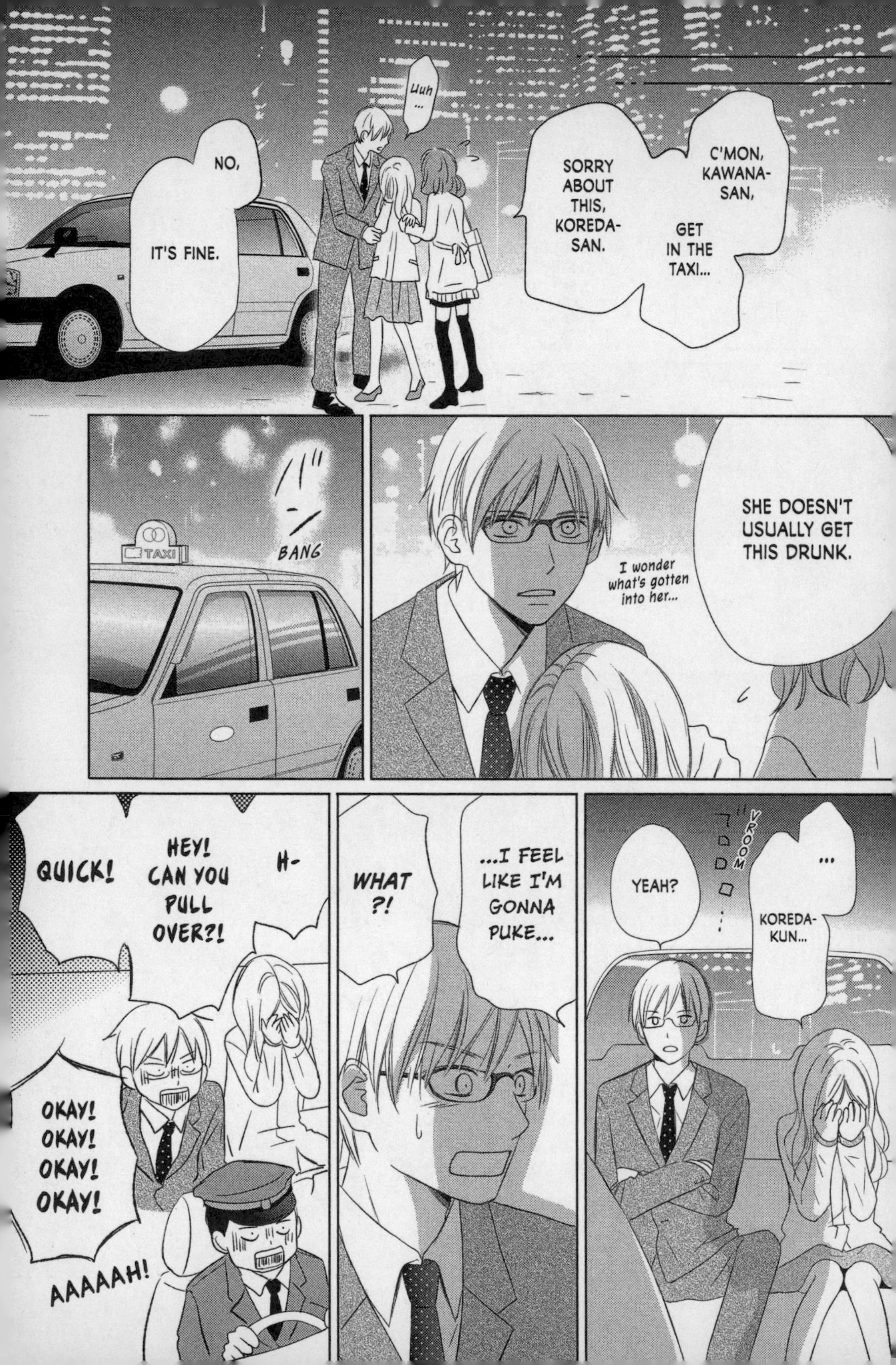
C'MON, KAWANA-SAN, GET IN THE TAXI...
SORRY ABOUT THIS, KOREDA-SAN.
Uuh ...
NO, IT'S FINE.
SHE DOESN'T USUALLY GET THIS DRUNK.
I wonder what's gotten into her...
BANG
TAXI
...
KOREDA-KUN...
VROOM
YEAH?
...I FEEL LIKE I'M GONNA PUKE...
WHAT?!
H-
HEY! CAN YOU PULL OVER?!
QUICK!
OKAY! OKAY! OKAY! OKAY!
AAAAAH!

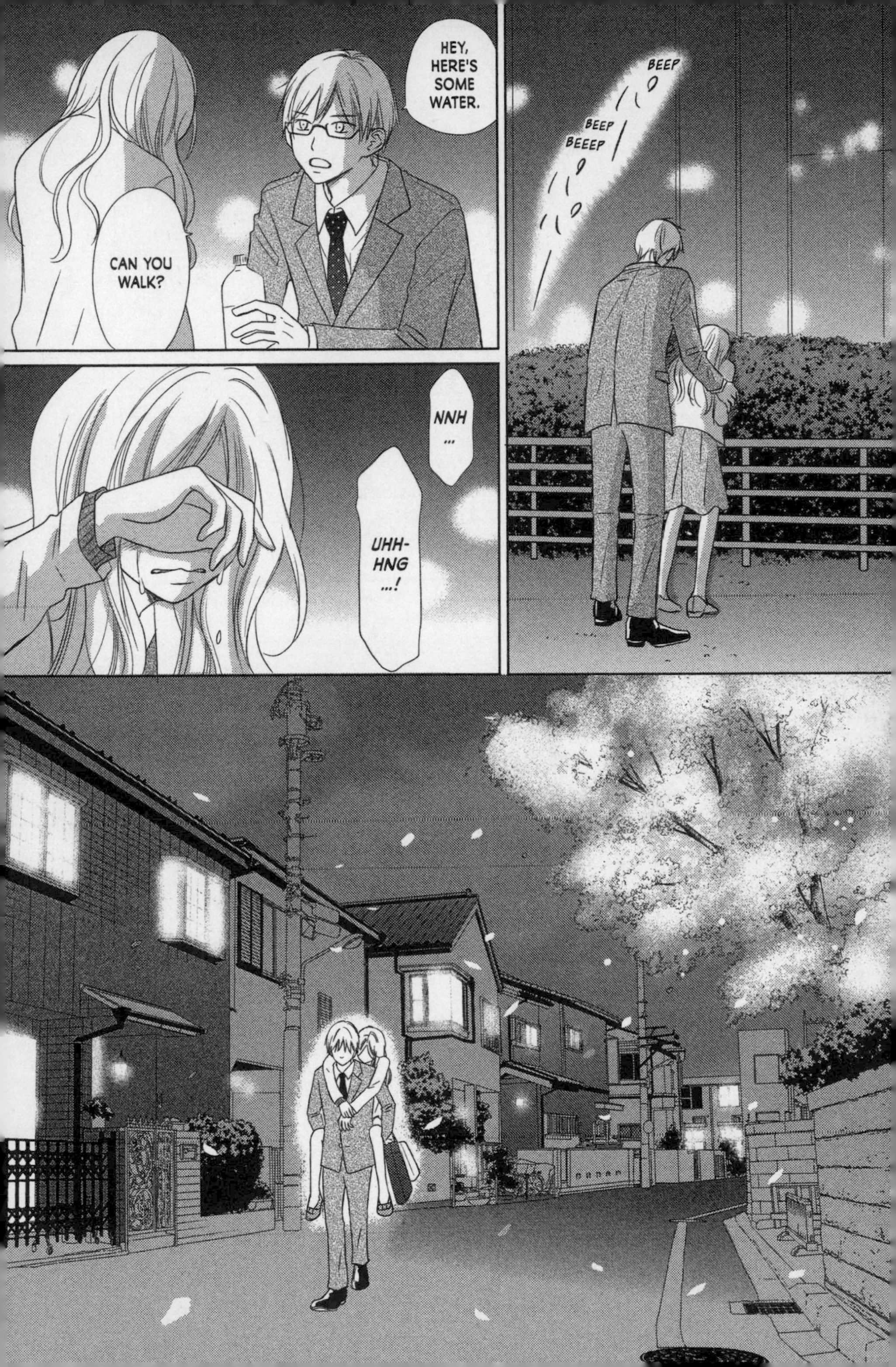
BEEP
BEEP BEEEP
HEY, HERE'S SOME WATER.
CAN YOU WALK?
NNH ...
UHH-HNG ...!

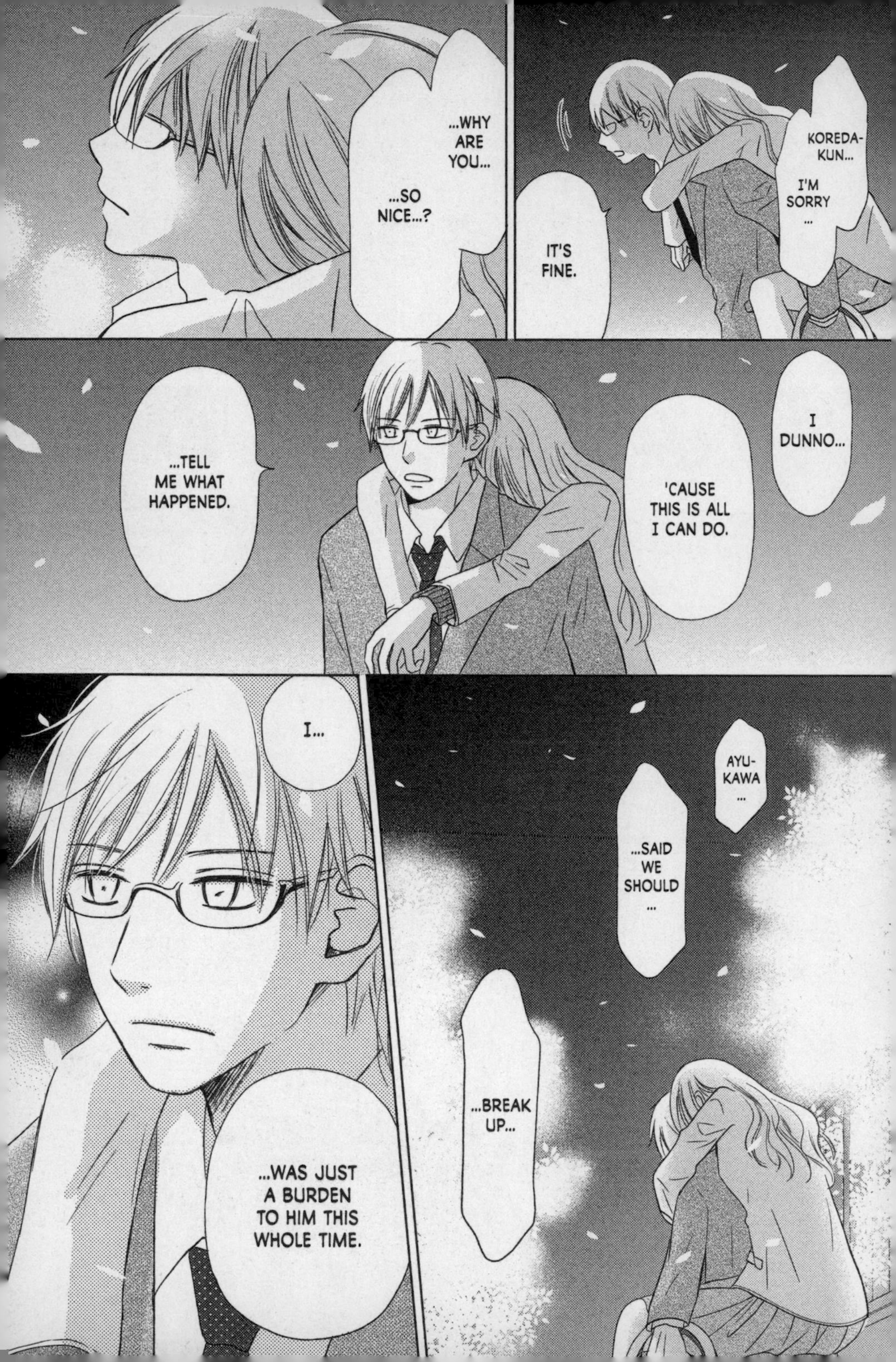
KOREDA-KUN...
I'M SORRY ...
IT'S FINE.
...WHY ARE YOU...
...SO NICE...?
I DUNNO...
'CAUSE THIS IS ALL I CAN DO.
...TELL ME WHAT HAPPENED.
AYU-KAWA ...
...SAID WE SHOULD ...
...BREAK UP...
I...
...WAS JUST A BURDEN TO HIM THIS WHOLE TIME.

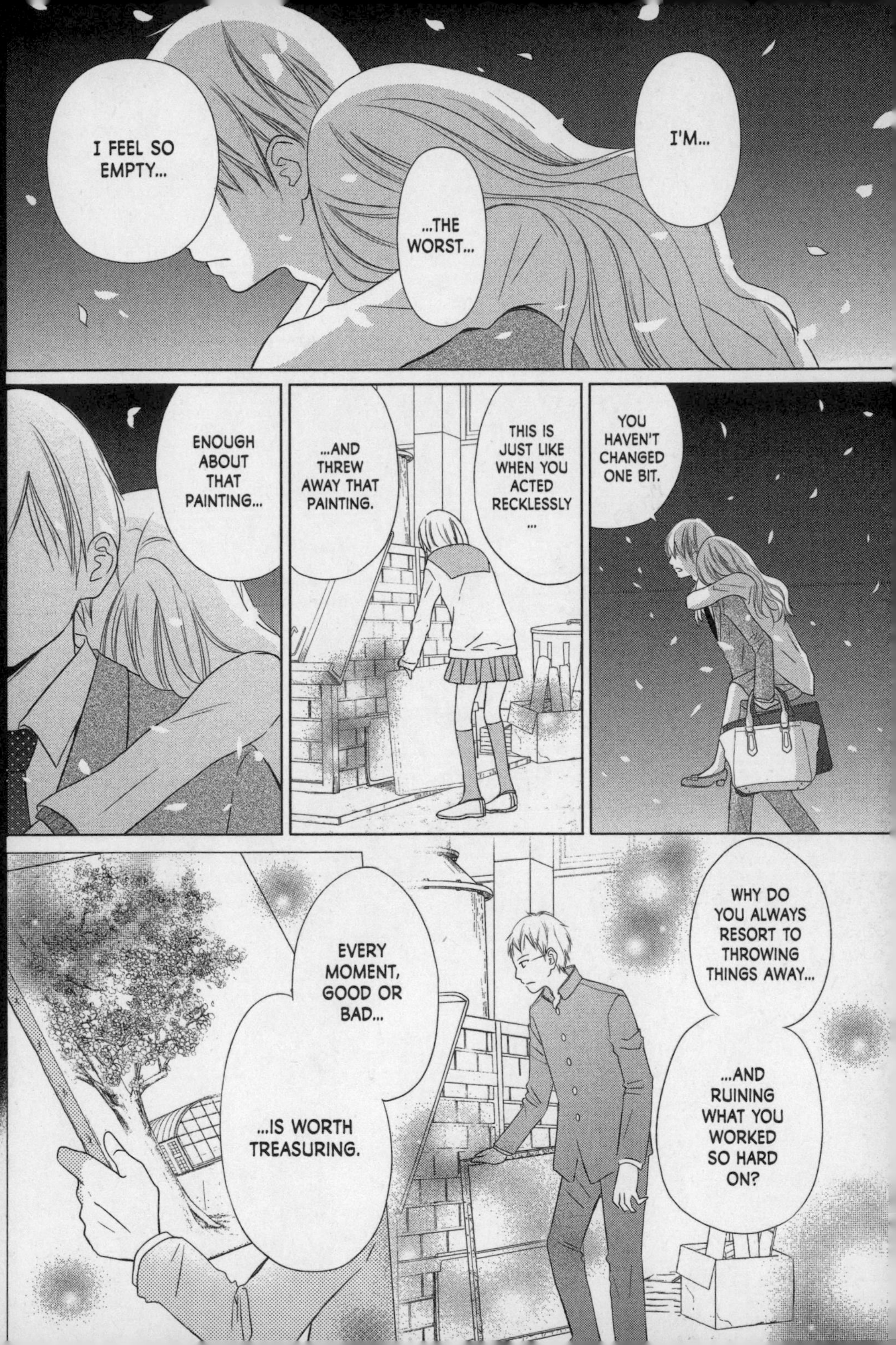
I'M...
...THE WORST...
I FEEL SO EMPTY...
YOU HAVEN'T CHANGED ONE BIT.
THIS IS JUST LIKE WHEN YOU ACTED RECKLESSLY ...
...AND THREW AWAY THAT PAINTING.
ENOUGH ABOUT THAT PAINTING...
WHY DO YOU ALWAYS RESORT TO THROWING THINGS AWAY...
...AND RUINING WHAT YOU WORKED SO HARD ON?
EVERY MOMENT, GOOD OR BAD...
...IS WORTH TREASURING.

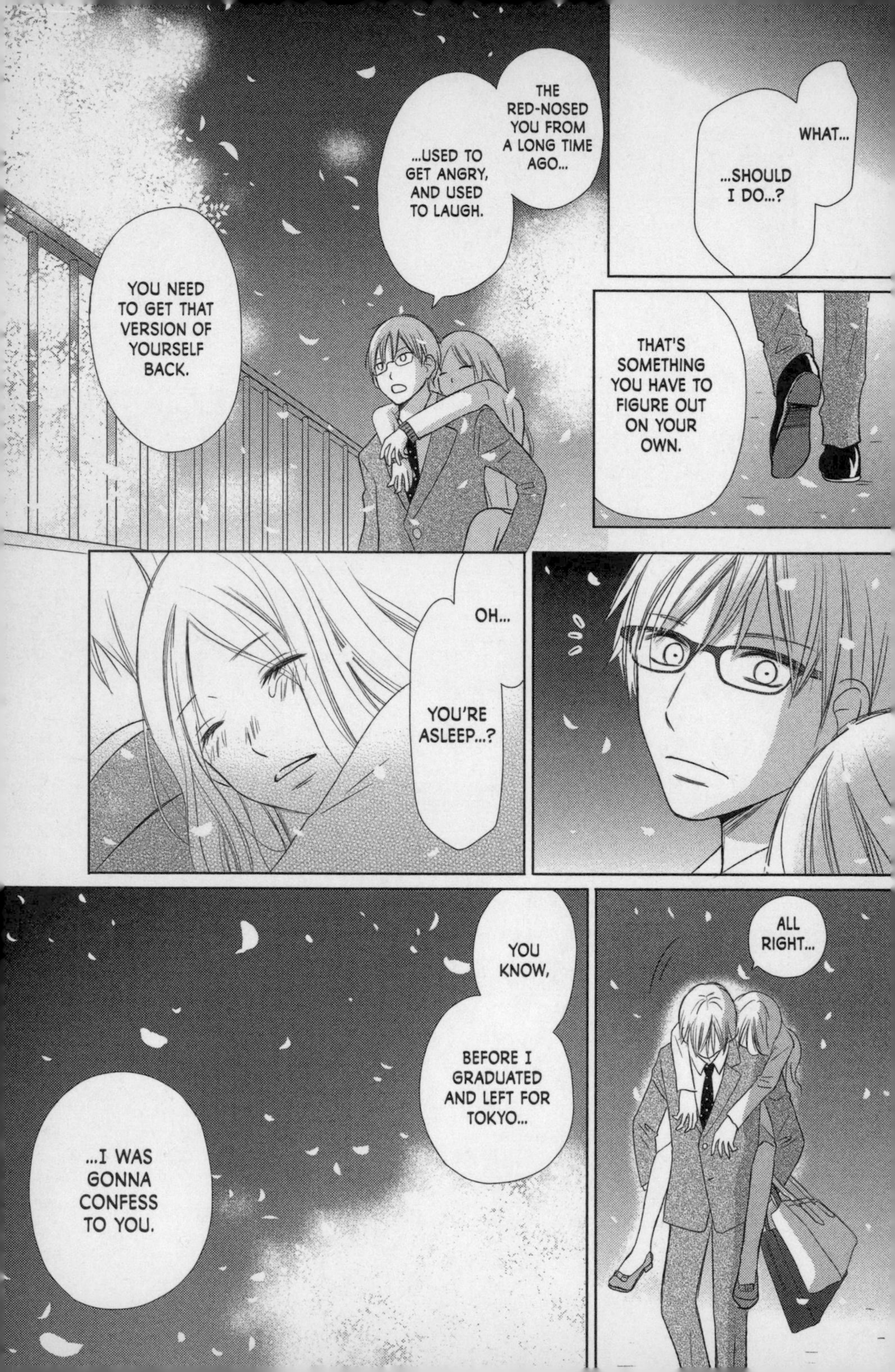
WHAT...
...SHOULD I DO...?
THAT'S SOMETHING YOU HAVE TO FIGURE OUT ON YOUR OWN.
THE RED-NOSED YOU FROM A LONG TIME AGO...
...USED TO GET ANGRY, AND USED TO LAUGH.
YOU NEED TO GET THAT VERSION OF YOURSELF BACK.
OH...
YOU'RE ASLEEP...?
ALL RIGHT...
YOU KNOW,
BEFORE I GRADUATED AND LEFT FOR TOKYO...
...I WAS GONNA CONFESS TO YOU.

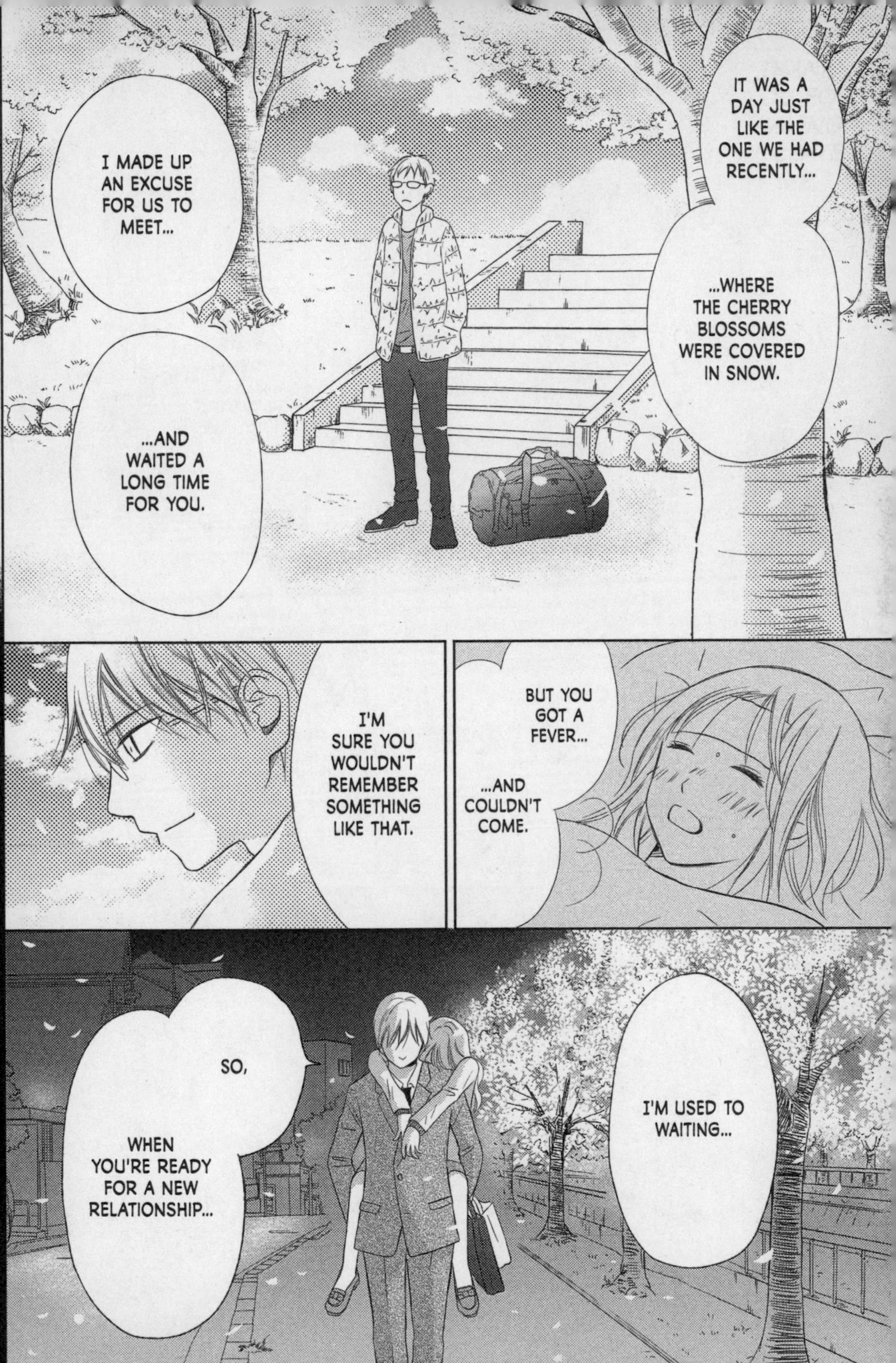
IT WAS A DAY JUST LIKE THE ONE WE HAD RECENTLY...
...WHERE THE CHERRY BLOSSOMS WERE COVERED IN SNOW.
I MADE UP AN EXCUSE FOR US TO MEET...
...AND WAITED A LONG TIME FOR YOU.
BUT YOU GOT A FEVER...
...AND COULDN'T COME.
I'M SURE YOU WOULDN'T REMEMBER SOMETHING LIKE THAT.
I'M USED TO WAITING...
SO,
WHEN YOU'RE READY FOR A NEW RELATIONSHIP...

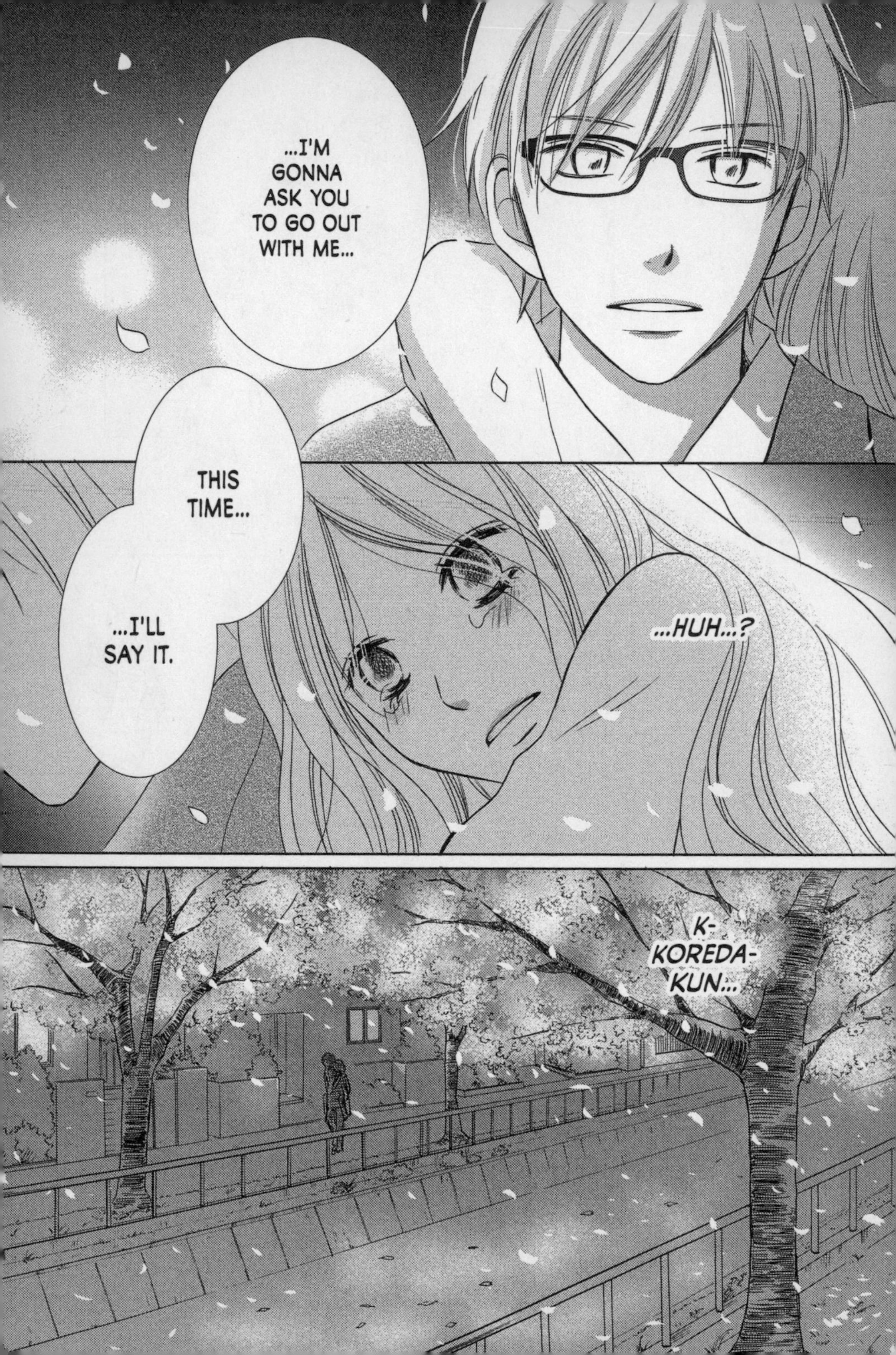
...I'M GONNA ASK YOU TO GO OUT WITH ME...
THIS TIME...
...I'LL SAY IT.
...HUH...?
K-KOREDA-KUN...

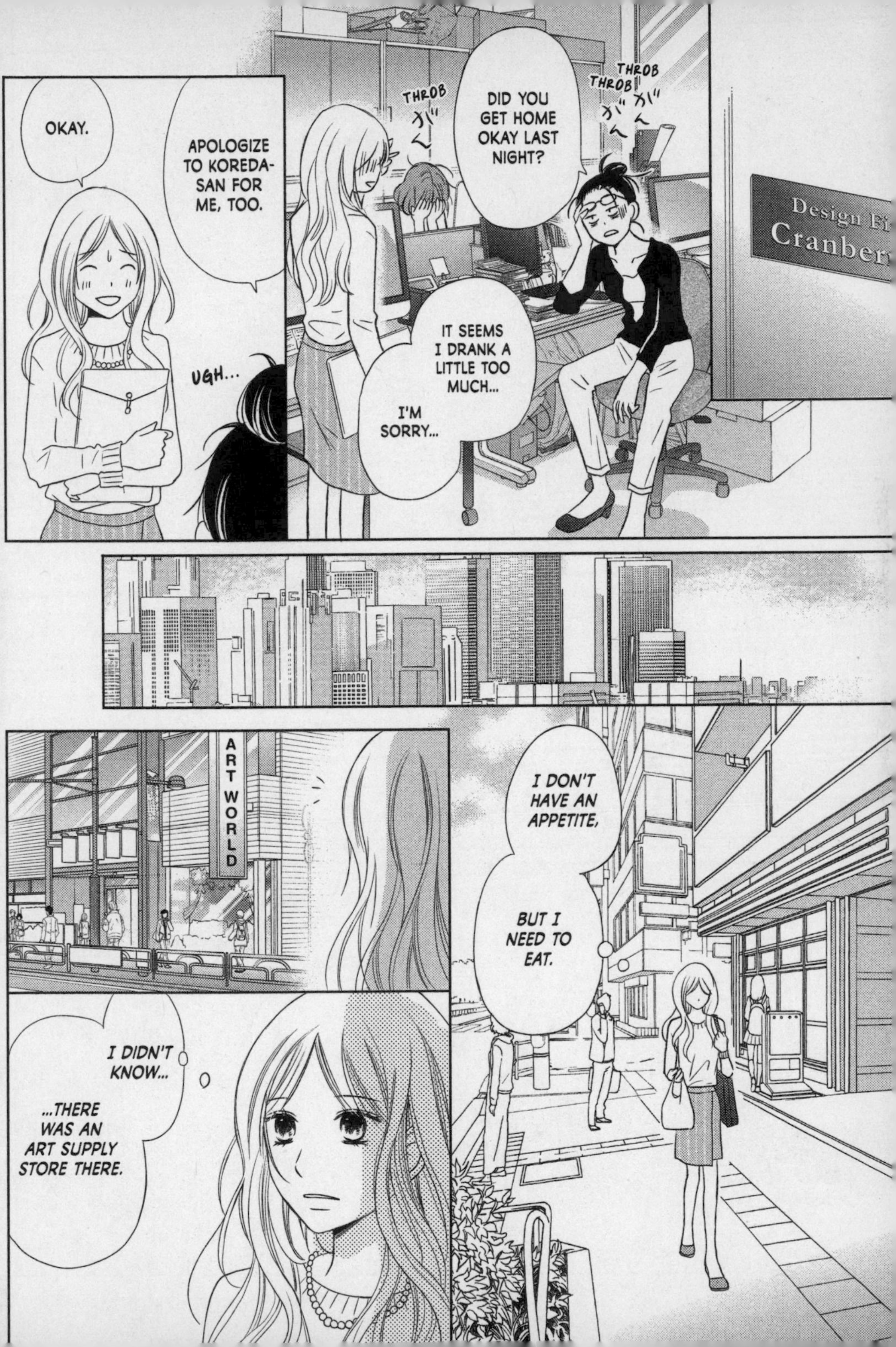
THROB THROB
DID YOU GET HOME OKAY LAST NIGHT?
THROB
IT SEEMS I DRANK A LITTLE TOO MUCH...
I'M SORRY...
APOLOGIZE TO KOREDA-SAN FOR ME, TOO.
UGH...
OKAY.
I DON'T HAVE AN APPETITE,
BUT I NEED TO EAT.
ART WORLD
I DIDN'T KNOW...
...THERE WAS AN ART SUPPLY STORE THERE.

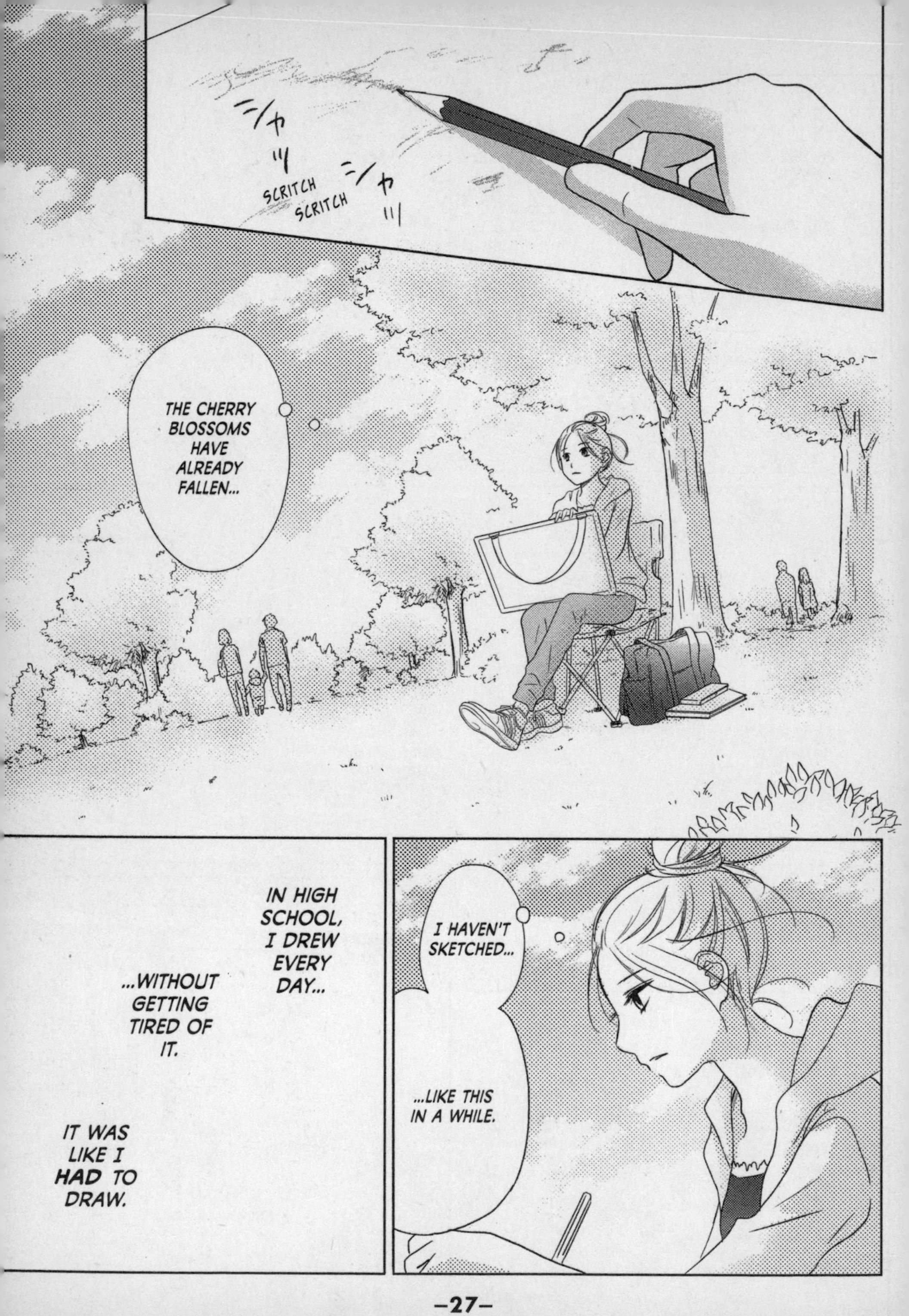
シャッ
SCRITCH
シャッ
SCRITCH
THE CHERRY BLOSSOMS HAVE ALREADY FALLEN...
I HAVEN'T SKETCHED...
...LIKE THIS IN A WHILE.
IN HIGH SCHOOL, I DREW EVERY DAY...
...WITHOUT GETTING TIRED OF IT.
IT WAS LIKE I HAD TO DRAW.

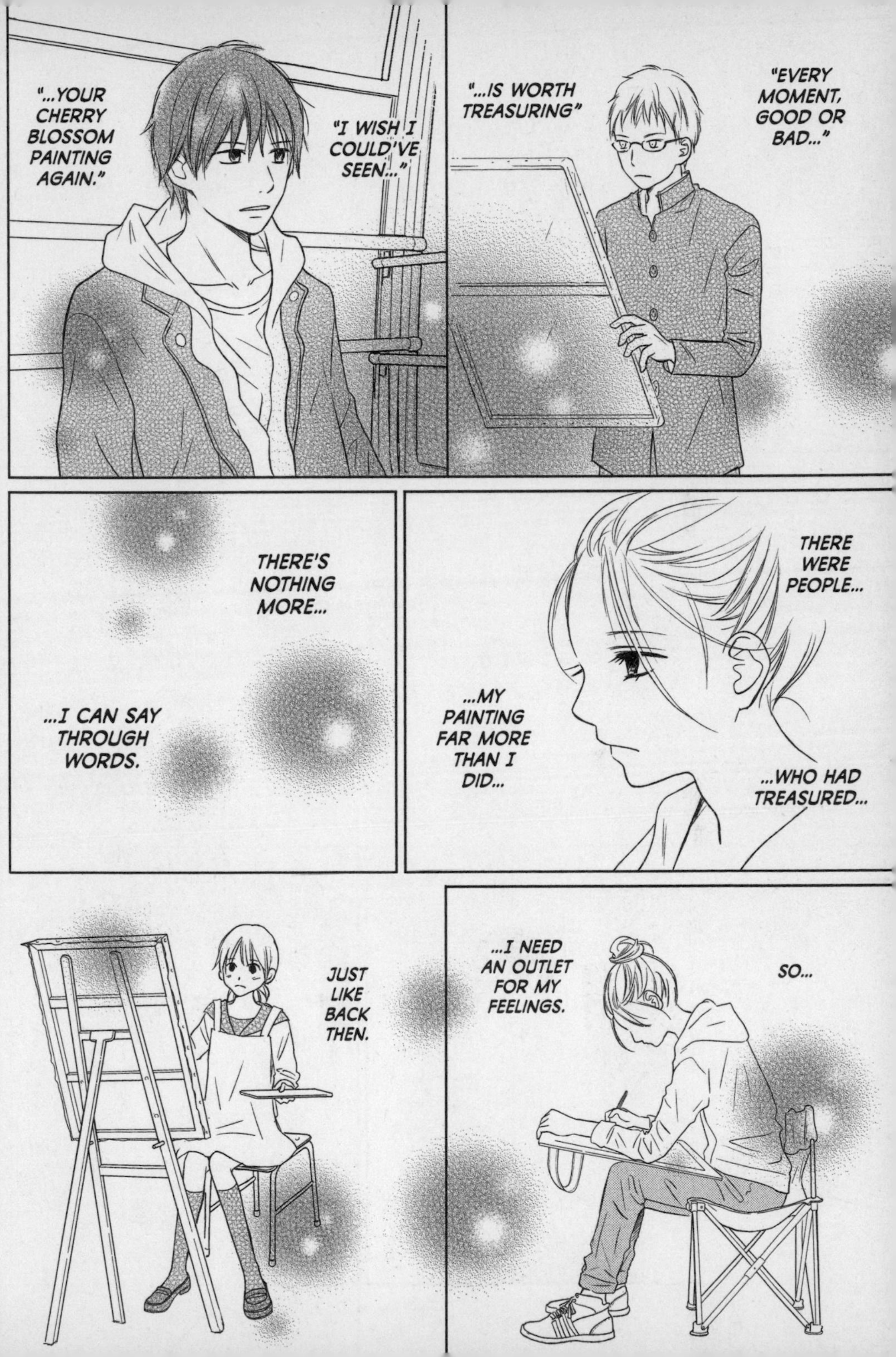
"EVERY MOMENT, GOOD OR BAD..."
"...IS WORTH TREASURING"
"I WISH I COULD'VE SEEN..."
"...YOUR CHERRY BLOSSOM PAINTING AGAIN."
THERE WERE PEOPLE...
...WHO HAD TREASURED...
...MY PAINTING FAR MORE THAN I DID...
THERE'S NOTHING MORE...
...I CAN SAY THROUGH WORDS.
SO...
...I NEED AN OUTLET FOR MY FEELINGS.
JUST LIKE BACK THEN.

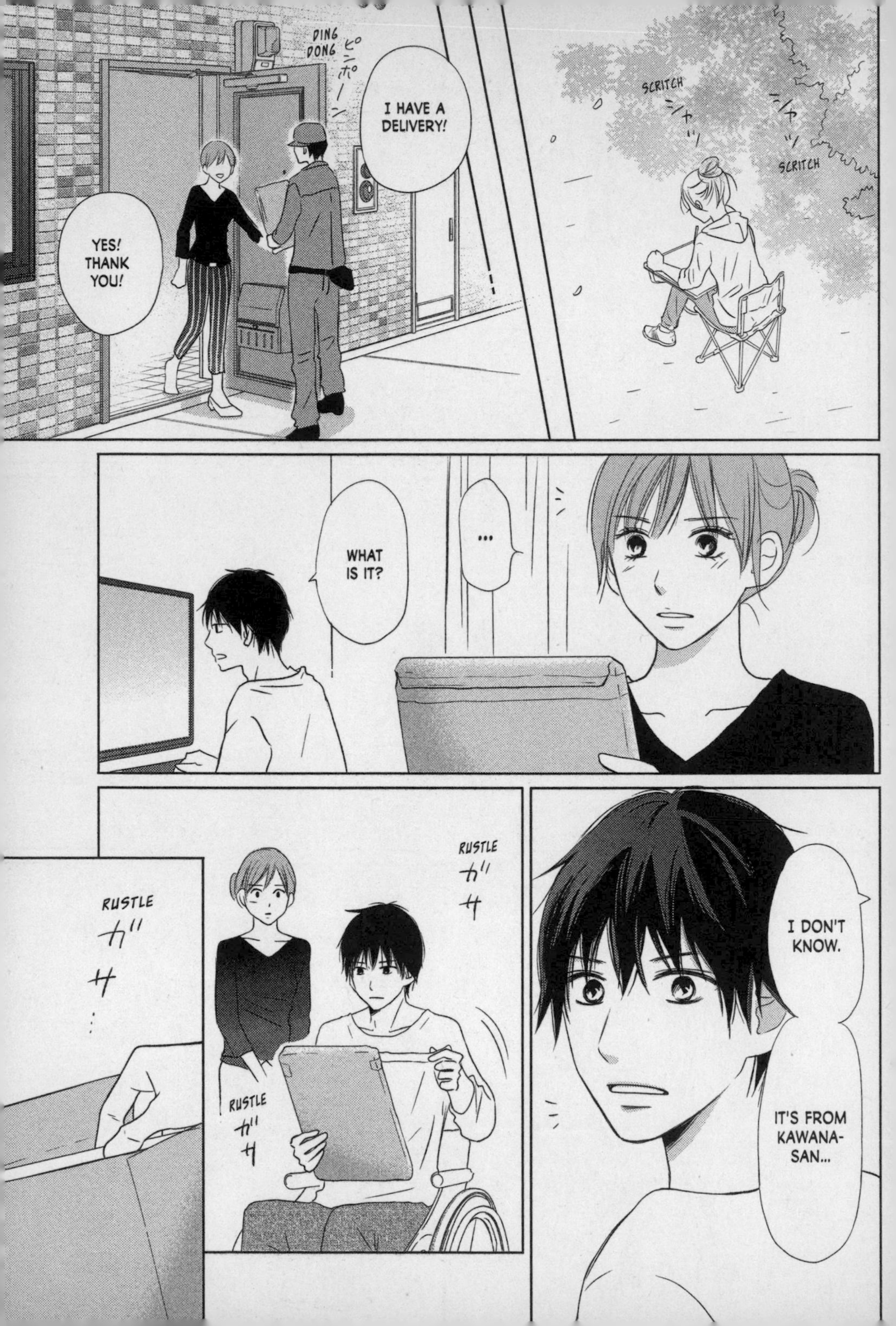
SCRITCH
SCRITCH
DING DONG
I HAVE A DELIVERY!
YES! THANK YOU!
...
WHAT IS IT?
I DON'T KNOW.
IT'S FROM KAWANA-SAN...
RUSTLE
RUSTLE
RUSTLE

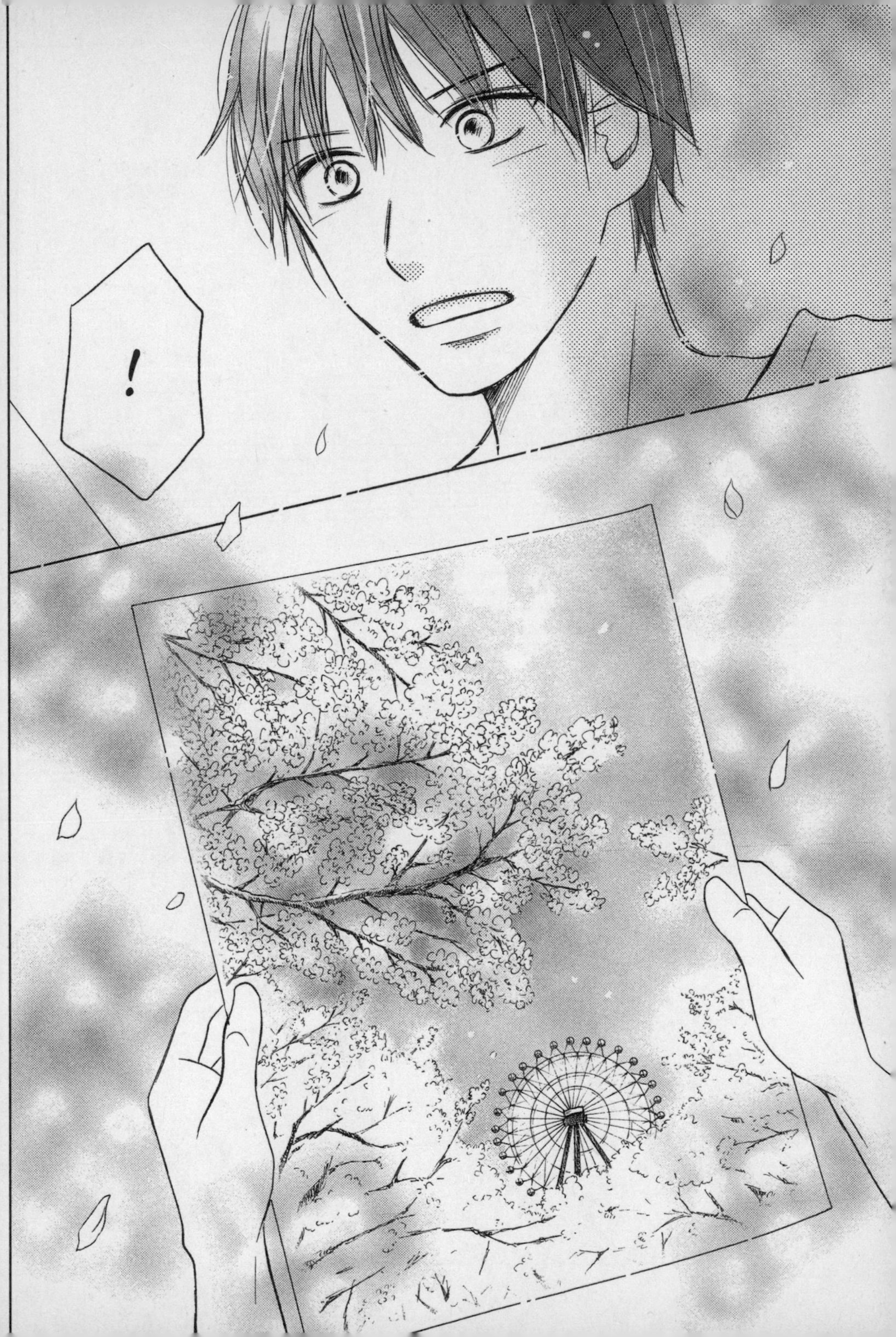
!

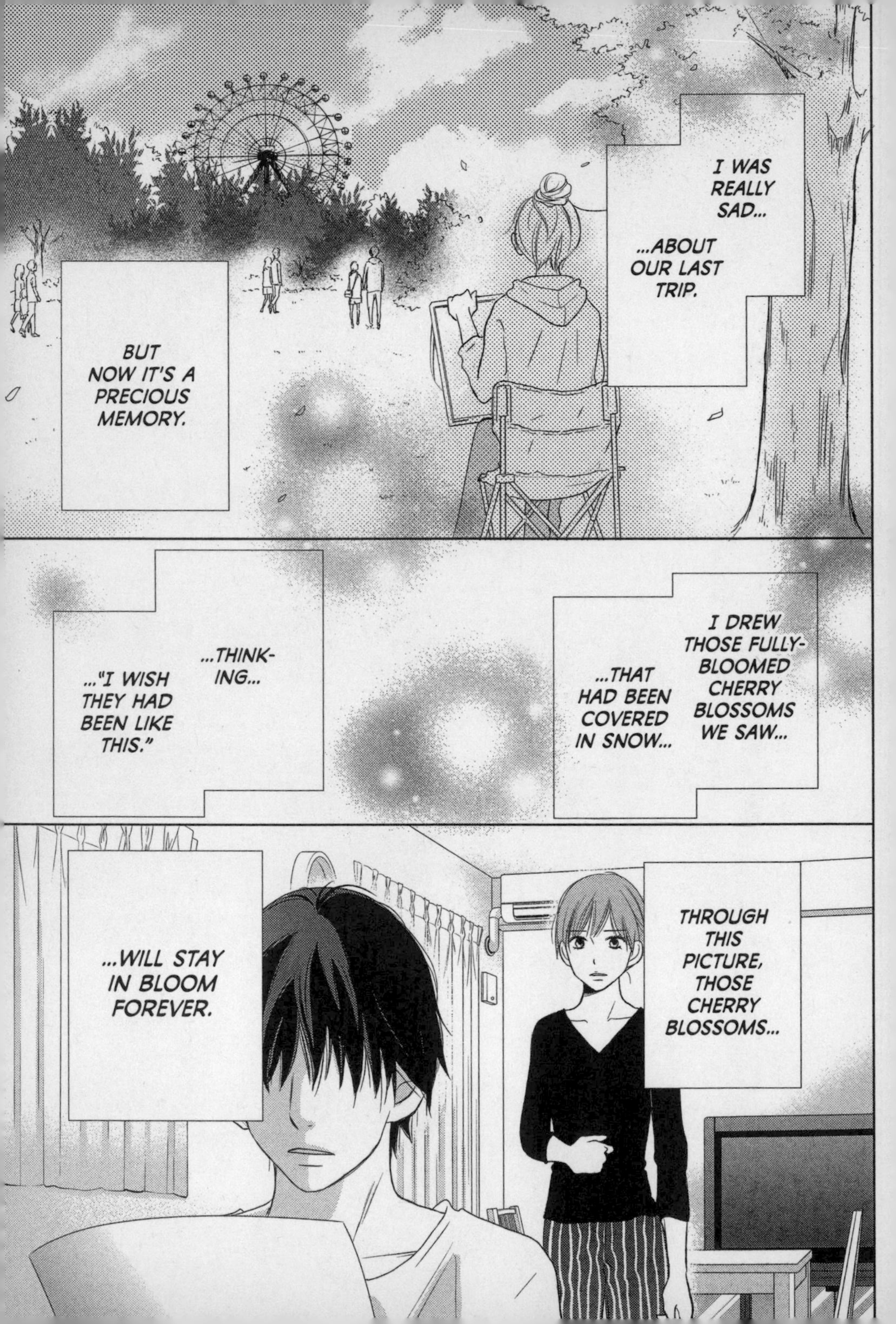
I WAS REALLY SAD...
...ABOUT OUR LAST TRIP.
BUT NOW IT'S A PRECIOUS MEMORY.
I DREW THOSE FULLY-BLOOMED CHERRY BLOSSOMS WE SAW...
...THAT HAD BEEN COVERED IN SNOW...
...THINKING...
..."I WISH THEY HAD BEEN LIKE THIS."
THROUGH THIS PICTURE, THOSE CHERRY BLOSSOMS...
...WILL STAY IN BLOOM FOREVER.

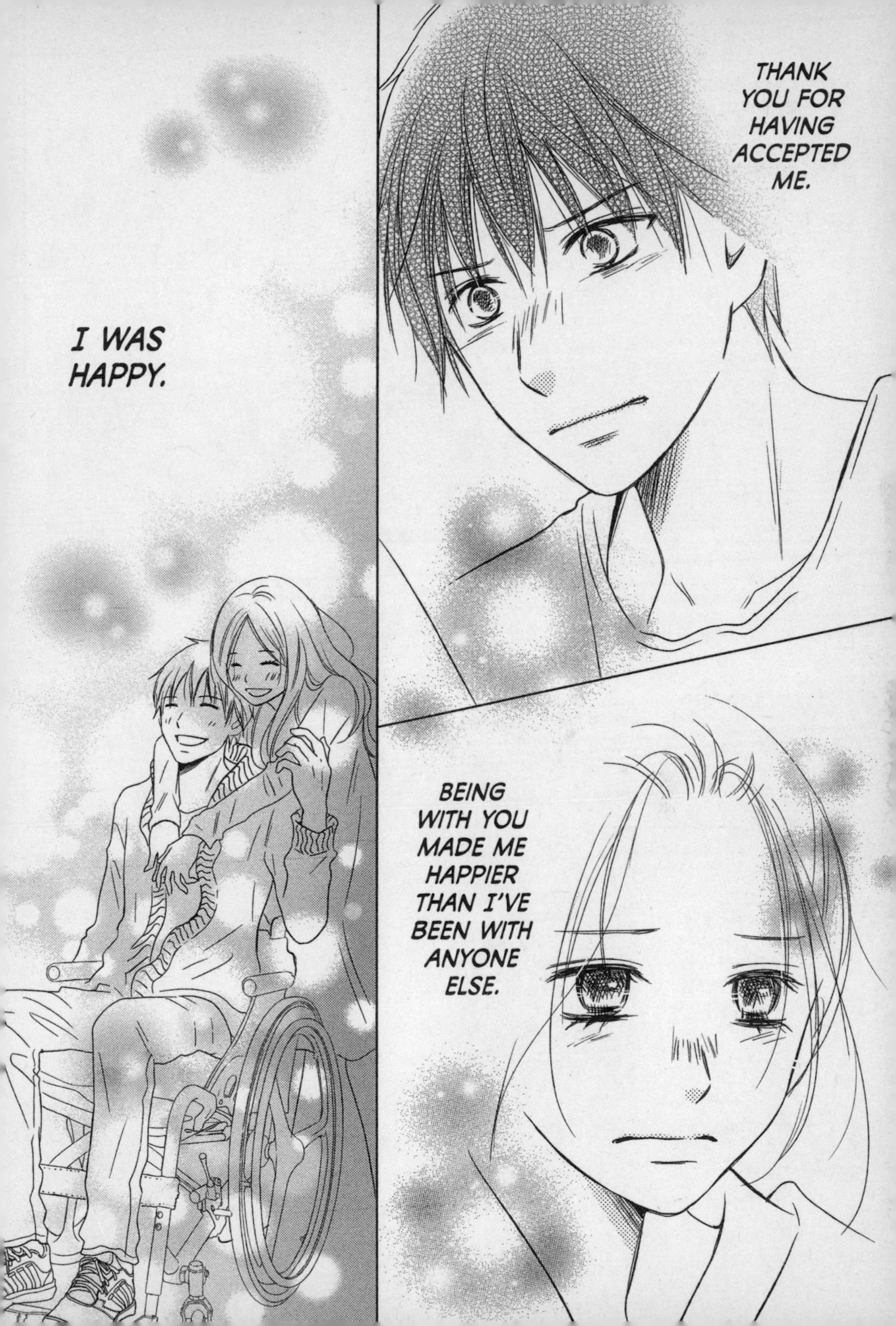
THANK YOU FOR HAVING ACCEPTED ME.
BEING WITH YOU MADE ME HAPPIER THAN I'VE BEEN WITH ANYONE ELSE.
I WAS HAPPY.

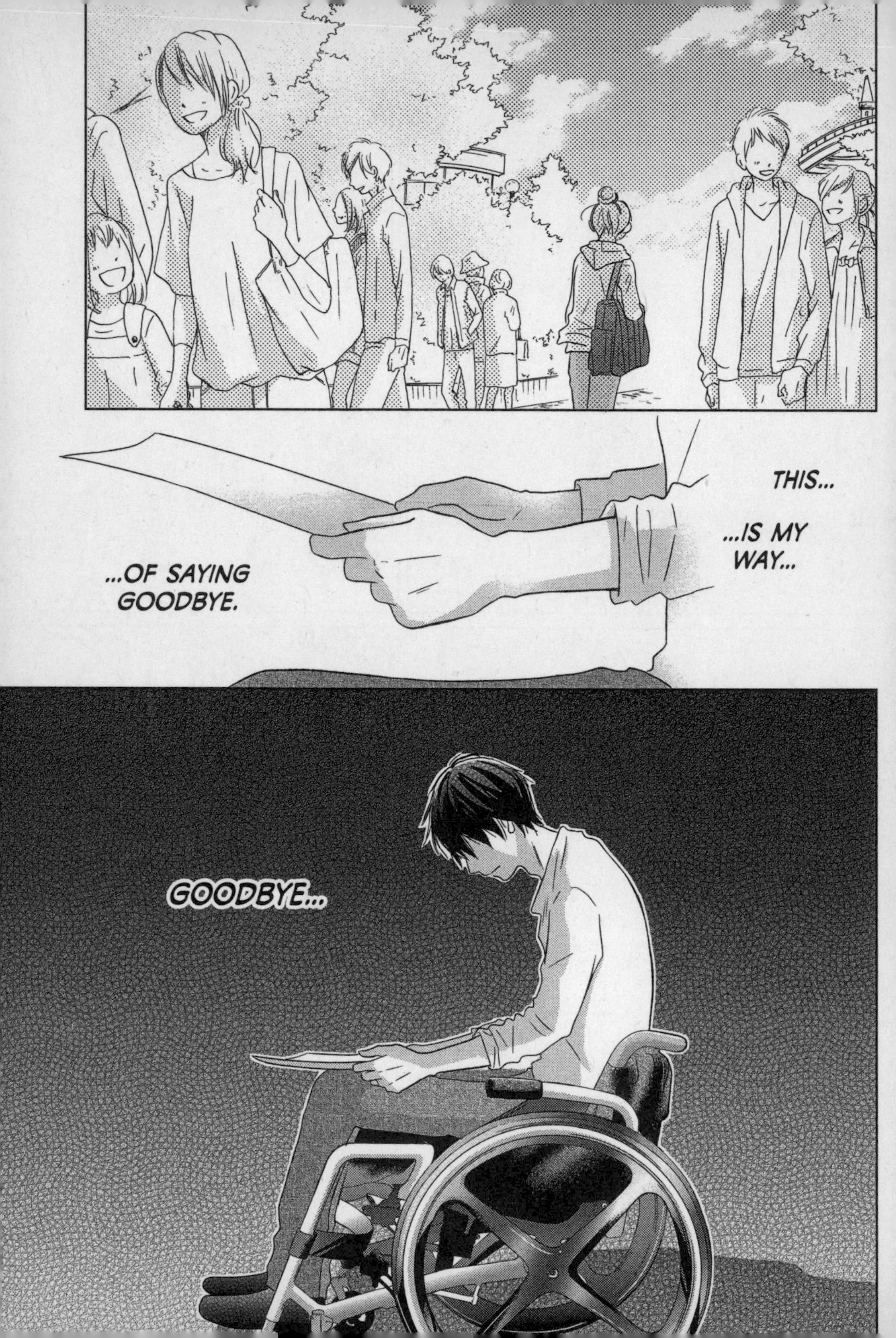
THIS...
...IS MY WAY...
...OF SAYING GOODBYE.
GOODBYE...

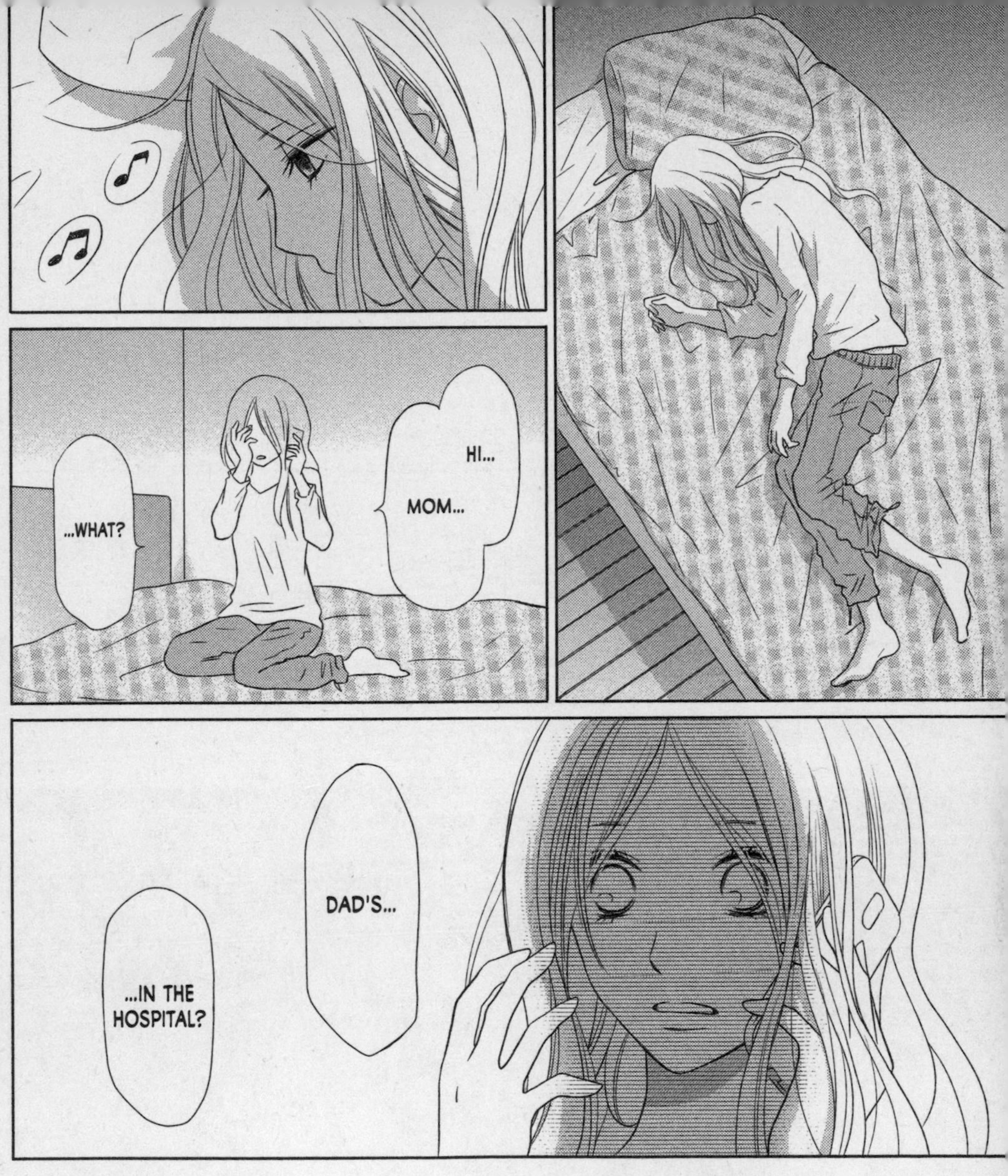
HI... MOM...
...WHAT?
DAD'S...
...IN THE HOSPITAL?

AND THEN...

...I HAD ANOTHER HUGE DECISION...

...TO MAKE.

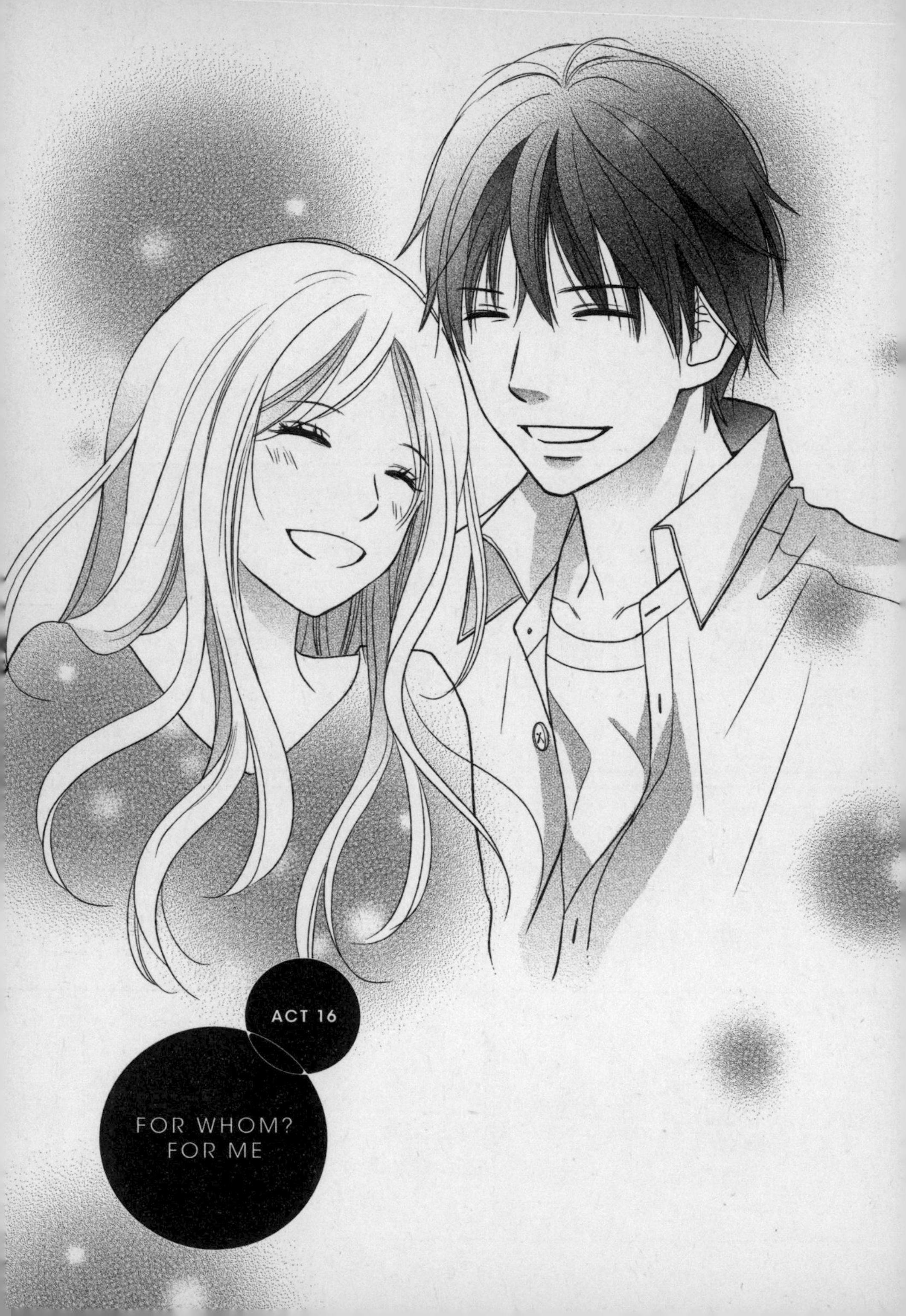
ACT 16
FOR WHOM? FOR ME

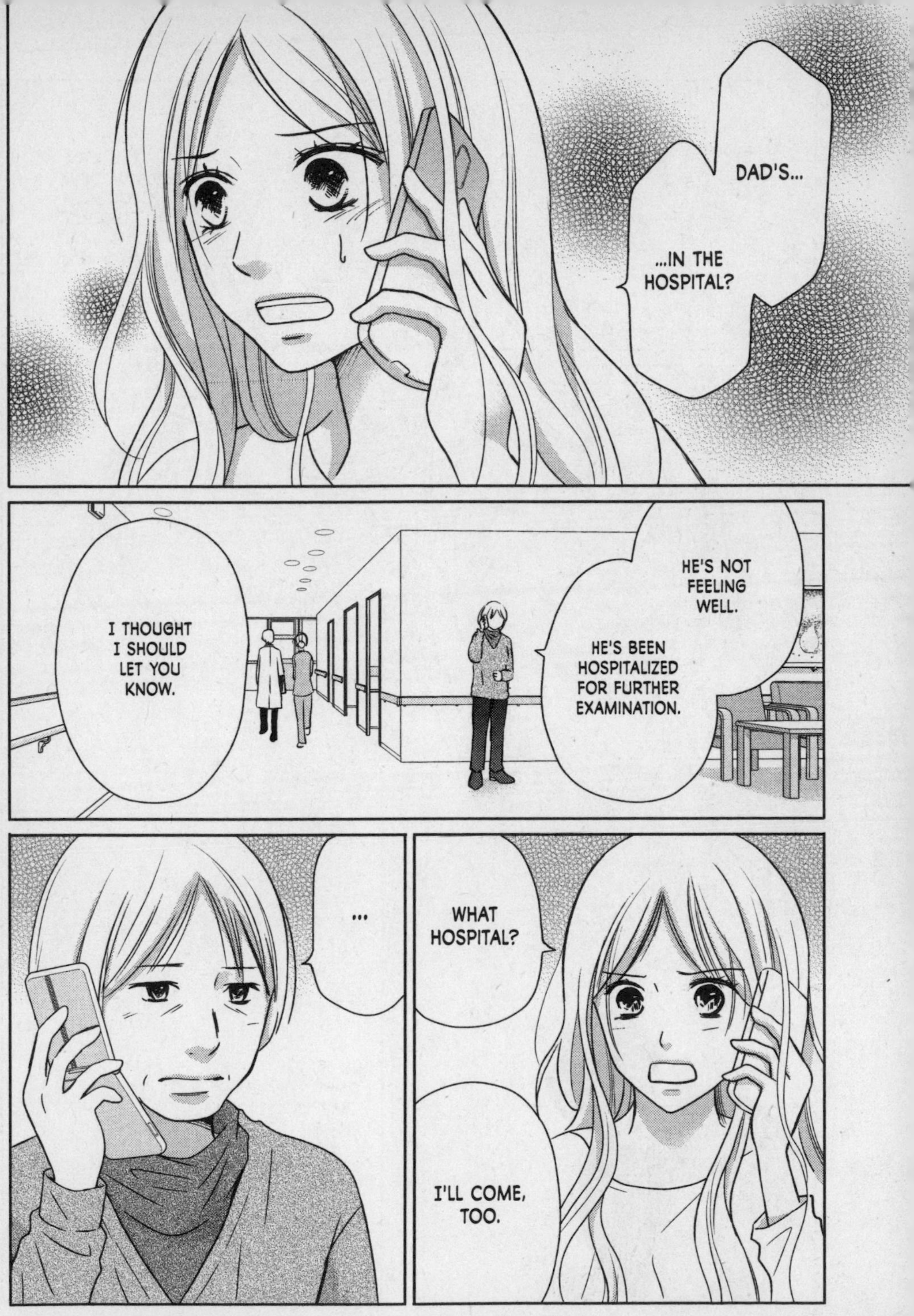
DAD'S...
...IN THE HOSPITAL?
HE'S NOT FEELING WELL.
HE'S BEEN HOSPITALIZED FOR FURTHER EXAMINATION.
I THOUGHT I SHOULD LET YOU KNOW.
WHAT HOSPITAL?
I'LL COME, TOO.
...

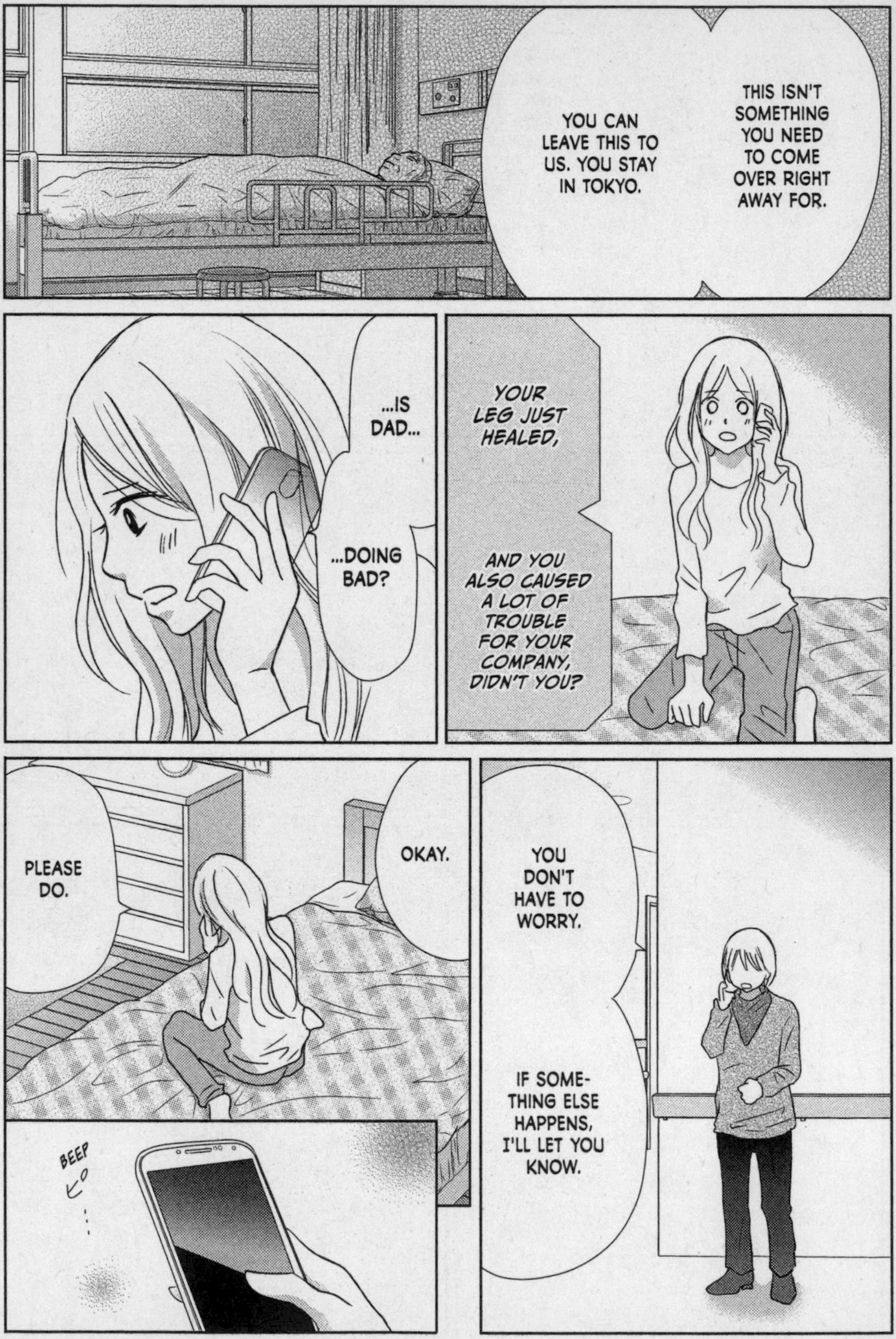
THIS ISN'T SOMETHING YOU NEED TO COME OVER RIGHT AWAY FOR.
YOU CAN LEAVE THIS TO US. YOU STAY IN TOKYO.
YOUR LEG JUST HEALED,
AND YOU ALSO CAUSED A LOT OF TROUBLE FOR YOUR COMPANY, DIDN'T YOU?
...IS DAD...
...DOING BAD?
YOU DON'T HAVE TO WORRY.
IF SOME-THING ELSE HAPPENS, I'LL LET YOU KNOW.
OKAY.
PLEASE DO.
BEEP
ピ

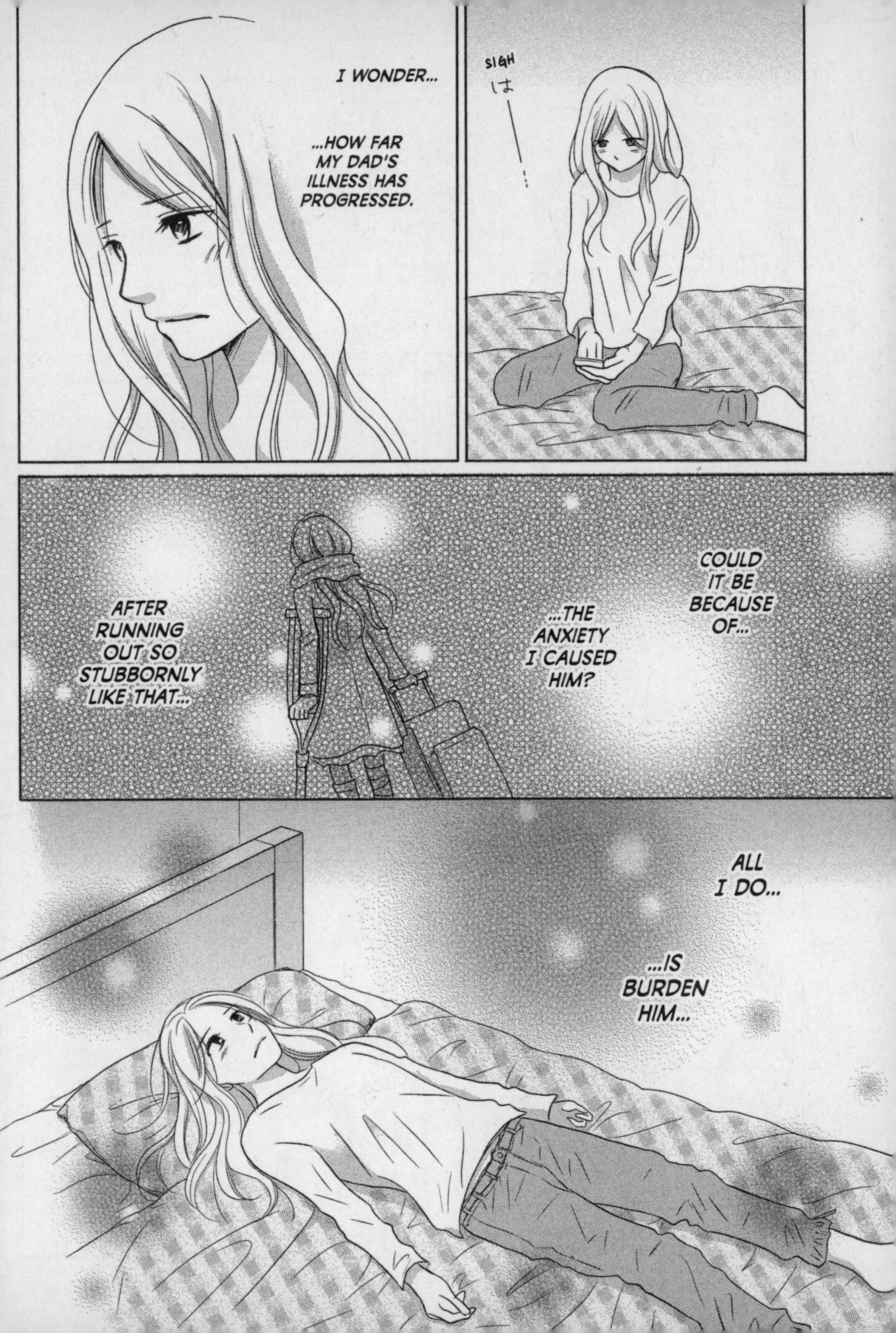
SIGH
は
I WONDER...
...HOW FAR MY DAD'S ILLNESS HAS PROGRESSED.
COULD IT BE BECAUSE OF...
...THE ANXIETY I CAUSED HIM?
AFTER RUNNING OUT SO STUBBORNLY LIKE THAT...
ALL I DO...
...IS BURDEN HIM...

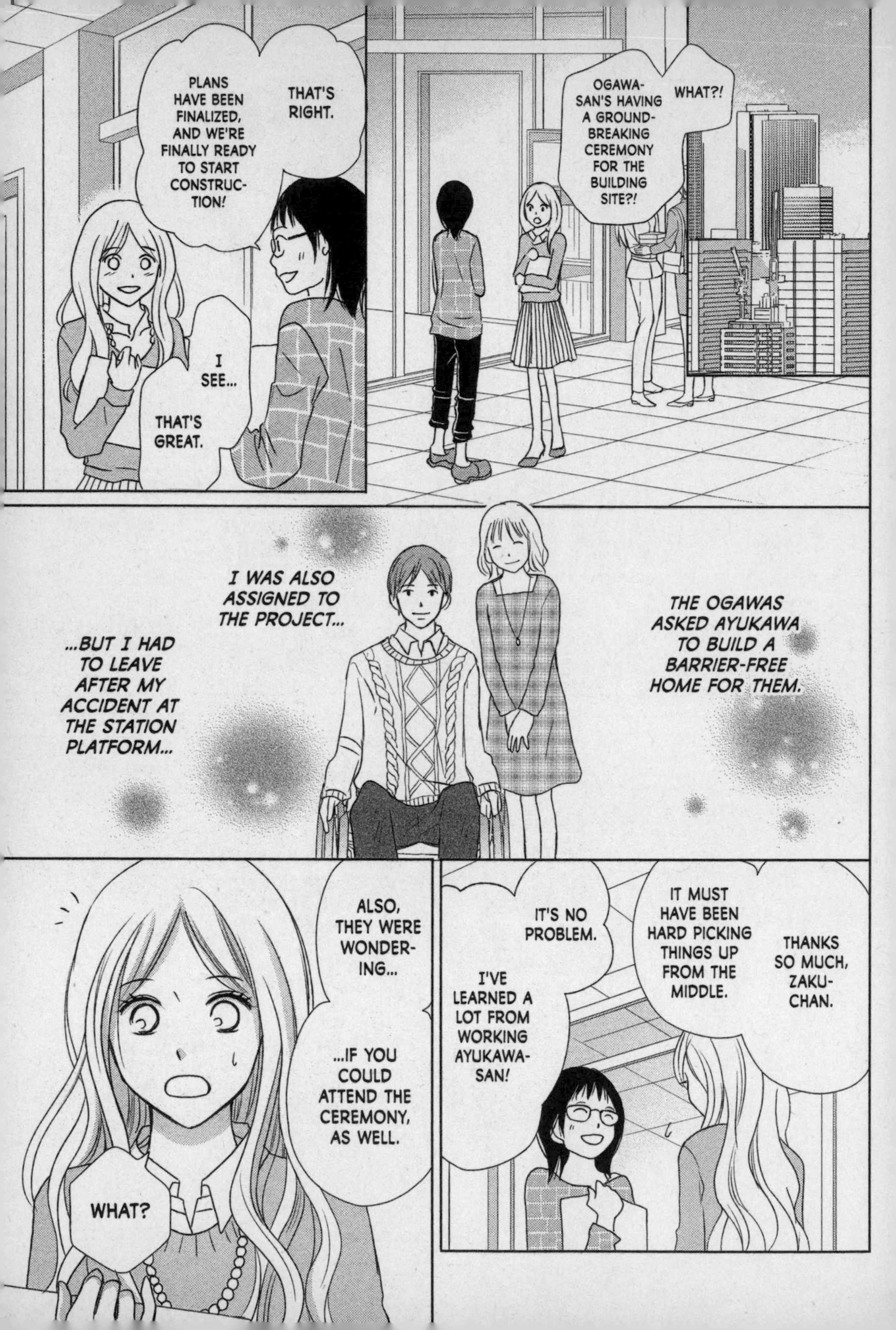
WHAT?!
OGAWA-SAN'S HAVING A GROUND-BREAKING CEREMONY FOR THE BUILDING SITE?!
THAT'S RIGHT.
PLANS HAVE BEEN FINALIZED, AND WE'RE FINALLY READY TO START CONSTRUCTION!
I SEE...
THAT'S GREAT.
THE OGAWAS ASKED AYUKAWA TO BUILD A BARRIER-FREE HOME FOR THEM.
I WAS ALSO ASSIGNED TO THE PROJECT...
...BUT I HAD TO LEAVE AFTER MY ACCIDENT AT THE STATION PLATFORM...
THANKS SO MUCH, ZAKU-CHAN.
IT MUST HAVE BEEN HARD PICKING THINGS UP FROM THE MIDDLE.
IT'S NO PROBLEM.
I'VE LEARNED A LOT FROM WORKING AYUKAWA-SAN!
ALSO, THEY WERE WONDERING...
...IF YOU COULD ATTEND THE CEREMONY, AS WELL.
WHAT?

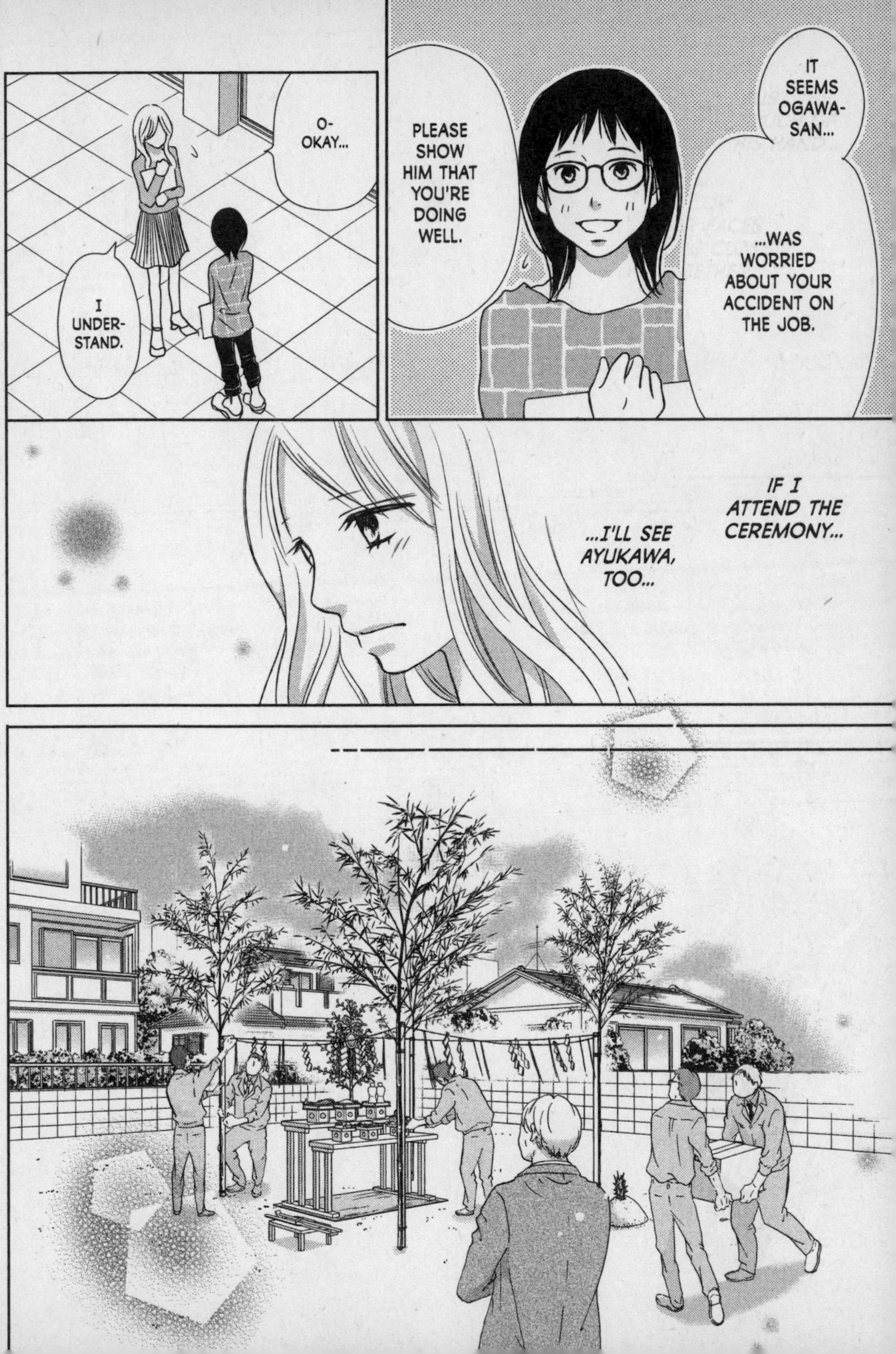
IT SEEMS OGAWA-SAN...
...WAS WORRIED ABOUT YOUR ACCIDENT ON THE JOB.
PLEASE SHOW HIM THAT YOU'RE DOING WELL.
O-OKAY...
I UNDER-STAND.
IF I ATTEND THE CEREMONY...
...I'LL SEE AYUKAWA, TOO...

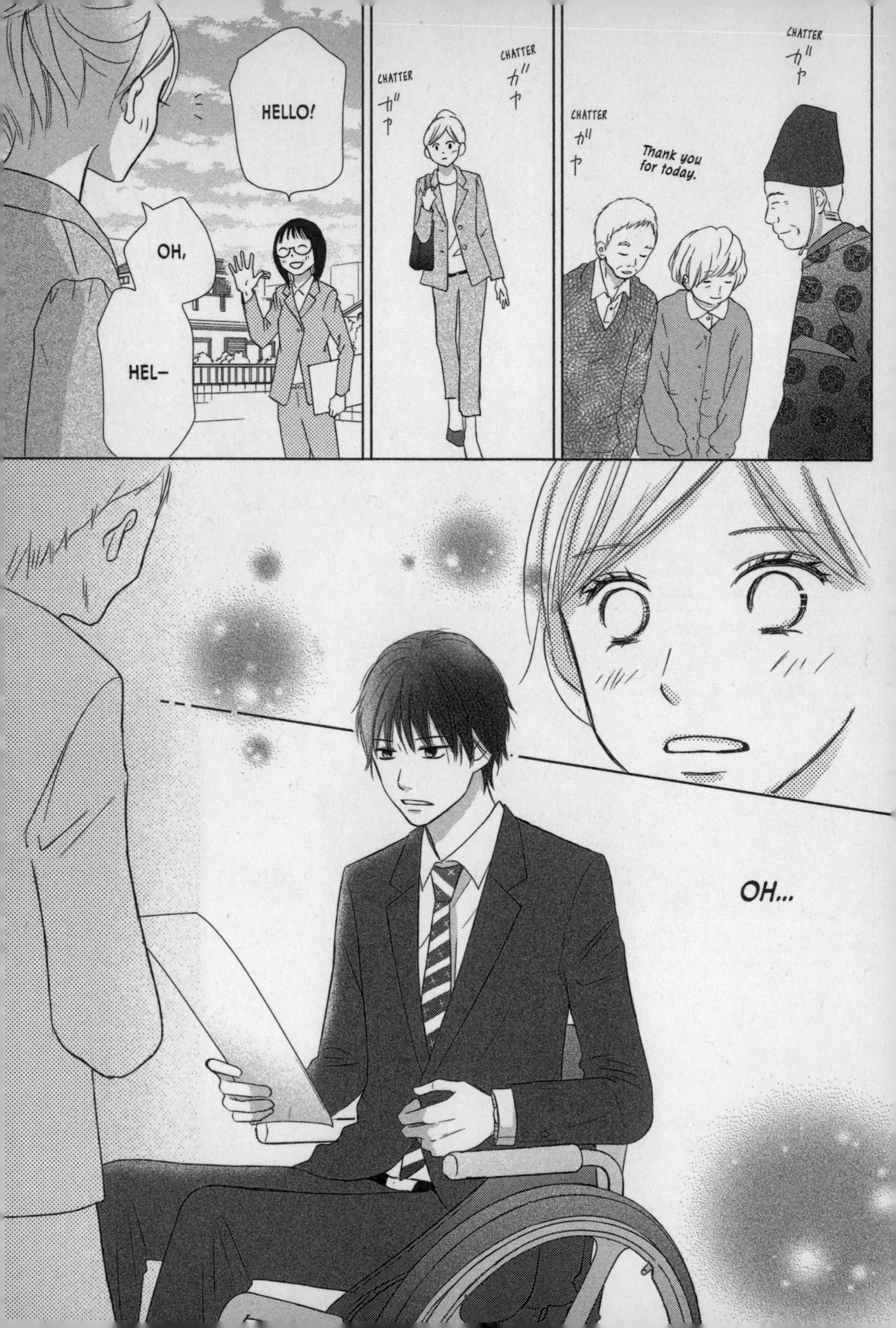
CHATTER
ガヤ
Thank you for today.
CHATTER
ガヤ
CHATTER
ガヤ
CHATTER
ガヤ
HELLO!
OH,
HEL–
OH...

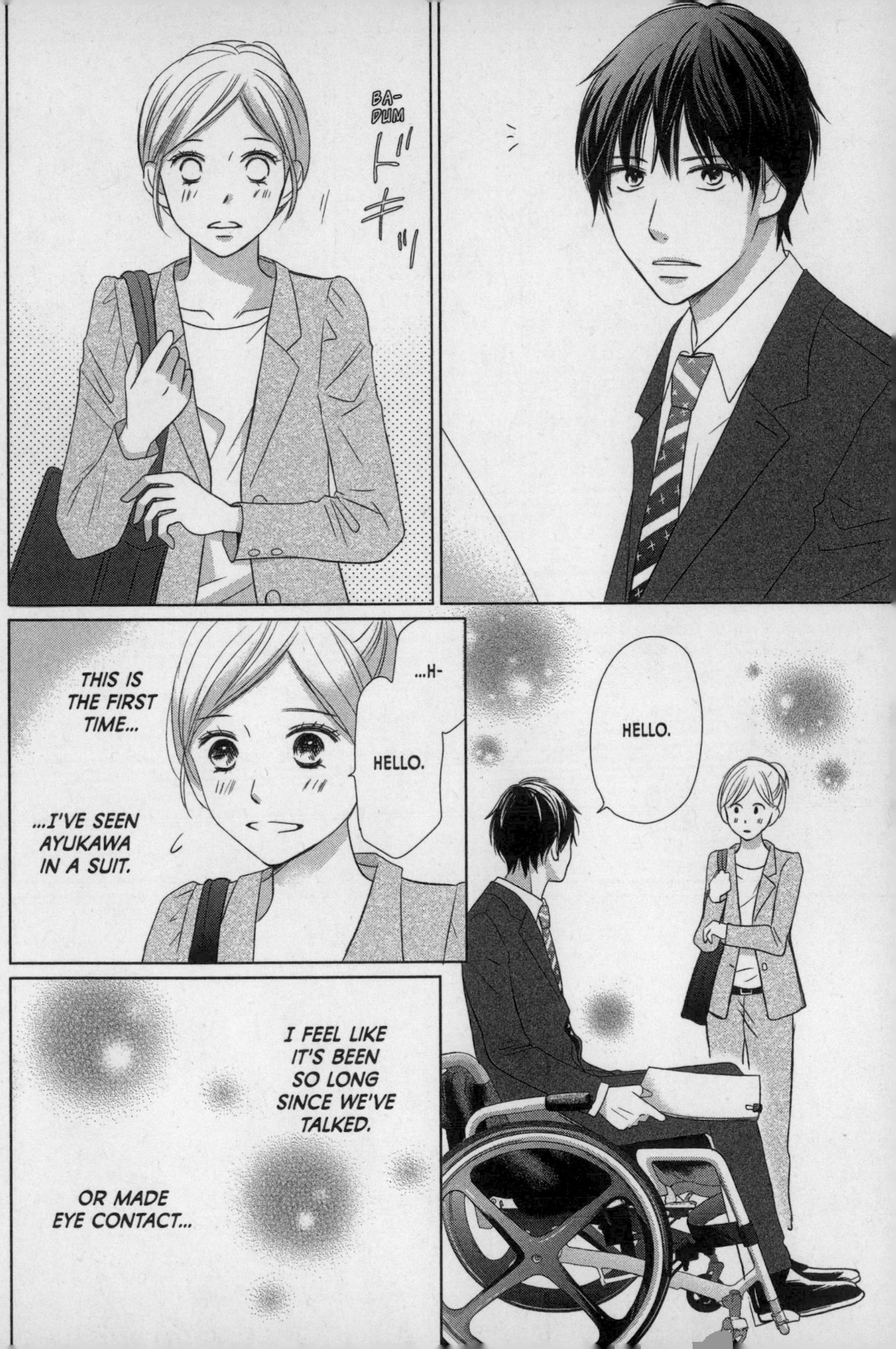

BA-DUM
ドキッ
HELLO.
...H- HELLO.
THIS IS THE FIRST TIME...
...I'VE SEEN AYUKAWA IN A SUIT.
I FEEL LIKE IT'S BEEN SO LONG SINCE WE'VE TALKED.
OR MADE EYE CONTACT...

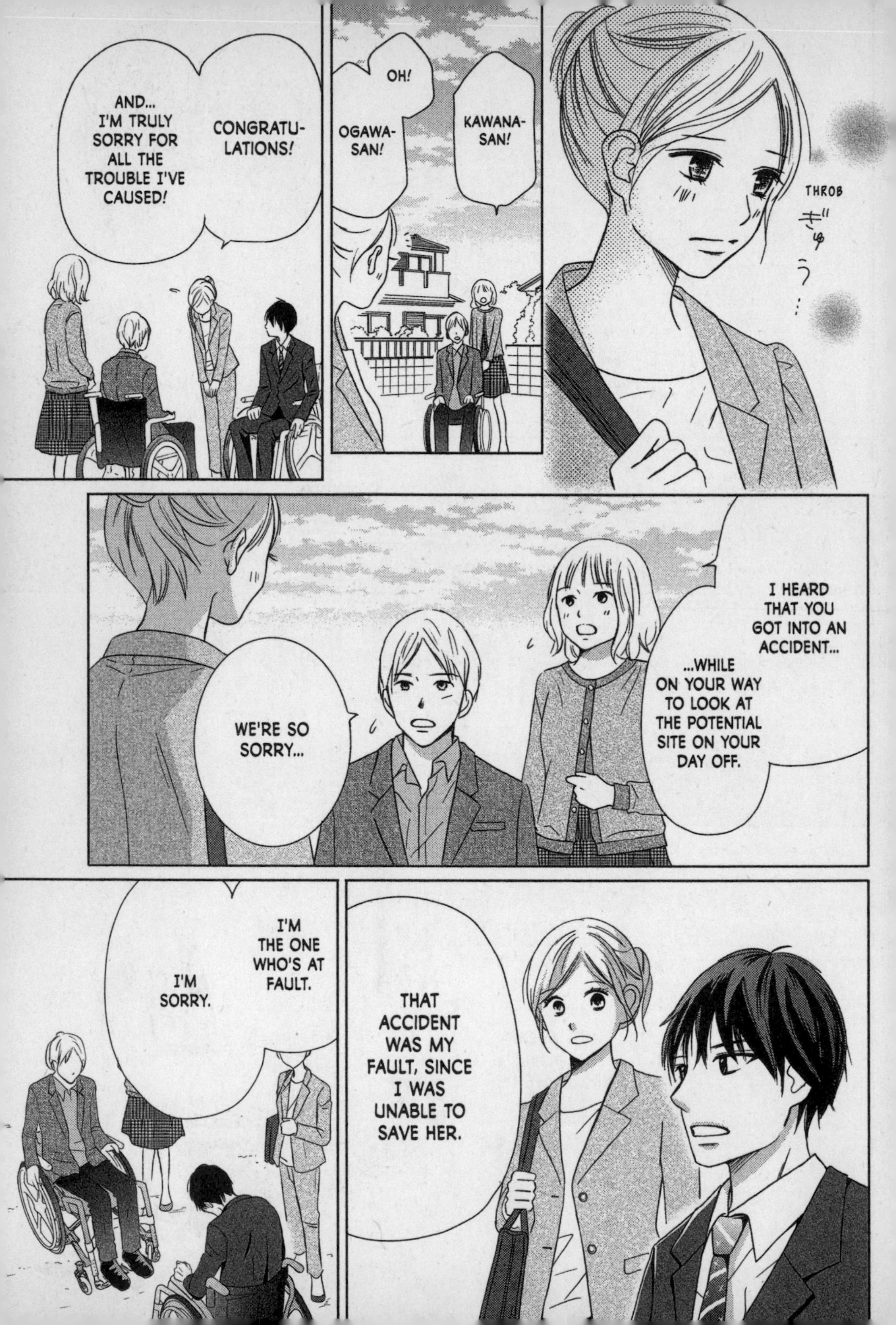
THROB
KAWANA-SAN!
OH!
OGAWA-SAN!
CONGRATULATIONS!
AND... I'M TRULY SORRY FOR ALL THE TROUBLE I'VE CAUSED!
I HEARD THAT YOU GOT INTO AN ACCIDENT...
...WHILE ON YOUR WAY TO LOOK AT THE POTENTIAL SITE ON YOUR DAY OFF.
WE'RE SO SORRY...
THAT ACCIDENT WAS MY FAULT, SINCE I WAS UNABLE TO SAVE HER.
I'M THE ONE WHO'S AT FAULT.
I'M SORRY.

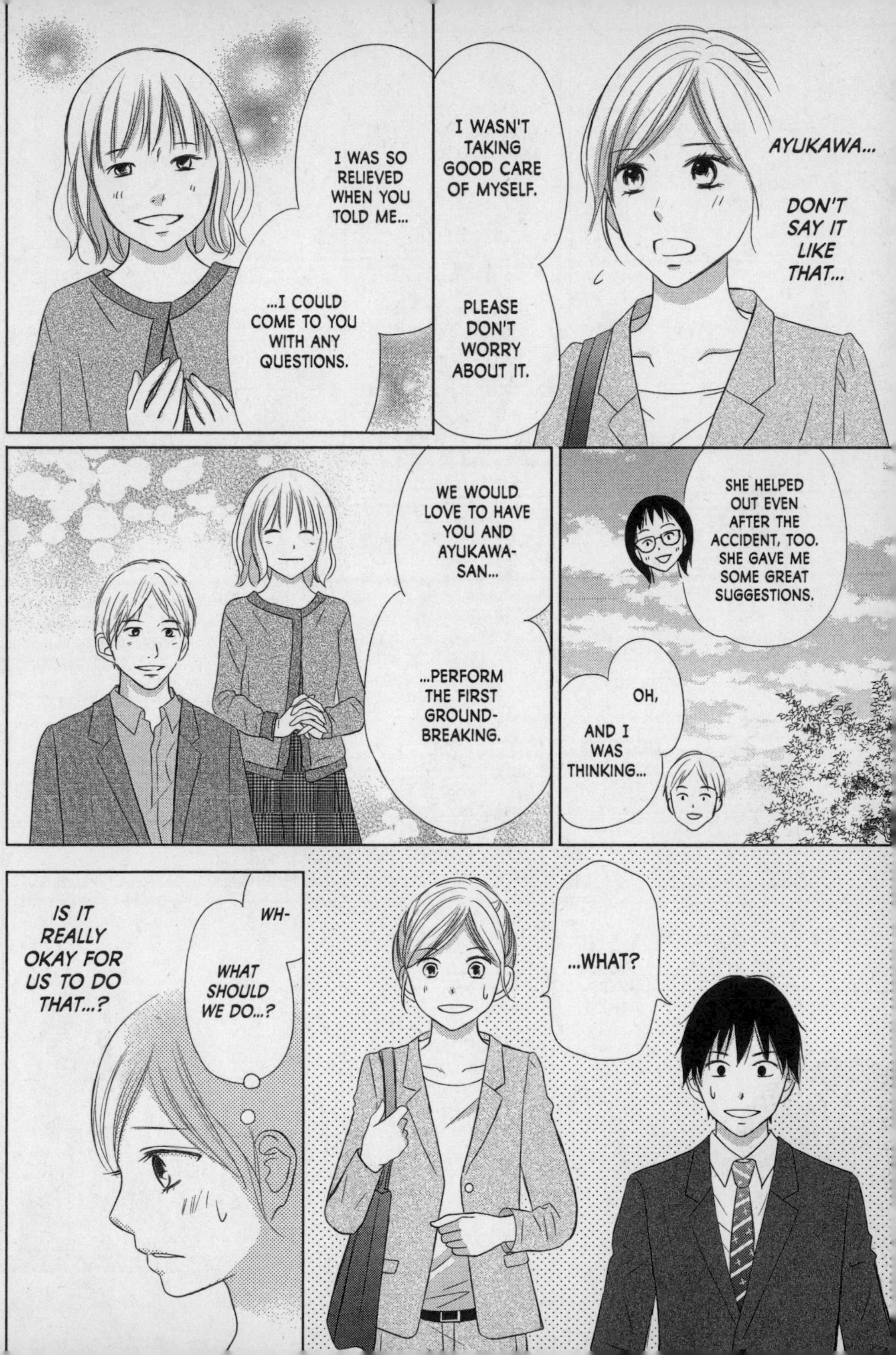
AYUKAWA...
DON'T SAY IT LIKE THAT...
I WASN'T TAKING GOOD CARE OF MYSELF.
PLEASE DON'T WORRY ABOUT IT.
I WAS SO RELIEVED WHEN YOU TOLD ME...
...I COULD COME TO YOU WITH ANY QUESTIONS.
SHE HELPED OUT EVEN AFTER THE ACCIDENT, TOO. SHE GAVE ME SOME GREAT SUGGESTIONS.
OH,
AND I WAS THINKING...
WE WOULD LOVE TO HAVE YOU AND AYUKAWA-SAN...
...PERFORM THE FIRST GROUND-BREAKING.
...WHAT?
WH-
WHAT SHOULD WE DO...?
IS IT REALLY OKAY FOR US TO DO THAT...?

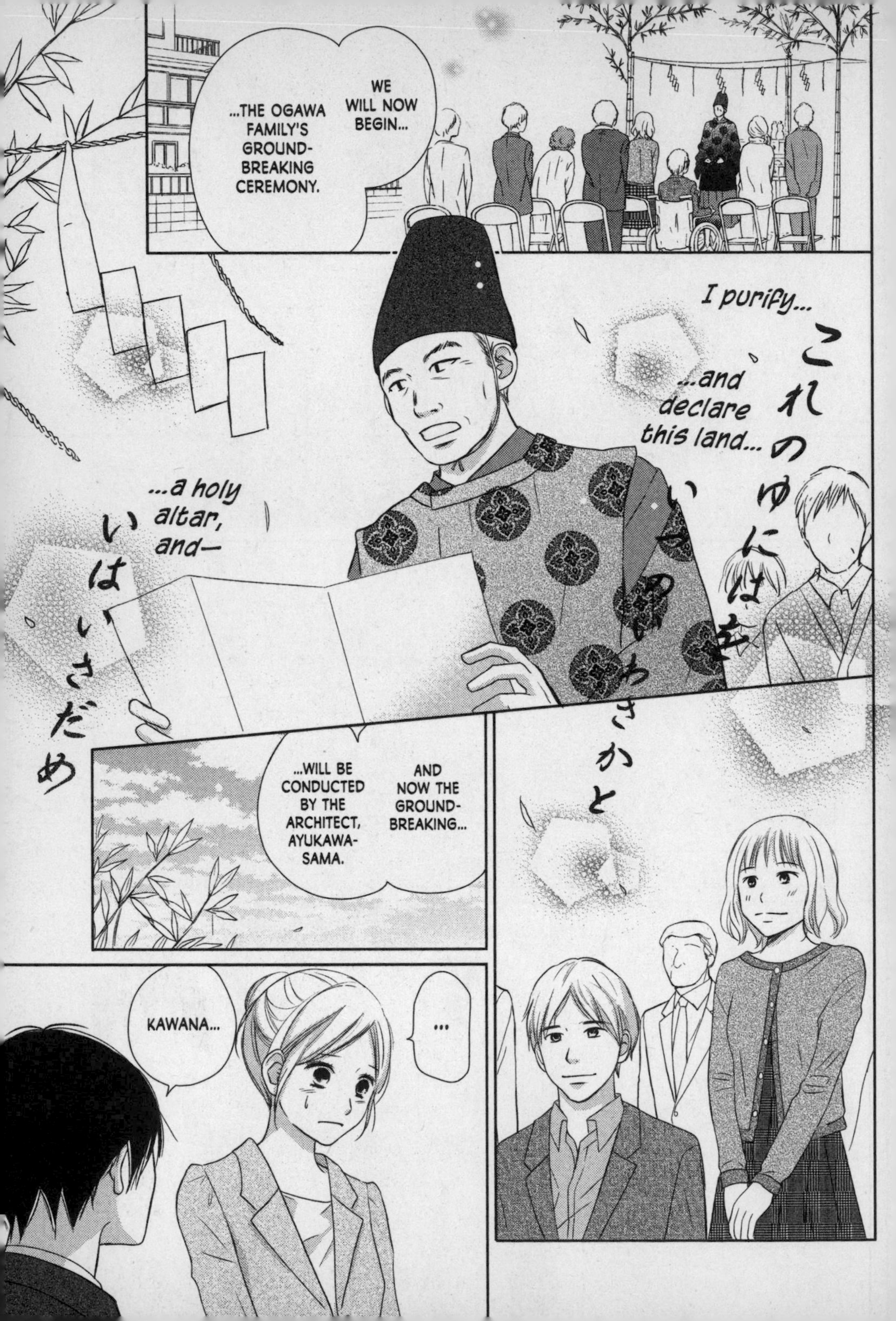
WE WILL NOW BEGIN...
...THE OGAWA FAMILY'S GROUND-BREAKING CEREMONY.
I purify...
これのゆにはを
...and declare this land...
...a holy altar, and—
いはいさだめ
AND NOW THE GROUND-BREAKING...
...WILL BE CONDUCTED BY THE ARCHITECT, AYUKAWA-SAMA.
...
KAWANA...

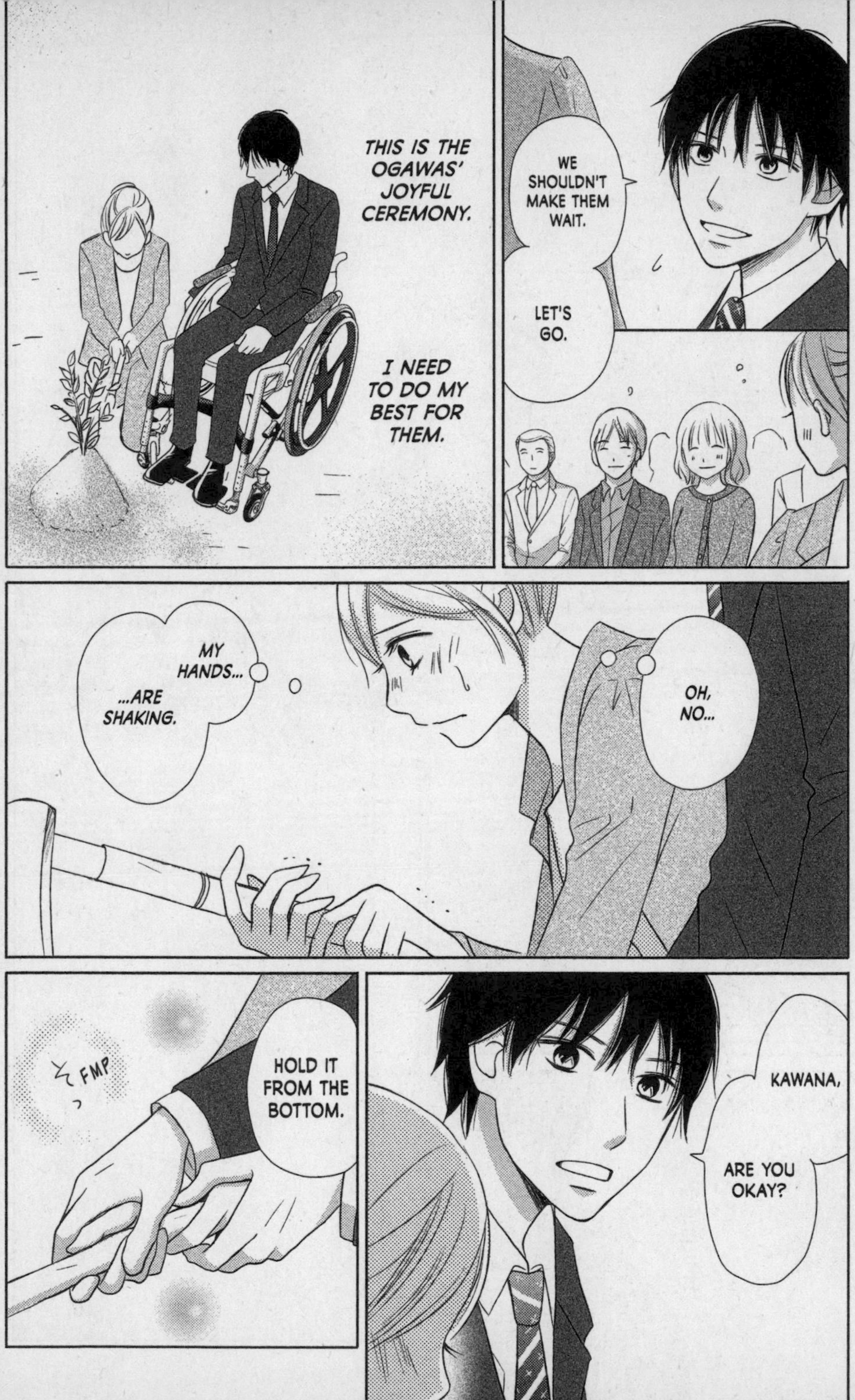
WE SHOULDN'T MAKE THEM WAIT.
LET'S GO.
THIS IS THE OGAWAS' JOYFUL CEREMONY.
I NEED TO DO MY BEST FOR THEM.
OH, NO...
MY HANDS...
...ARE SHAKING.
KAWANA,
ARE YOU OKAY?
HOLD IT FROM THE BOTTOM.
FMP

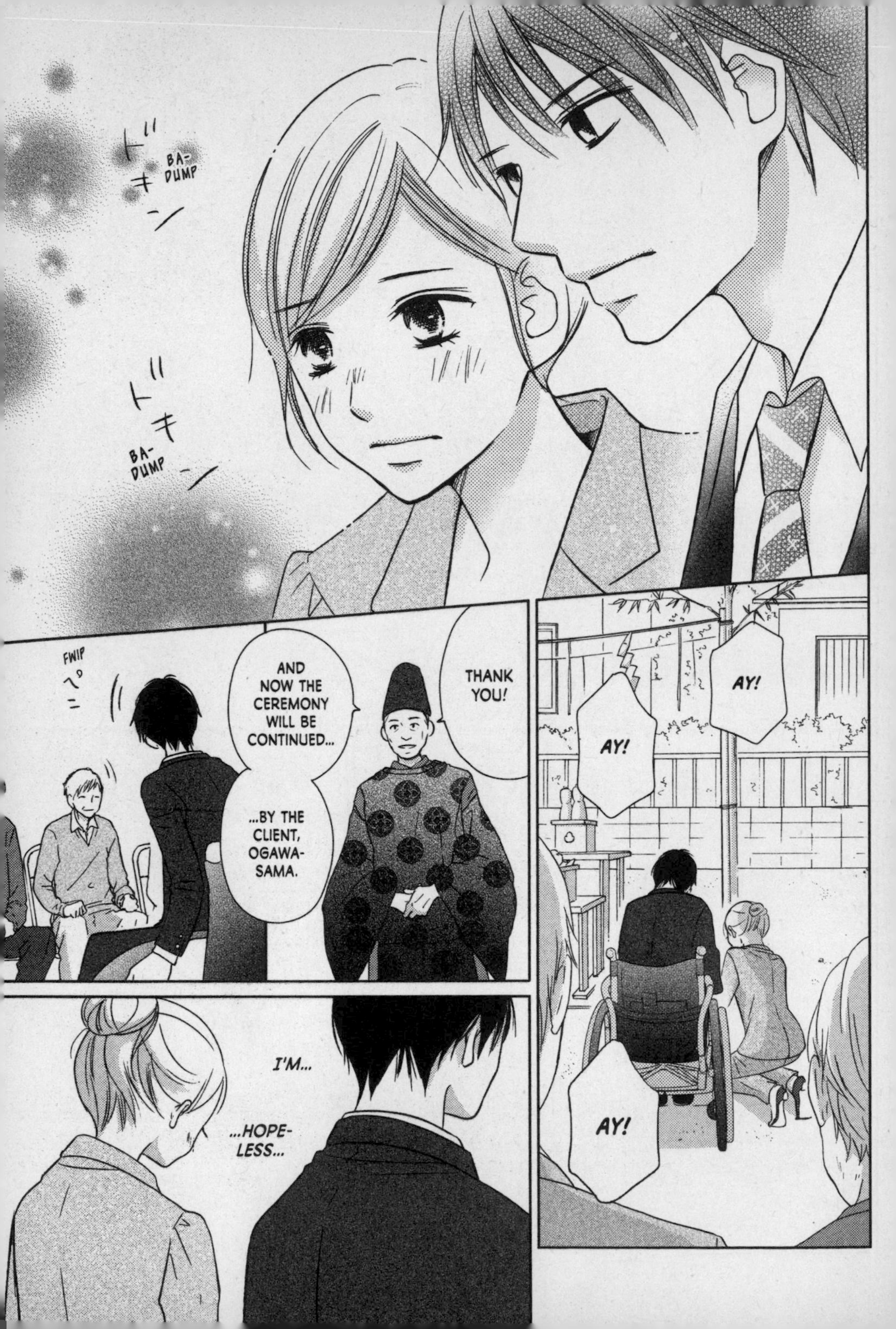
ドキン
BA-DUMP
ドキン
BA-DUMP
AY!
AY!
AY!
THANK YOU!
AND NOW THE CEREMONY WILL BE CONTINUED...
...BY THE CLIENT, OGAWA-SAMA.
ぺこ
FWIP
I'M...
...HOPE-LESS...

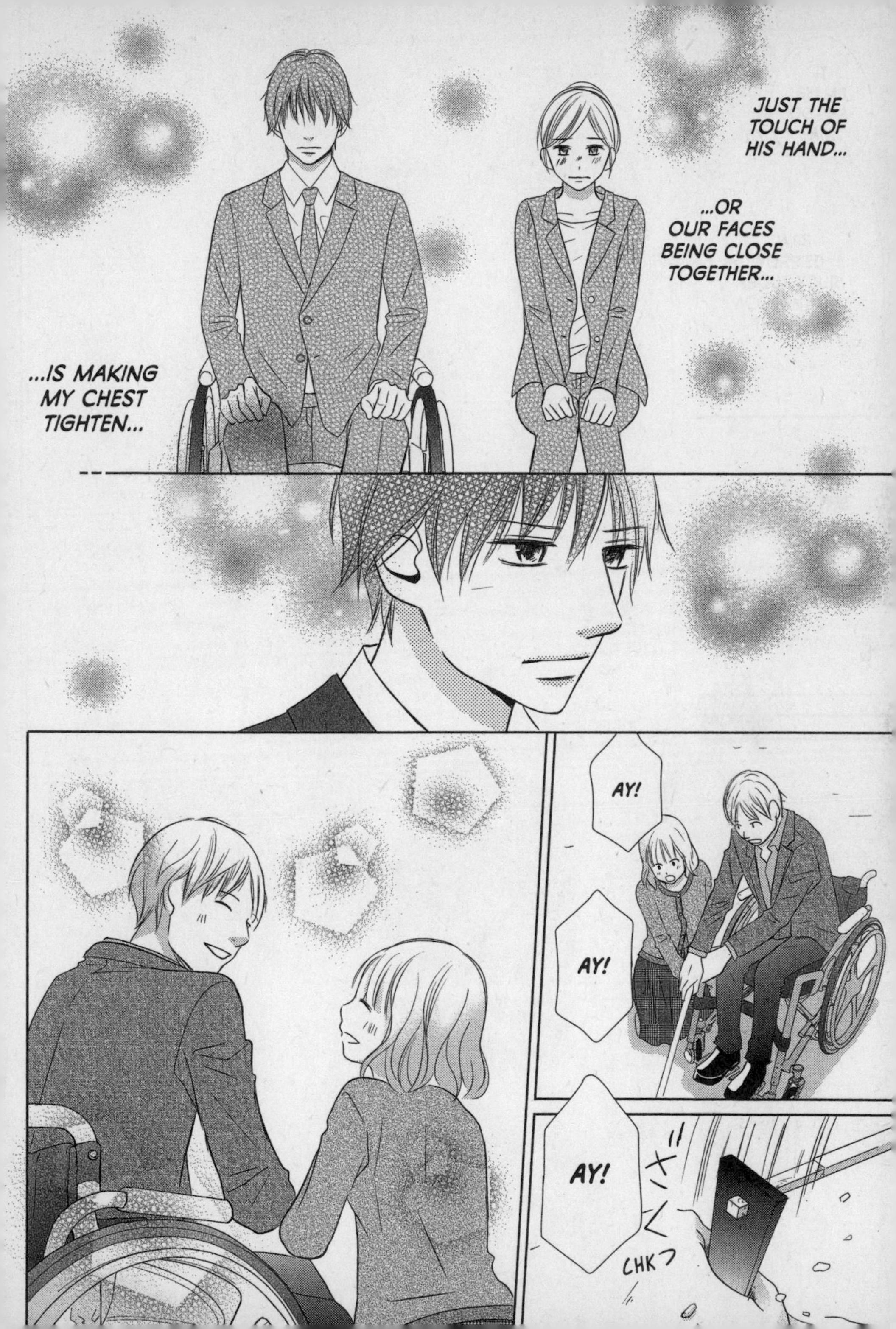
JUST THE TOUCH OF HIS HAND...
...OR OUR FACES BEING CLOSE TOGETHER...
...IS MAKING MY CHEST TIGHTEN...
AY!
AY!
AY!
CHK

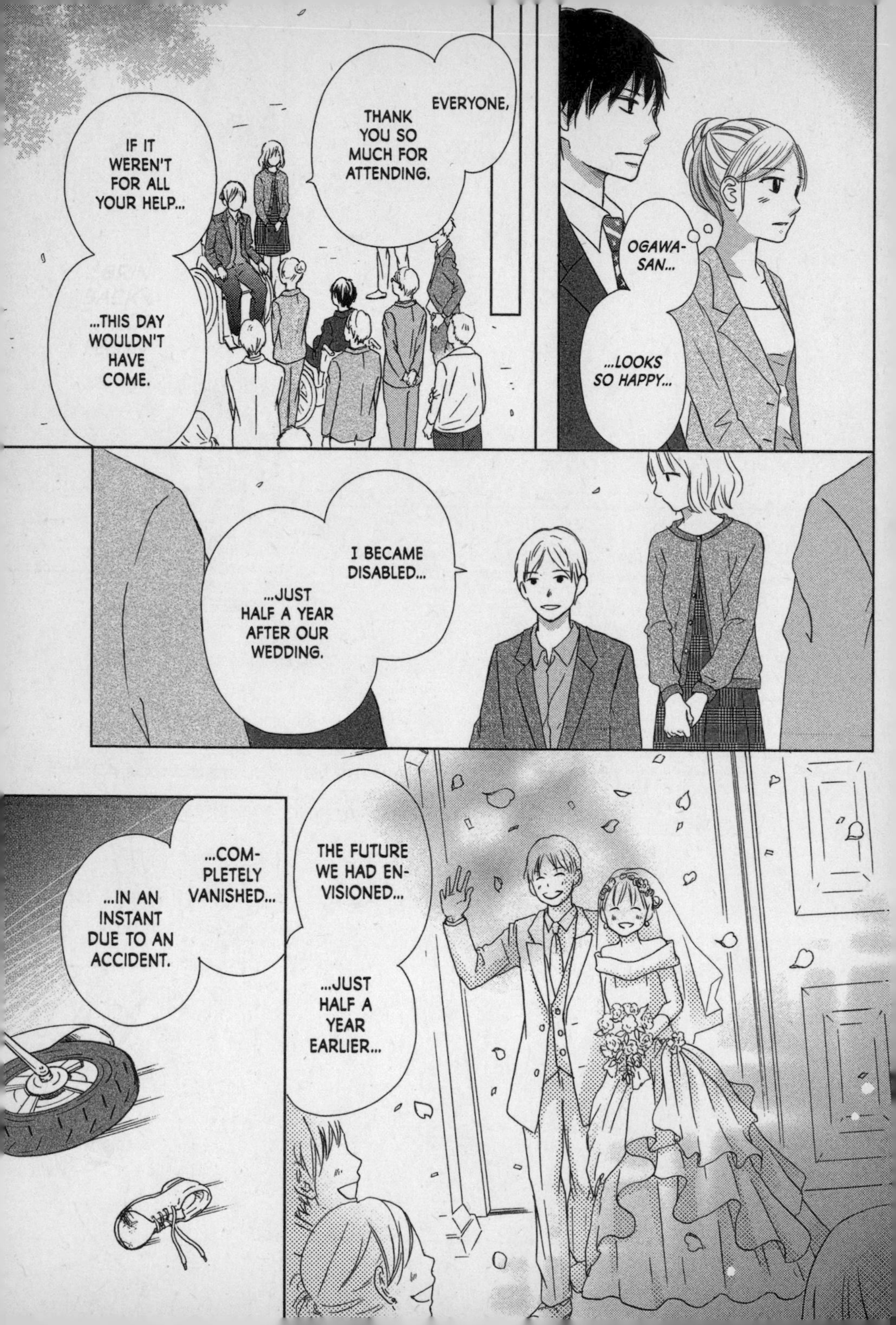
OGAWA-SAN...
...LOOKS SO HAPPY...
EVERYONE,
THANK YOU SO MUCH FOR ATTENDING.
IF IT WEREN'T FOR ALL YOUR HELP...
...THIS DAY WOULDN'T HAVE COME.
I BECAME DISABLED...
...JUST HALF A YEAR AFTER OUR WEDDING.
THE FUTURE WE HAD EN-VISIONED...
...JUST HALF A YEAR EARLIER...
...COM-PLETELY VANISHED...
...IN AN INSTANT DUE TO AN ACCIDENT.

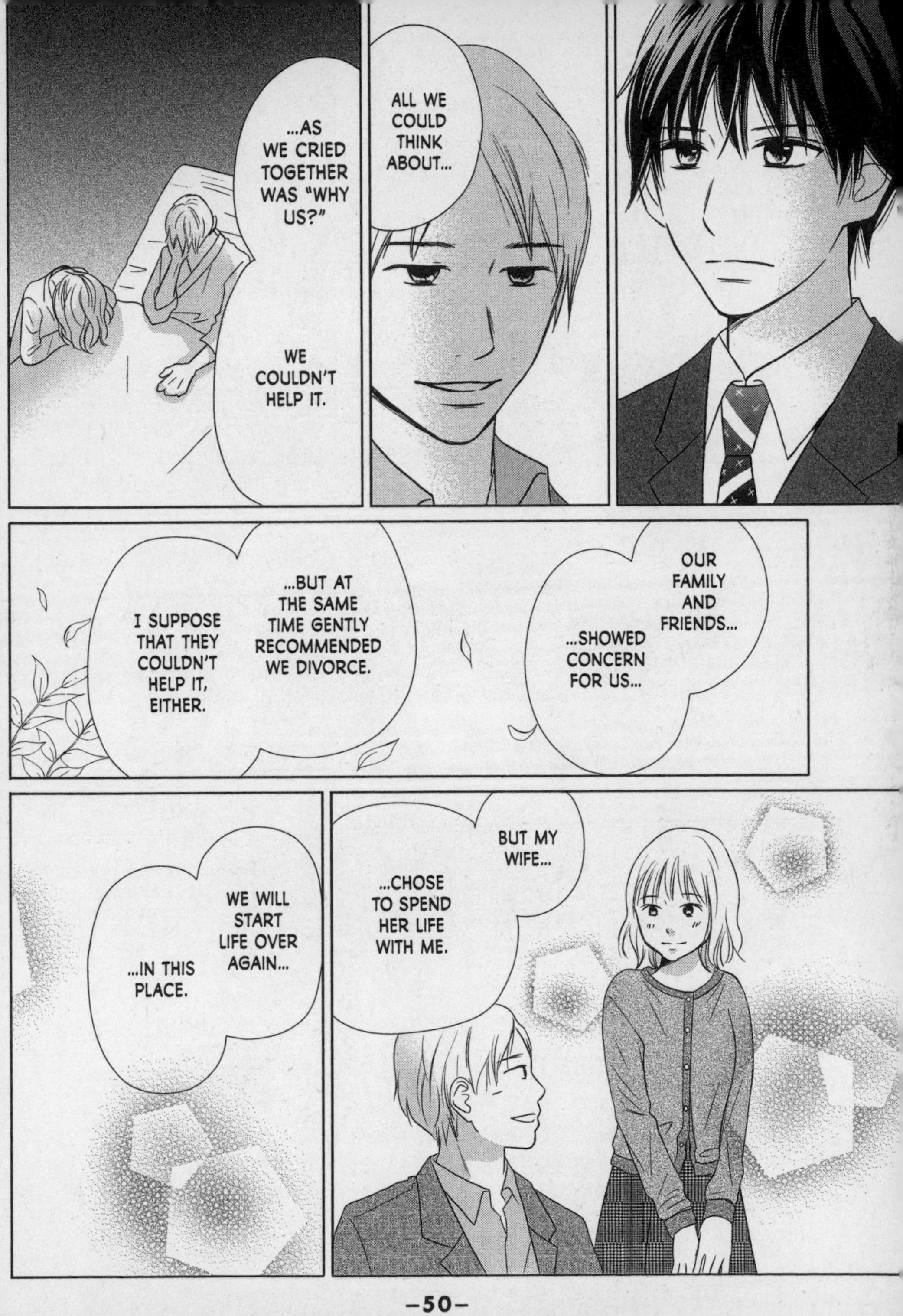
ALL WE COULD THINK ABOUT...
...AS WE CRIED TOGETHER WAS "WHY US?"
WE COULDN'T HELP IT.
OUR FAMILY AND FRIENDS...
...SHOWED CONCERN FOR US...
...BUT AT THE SAME TIME GENTLY RECOMMENDED WE DIVORCE.
I SUPPOSE THAT THEY COULDN'T HELP IT, EITHER.
BUT MY WIFE...
...CHOSE TO SPEND HER LIFE WITH ME.
WE WILL START LIFE OVER AGAIN...
...IN THIS PLACE.

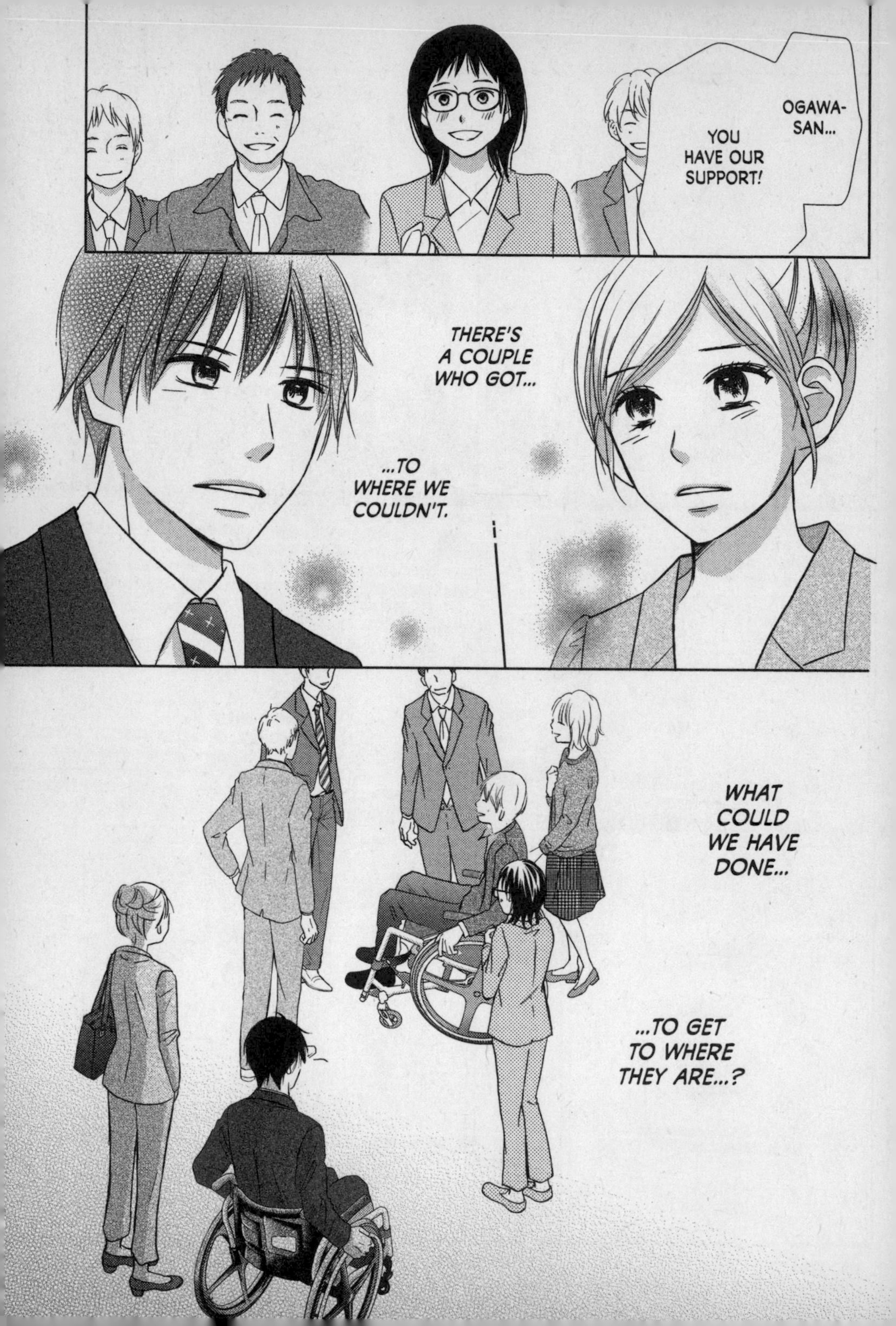
OGAWA-SAN...
YOU HAVE OUR SUPPORT!
THERE'S A COUPLE WHO GOT...
...TO WHERE WE COULDN'T.
WHAT COULD WE HAVE DONE...
...TO GET TO WHERE THEY ARE...?

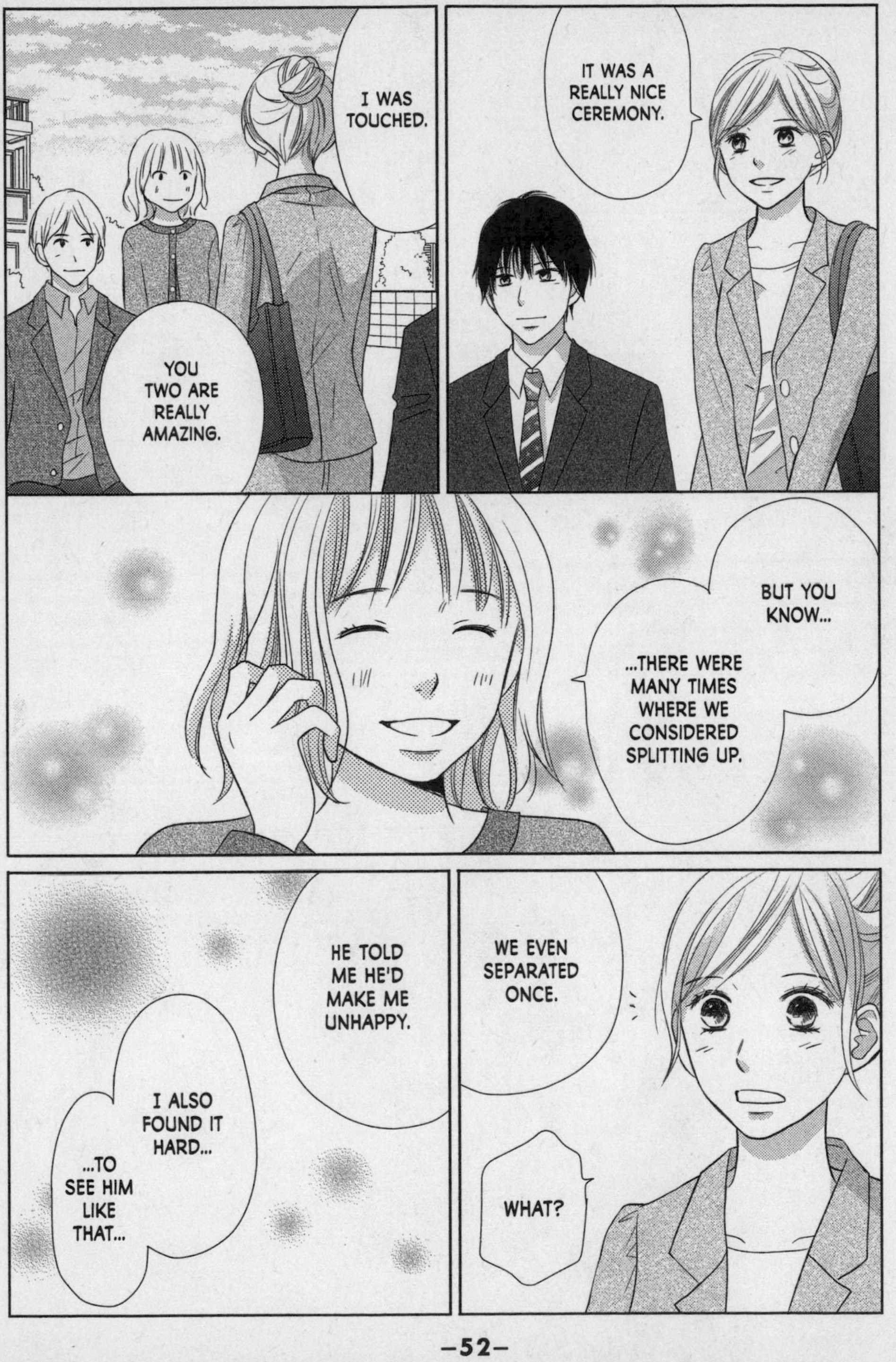
IT WAS A REALLY NICE CEREMONY.
I WAS TOUCHED.
YOU TWO ARE REALLY AMAZING.
BUT YOU KNOW...
...THERE WERE MANY TIMES WHERE WE CONSIDERED SPLITTING UP.
WE EVEN SEPARATED ONCE.
WHAT?
HE TOLD ME HE'D MAKE ME UNHAPPY.
I ALSO FOUND IT HARD...
...TO SEE HIM LIKE THAT...

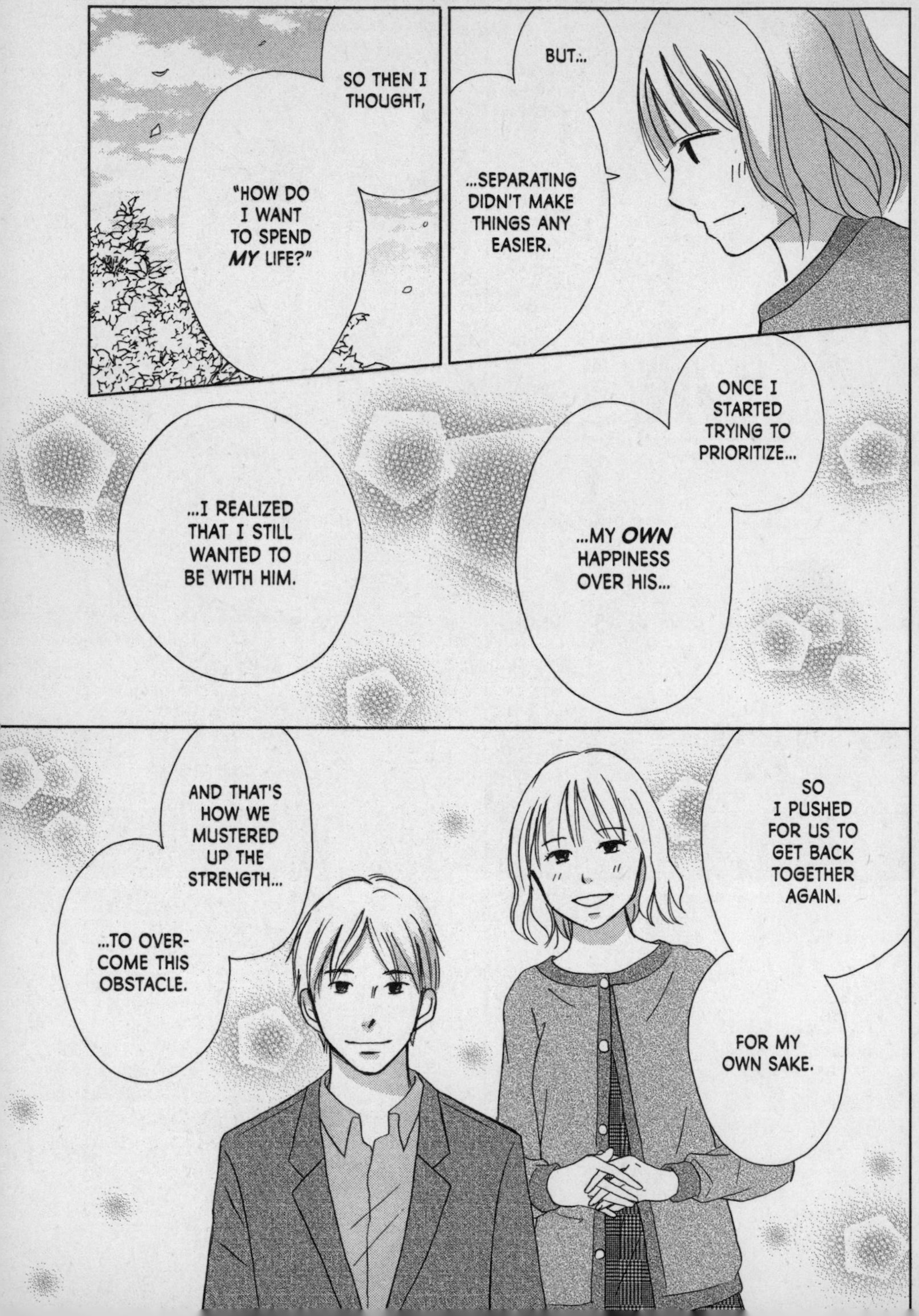
BUT...
...SEPARATING DIDN'T MAKE THINGS ANY EASIER.
SO THEN I THOUGHT,
"HOW DO I WANT TO SPEND *MY* LIFE?"
ONCE I STARTED TRYING TO PRIORITIZE...
...MY ***OWN*** HAPPINESS OVER HIS...
...I REALIZED THAT I STILL WANTED TO BE WITH HIM.
SO I PUSHED FOR US TO GET BACK TOGETHER AGAIN.
FOR MY OWN SAKE.
AND THAT'S HOW WE MUSTERED UP THE STRENGTH...
...TO OVER-COME THIS OBSTACLE.

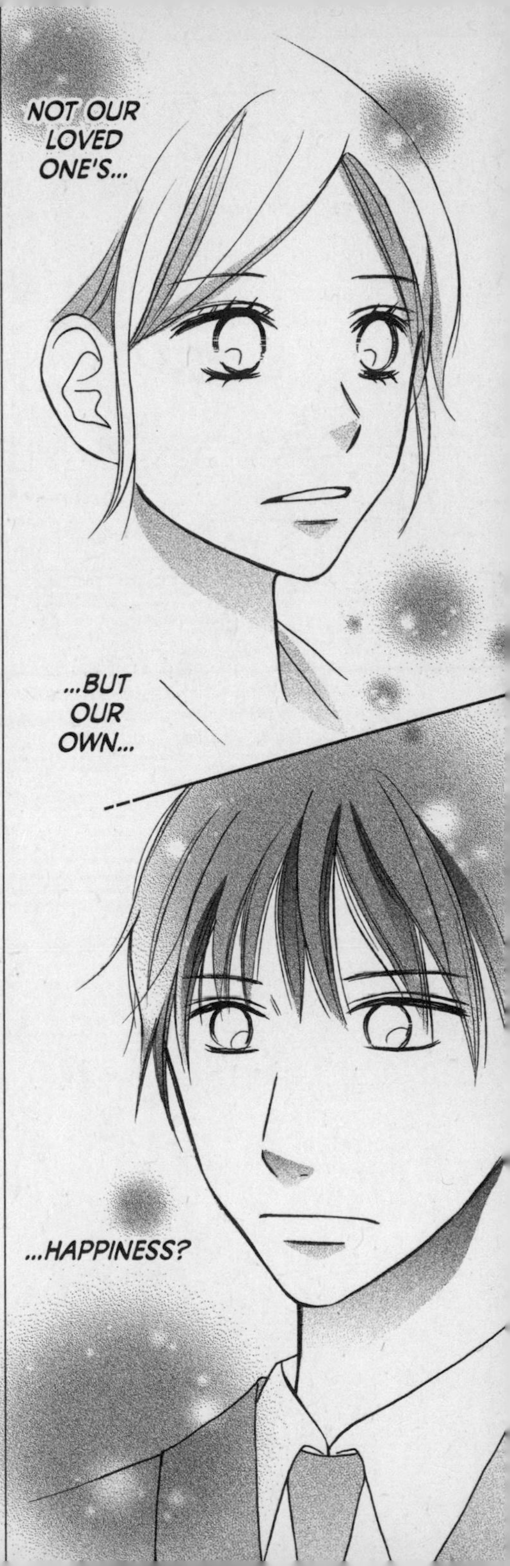
NOT OUR LOVED ONE'S...
...BUT OUR OWN...
...HAPPINESS?

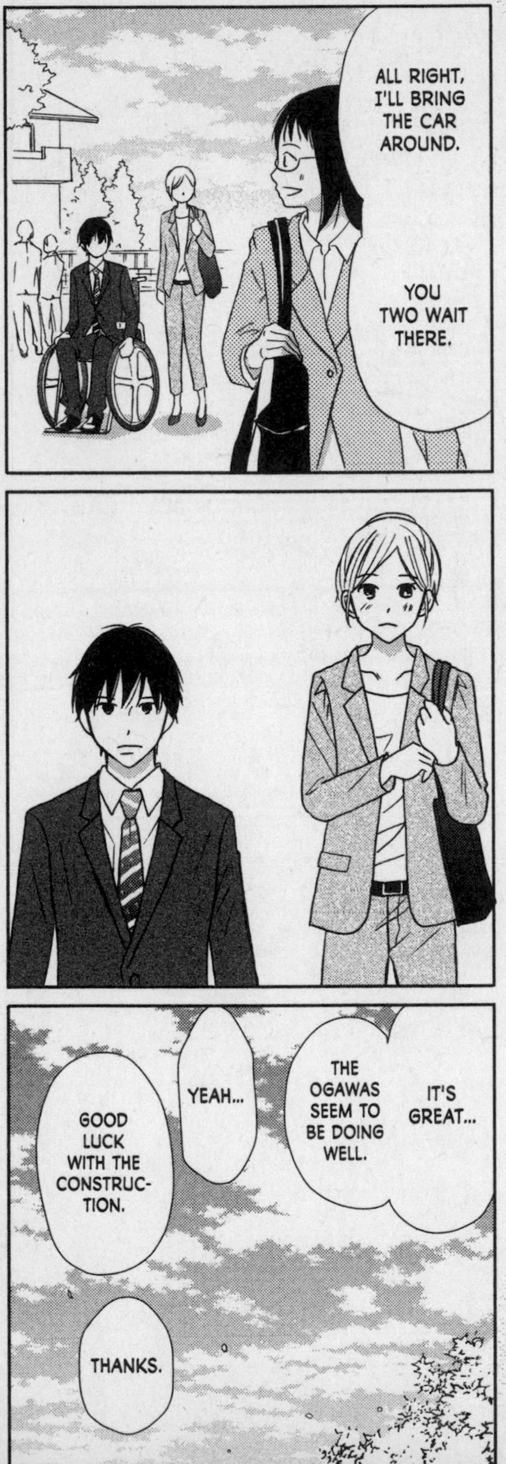
ALL RIGHT, I'LL BRING THE CAR AROUND.
YOU TWO WAIT THERE.
IT'S GREAT...
THE OGAWAS SEEM TO BE DOING WELL.
YEAH...
GOOD LUCK WITH THE CONSTRUC-TION.
THANKS.

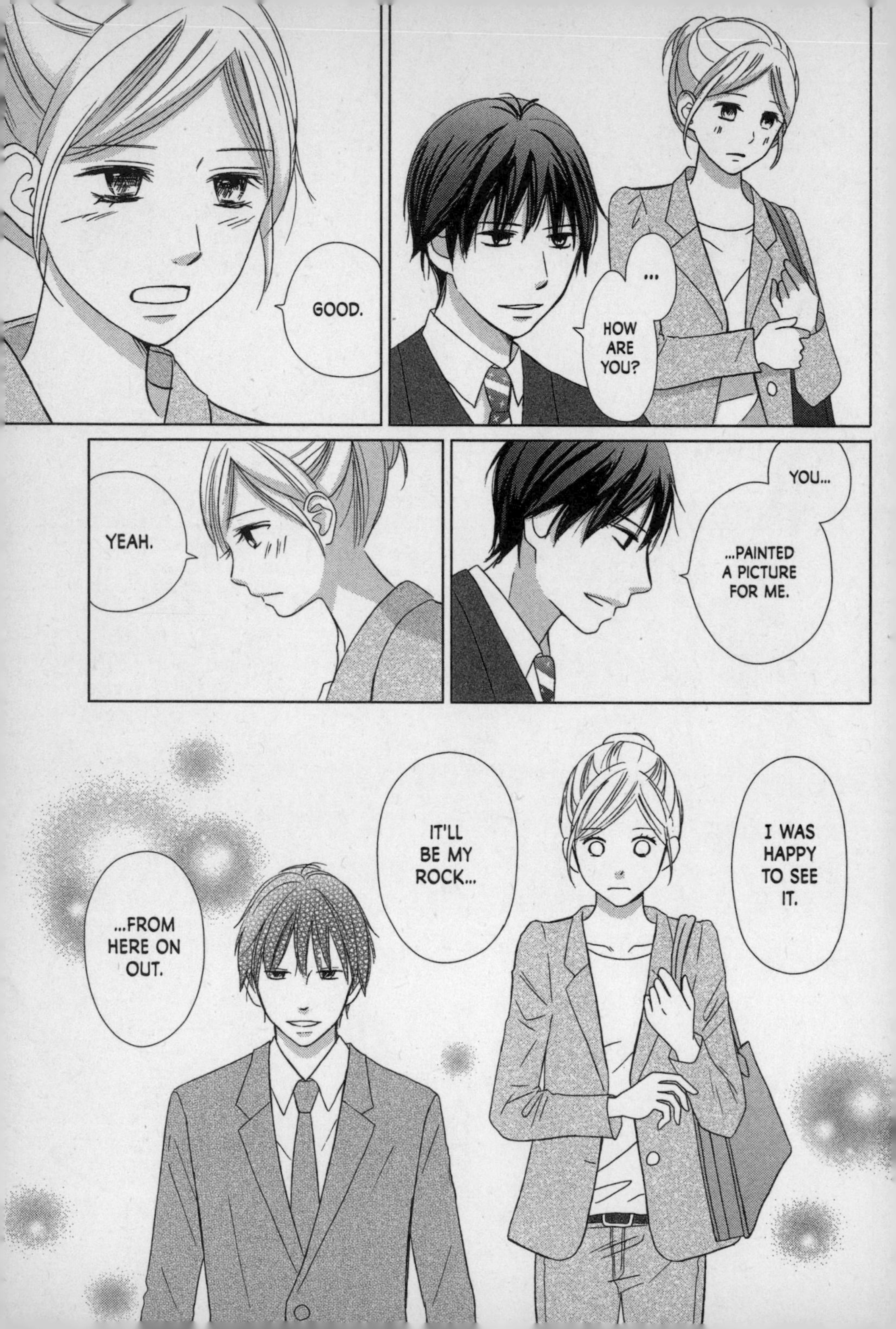
...
HOW ARE YOU?
GOOD.
YOU...
...PAINTED A PICTURE FOR ME.
YEAH.
I WAS HAPPY TO SEE IT.
IT'LL BE MY ROCK...
...FROM HERE ON OUT.

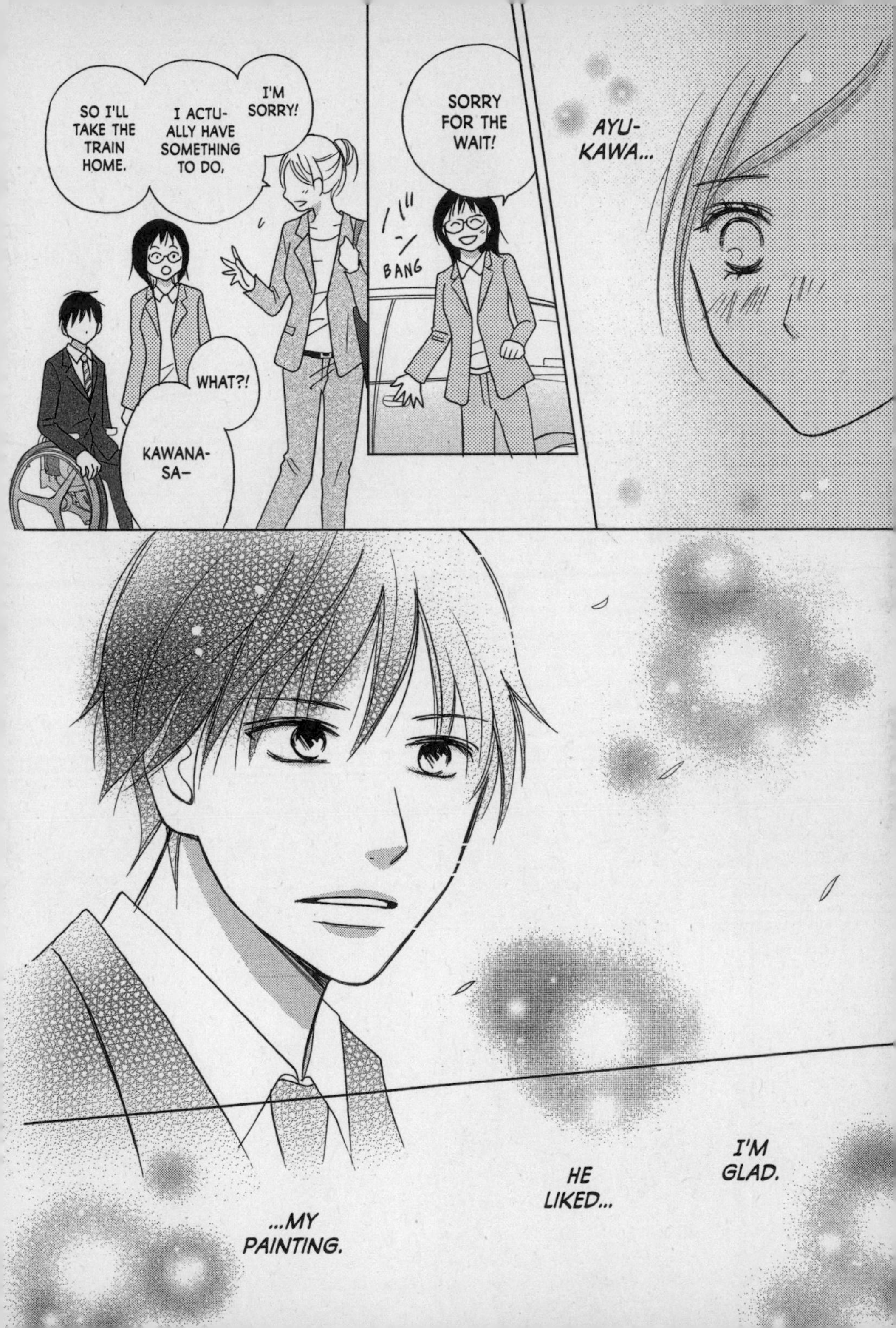
AYU-KAWA...
SORRY FOR THE WAIT!
BANG
I'M SORRY!
I ACTU-ALLY HAVE SOMETHING TO DO,
SO I'LL TAKE THE TRAIN HOME.
WHAT?!
KAWANA-SA-
I'M GLAD.
HE LIKED...
...MY PAINTING.

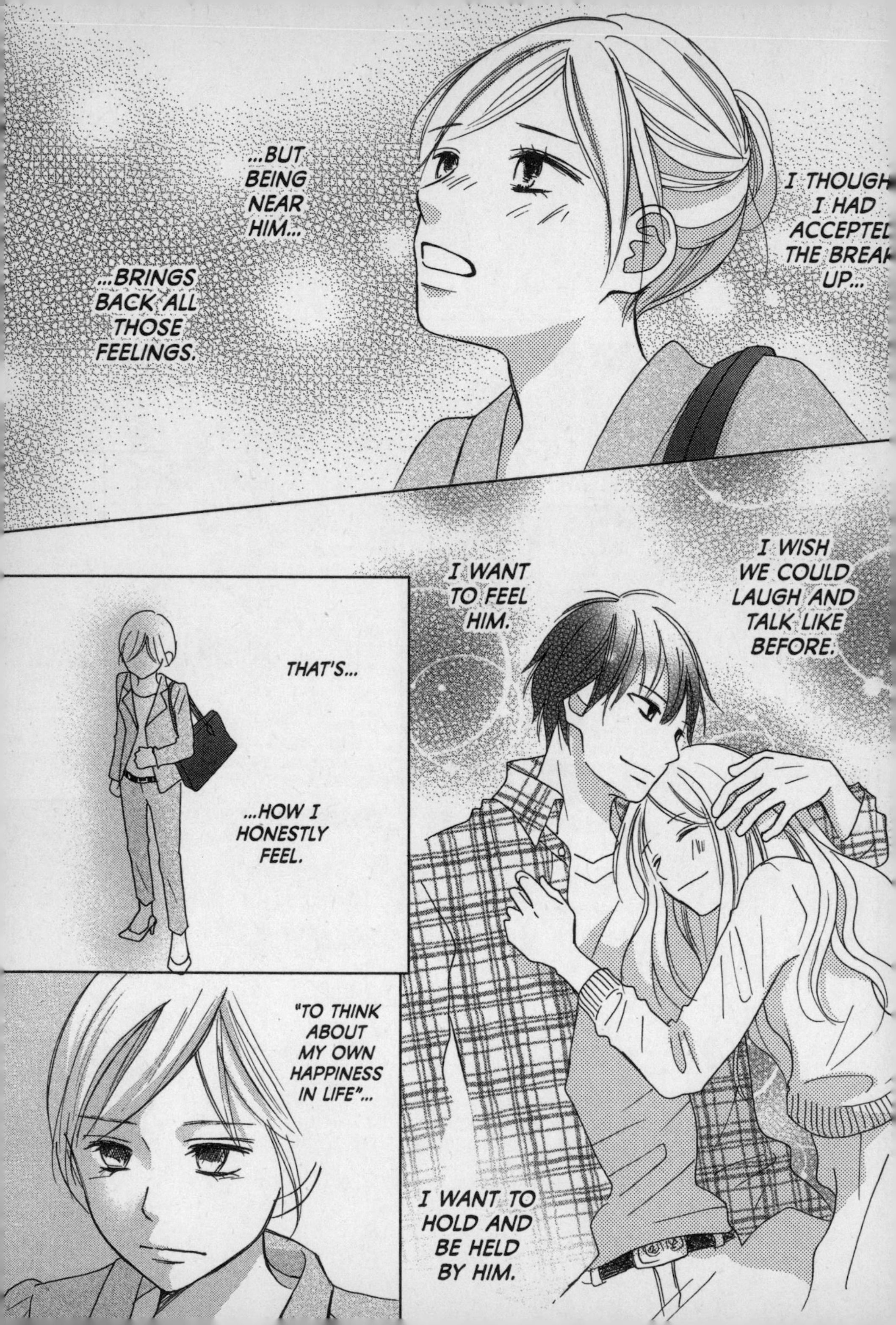
I THOUGH I HAD ACCEPTE THE BREA UP...
...BUT BEING NEAR HIM...
...BRINGS BACK ALL THOSE FEELINGS.
I WISH WE COULD LAUGH AND TALK LIKE BEFORE.
I WANT TO FEEL HIM.
I WANT TO HOLD AND BE HELD BY HIM.
THAT'S...
...HOW I HONESTLY FEEL.
"TO THINK ABOUT MY OWN HAPPINESS IN LIFE"...

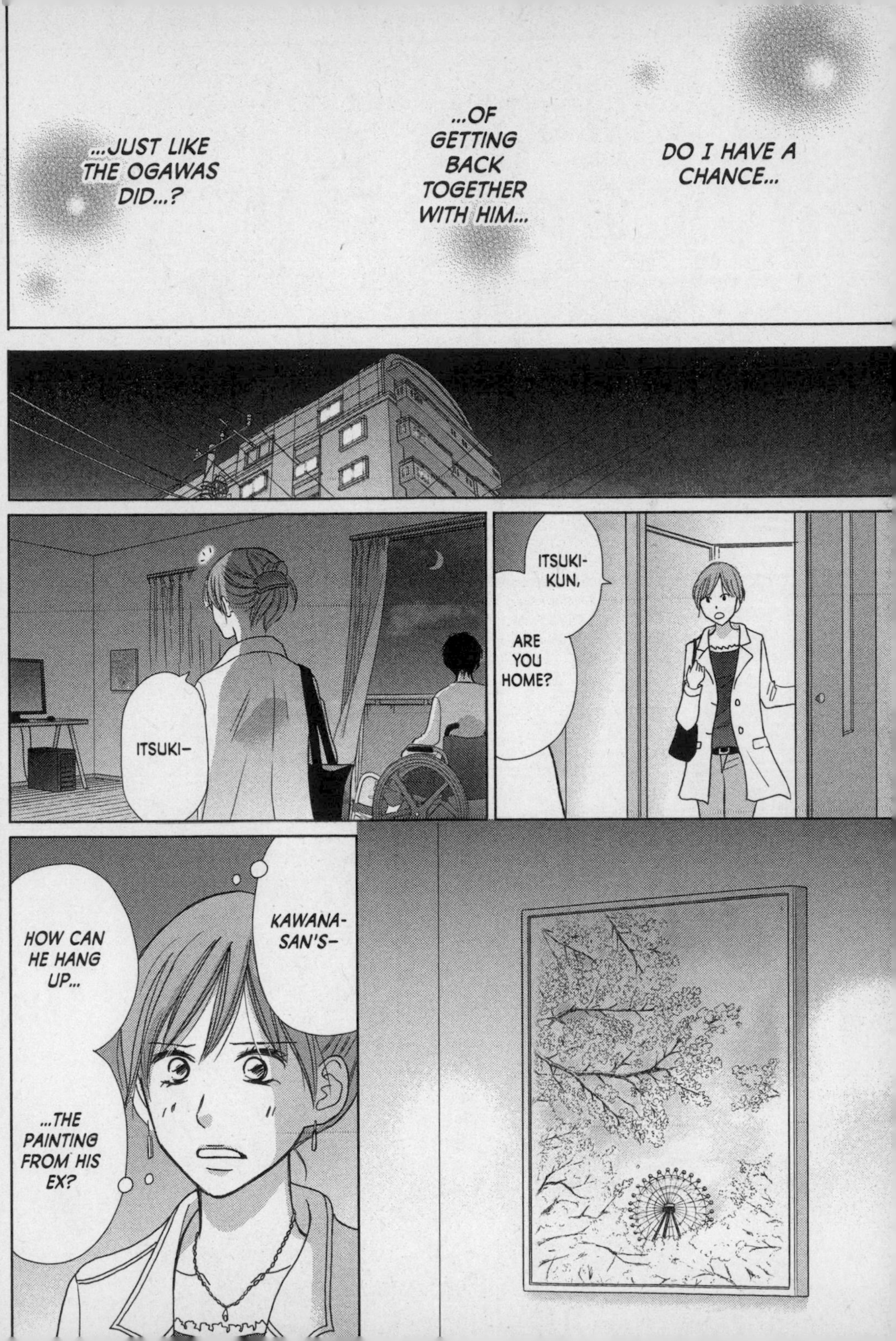
DO I HAVE A CHANCE...
...OF GETTING BACK TOGETHER WITH HIM...
...JUST LIKE THE OGAWAS DID...?
ITSUKI-KUN,
ARE YOU HOME?
ITSUKI–
KAWANA-SAN'S–
HOW CAN HE HANG UP...
...THE PAINTING FROM HIS EX?

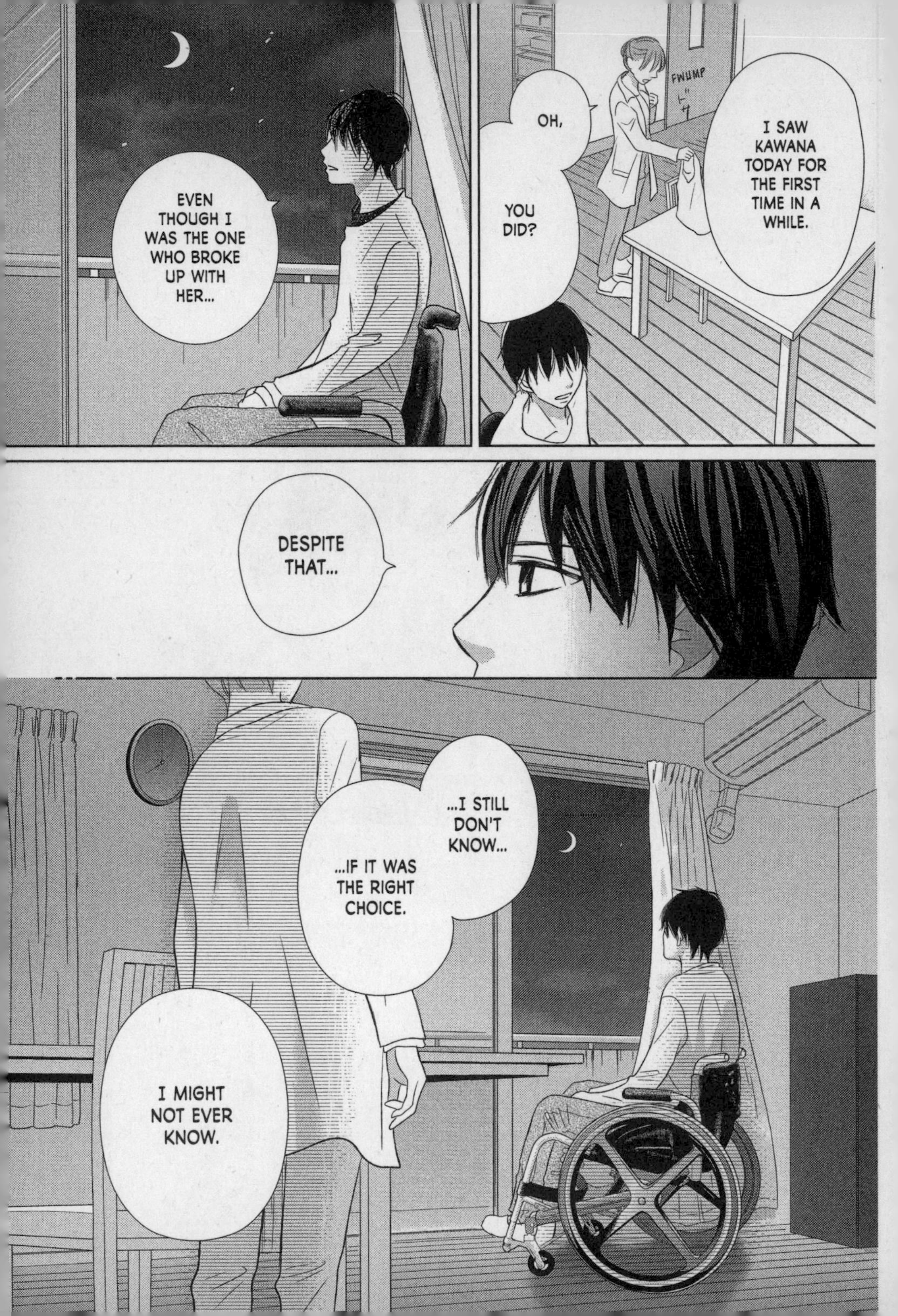
FWUMP
I SAW KAWANA TODAY FOR THE FIRST TIME IN A WHILE.
OH,
YOU DID?
EVEN THOUGH I WAS THE ONE WHO BROKE UP WITH HER...
DESPITE THAT...
...I STILL DON'T KNOW...
...IF IT WAS THE RIGHT CHOICE.
I MIGHT NOT EVER KNOW.

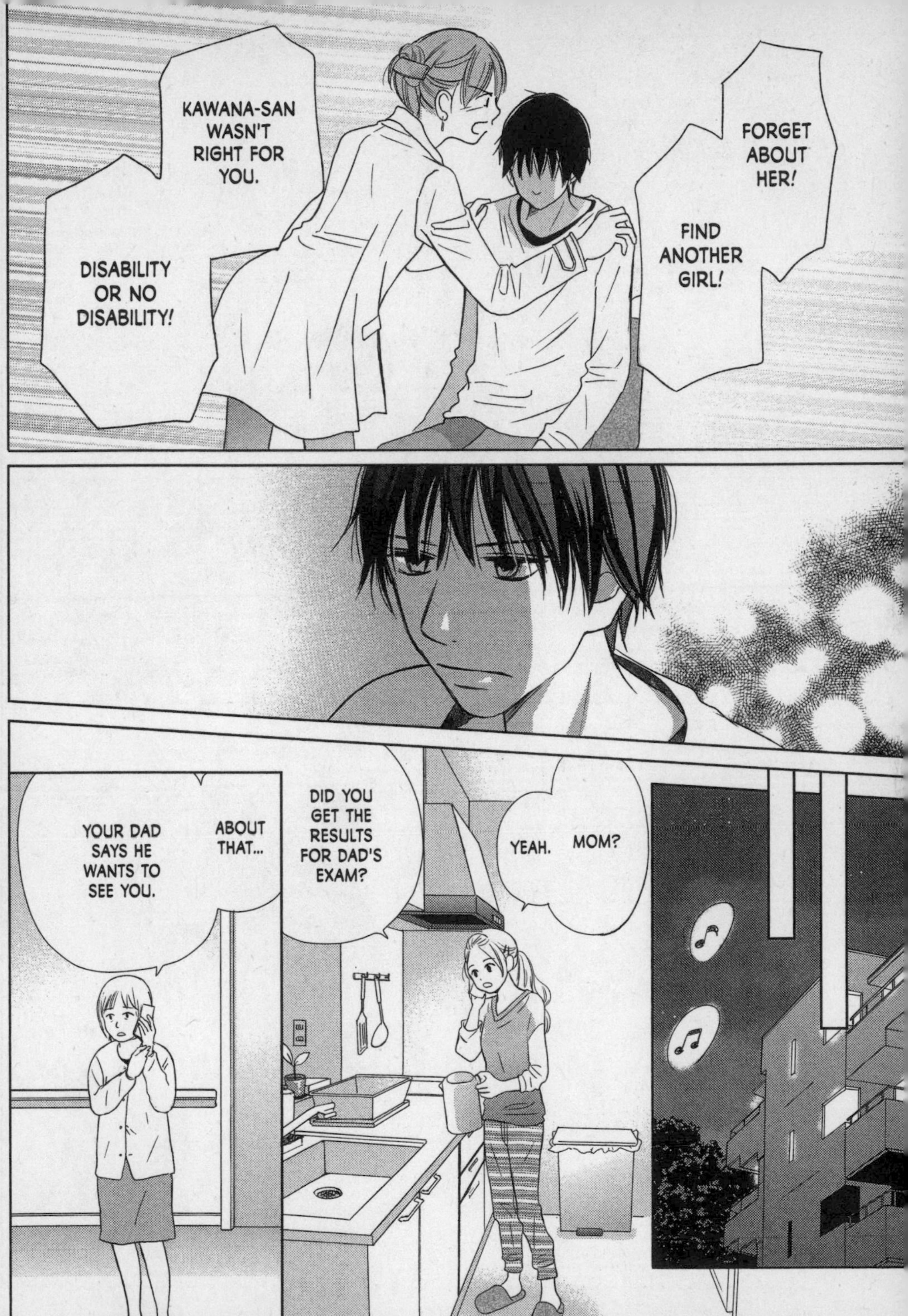
FORGET ABOUT HER!
FIND ANOTHER GIRL!
KAWANA-SAN WASN'T RIGHT FOR YOU.
DISABILITY OR NO DISABILITY!
MOM?
YEAH.
DID YOU GET THE RESULTS FOR DAD'S EXAM?
ABOUT THAT...
YOUR DAD SAYS HE WANTS TO SEE YOU.

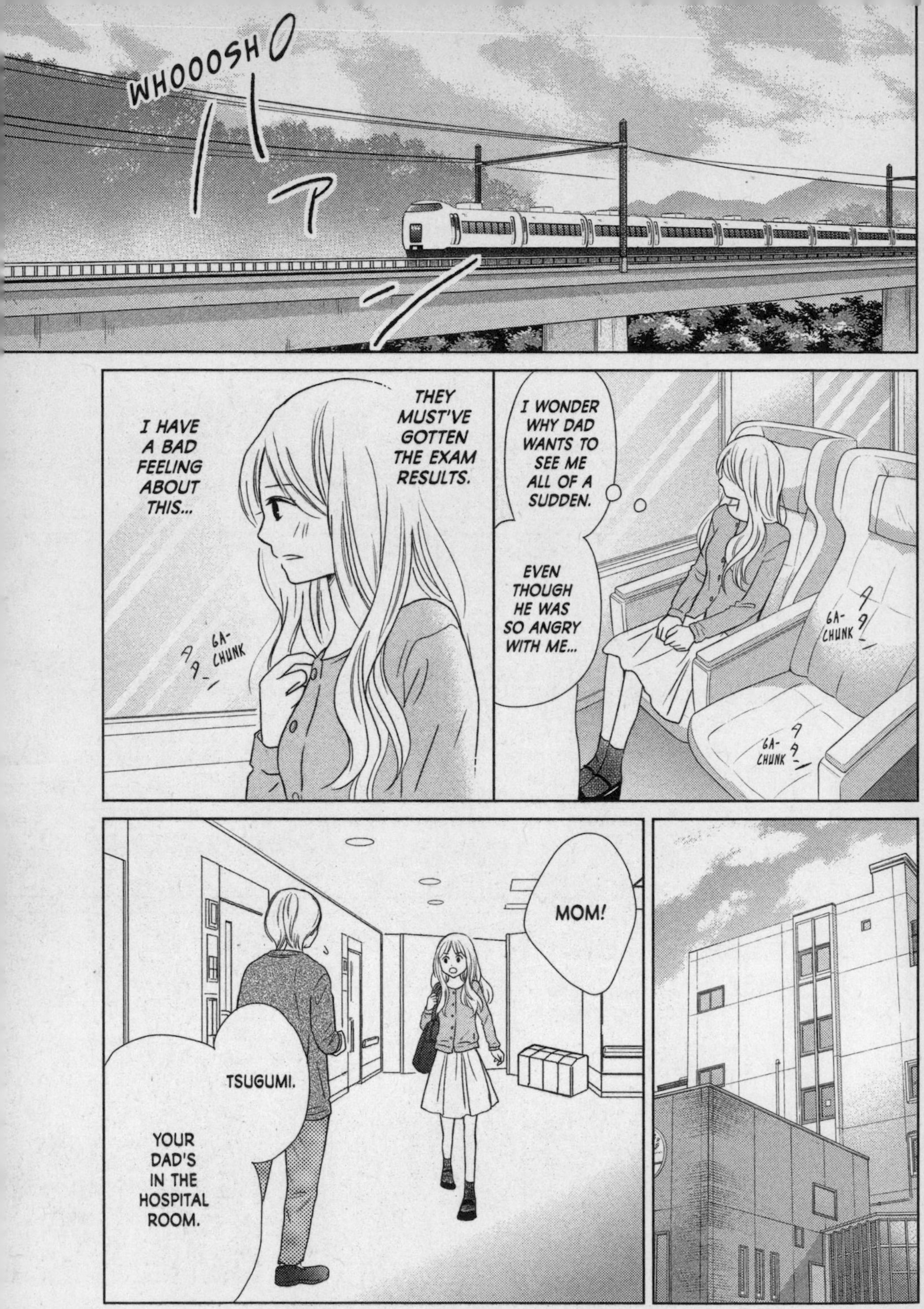
WHOOOSH
I WONDER WHY DAD WANTS TO SEE ME ALL OF A SUDDEN.
EVEN THOUGH HE WAS SO ANGRY WITH ME...
GA-CHUNK
GA-CHUNK
THEY MUST'VE GOTTEN THE EXAM RESULTS.
I HAVE A BAD FEELING ABOUT THIS...
GA-CHUNK
MOM!
TSUGUMI.
YOUR DAD'S IN THE HOSPITAL ROOM.

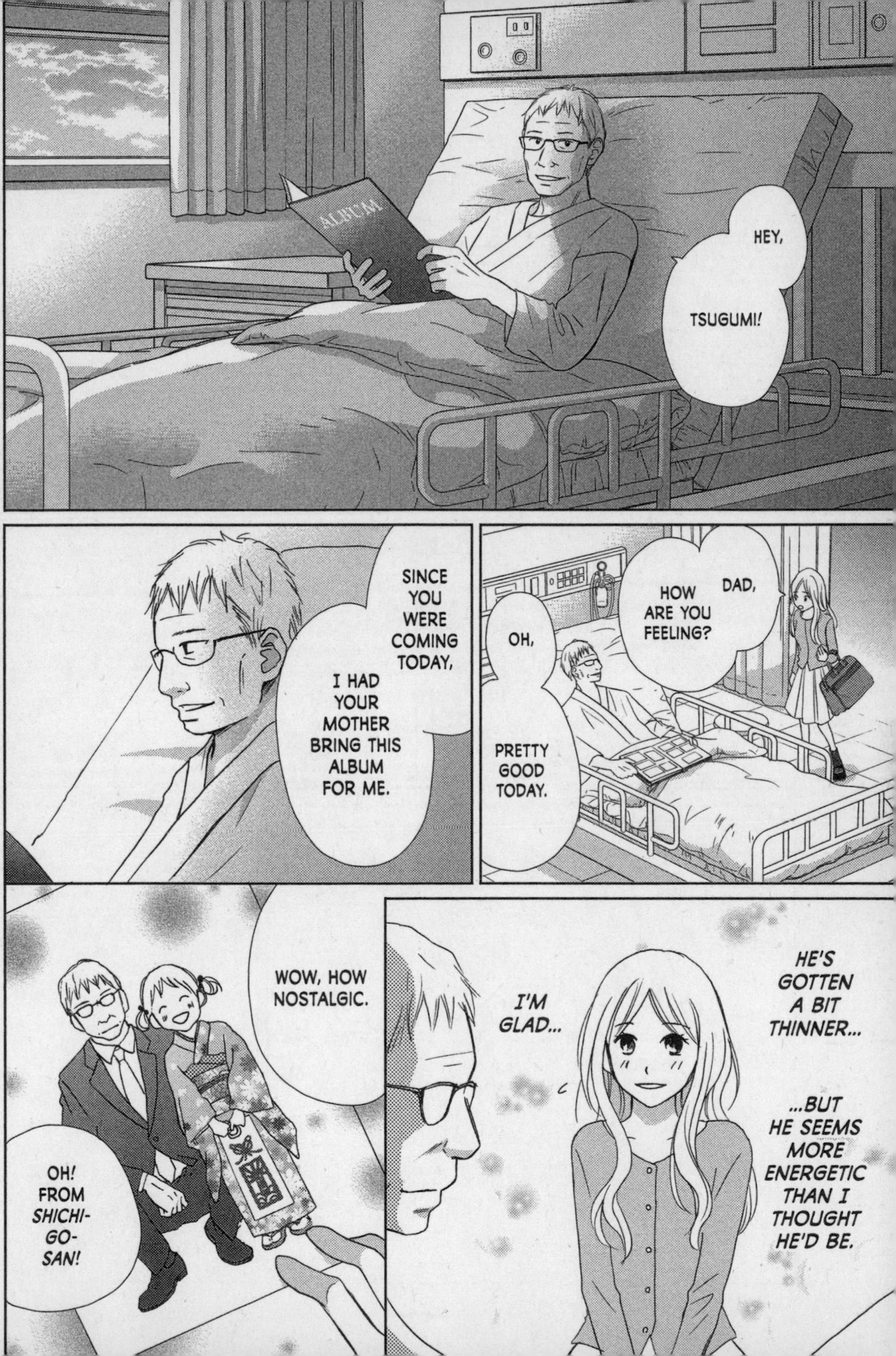
ALBUM
HEY,
TSUGUMI!
DAD,
HOW ARE YOU FEELING?
OH,
PRETTY GOOD TODAY.
SINCE YOU WERE COMING TODAY,
I HAD YOUR MOTHER BRING THIS ALBUM FOR ME.
HE'S GOTTEN A BIT THINNER...
...BUT HE SEEMS MORE ENERGETIC THAN I THOUGHT HE'D BE.
I'M GLAD...
WOW, HOW NOSTALGIC.
OH! FROM SHICHI-GO-SAN!

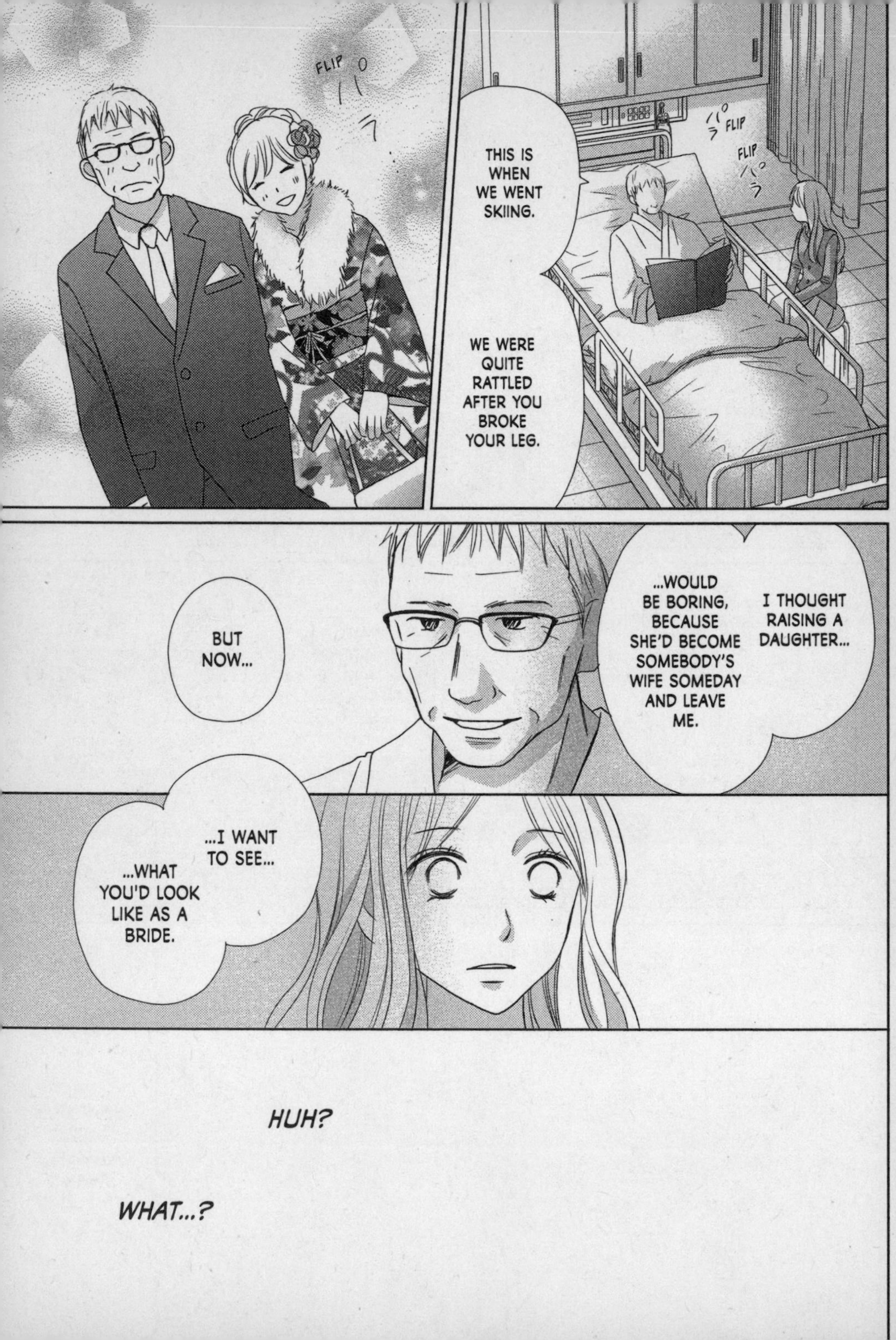
FLIP
FLIP
THIS IS WHEN WE WENT SKIING.
WE WERE QUITE RATTLED AFTER YOU BROKE YOUR LEG.
FLIP
I THOUGHT RAISING A DAUGHTER...
...WOULD BE BORING, BECAUSE SHE'D BECOME SOMEBODY'S WIFE SOMEDAY AND LEAVE ME.
BUT NOW...
...I WANT TO SEE...
...WHAT YOU'D LOOK LIKE AS A BRIDE.
HUH?
WHAT...?

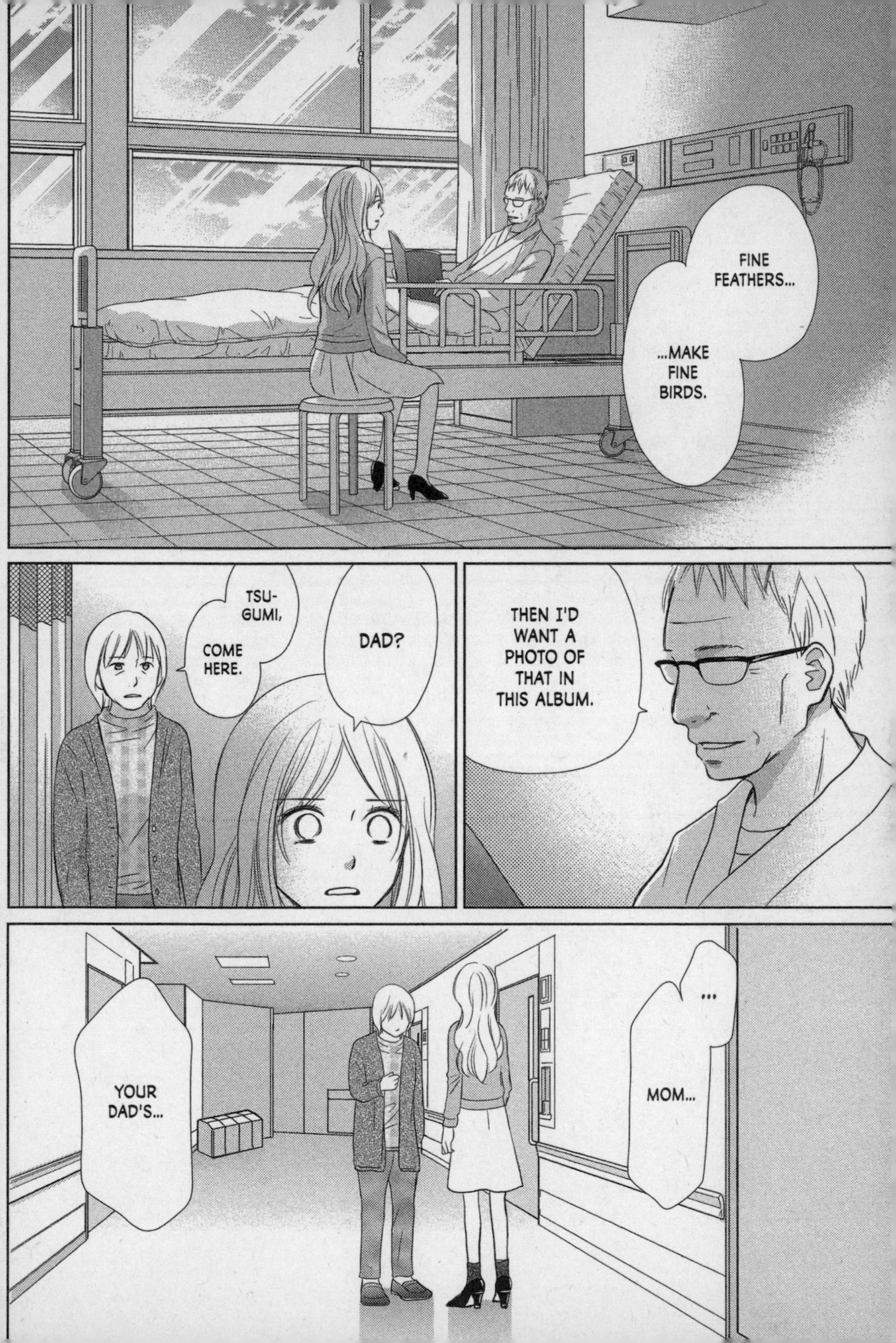
FINE FEATHERS...
...MAKE FINE BIRDS.
THEN I'D WANT A PHOTO OF THAT IN THIS ALBUM.
DAD?
TSU-GUMI,
COME HERE.
...
MOM...
YOUR DAD'S...

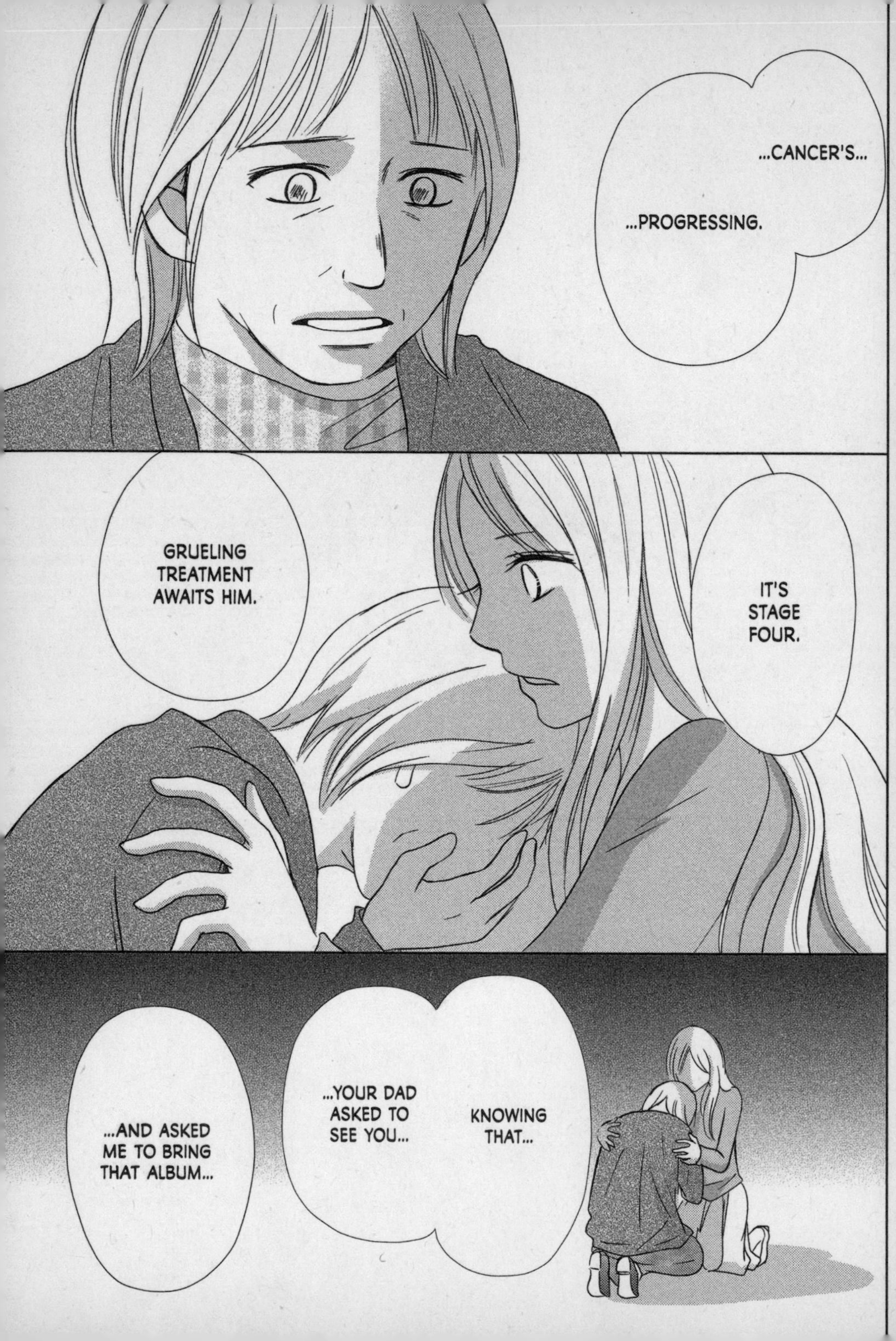
...CANCER'S...
...PROGRESSING.
IT'S STAGE FOUR.
GRUELING TREATMENT AWAITS HIM.
KNOWING THAT...
...YOUR DAD ASKED TO SEE YOU...
...AND ASKED ME TO BRING THAT ALBUM...

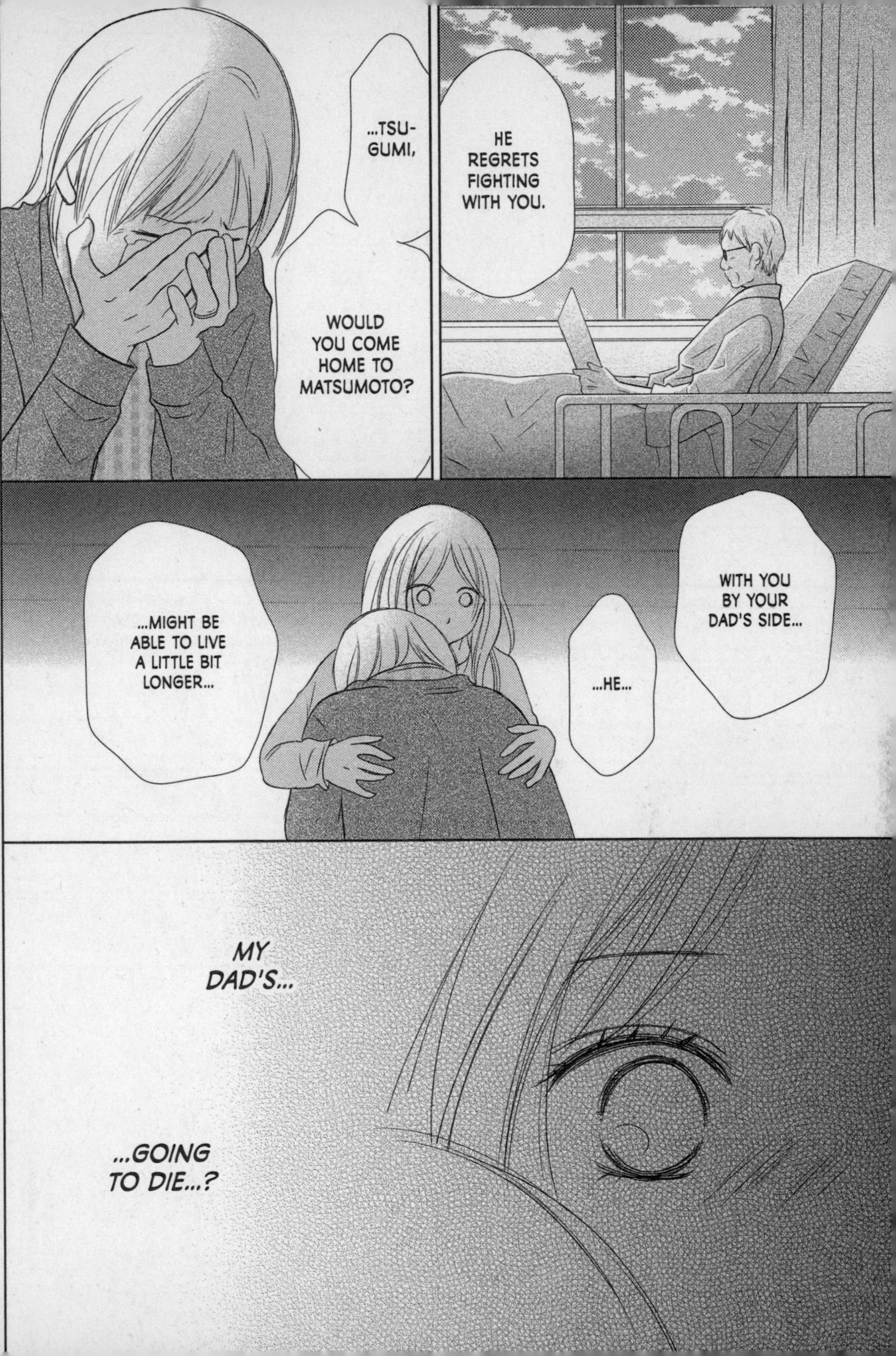
HE REGRETS FIGHTING WITH YOU.
...TSU-GUMI,
WOULD YOU COME HOME TO MATSUMOTO?
WITH YOU BY YOUR DAD'S SIDE...
...HE...
...MIGHT BE ABLE TO LIVE A LITTLE BIT LONGER...
MY DAD'S...
...GOING TO DIE...?

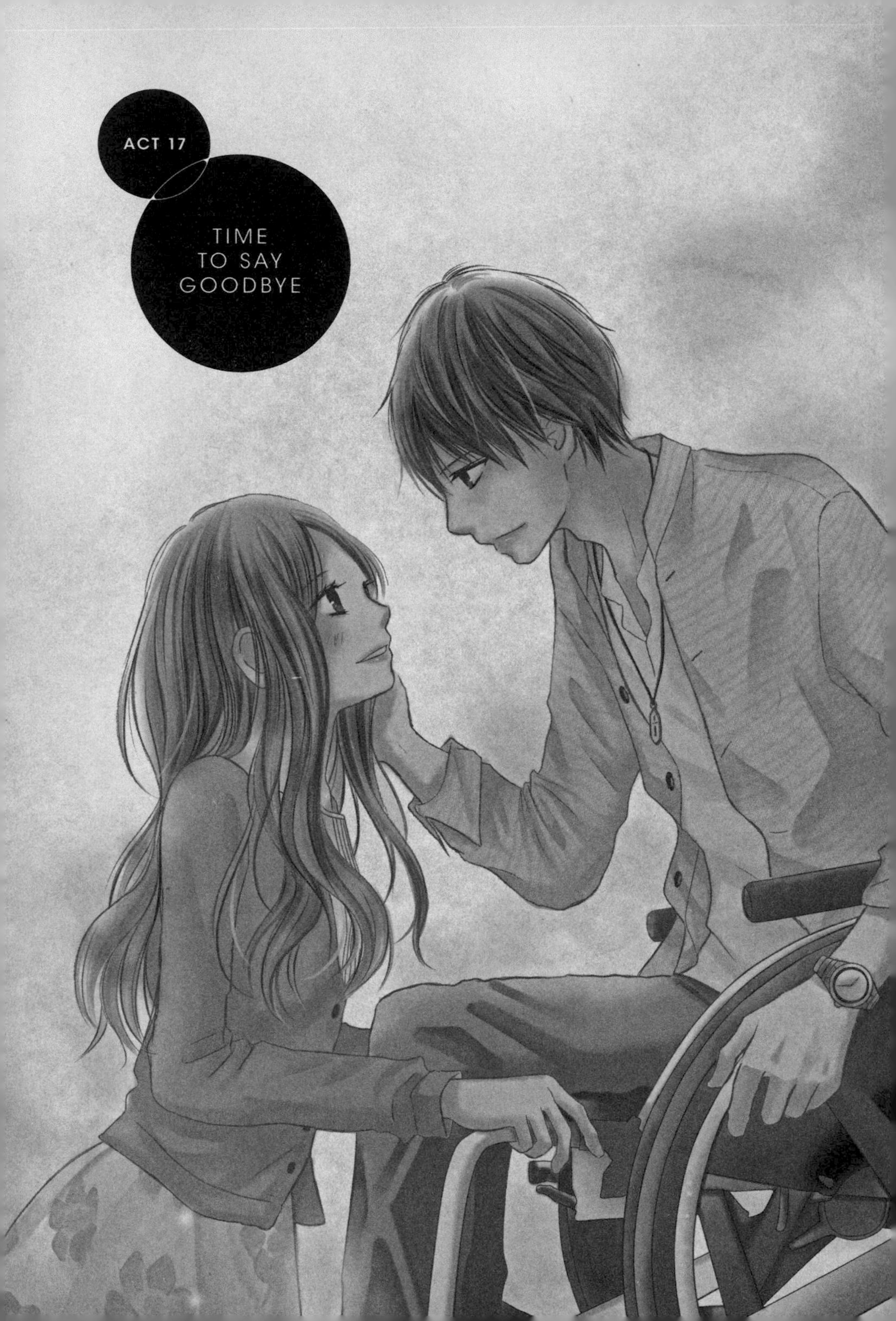
ACT 17
TIME TO SAY GOODBYE

PERFECT WORLD

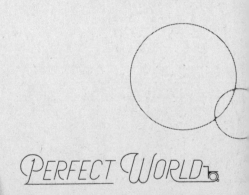

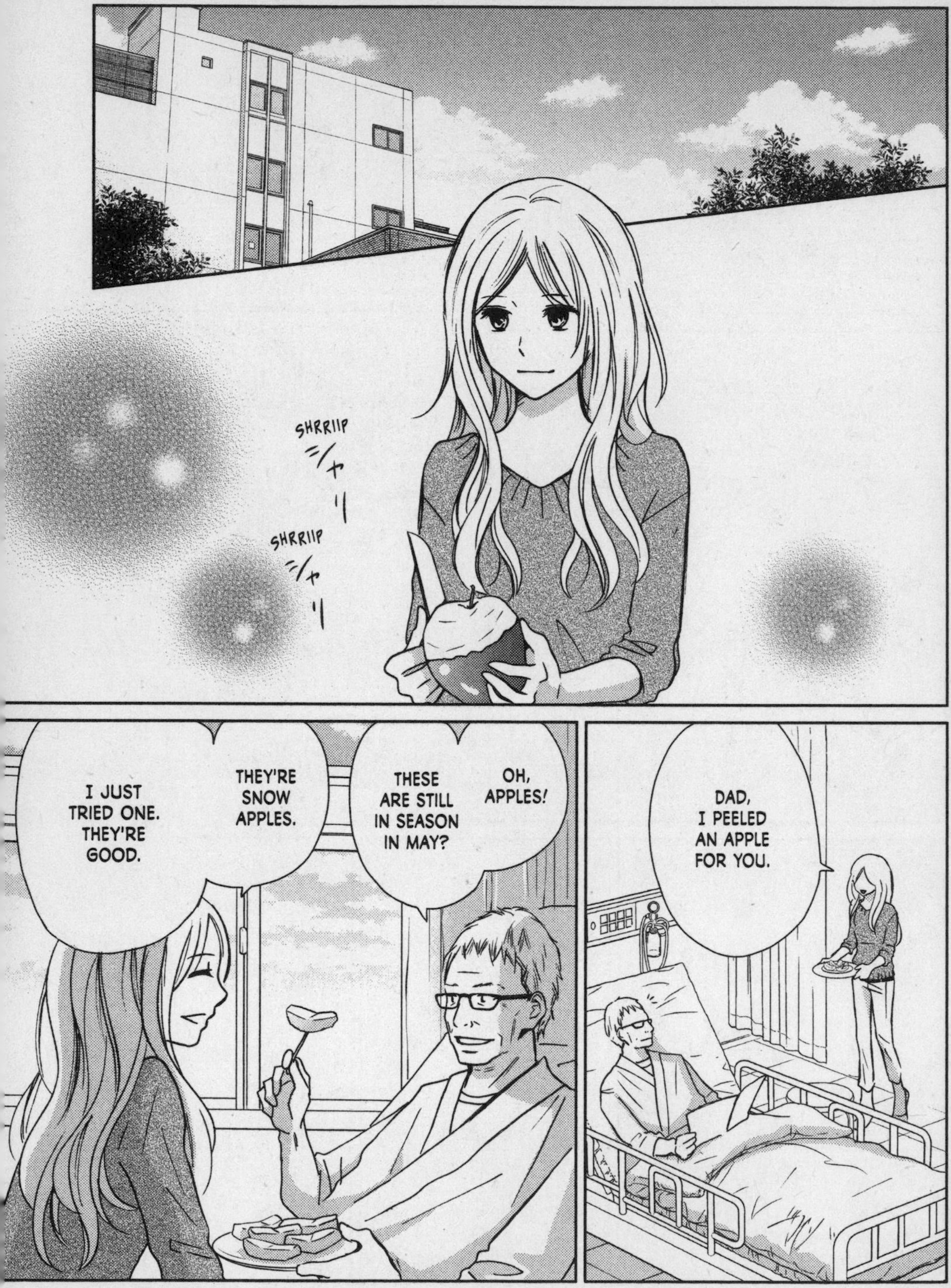
SHRRIIP
シャリ
SHRRIIP
シャリ
DAD, I PEELED AN APPLE FOR YOU.
OH, APPLES!
THESE ARE STILL IN SEASON IN MAY?
THEY'RE SNOW APPLES.
I JUST TRIED ONE. THEY'RE GOOD.

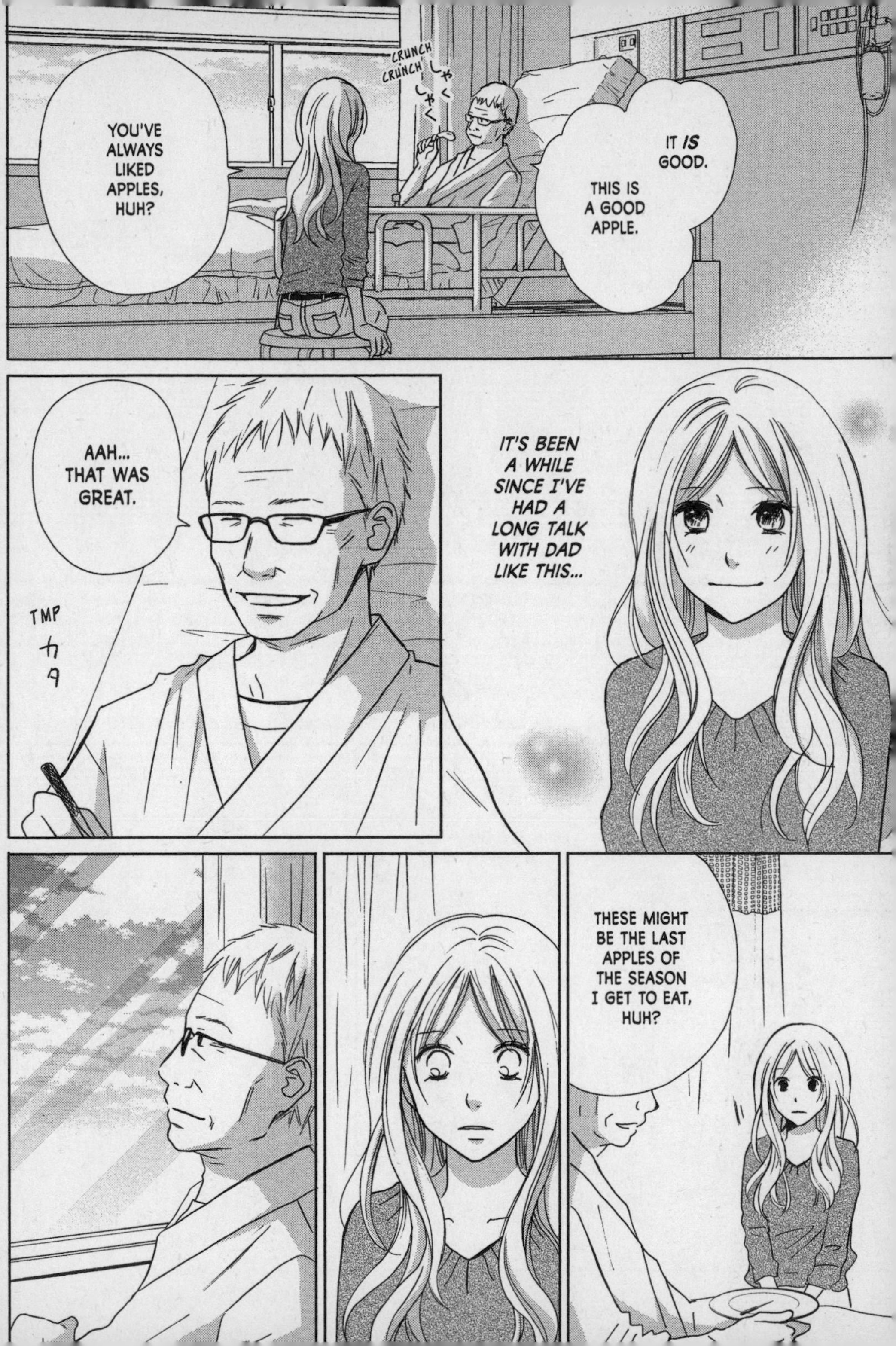
CRUNCH CRUNCH しゃく しゃく
IT *IS* GOOD.
THIS IS A GOOD APPLE.
YOU'VE ALWAYS LIKED APPLES, HUH?
IT'S BEEN A WHILE SINCE I'VE HAD A LONG TALK WITH DAD LIKE THIS...
AAH... THAT WAS GREAT.
TMP カタ
THESE MIGHT BE THE LAST APPLES OF THE SEASON I GET TO EAT, HUH?

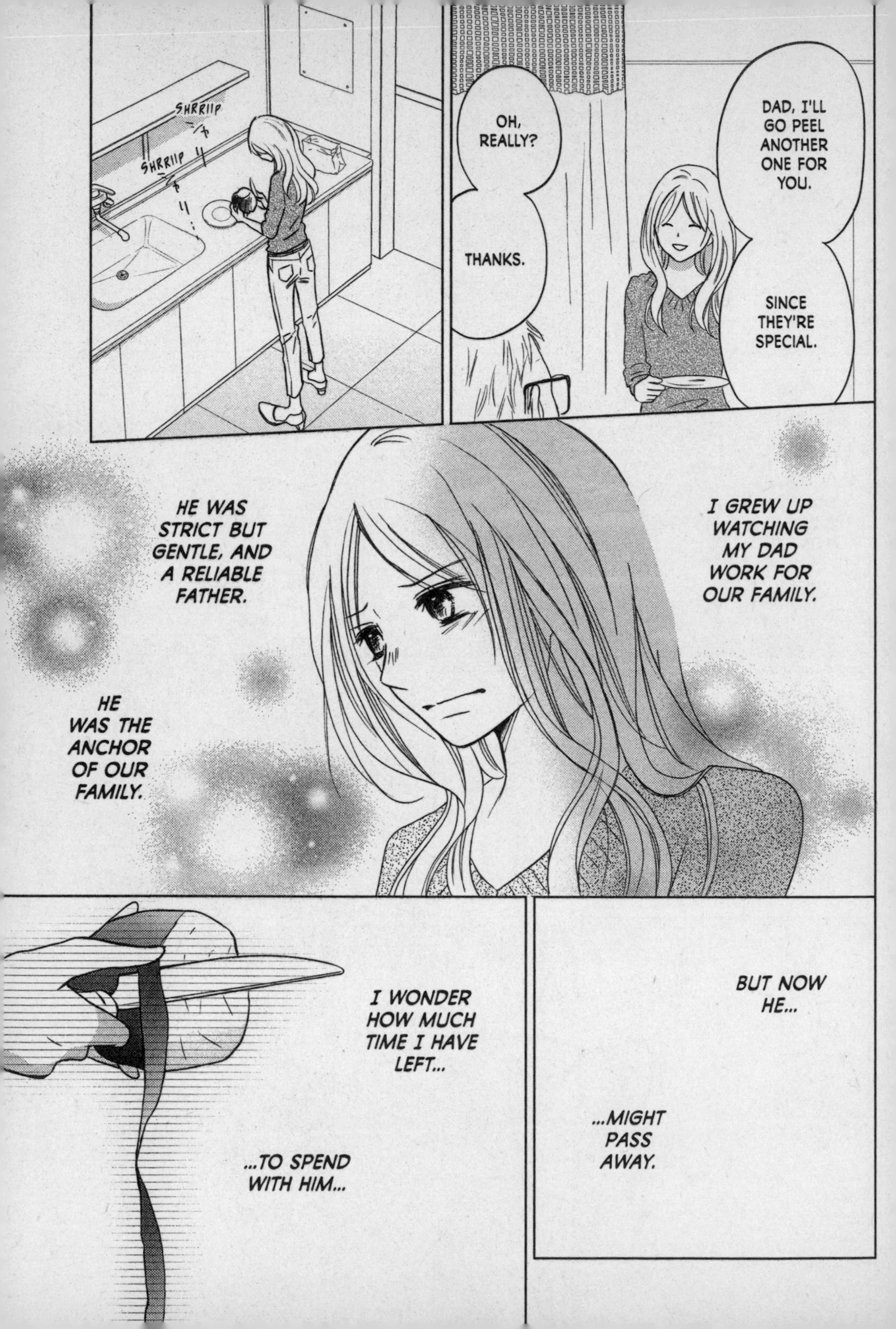

DAD, I'LL GO PEEL ANOTHER ONE FOR YOU.
SINCE THEY'RE SPECIAL.
OH, REALLY?
THANKS.
SHRRIIP
SHRRIP
I GREW UP WATCHING MY DAD WORK FOR OUR FAMILY.
HE WAS STRICT BUT GENTLE, AND A RELIABLE FATHER.
HE WAS THE ANCHOR OF OUR FAMILY.
BUT NOW HE...
...MIGHT PASS AWAY.
I WONDER HOW MUCH TIME I HAVE LEFT...
...TO SPEND WITH HIM...

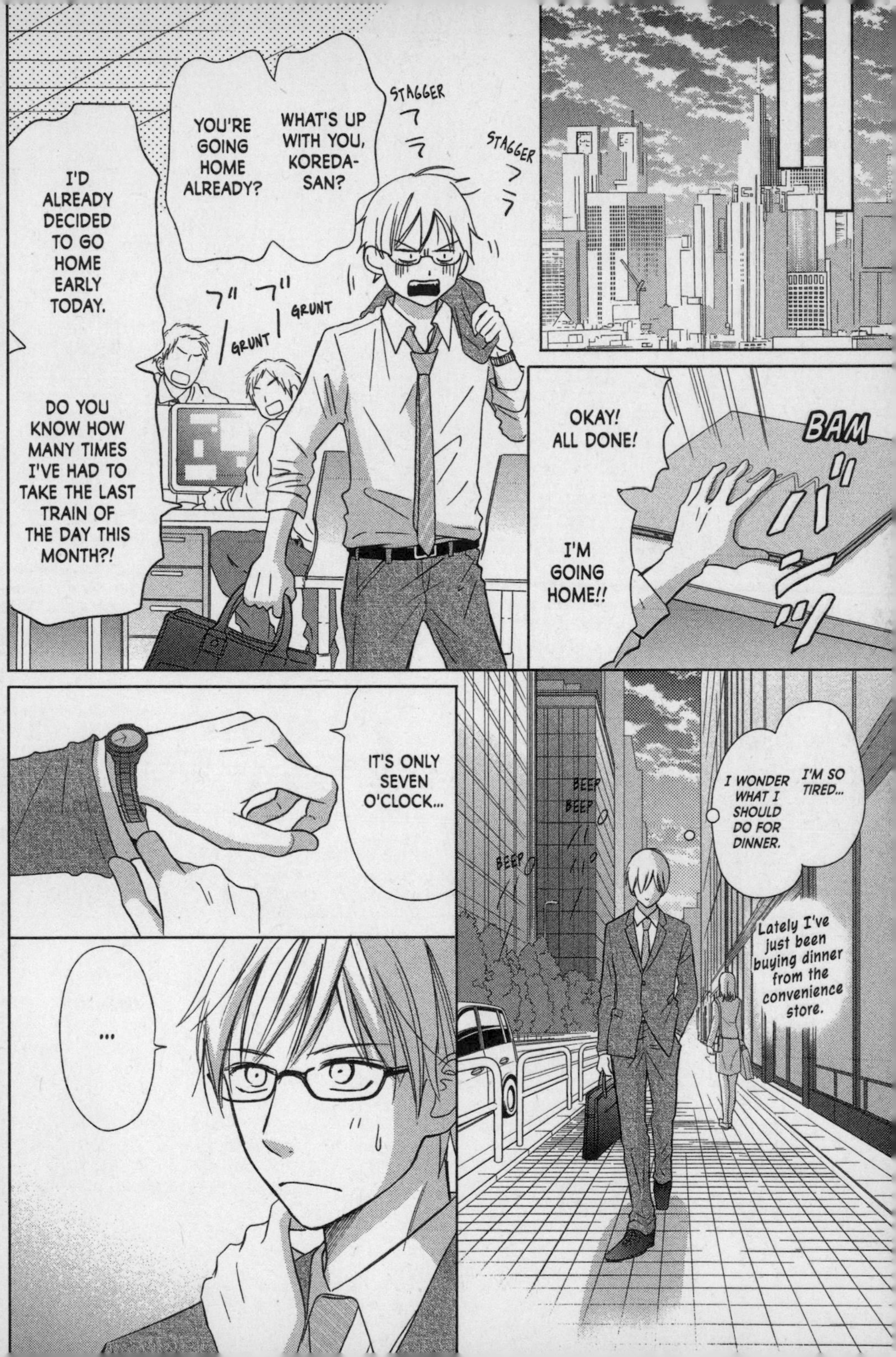
BAM
OKAY! ALL DONE!
I'M GOING HOME!!
STAGGER
STAGGER
WHAT'S UP WITH YOU, KOREDA-SAN?
YOU'RE GOING HOME ALREADY?
I'D ALREADY DECIDED TO GO HOME EARLY TODAY.
GRUNT
GRUNT
DO YOU KNOW HOW MANY TIMES I'VE HAD TO TAKE THE LAST TRAIN OF THE DAY THIS MONTH?!
I'M SO TIRED...
I WONDER WHAT I SHOULD DO FOR DINNER.
BEEP
BEEP
BEEP
Lately I've just been buying dinner from the convenience store.
IT'S ONLY SEVEN O'CLOCK...
...

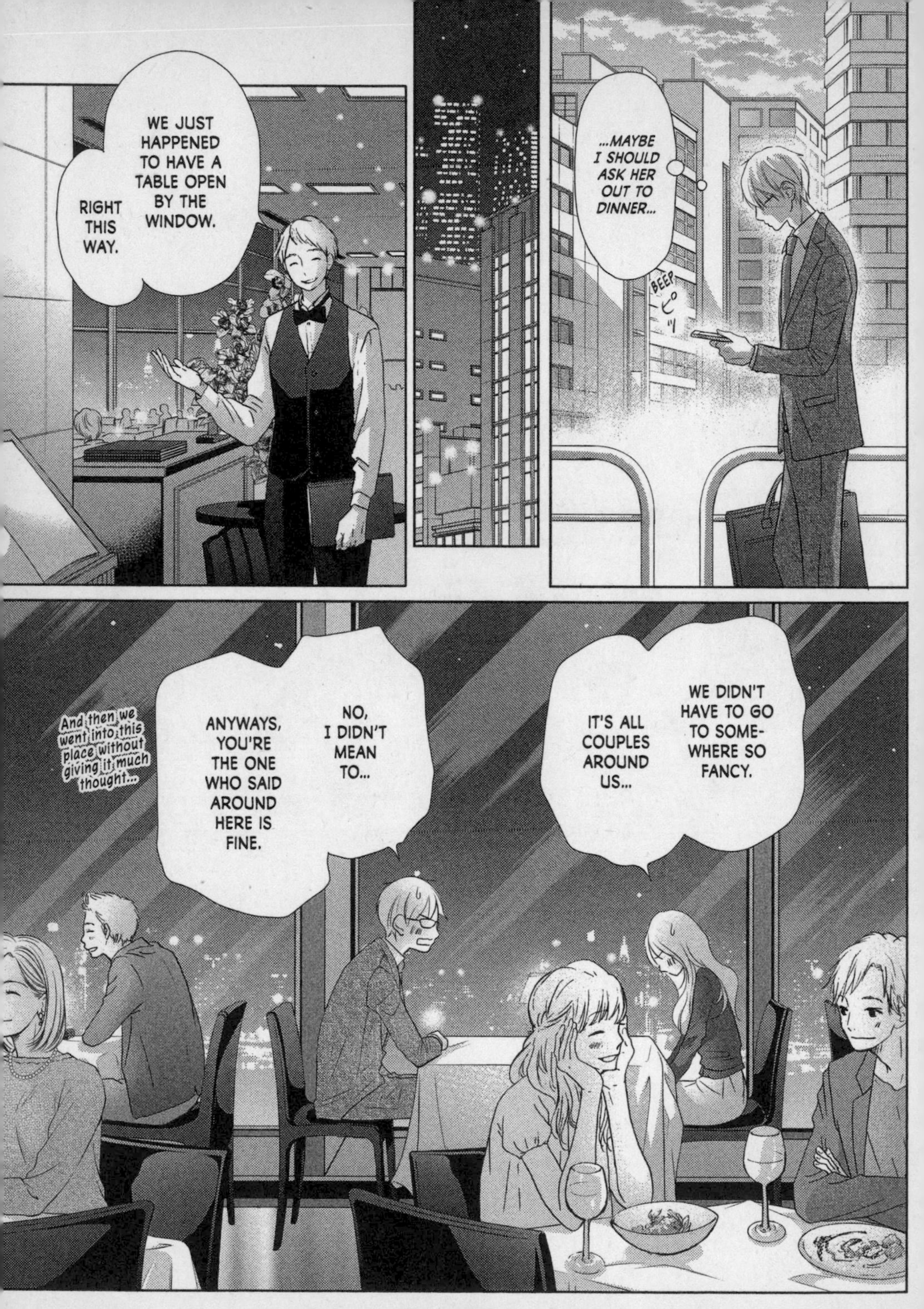
...MAYBE I SHOULD ASK HER OUT TO DINNER...
BEEP
ピッ
WE JUST HAPPENED TO HAVE A TABLE OPEN BY THE WINDOW.
RIGHT THIS WAY.
WE DIDN'T HAVE TO GO TO SOME-WHERE SO FANCY.
IT'S ALL COUPLES AROUND US...
NO, I DIDN'T MEAN TO...
ANYWAYS, YOU'RE THE ONE WHO SAID AROUND HERE IS FINE.
And then we went into this place without giving it much thought...

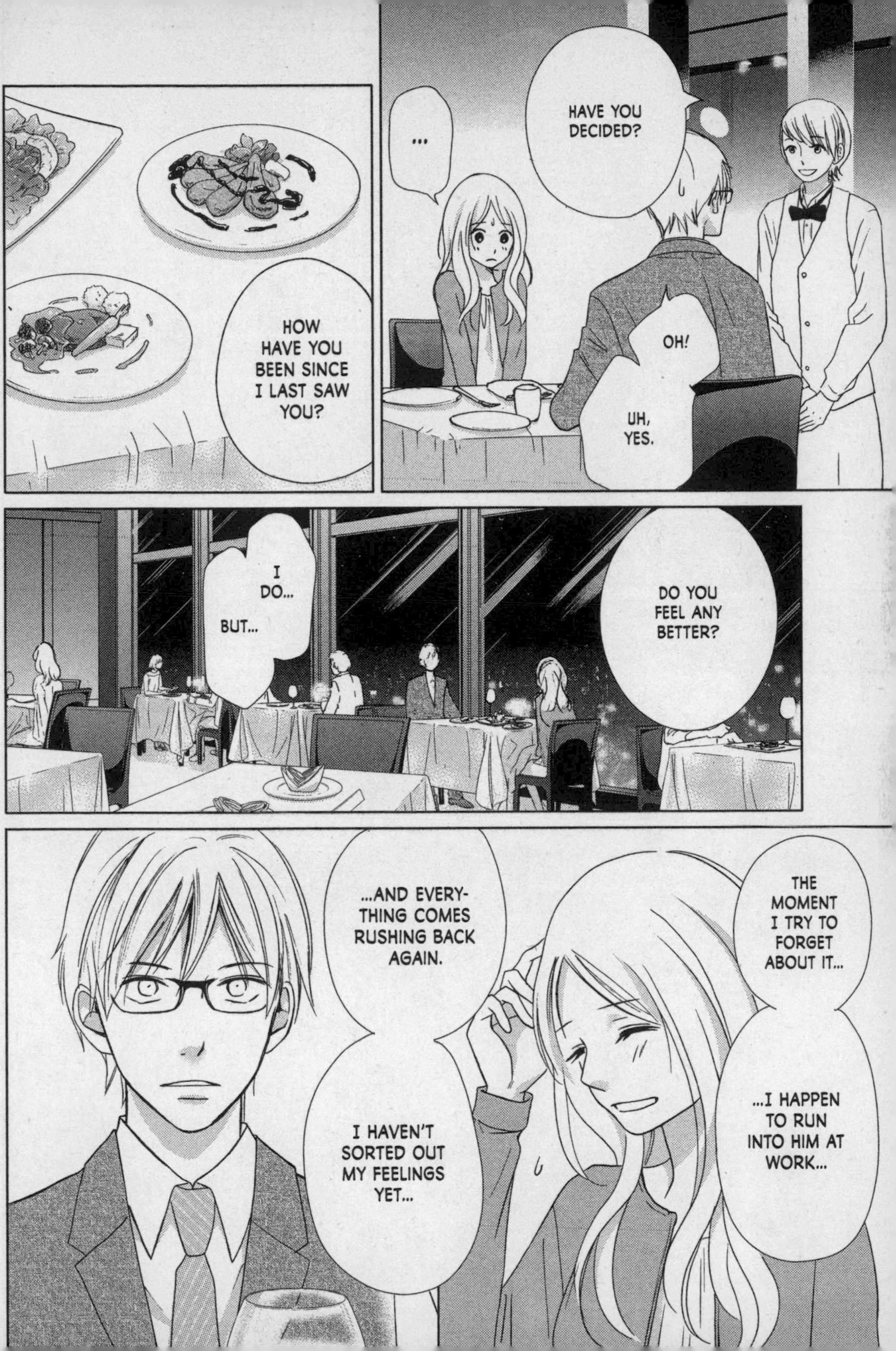
HAVE YOU DECIDED?
...
OH!
UH, YES.
HOW HAVE YOU BEEN SINCE I LAST SAW YOU?
DO YOU FEEL ANY BETTER?
I DO...
BUT...
THE MOMENT I TRY TO FORGET ABOUT IT...
...I HAPPEN TO RUN INTO HIM AT WORK...
...AND EVERY-THING COMES RUSHING BACK AGAIN.
I HAVEN'T SORTED OUT MY FEELINGS YET...

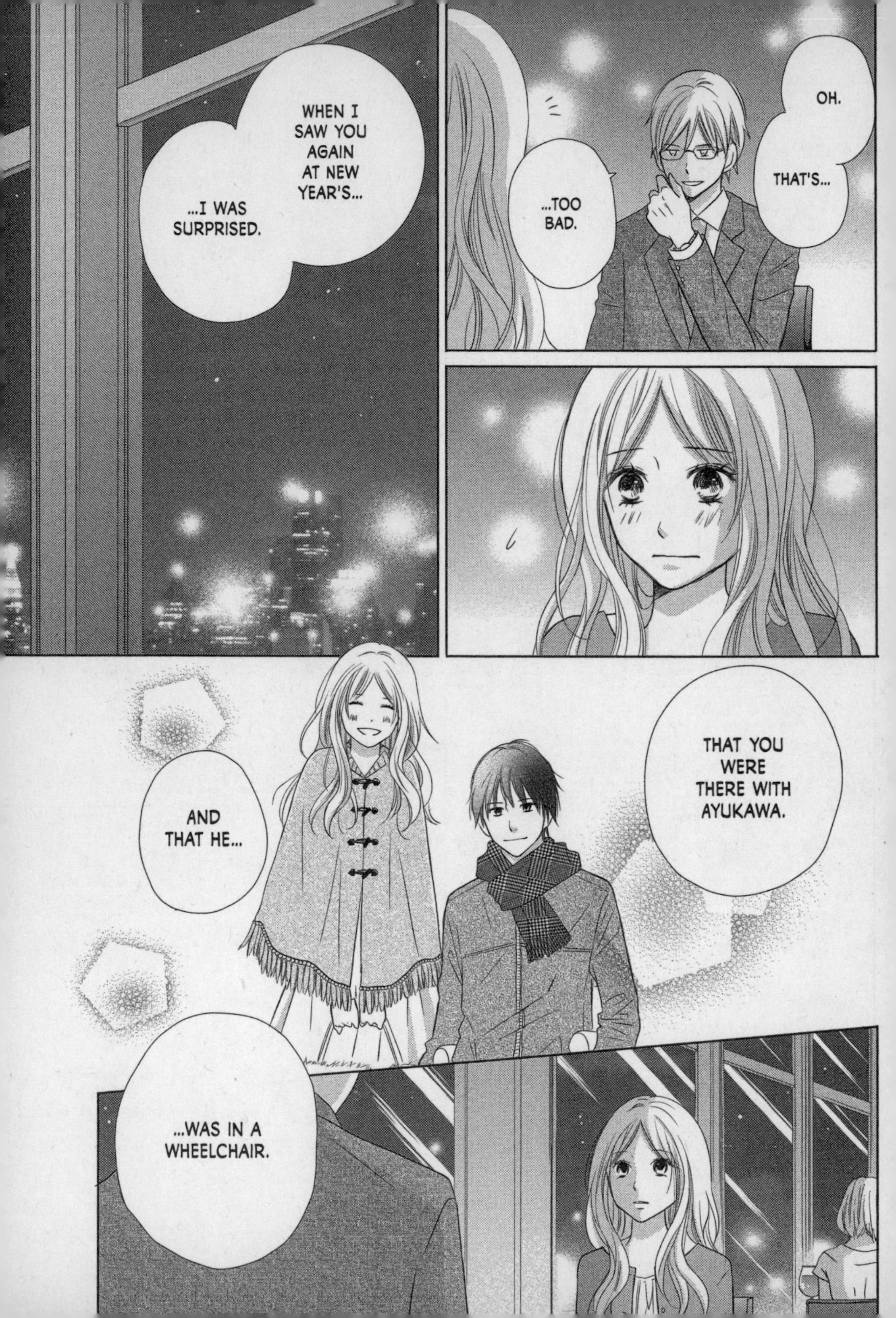
OH.
THAT'S...
...TOO BAD.
WHEN I SAW YOU AGAIN AT NEW YEAR'S...
...I WAS SURPRISED.
THAT YOU WERE THERE WITH AYUKAWA.
AND THAT HE...
...WAS IN A WHEELCHAIR.

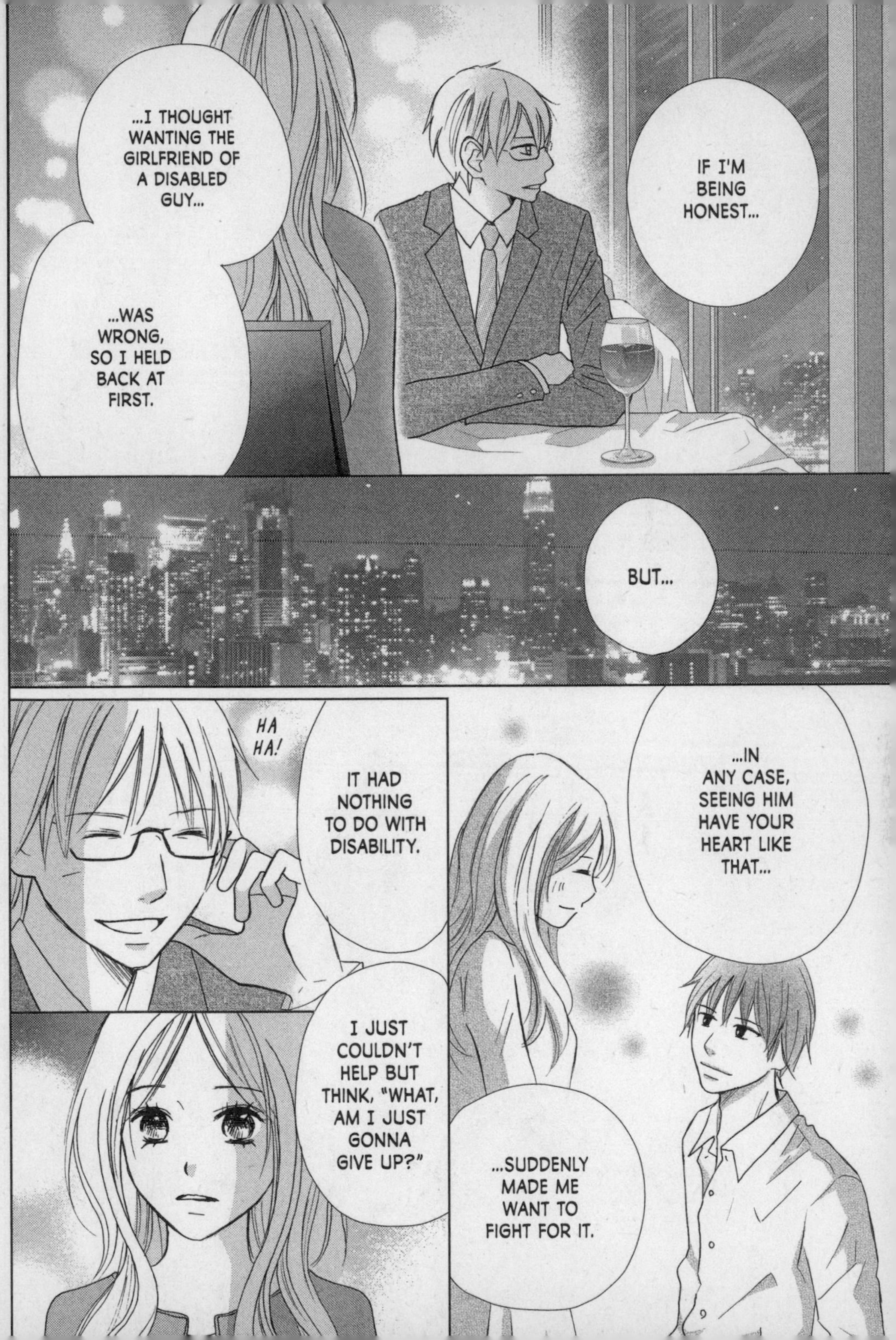
IF I'M BEING HONEST...
...I THOUGHT WANTING THE GIRLFRIEND OF A DISABLED GUY...
...WAS WRONG, SO I HELD BACK AT FIRST.
BUT...
...IN ANY CASE, SEEING HIM HAVE YOUR HEART LIKE THAT...
...SUDDENLY MADE ME WANT TO FIGHT FOR IT.
HA HA!
IT HAD NOTHING TO DO WITH DISABILITY.
I JUST COULDN'T HELP BUT THINK, "WHAT, AM I JUST GONNA GIVE UP?"

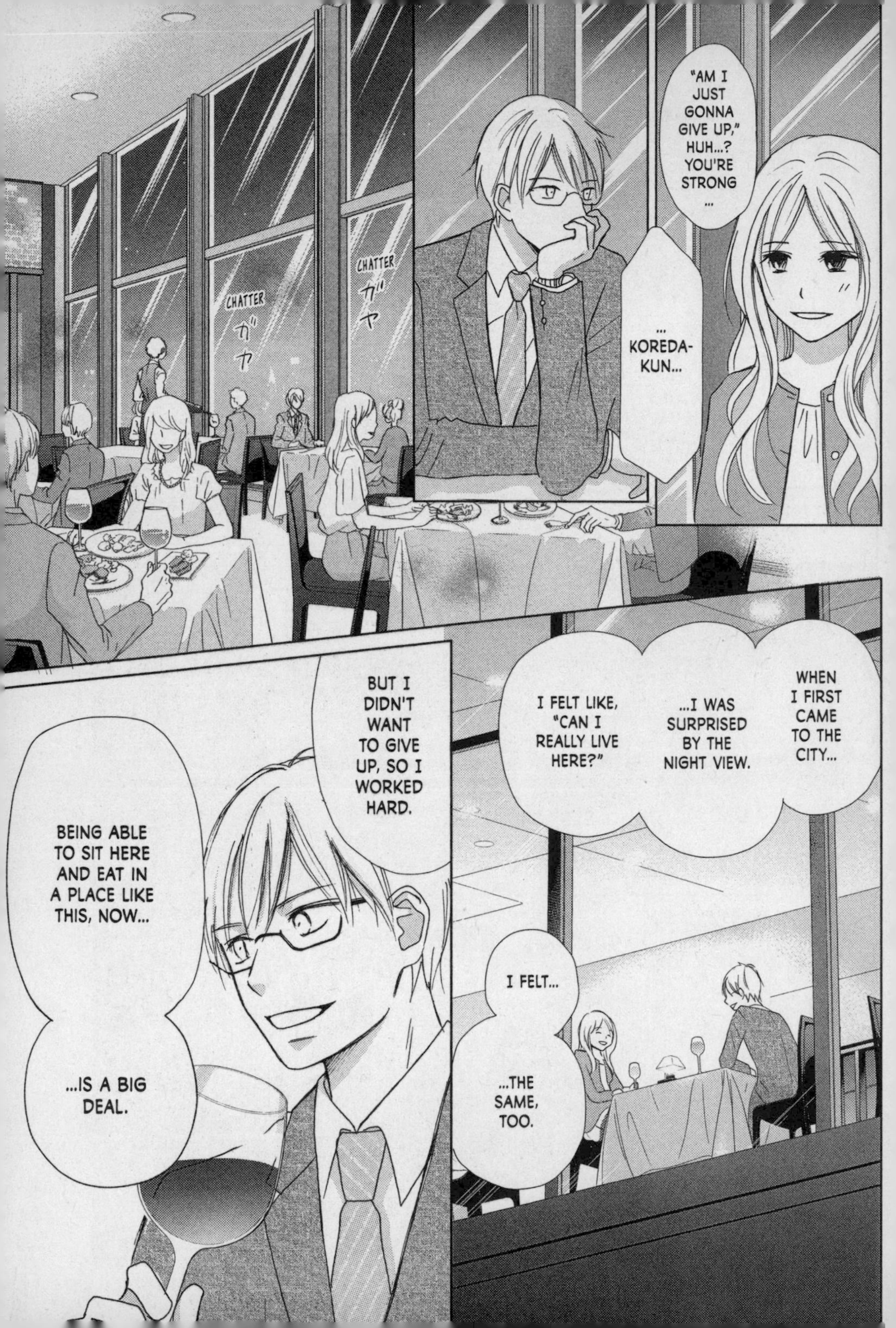
"AM I JUST GONNA GIVE UP," HUH...? YOU'RE STRONG ...
... KOREDA-KUN...
CHATTER
ガヤ
CHATTER
ガヤ
WHEN I FIRST CAME TO THE CITY...
...I WAS SURPRISED BY THE NIGHT VIEW.
I FELT LIKE, "CAN I REALLY LIVE HERE?"
I FELT...
...THE SAME, TOO.
BUT I DIDN'T WANT TO GIVE UP, SO I WORKED HARD.
BEING ABLE TO SIT HERE AND EAT IN A PLACE LIKE THIS, NOW...
...IS A BIG DEAL.

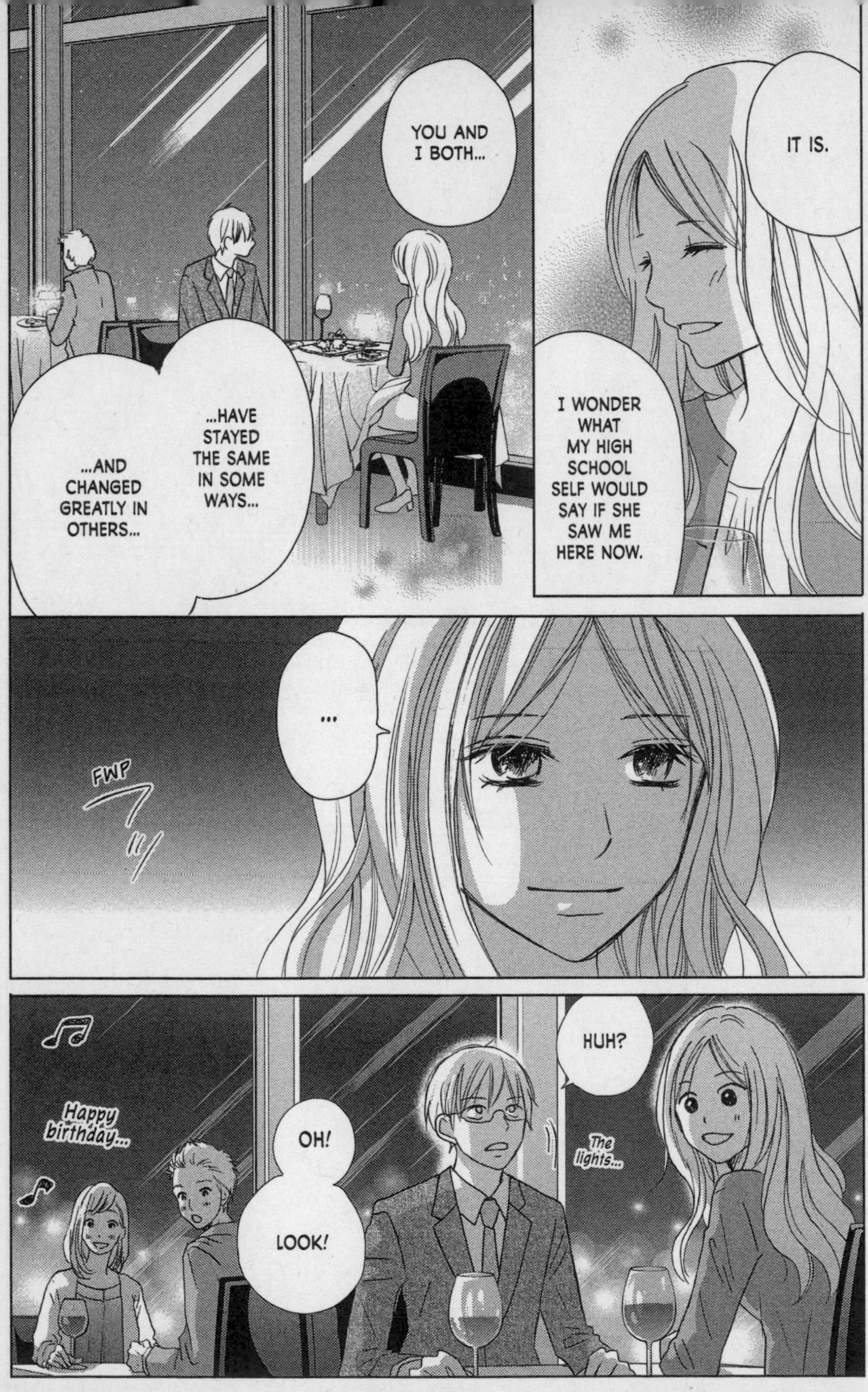
IT IS.
I WONDER WHAT MY HIGH SCHOOL SELF WOULD SAY IF SHE SAW ME HERE NOW.
YOU AND I BOTH...
...HAVE STAYED THE SAME IN SOME WAYS...
...AND CHANGED GREATLY IN OTHERS...
...
FWP
HUH?
The lights...
OH!
LOOK!
Happy birthday...

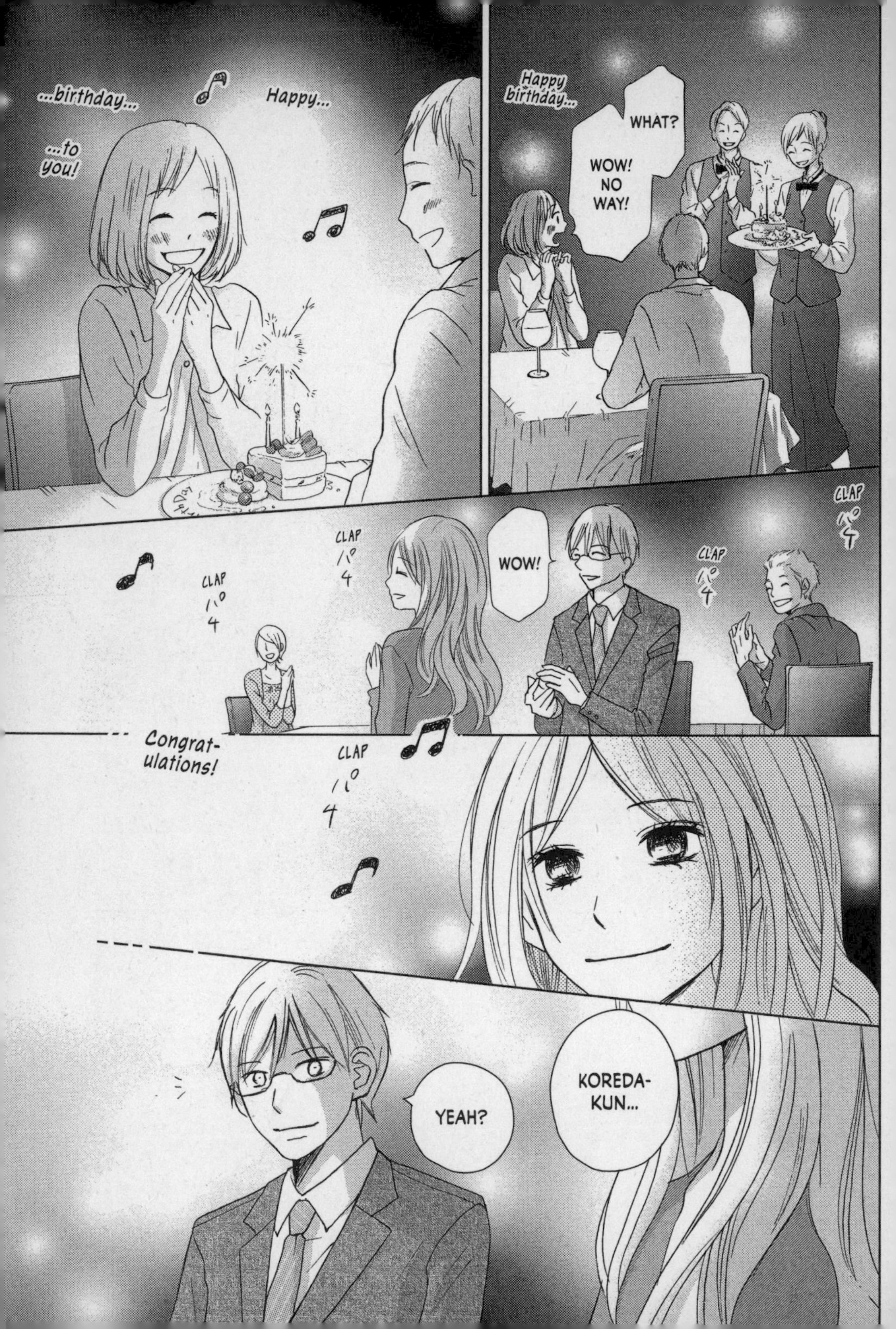
Happy birthday...
WHAT?
WOW! NO WAY!
Happy...
...birthday...
...to you!
CLAP パチ
CLAP パチ
WOW!
CLAP パチ
CLAP パチ
Congrat-ulations!
CLAP パチ
KOREDA-KUN...
YEAH?

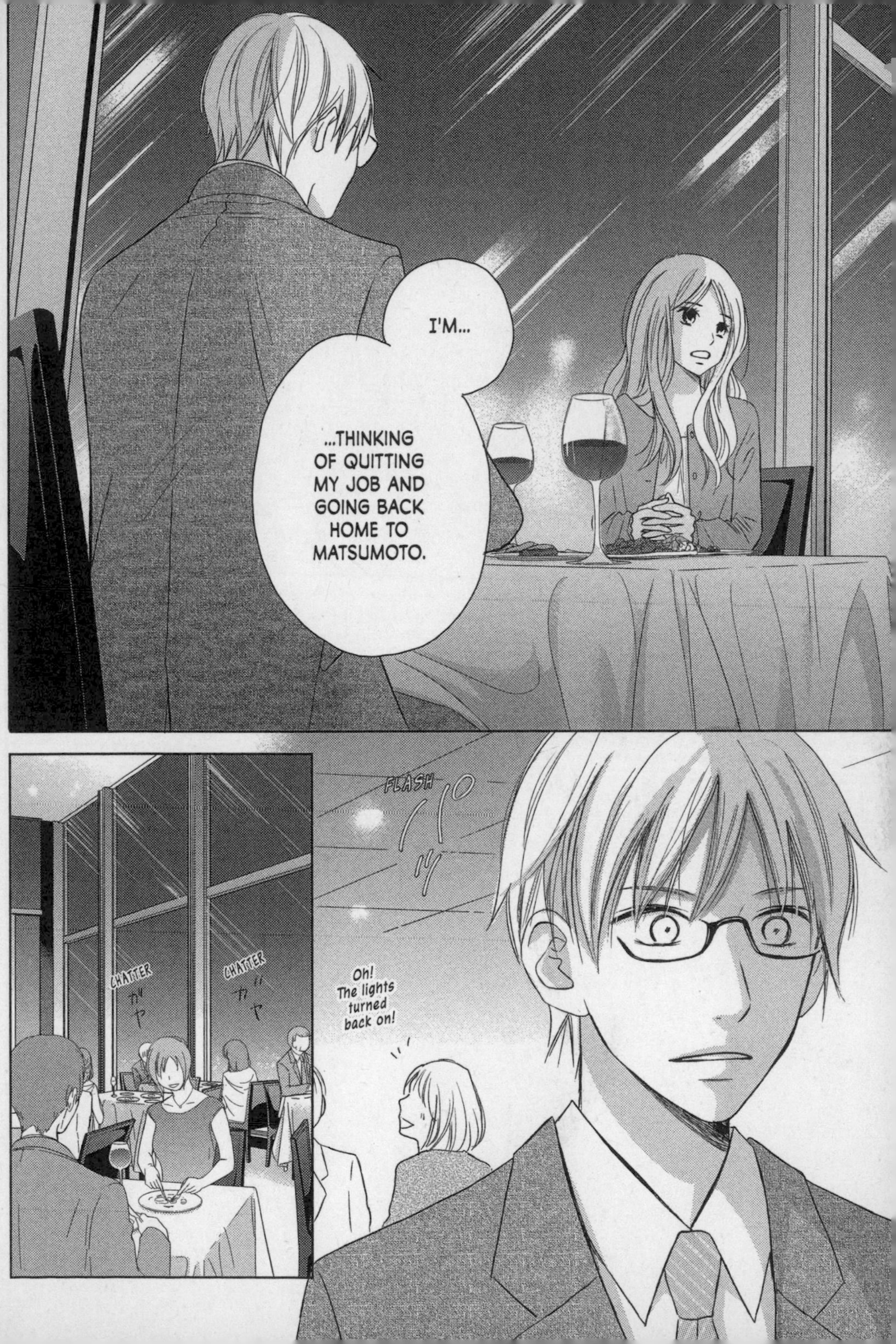
I'M...
...THINKING OF QUITTING MY JOB AND GOING BACK HOME TO MATSUMOTO.
FLASH
Oh! The lights turned back on!
CHATTER
CHATTER

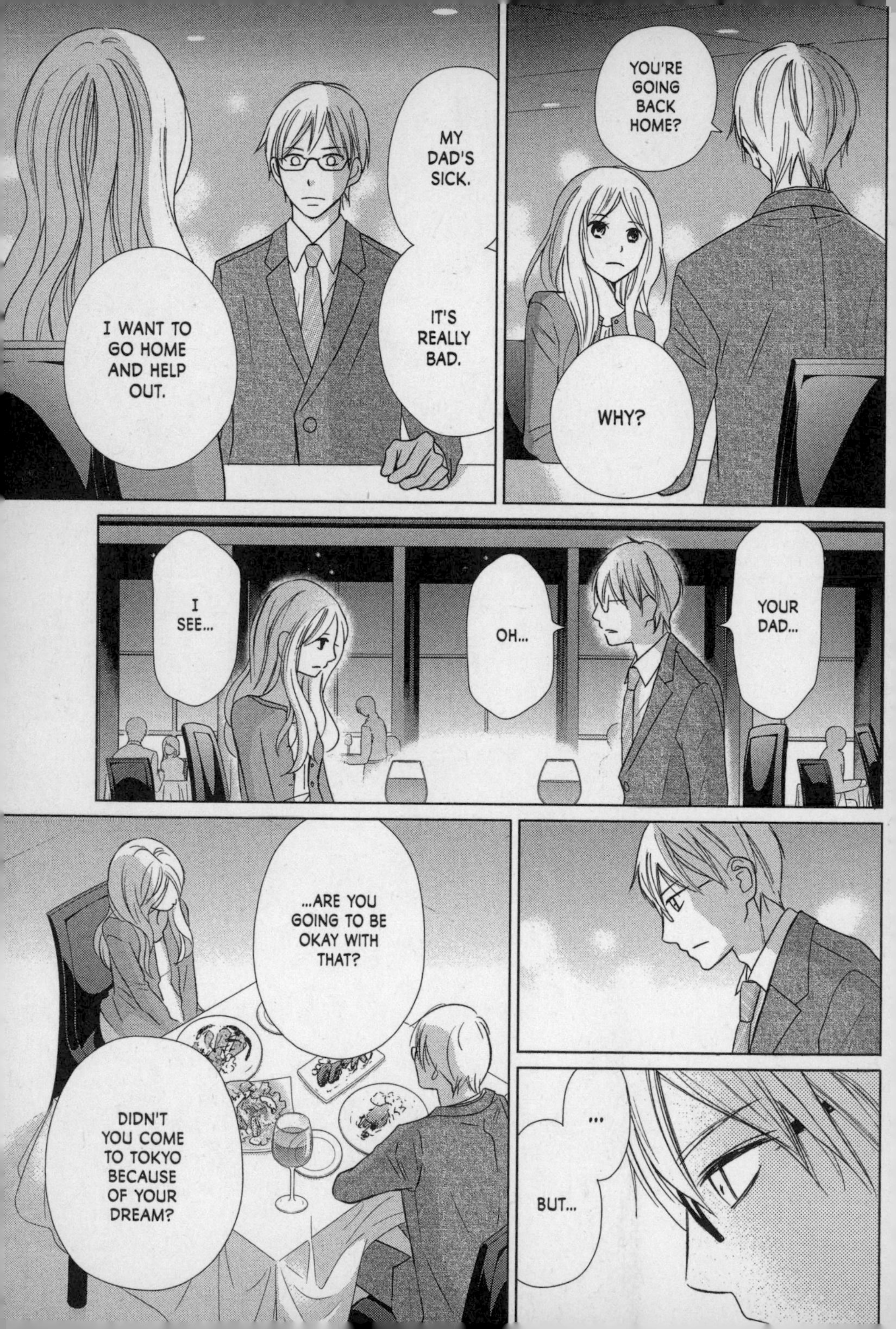
YOU'RE GOING BACK HOME?
WHY?
MY DAD'S SICK.
IT'S REALLY BAD.
I WANT TO GO HOME AND HELP OUT.
YOUR DAD...
OH...
I SEE...
...ARE YOU GOING TO BE OKAY WITH THAT?
DIDN'T YOU COME TO TOKYO BECAUSE OF YOUR DREAM?
...
BUT...

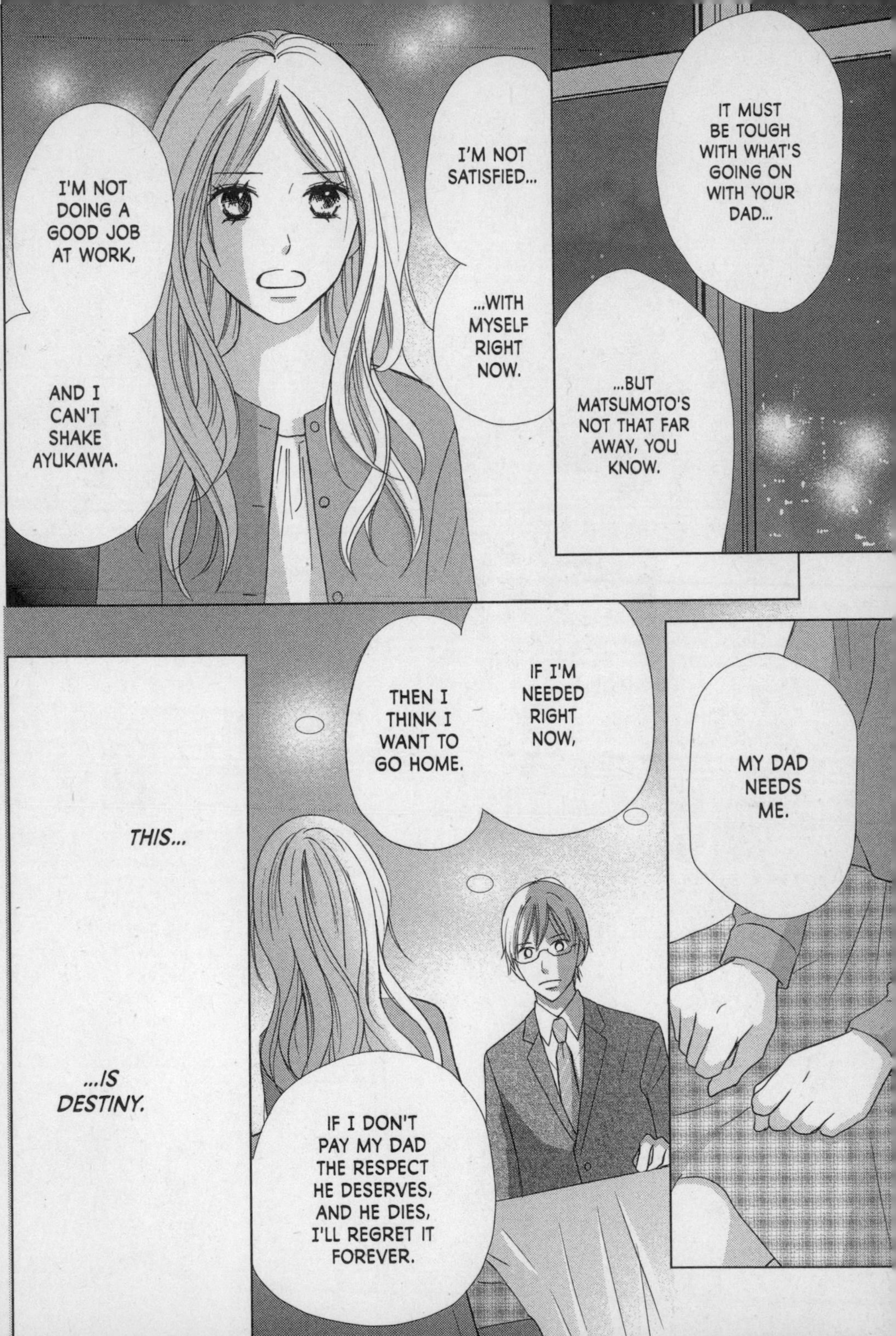
IT MUST BE TOUGH WITH WHAT'S GOING ON WITH YOUR DAD...
...BUT MATSUMOTO'S NOT THAT FAR AWAY, YOU KNOW.
I'M NOT SATISFIED...
...WITH MYSELF RIGHT NOW.
I'M NOT DOING A GOOD JOB AT WORK,
AND I CAN'T SHAKE AYUKAWA.
MY DAD NEEDS ME.
IF I'M NEEDED RIGHT NOW,
THEN I THINK I WANT TO GO HOME.
IF I DON'T PAY MY DAD THE RESPECT HE DESERVES, AND HE DIES, I'LL REGRET IT FOREVER.
THIS...
...IS DESTINY.

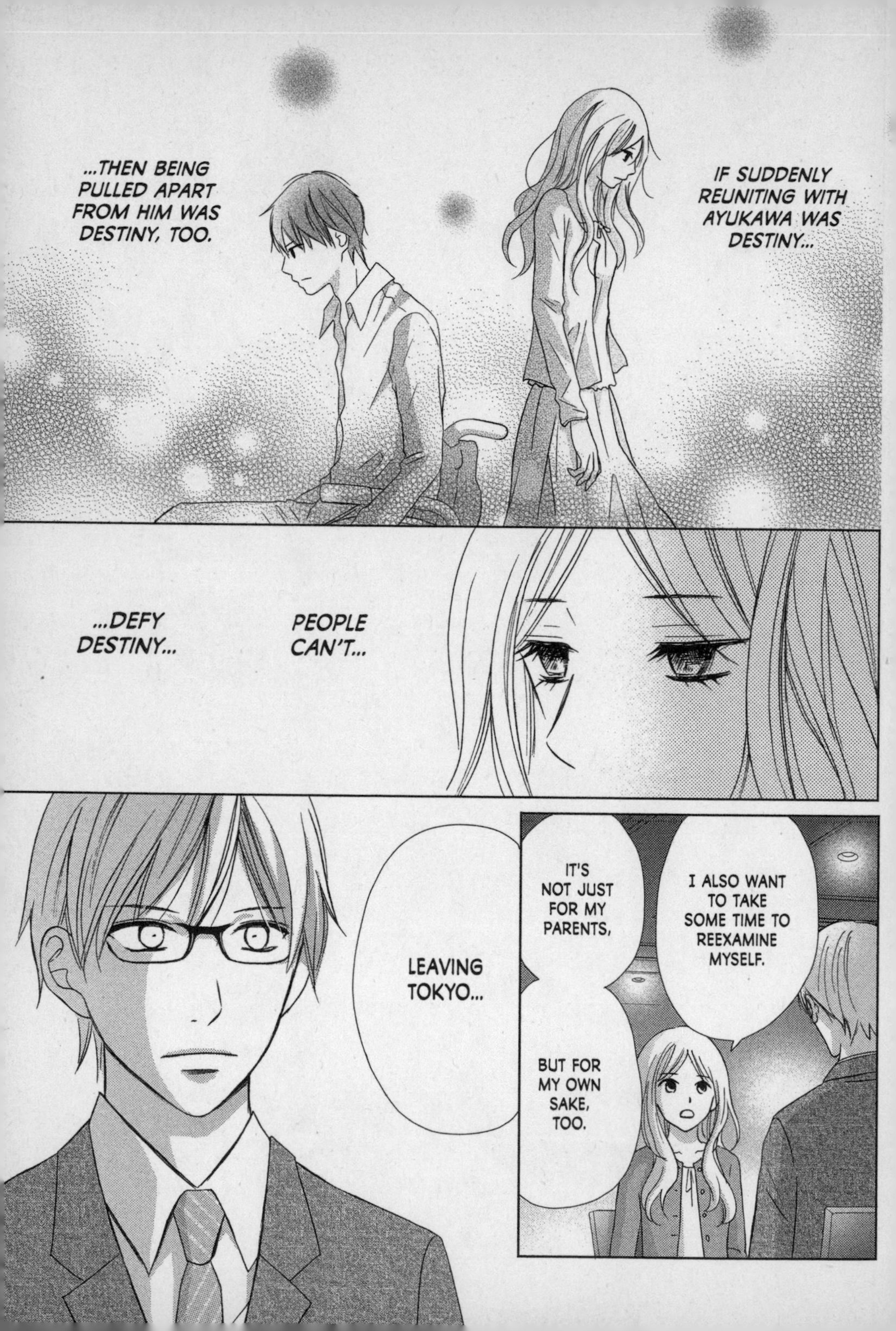
IF SUDDENLY REUNITING WITH AYUKAWA WAS DESTINY...
...THEN BEING PULLED APART FROM HIM WAS DESTINY, TOO.
PEOPLE CAN'T...
...DEFY DESTINY...
I ALSO WANT TO TAKE SOME TIME TO REEXAMINE MYSELF.
IT'S NOT JUST FOR MY PARENTS,
BUT FOR MY OWN SAKE, TOO.
LEAVING TOKYO...

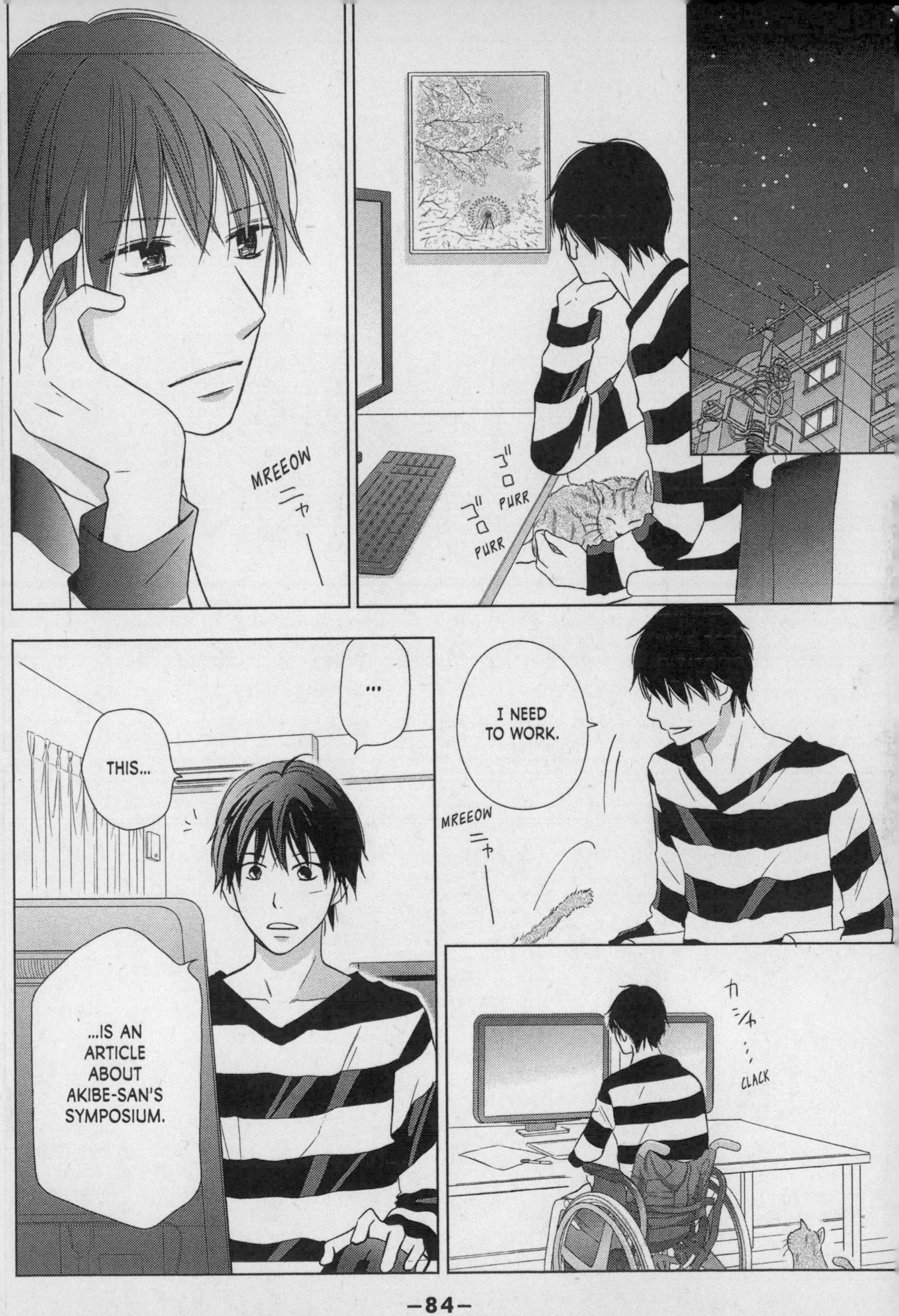

ゴロ
PURR
ゴロ
PURR
MREEOW
ニャー
I NEED TO WORK.
MREEOW
ニャー
カシャ…
CLACK
...
THIS...
...IS AN ARTICLE ABOUT AKIBE-SAN'S SYMPOSIUM.

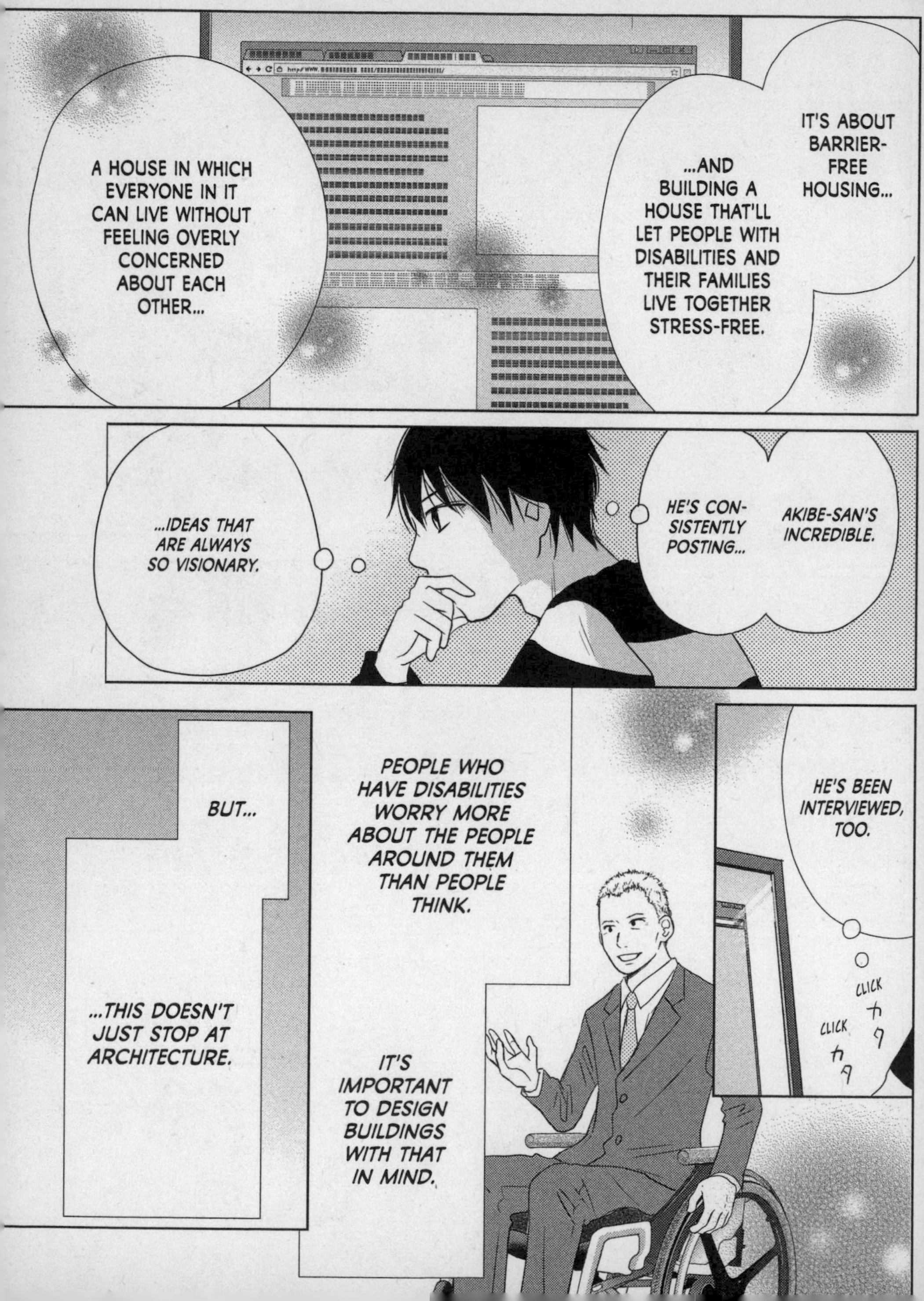
IT'S ABOUT BARRIER-FREE HOUSING...
...AND BUILDING A HOUSE THAT'LL LET PEOPLE WITH DISABILITIES AND THEIR FAMILIES LIVE TOGETHER STRESS-FREE.
A HOUSE IN WHICH EVERYONE IN IT CAN LIVE WITHOUT FEELING OVERLY CONCERNED ABOUT EACH OTHER...
AKIBE-SAN'S INCREDIBLE.
HE'S CON-SISTENTLY POSTING...
...IDEAS THAT ARE ALWAYS SO VISIONARY.
HE'S BEEN INTERVIEWED, TOO.
CLICK カタ
CLICK カタ
PEOPLE WHO HAVE DISABILITIES WORRY MORE ABOUT THE PEOPLE AROUND THEM THAN PEOPLE THINK.
IT'S IMPORTANT TO DESIGN BUILDINGS WITH THAT IN MIND.
BUT...
...THIS DOESN'T JUST STOP AT ARCHITECTURE.

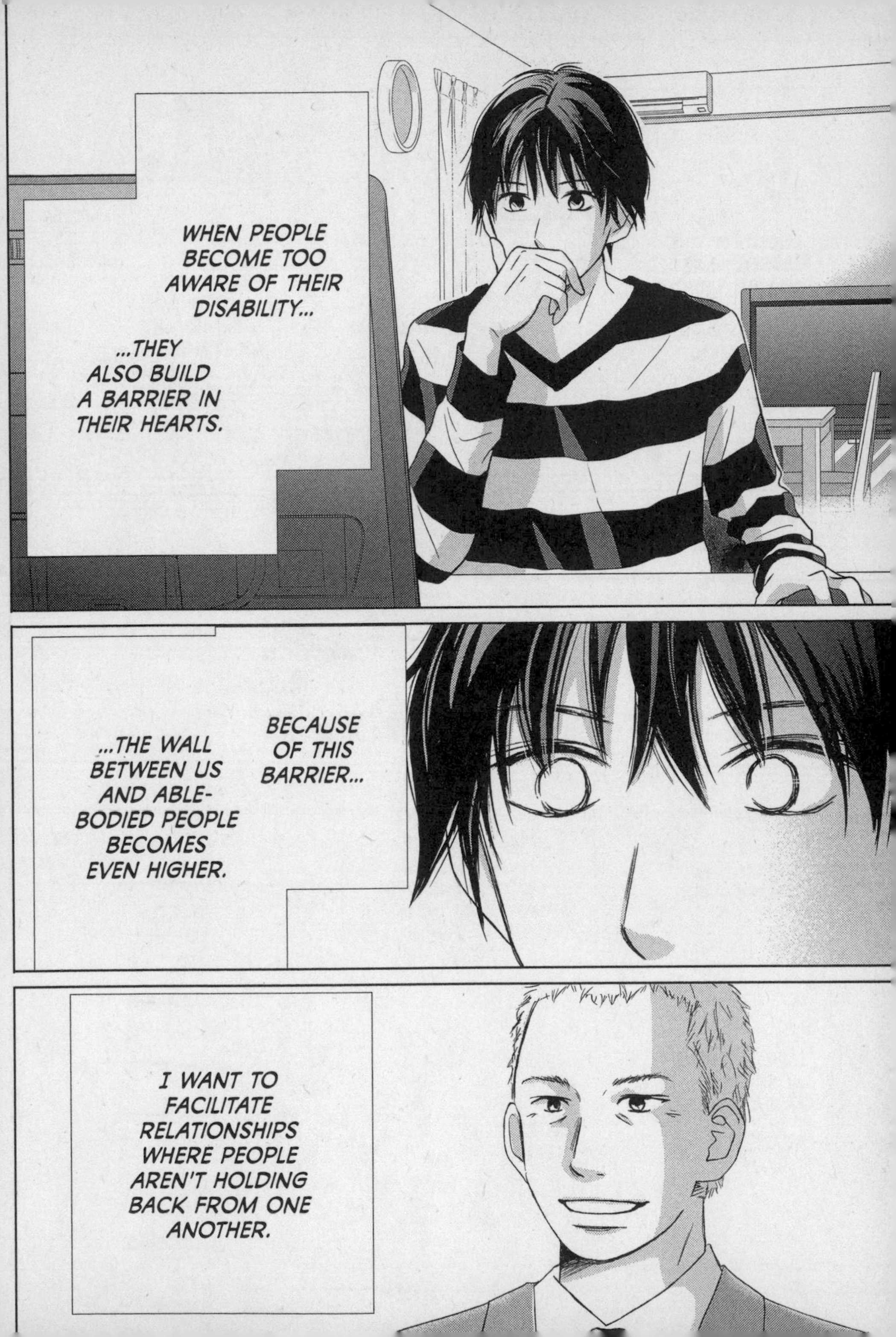
WHEN PEOPLE BECOME TOO AWARE OF THEIR DISABILITY...
...THEY ALSO BUILD A BARRIER IN THEIR HEARTS.
BECAUSE OF THIS BARRIER...
...THE WALL BETWEEN US AND ABLE-BODIED PEOPLE BECOMES EVEN HIGHER.
I WANT TO FACILITATE RELATIONSHIPS WHERE PEOPLE AREN'T HOLDING BACK FROM ONE ANOTHER.

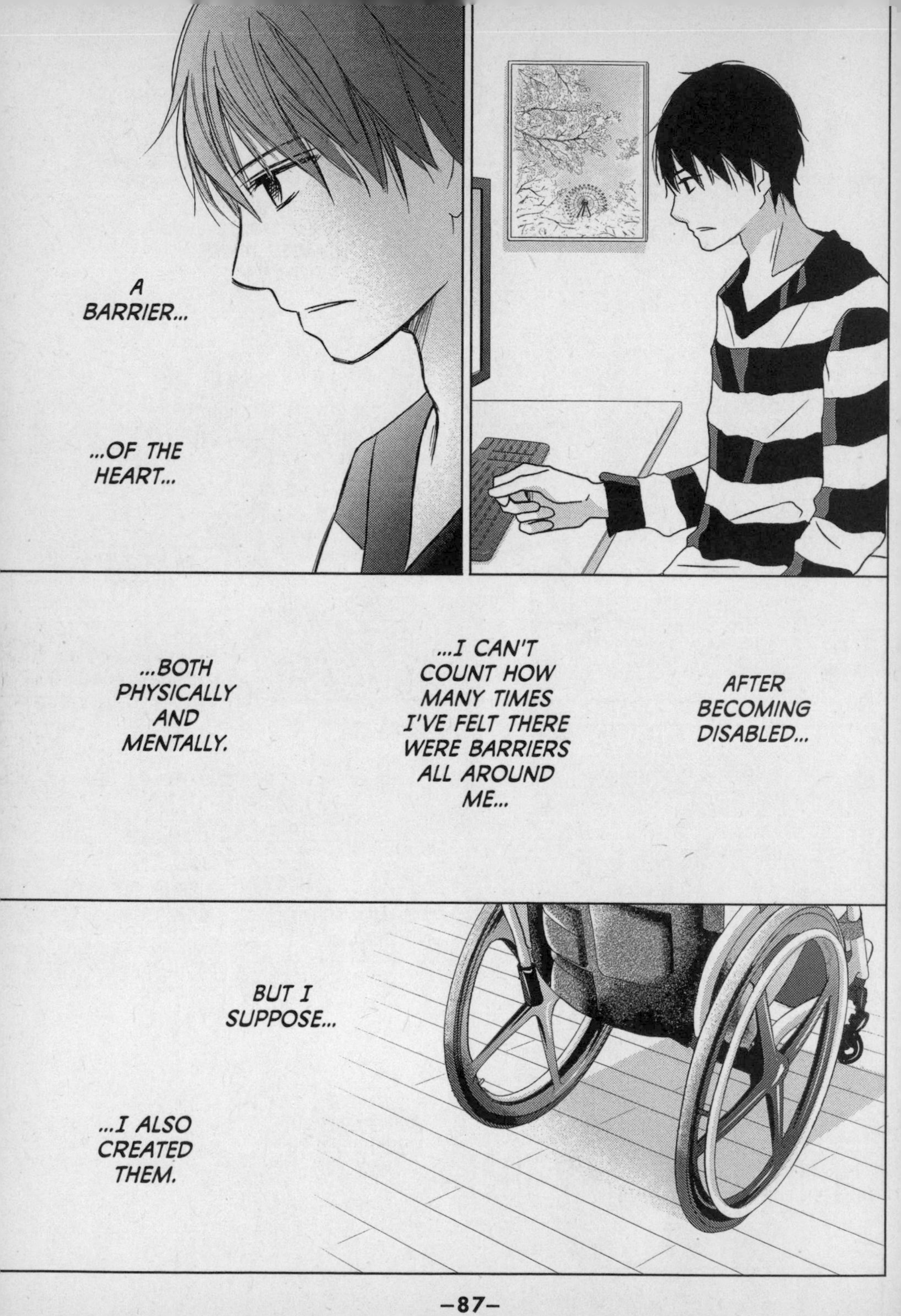
A BARRIER...
...OF THE HEART...
AFTER BECOMING DISABLED...
...I CAN'T COUNT HOW MANY TIMES I'VE FELT THERE WERE BARRIERS ALL AROUND ME...
...BOTH PHYSICALLY AND MENTALLY.
BUT I SUPPOSE...
...I ALSO CREATED THEM.

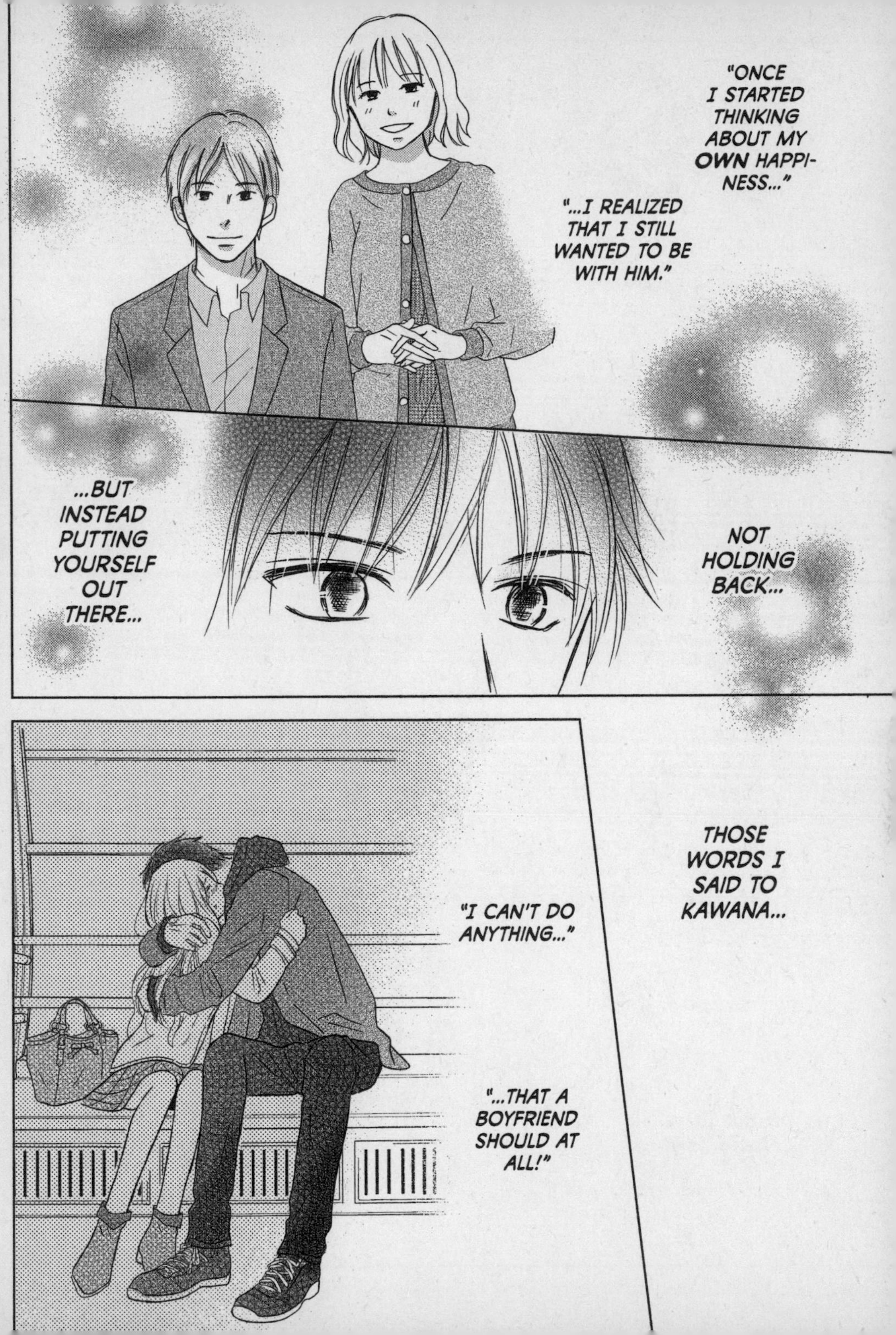
"ONCE I STARTED THINKING ABOUT MY OWN HAPPINESS..."
"...I REALIZED THAT I STILL WANTED TO BE WITH HIM."
NOT HOLDING BACK...
...BUT INSTEAD PUTTING YOURSELF OUT THERE...
THOSE WORDS I SAID TO KAWANA...
"I CAN'T DO ANYTHING..."
"...THAT A BOYFRIEND SHOULD AT ALL!"

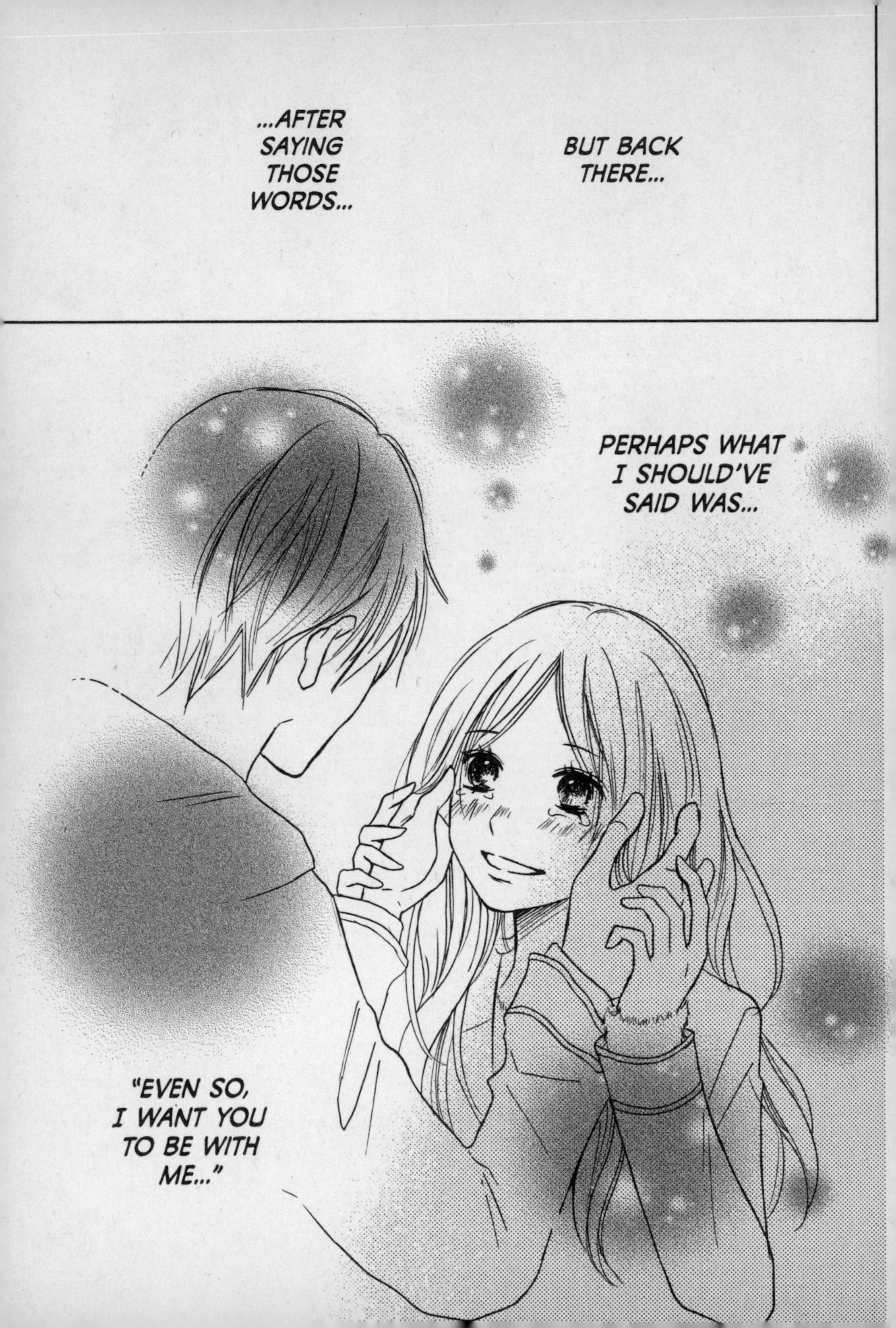
BUT BACK THERE...
...AFTER SAYING THOSE WORDS...
PERHAPS WHAT I SHOULD'VE SAID WAS...
"EVEN SO, I WANT YOU TO BE WITH ME..."

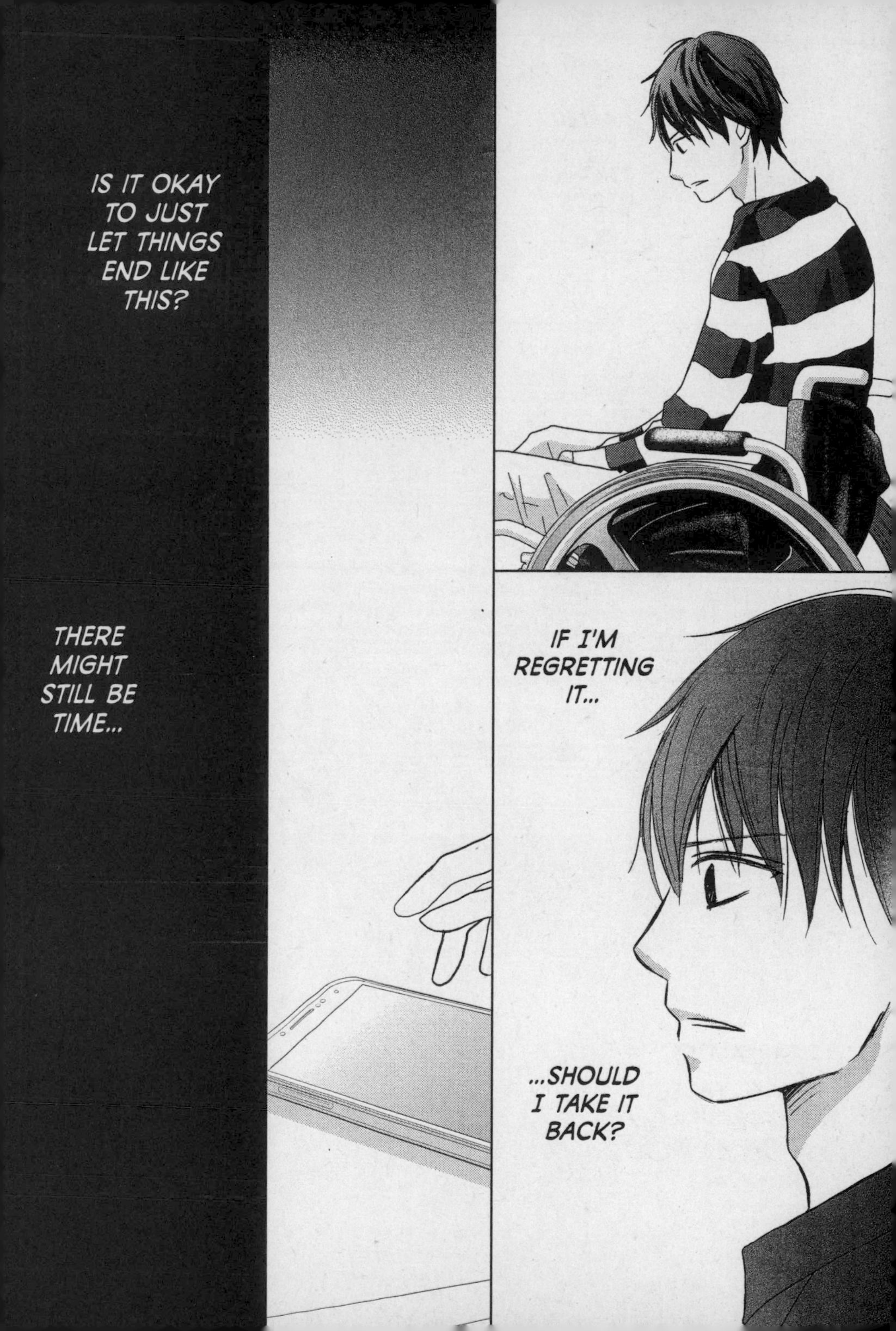
IF I'M REGRETTING IT...
...SHOULD I TAKE IT BACK?
IS IT OKAY TO JUST LET THINGS END LIKE THIS?
THERE MIGHT STILL BE TIME...

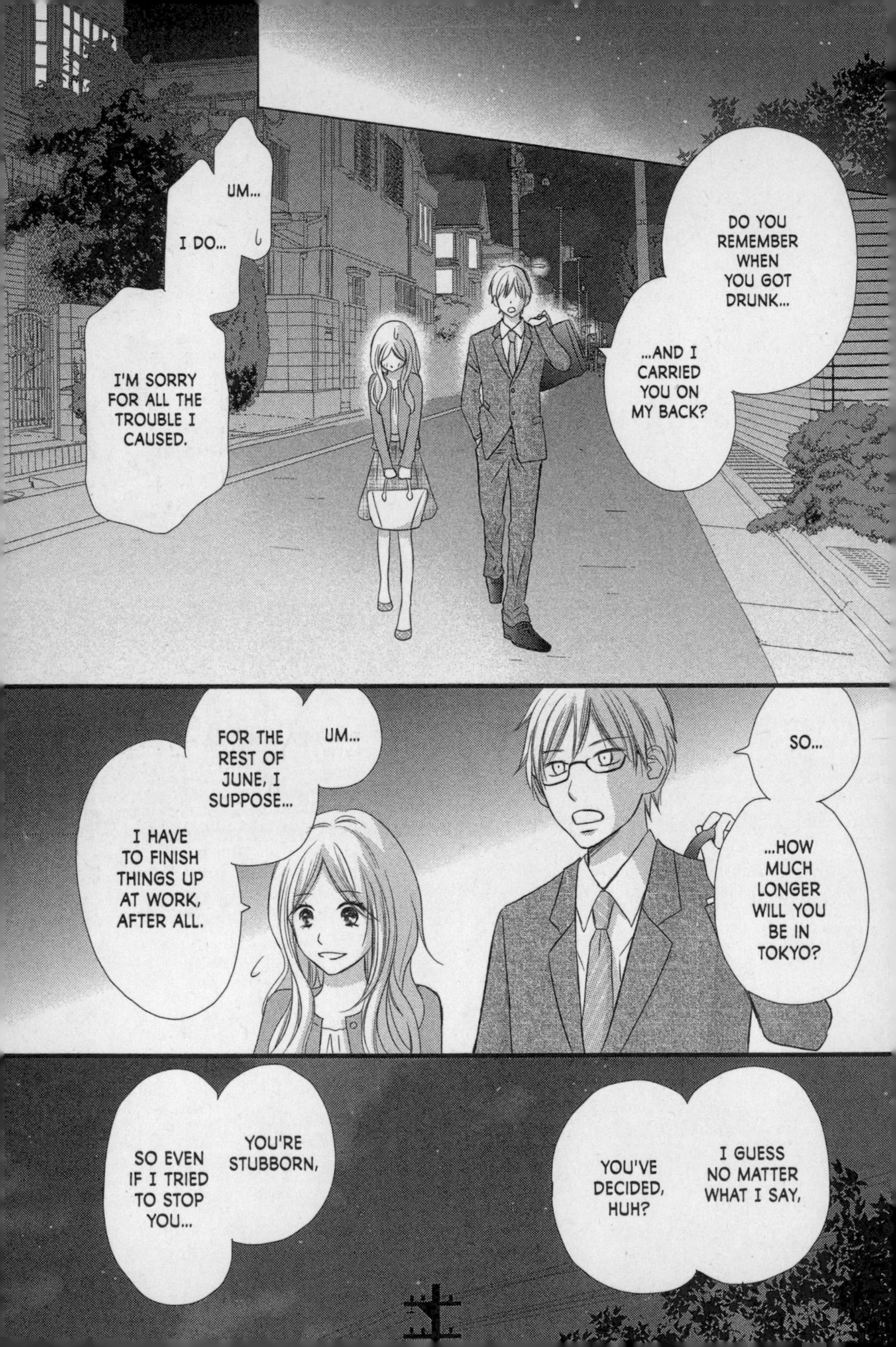
DO YOU REMEMBER WHEN YOU GOT DRUNK...
...AND I CARRIED YOU ON MY BACK?
UM...
I DO...
I'M SORRY FOR ALL THE TROUBLE I CAUSED.
SO...
...HOW MUCH LONGER WILL YOU BE IN TOKYO?
UM...
FOR THE REST OF JUNE, I SUPPOSE...
I HAVE TO FINISH THINGS UP AT WORK, AFTER ALL.
I GUESS NO MATTER WHAT I SAY,
YOU'VE DECIDED, HUH?
YOU'RE STUBBORN,
SO EVEN IF I TRIED TO STOP YOU...

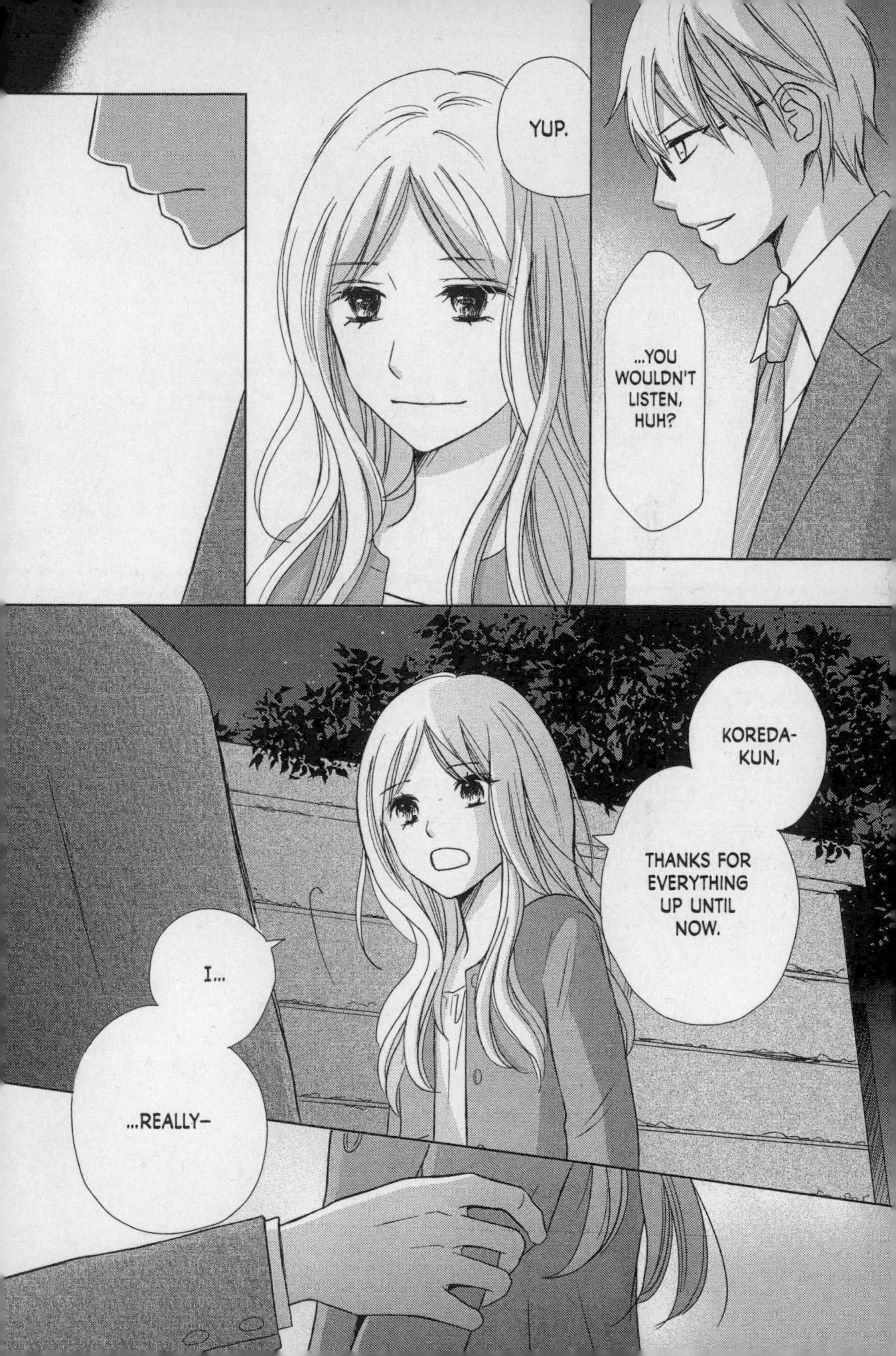
...YOU WOULDN'T LISTEN, HUH?
YUP.
KOREDA-KUN,
THANKS FOR EVERYTHING UP UNTIL NOW.
I...
...REALLY—

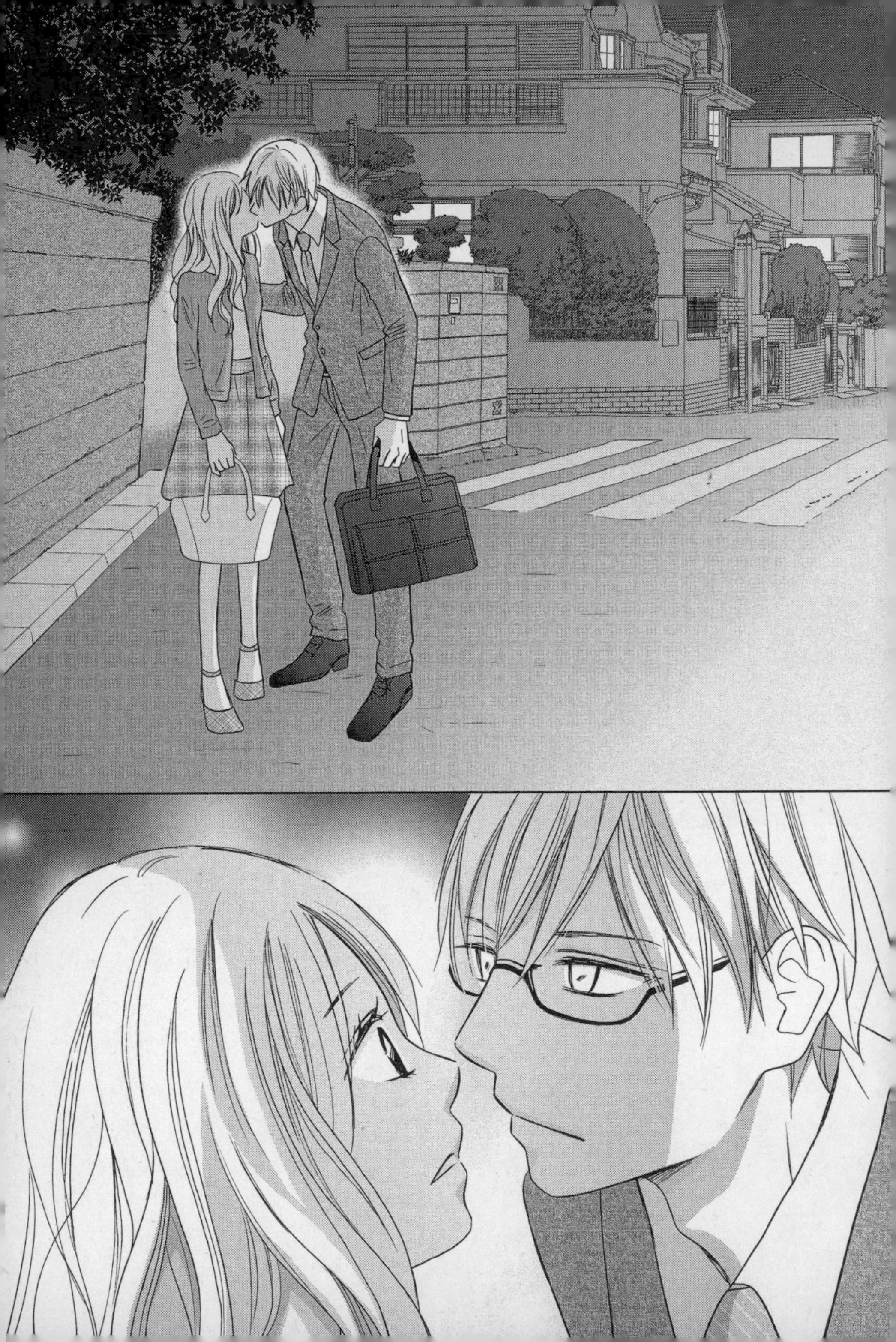

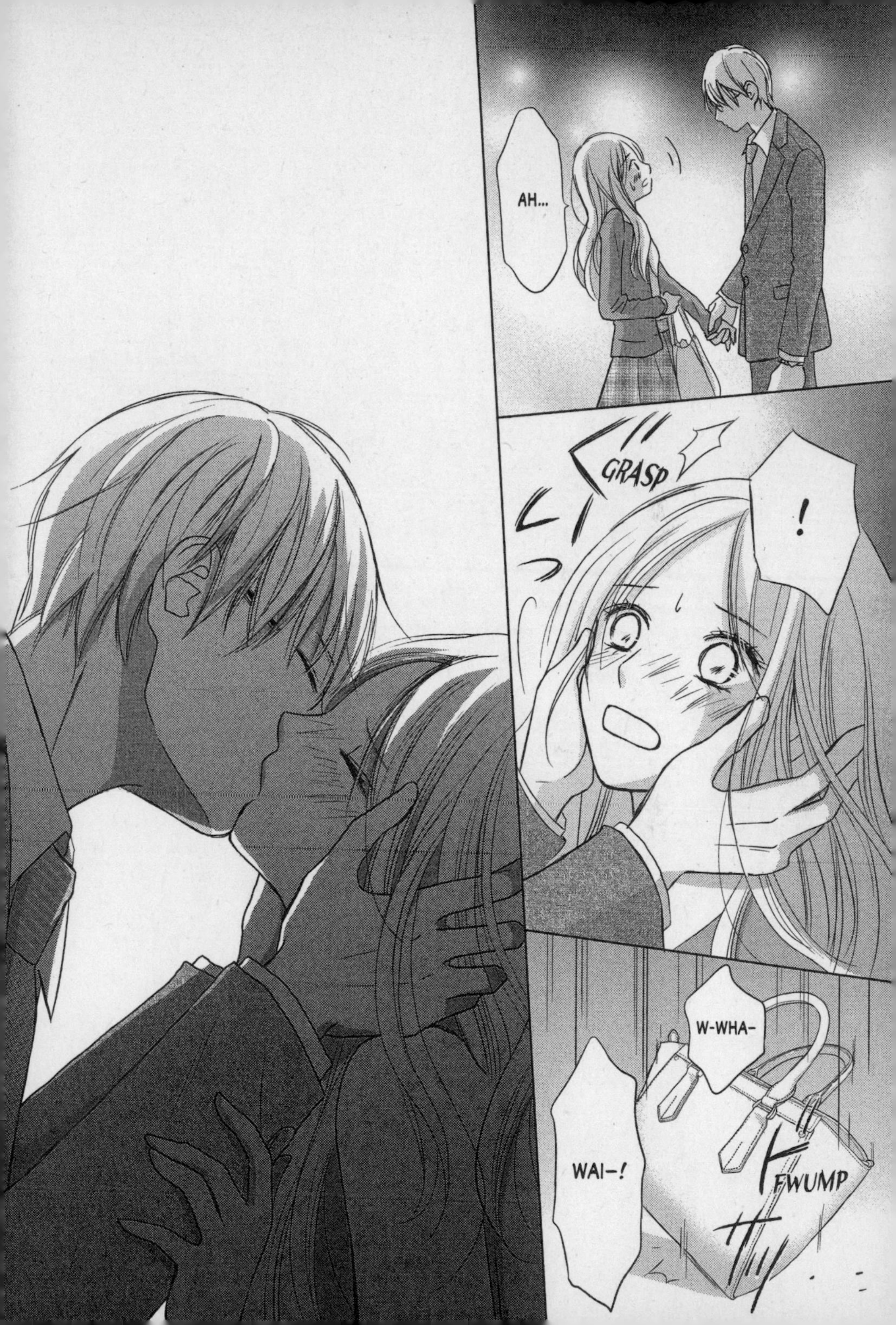
AH...
GRASP
!
W-WHA-
WAI-!
FWUMP

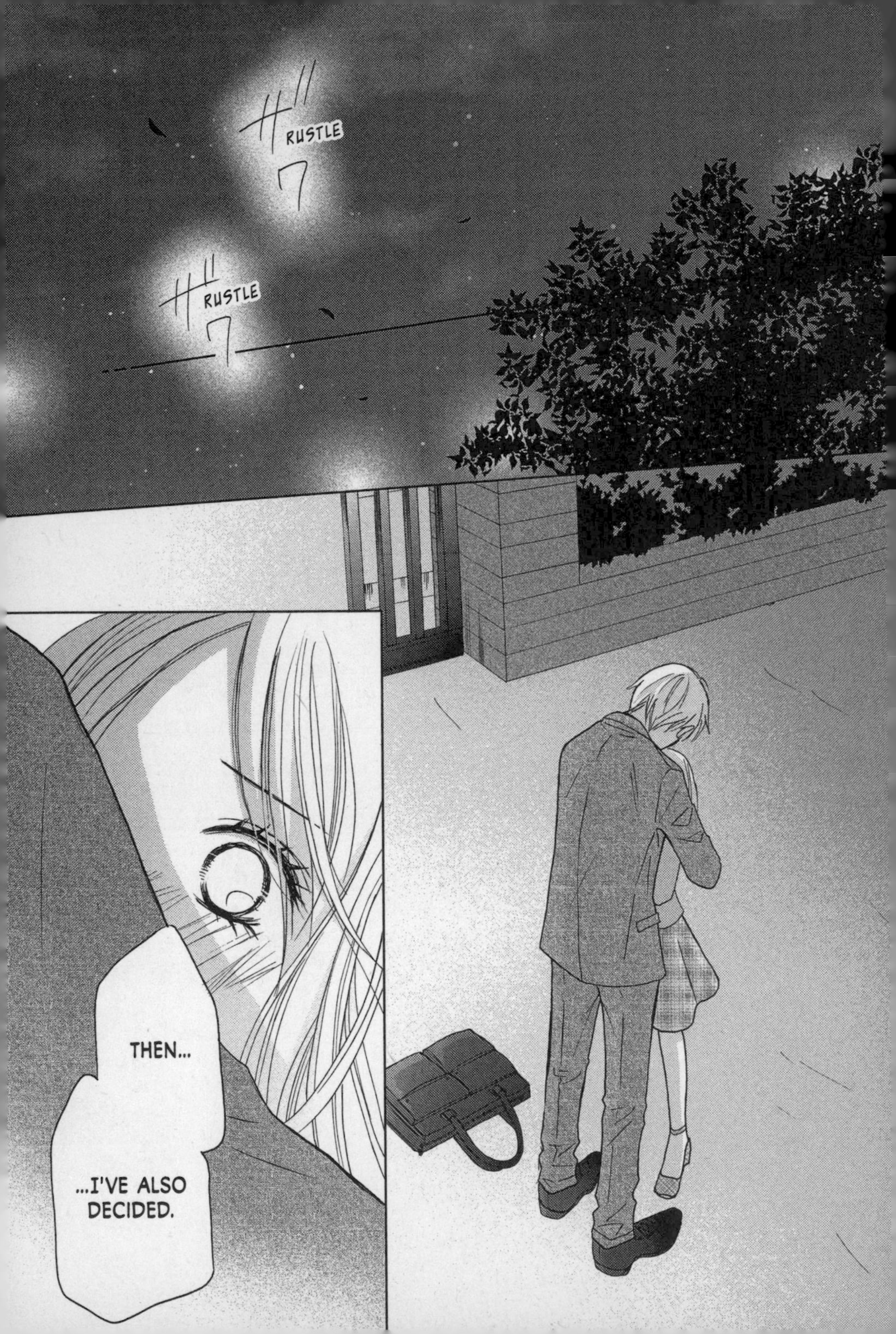
RUSTLE
RUSTLE
THEN...
...I'VE ALSO DECIDED.

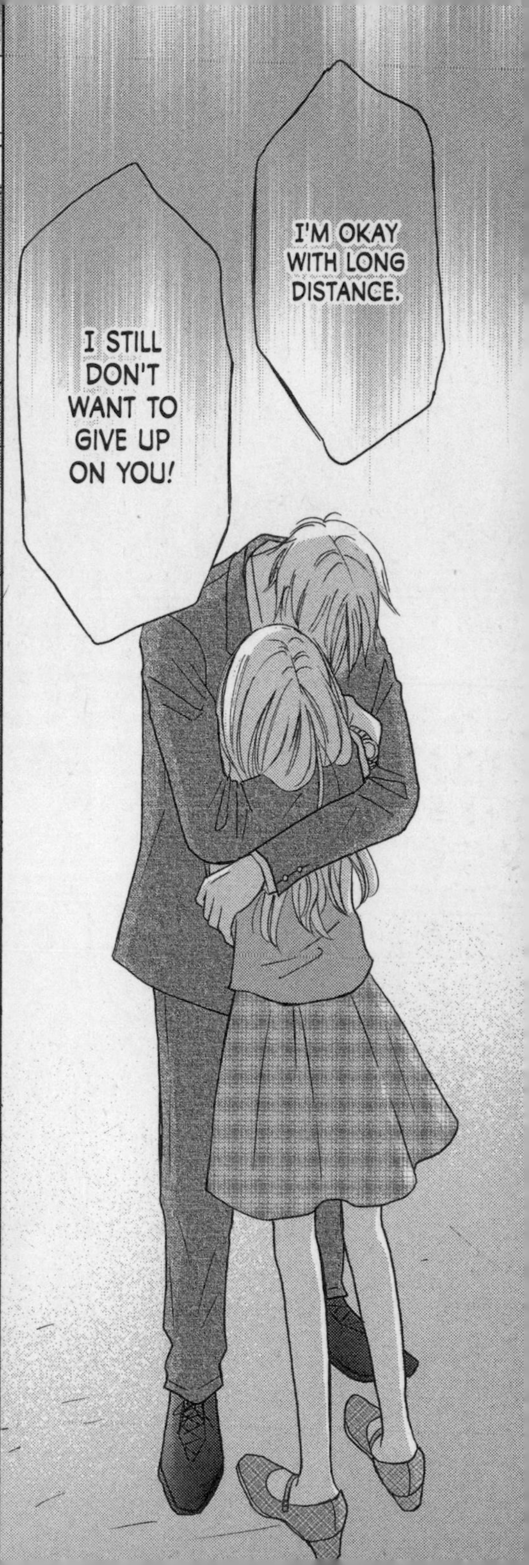
I'M OKAY WITH LONG DISTANCE.
I STILL DON'T WANT TO GIVE UP ON YOU!
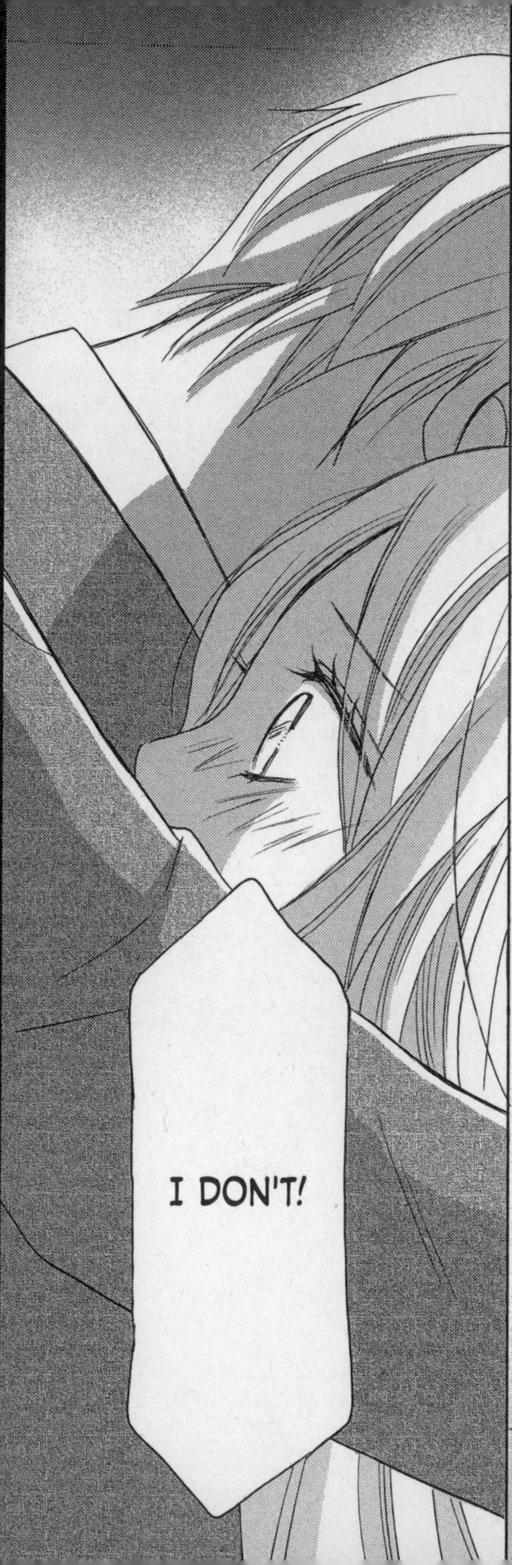
I DON'T!

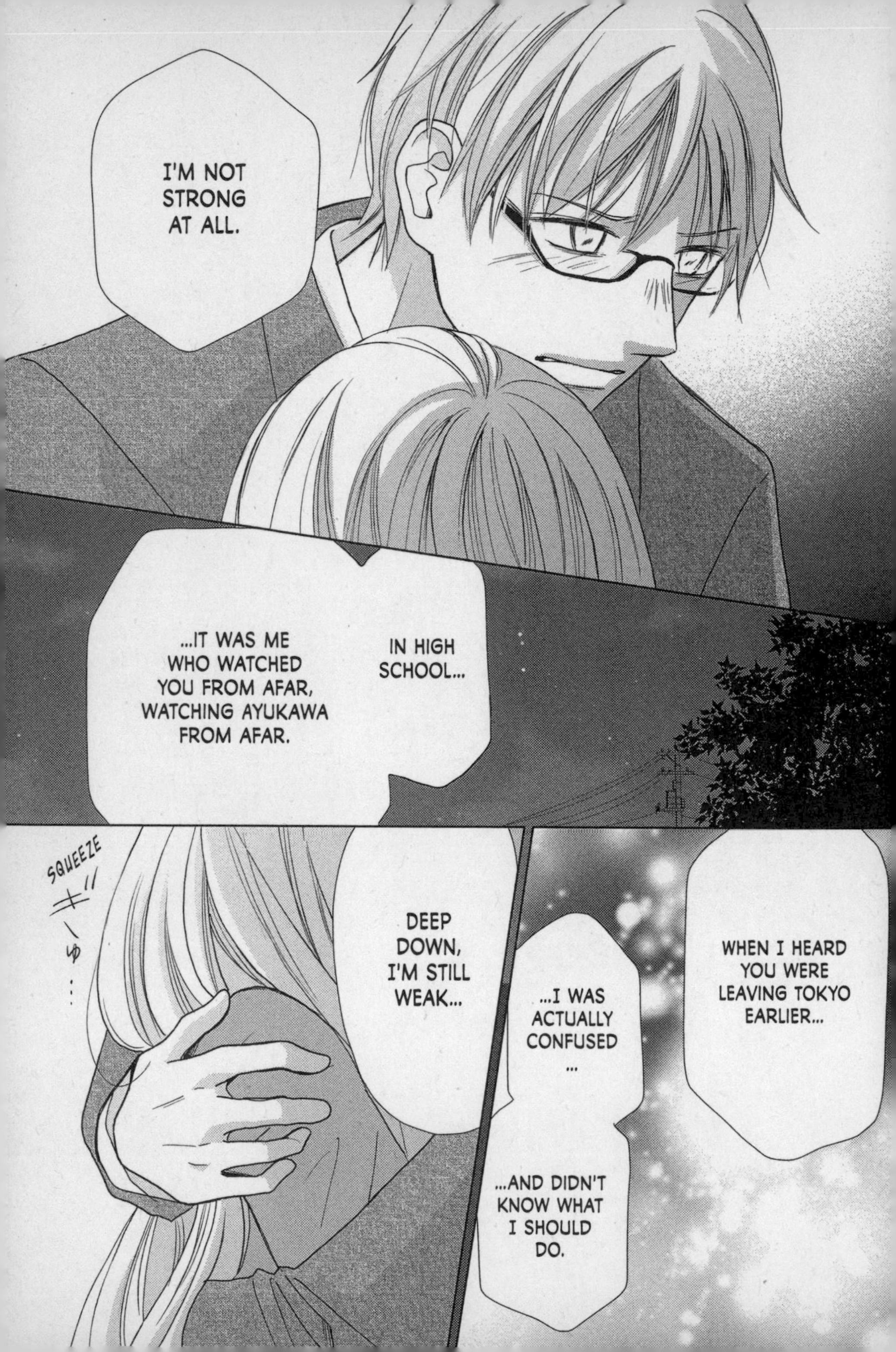
I'M NOT STRONG AT ALL.
IN HIGH SCHOOL...
...IT WAS ME WHO WATCHED YOU FROM AFAR, WATCHING AYUKAWA FROM AFAR.
WHEN I HEARD YOU WERE LEAVING TOKYO EARLIER...
...I WAS ACTUALLY CONFUSED ...
...AND DIDN'T KNOW WHAT I SHOULD DO.
DEEP DOWN, I'M STILL WEAK...
SQUEEZE

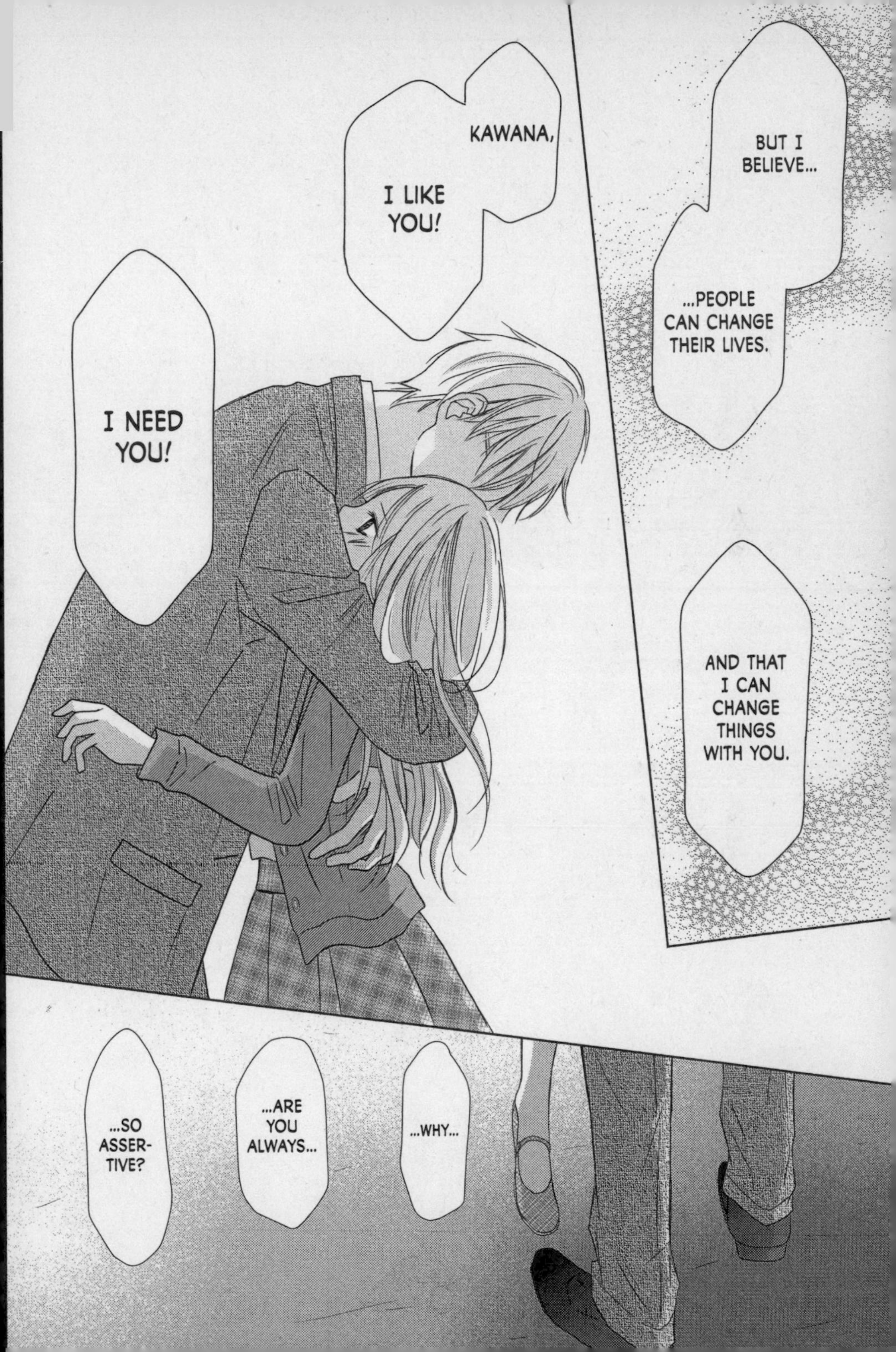
BUT I BELIEVE...
...PEOPLE CAN CHANGE THEIR LIVES.
AND THAT I CAN CHANGE THINGS WITH YOU.
KAWANA,
I LIKE YOU!
I NEED YOU!
...WHY...
...ARE YOU ALWAYS...
...SO ASSER-TIVE?

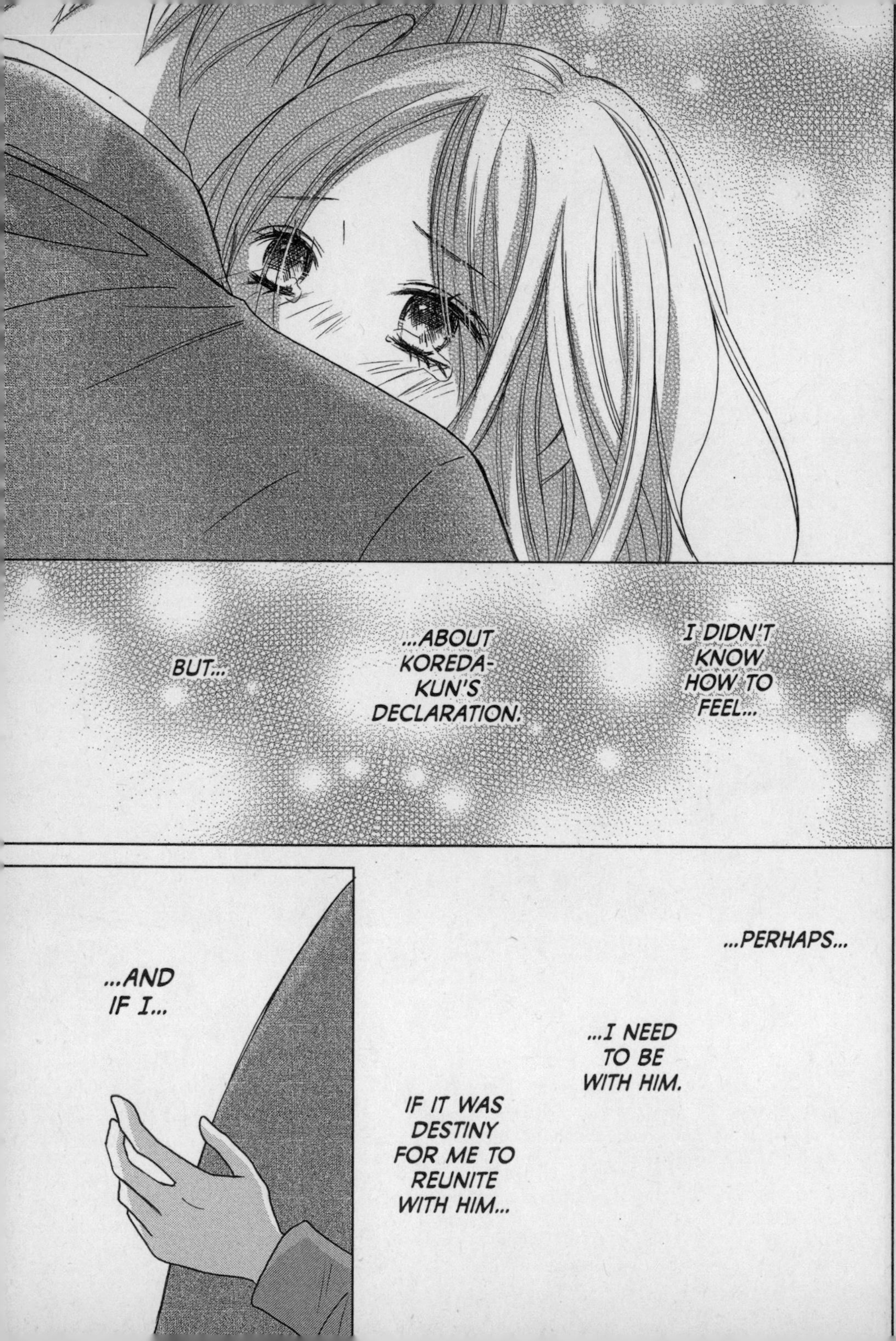
I DIDN'T KNOW HOW TO FEEL...
...ABOUT KOREDA-KUN'S DECLARATION.
BUT...
...PERHAPS...
...I NEED TO BE WITH HIM.
IF IT WAS DESTINY FOR ME TO REUNITE WITH HIM...
...AND IF I...

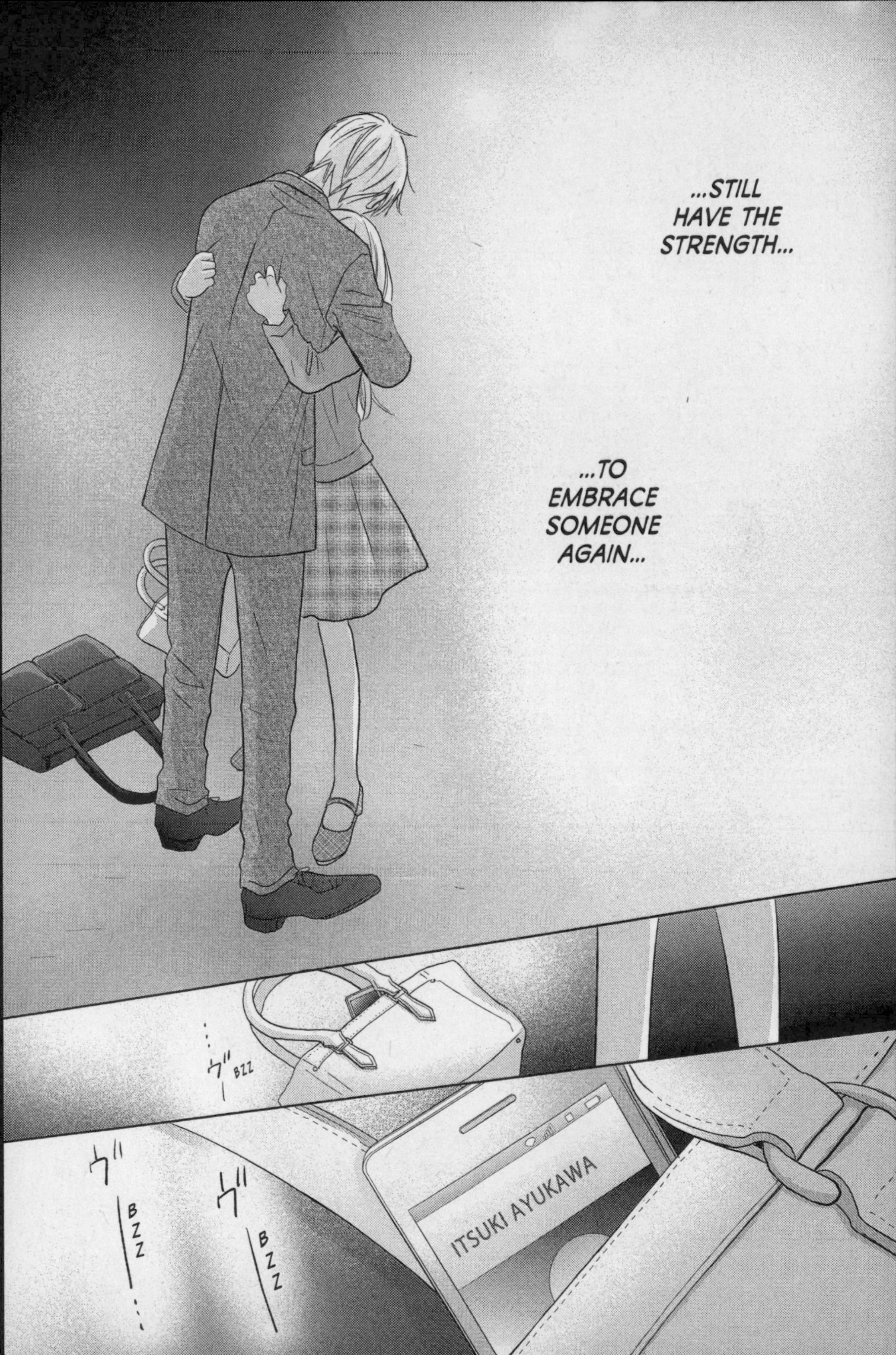
...STILL HAVE THE STRENGTH...
...TO EMBRACE SOMEONE AGAIN...
...ヴ BZZ
ITSUKI AYUKAWA
ヴ BZZ
ヴ BZZ
...

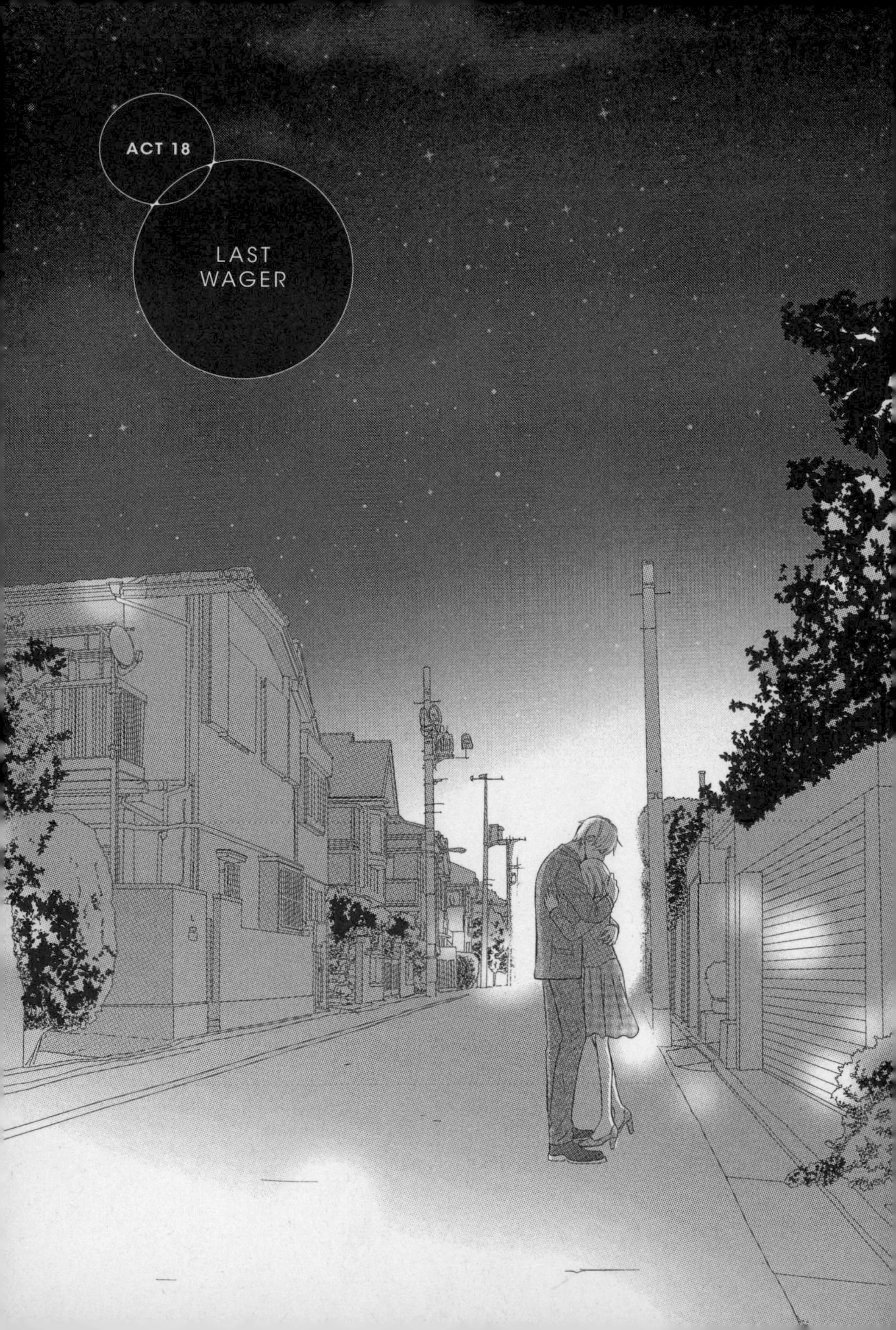
ACT 18
LAST WAGER

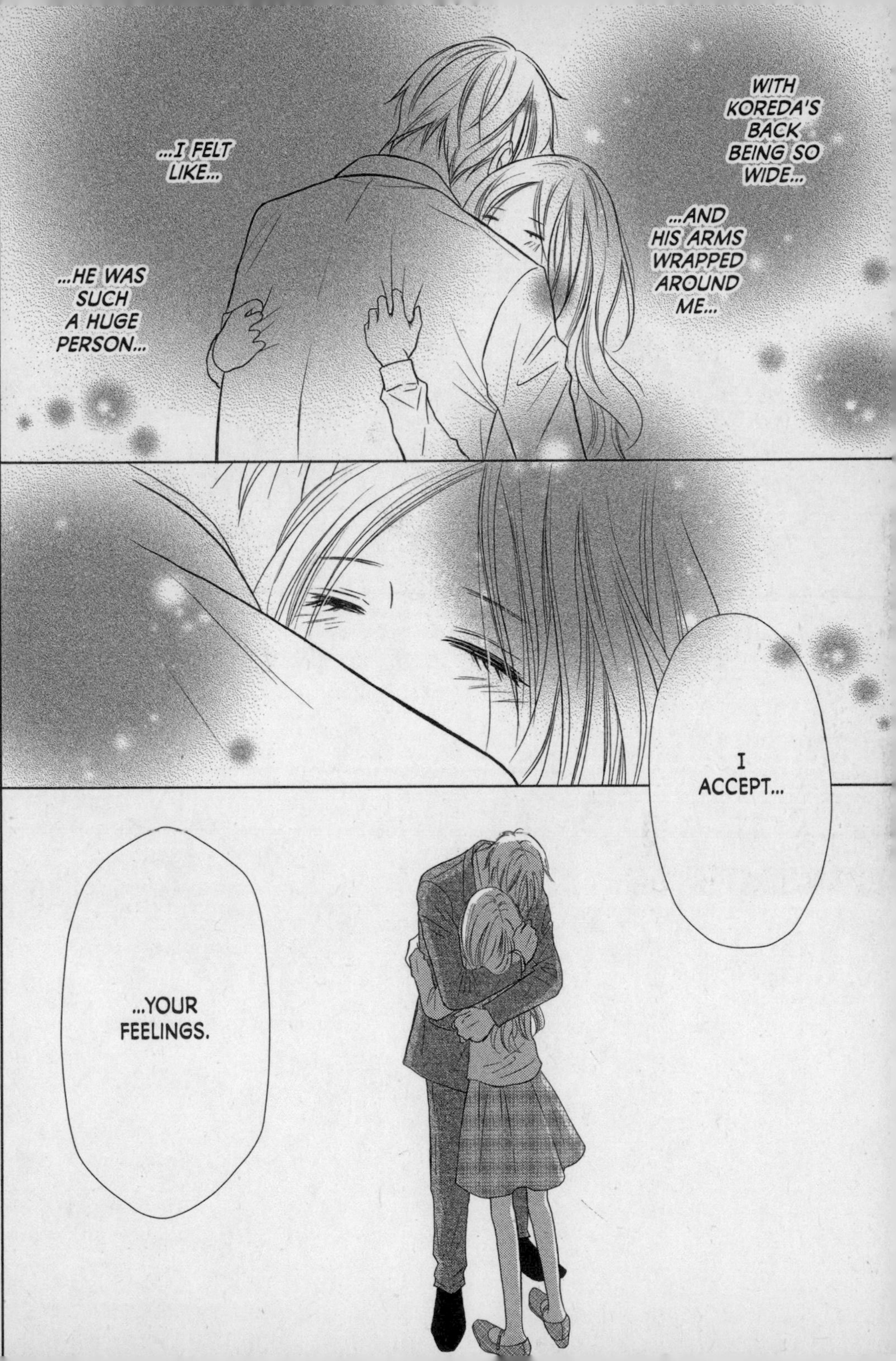
WITH KOREDA'S BACK BEING SO WIDE...
...AND HIS ARMS WRAPPED AROUND ME...
...I FELT LIKE...
...HE WAS SUCH A HUGE PERSON...
I ACCEPT...
...YOUR FEELINGS.

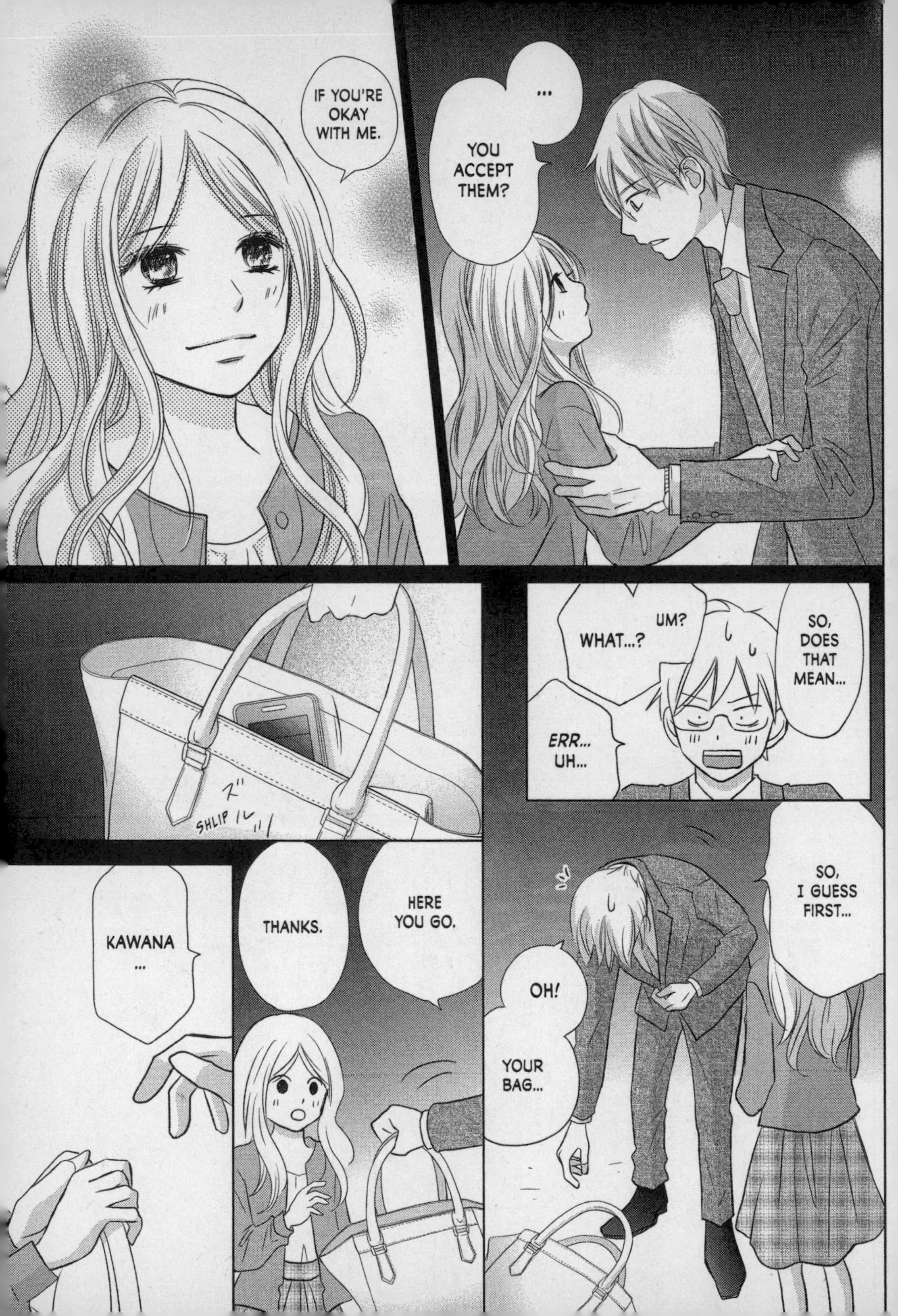
...
YOU ACCEPT THEM?
IF YOU'RE OKAY WITH ME.
SO, DOES THAT MEAN...
UM?
WHAT...?
ERR... UH...
SHLIP
SO, I GUESS FIRST...
OH!
YOUR BAG...
HERE YOU GO.
THANKS.
KAWANA ...

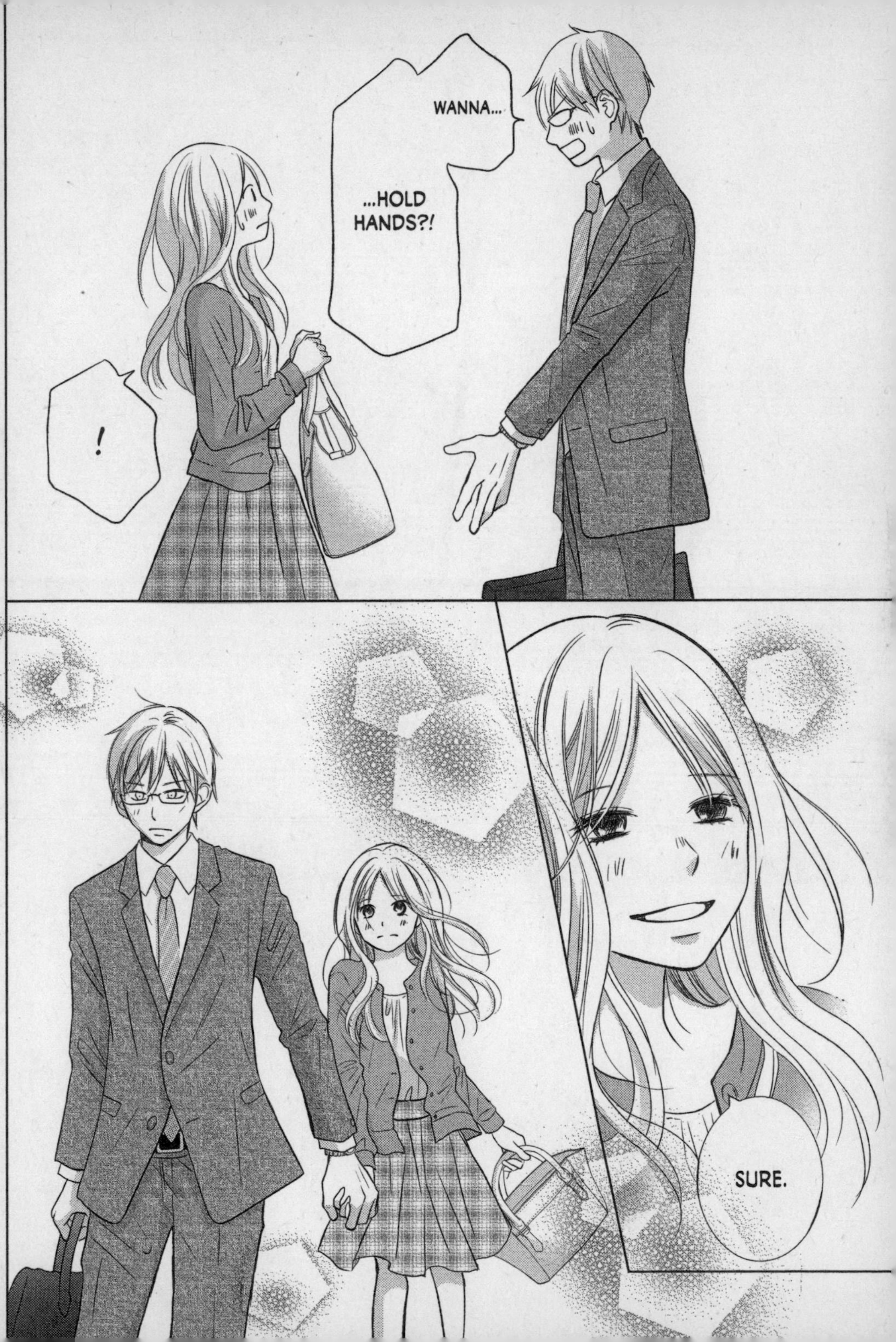
WANNA... ...HOLD HANDS?!
!
SURE.

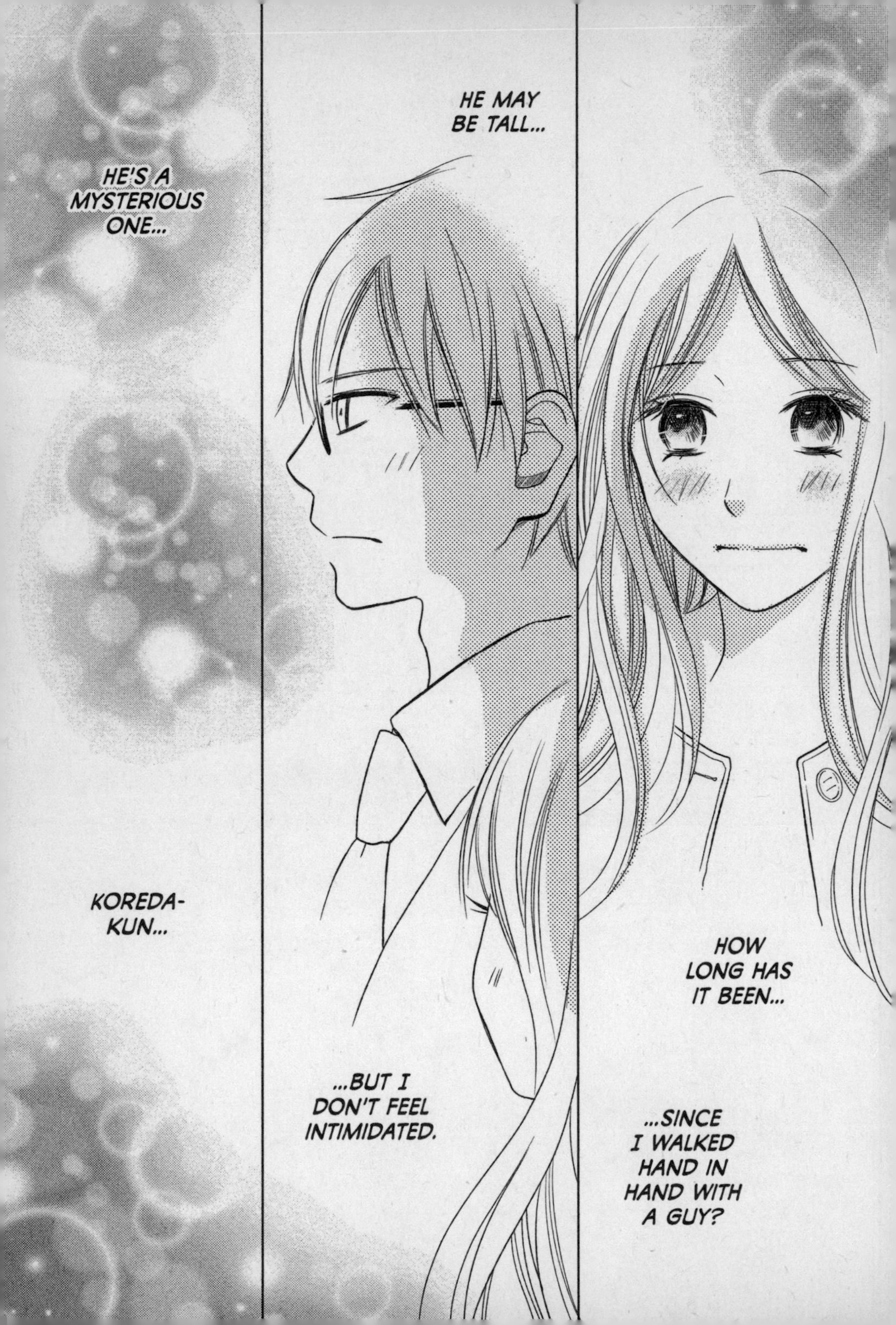
HOW LONG HAS IT BEEN...
...SINCE I WALKED HAND IN HAND WITH A GUY?
HE MAY BE TALL...
...BUT I DON'T FEEL INTIMIDATED.
HE'S A MYSTERIOUS ONE...
KOREDA-KUN...

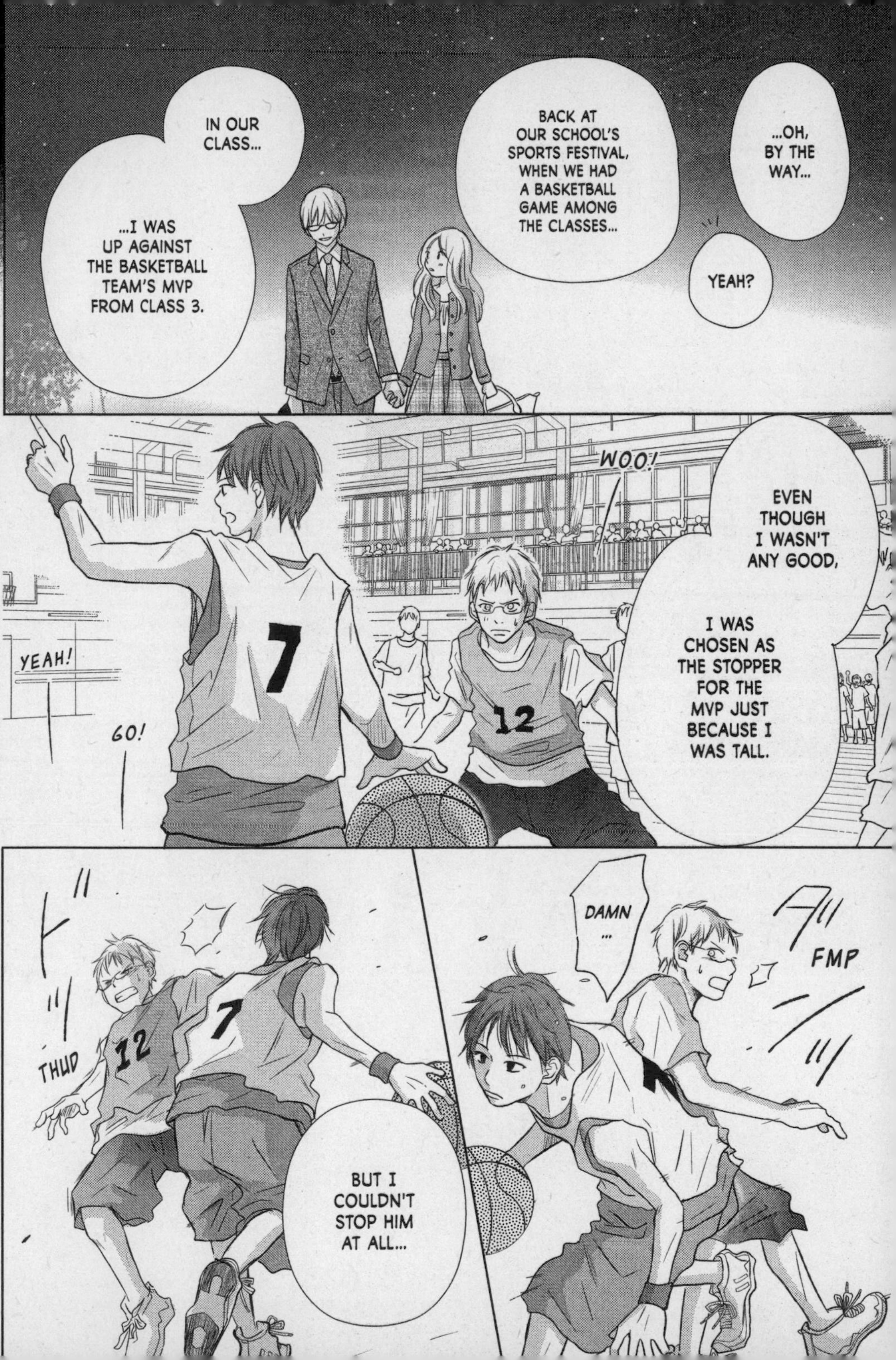
...OH, BY THE WAY...
YEAH?
BACK AT OUR SCHOOL'S SPORTS FESTIVAL, WHEN WE HAD A BASKETBALL GAME AMONG THE CLASSES...
IN OUR CLASS...
...I WAS UP AGAINST THE BASKETBALL TEAM'S MVP FROM CLASS 3.
WOO!
EVEN THOUGH I WASN'T ANY GOOD,
I WAS CHOSEN AS THE STOPPER FOR THE MVP JUST BECAUSE I WAS TALL.
YEAH!
GO!
FMP
DAMN...
BUT I COULDN'T STOP HIM AT ALL...
THUD

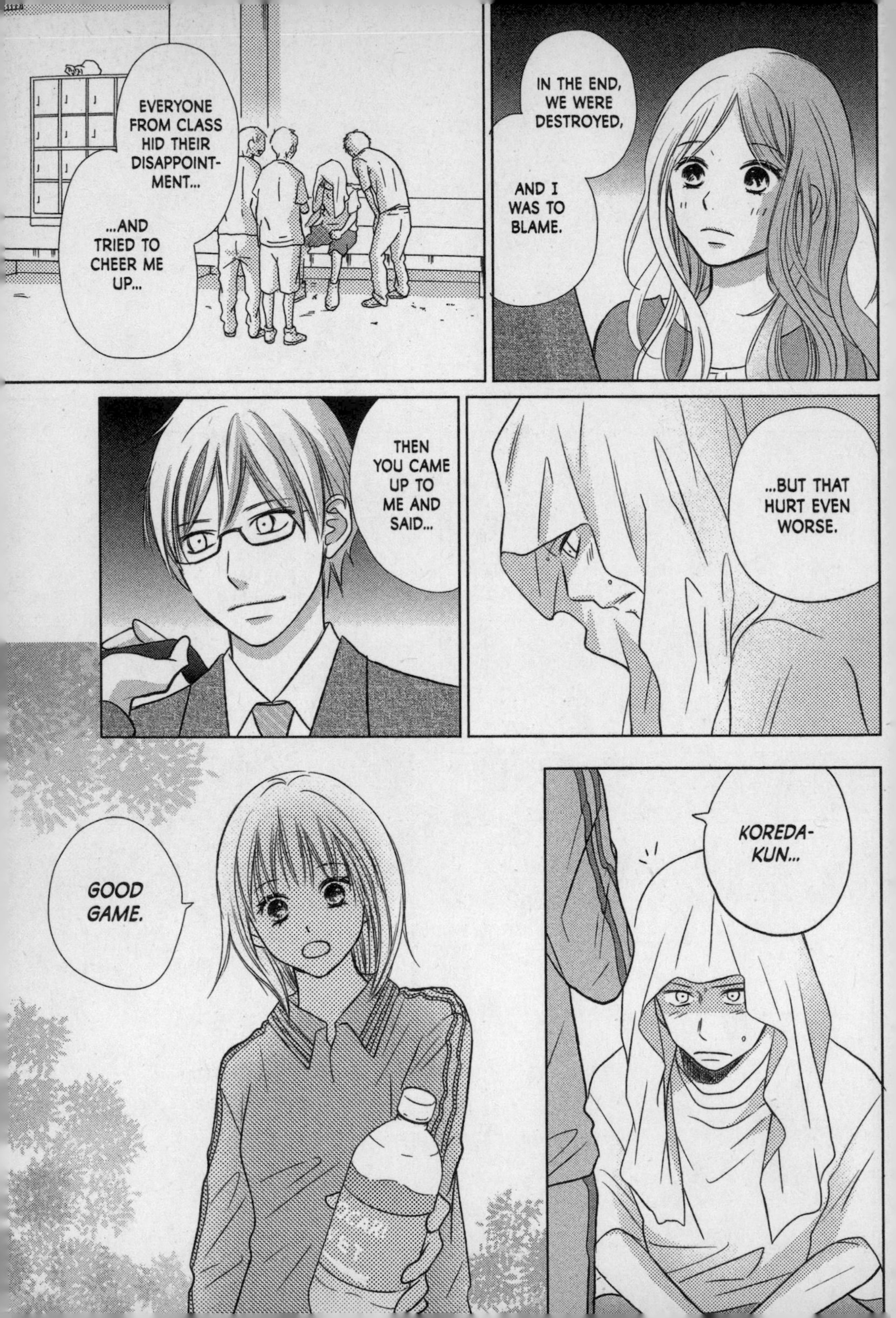
IN THE END, WE WERE DESTROYED,
AND I WAS TO BLAME.
EVERYONE FROM CLASS HID THEIR DISAPPOINT-MENT...
...AND TRIED TO CHEER ME UP...
...BUT THAT HURT EVEN WORSE.
THEN YOU CAME UP TO ME AND SAID...
KOREDA-KUN...
GOOD GAME.

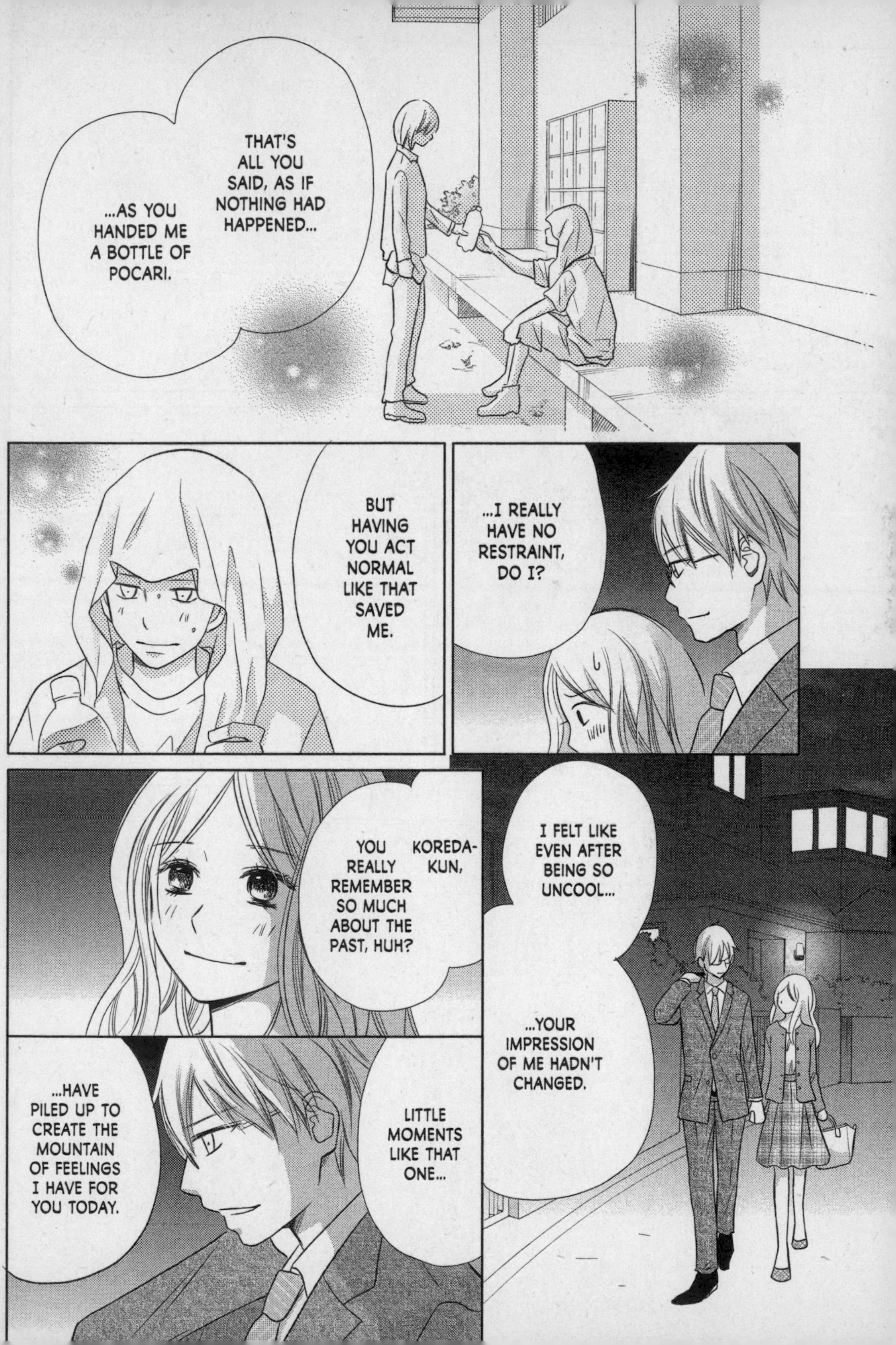
THAT'S ALL YOU SAID, AS IF NOTHING HAD HAPPENED...
...AS YOU HANDED ME A BOTTLE OF POCARI.
...I REALLY HAVE NO RESTRAINT, DO I?
BUT HAVING YOU ACT NORMAL LIKE THAT SAVED ME.
I FELT LIKE EVEN AFTER BEING SO UNCOOL...
...YOUR IMPRESSION OF ME HADN'T CHANGED.
KOREDA-KUN, YOU REALLY REMEMBER SO MUCH ABOUT THE PAST, HUH?
LITTLE MOMENTS LIKE THAT ONE...
...HAVE PILED UP TO CREATE THE MOUNTAIN OF FEELINGS I HAVE FOR YOU TODAY.

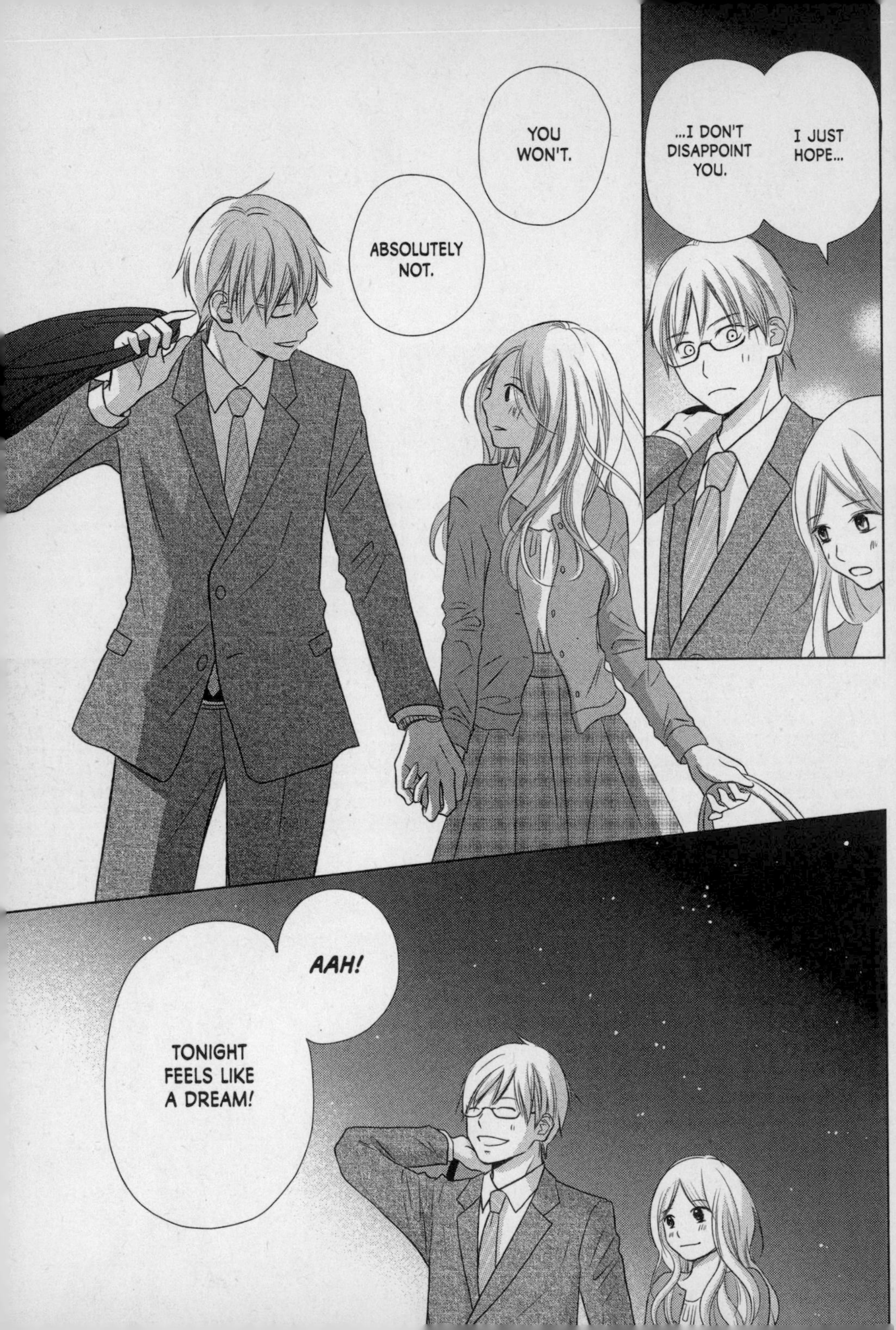
I JUST HOPE...
...I DON'T DISAPPOINT YOU.
YOU WON'T.
ABSOLUTELY NOT.
AAH!
TONIGHT FEELS LIKE A DREAM!

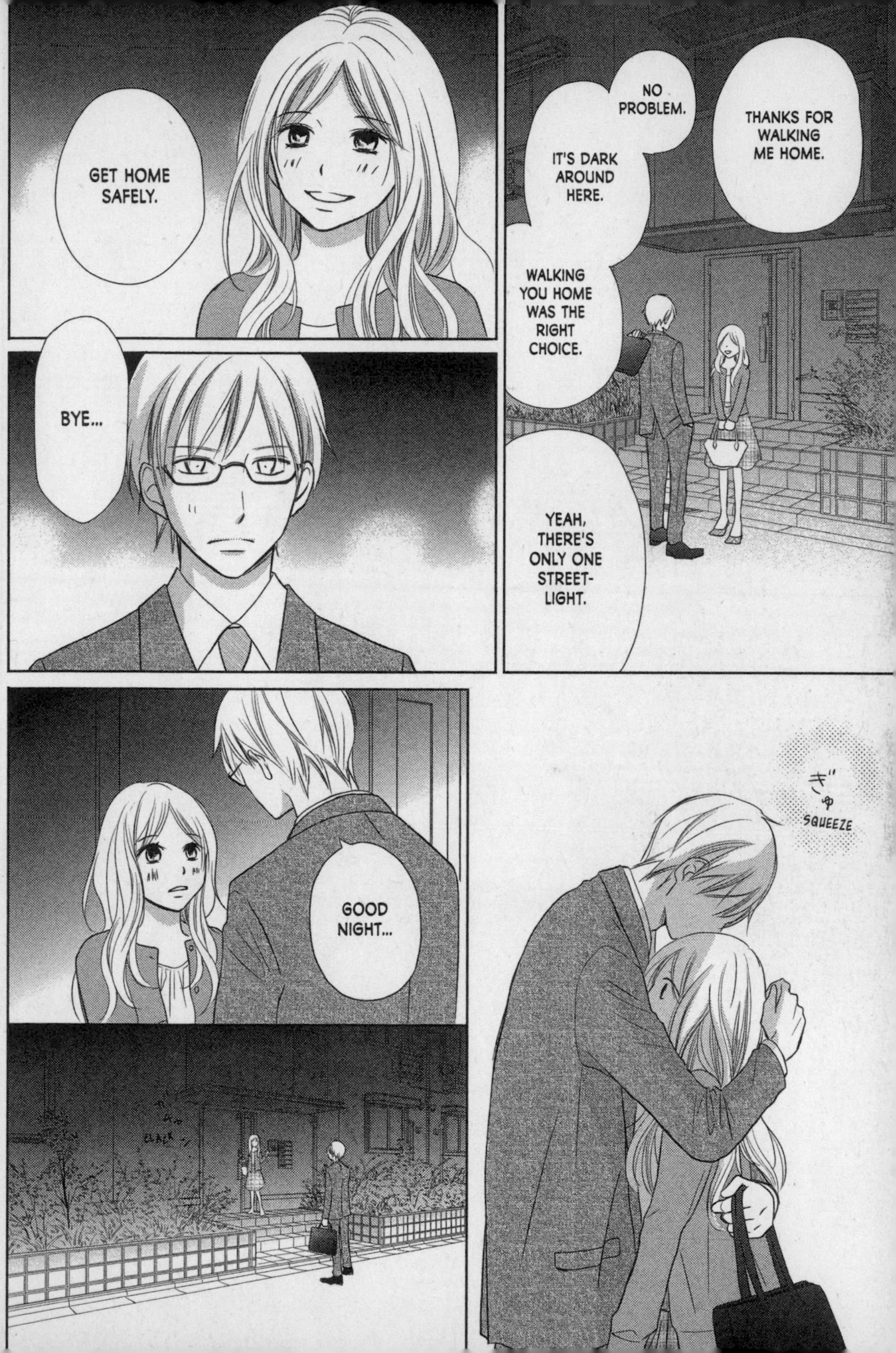
THANKS FOR WALKING ME HOME.
NO PROBLEM.
IT'S DARK AROUND HERE.
WALKING YOU HOME WAS THE RIGHT CHOICE.
YEAH, THERE'S ONLY ONE STREET-LIGHT.
GET HOME SAFELY.
BYE...
ぎゅ
SQUEEZE
GOOD NIGHT...
CLACK

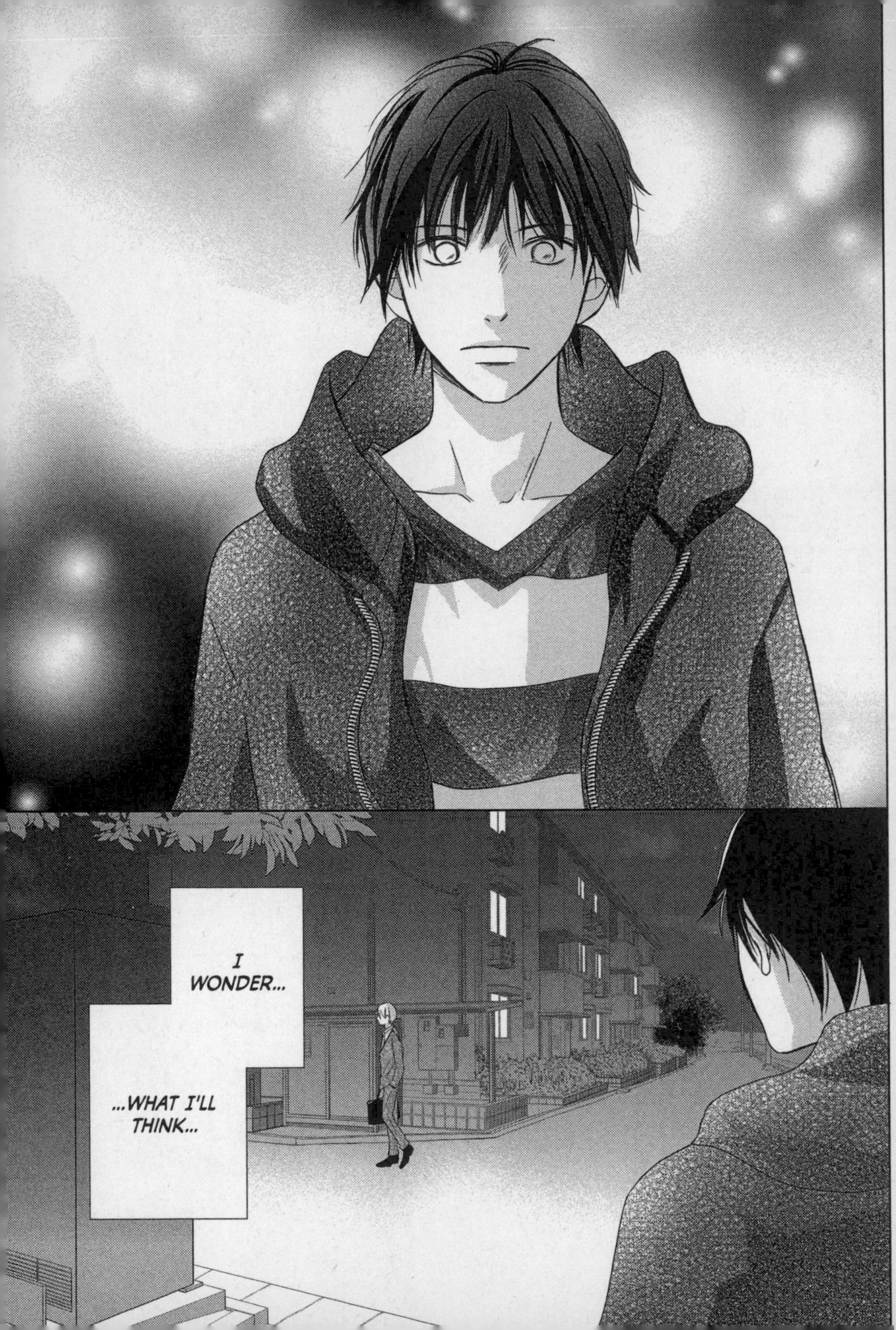
I WONDER...
...WHAT I'LL THINK...

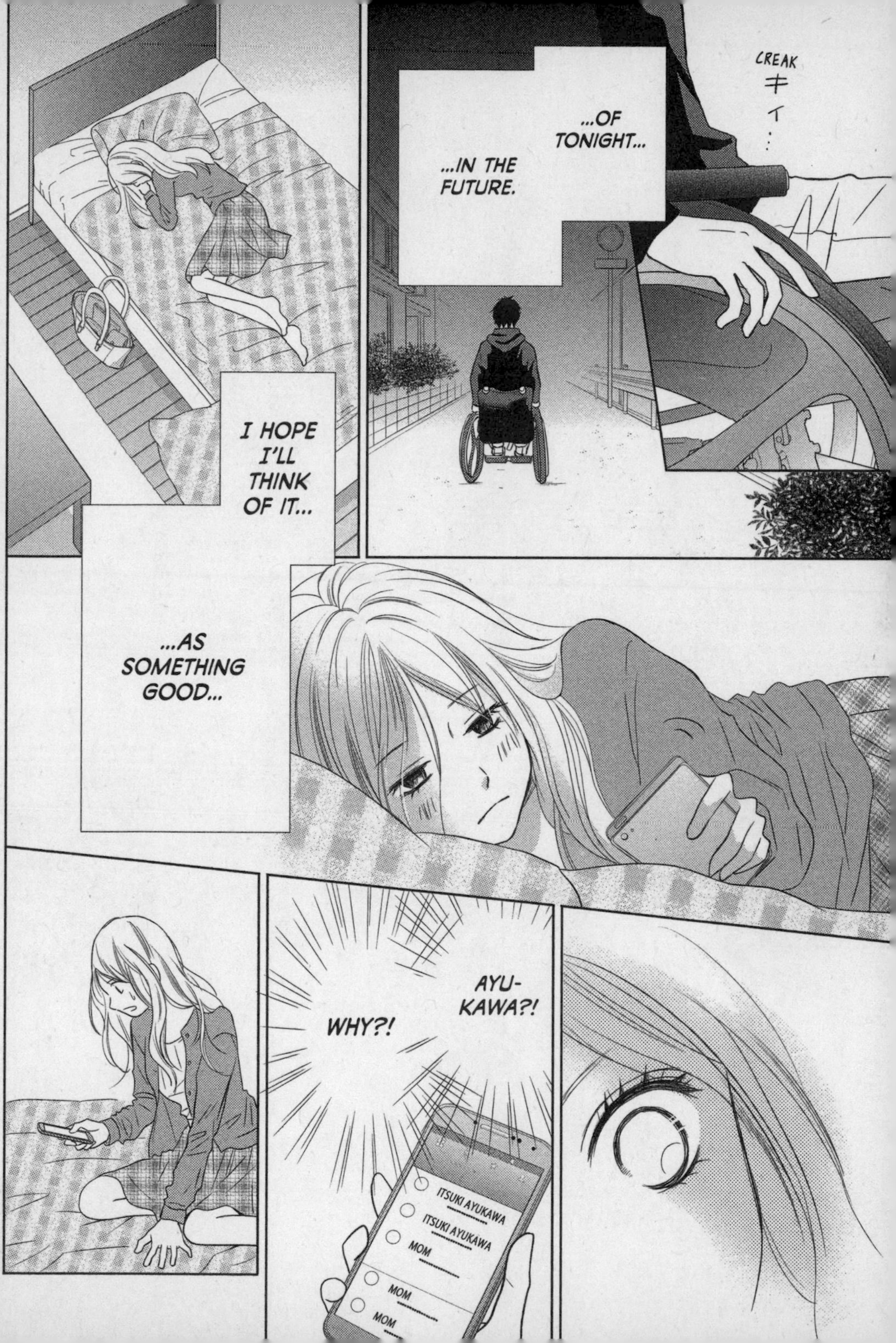
CREAK
キイ…
...OF TONIGHT...
...IN THE FUTURE.
I HOPE I'LL THINK OF IT...
...AS SOMETHING GOOD...
AYU-KAWA?!
WHY?!
ITSUKI AYUKAWA
ITSUKI AYUKAWA
MOM
MOM
MOM

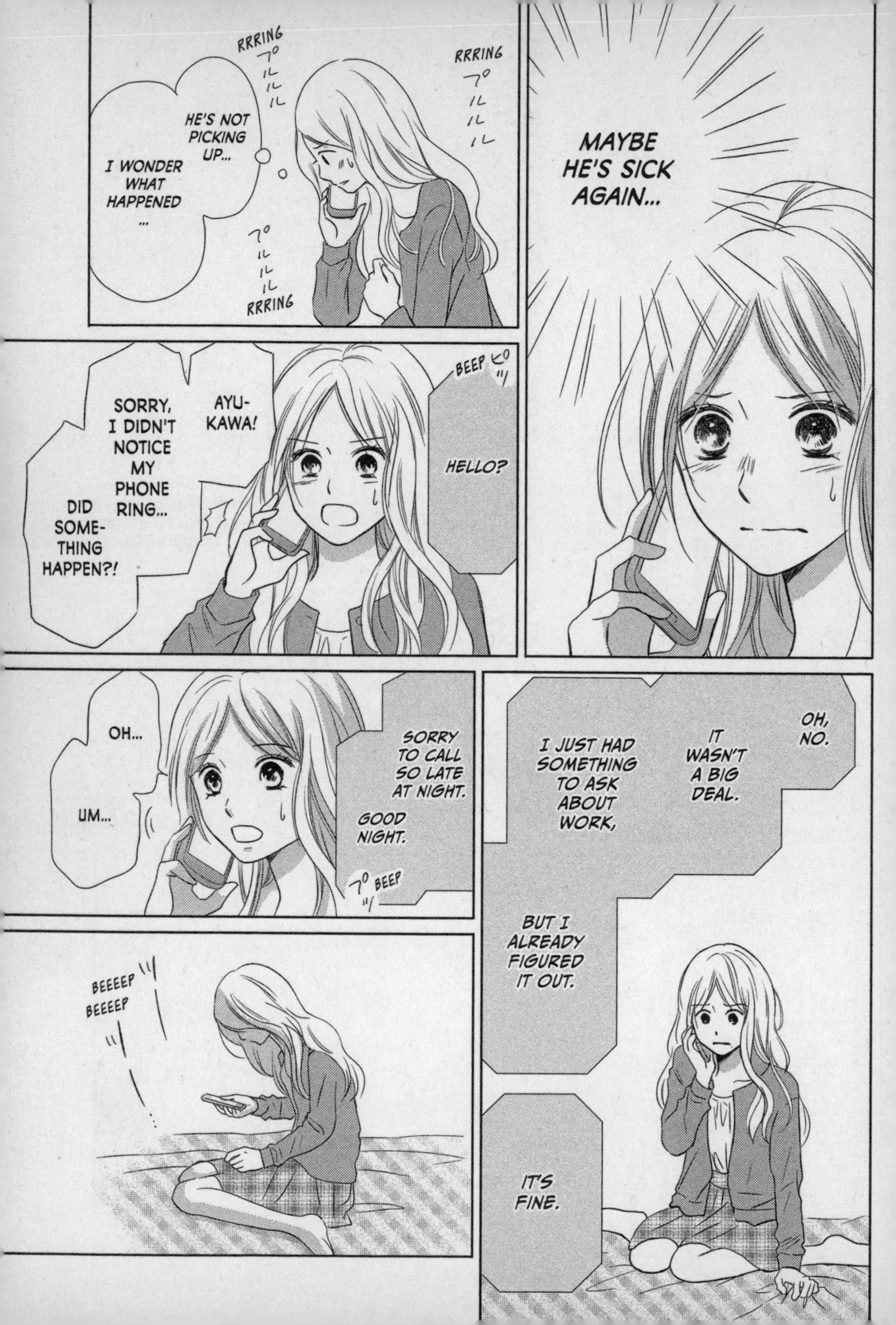
MAYBE HE'S SICK AGAIN...
RRRING プルル
RRRING プルル
HE'S NOT PICKING UP...
I WONDER WHAT HAPPENED...
プルル RRRING
BEEP ピッ
HELLO?
AYU-KAWA!
SORRY, I DIDN'T NOTICE MY PHONE RING...
DID SOME-THING HAPPEN?!
OH, NO.
IT WASN'T A BIG DEAL.
I JUST HAD SOMETHING TO ASK ABOUT WORK,
BUT I ALREADY FIGURED IT OUT.
IT'S FINE.
SORRY TO CALL SO LATE AT NIGHT.
GOOD NIGHT.
OH...
UM...
プッ BEEP
BEEEEP
BEEEEP

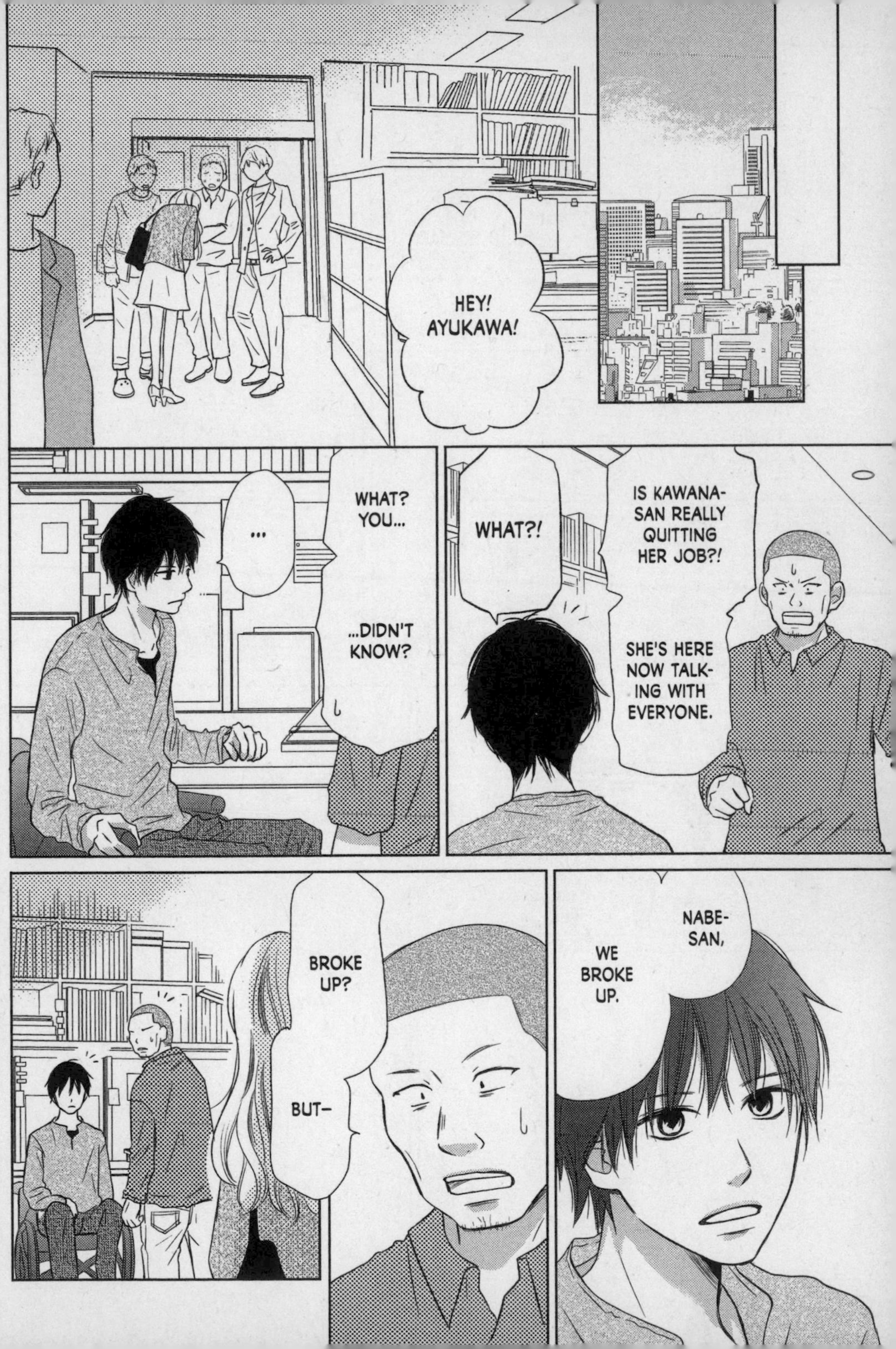
HEY! AYUKAWA!
IS KAWANA-SAN REALLY QUITTING HER JOB?!
SHE'S HERE NOW TALKING WITH EVERYONE.
WHAT?!
WHAT? YOU...
...DIDN'T KNOW?
...
NABE-SAN,
WE BROKE UP.
BROKE UP?
BUT–

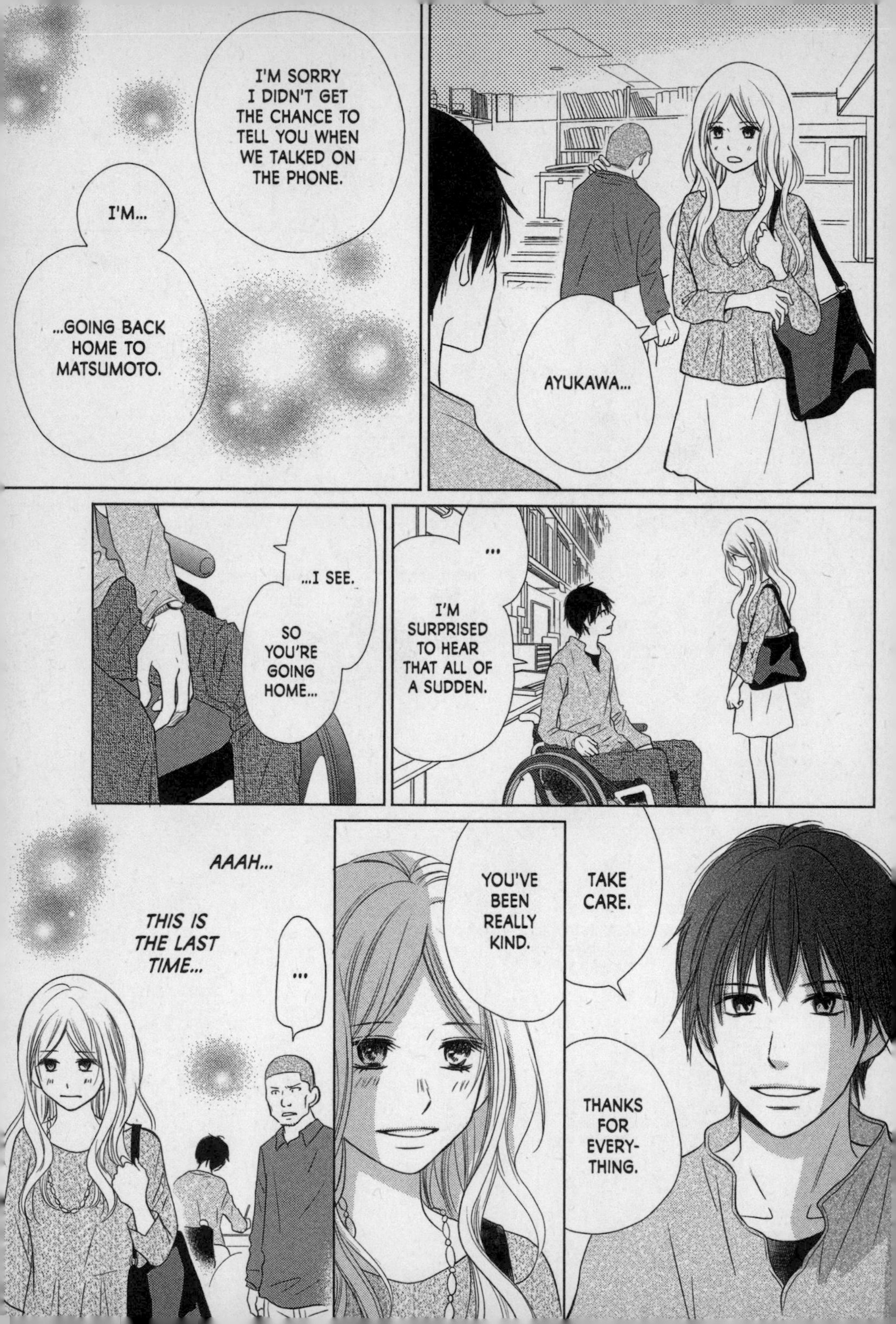
AYUKAWA...
I'M SORRY I DIDN'T GET THE CHANCE TO TELL YOU WHEN WE TALKED ON THE PHONE.
I'M...
...GOING BACK HOME TO MATSUMOTO.
...
I'M SURPRISED TO HEAR THAT ALL OF A SUDDEN.
...I SEE.
SO YOU'RE GOING HOME...
TAKE CARE.
YOU'VE BEEN REALLY KIND.
THANKS FOR EVERYTHING.
AAAH...
THIS IS THE LAST TIME...
...

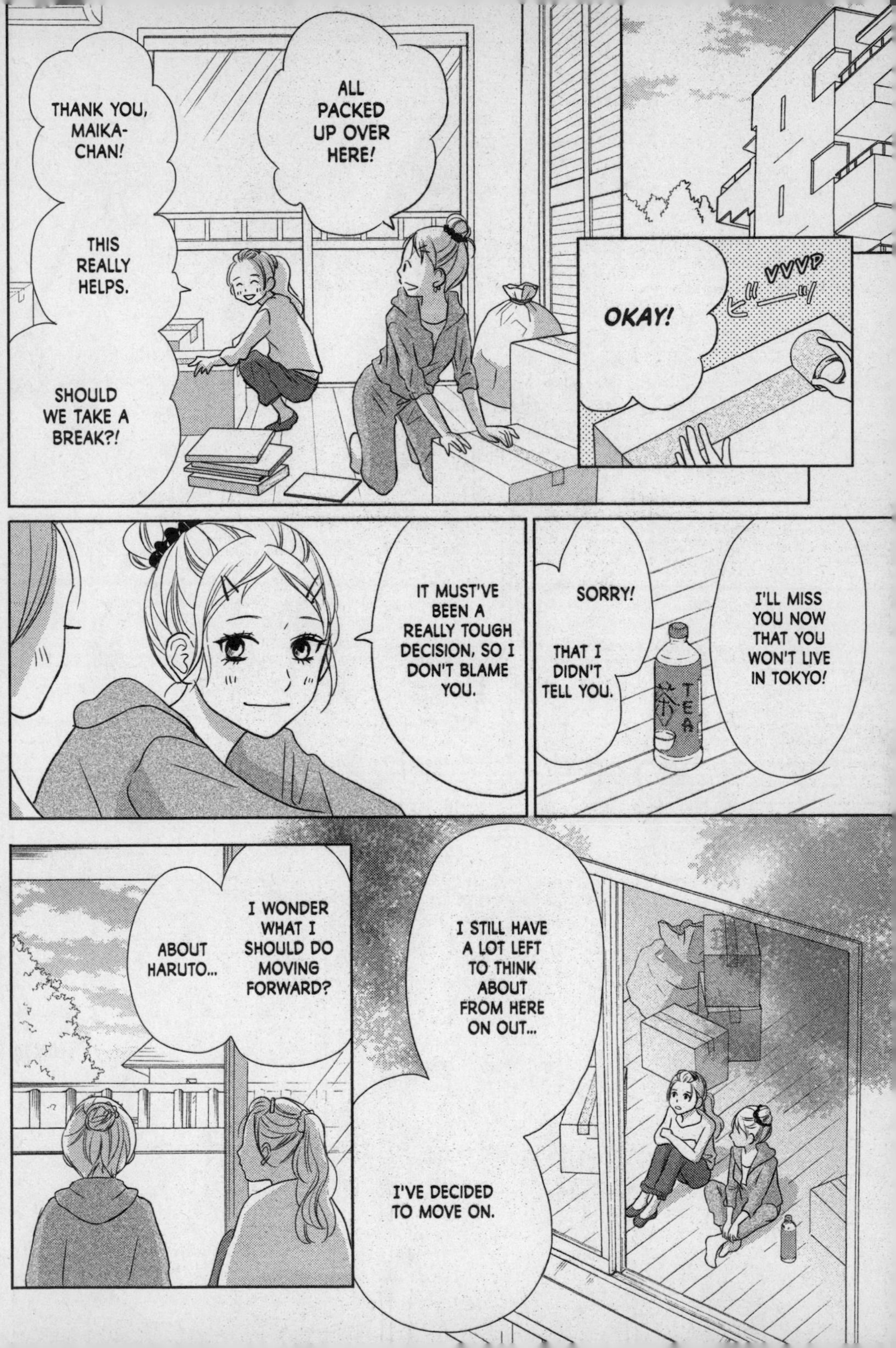
ALL PACKED UP OVER HERE!
OKAY!
VVVP
THANK YOU, MAIKA-CHAN!
THIS REALLY HELPS.
SHOULD WE TAKE A BREAK?!
I'LL MISS YOU NOW THAT YOU WON'T LIVE IN TOKYO!
SORRY!
THAT I DIDN'T TELL YOU.
茶 TEA
IT MUST'VE BEEN A REALLY TOUGH DECISION, SO I DON'T BLAME YOU.
I STILL HAVE A LOT LEFT TO THINK ABOUT FROM HERE ON OUT...
I'VE DECIDED TO MOVE ON.
I WONDER WHAT I SHOULD DO MOVING FORWARD?
ABOUT HARUTO...

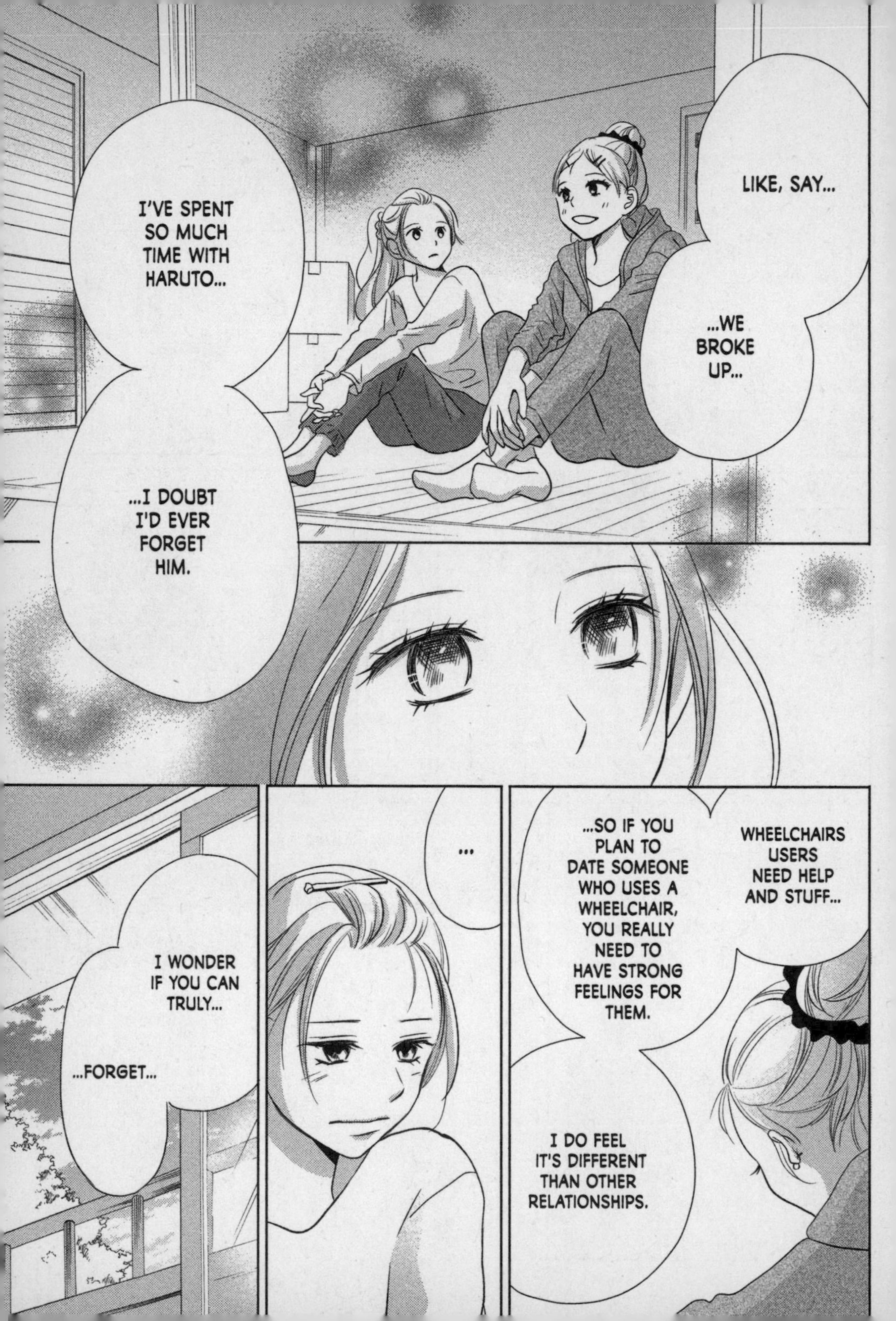
LIKE, SAY...
...WE BROKE UP...
I'VE SPENT SO MUCH TIME WITH HARUTO...
...I DOUBT I'D EVER FORGET HIM.
WHEELCHAIRS USERS NEED HELP AND STUFF...
...SO IF YOU PLAN TO DATE SOMEONE WHO USES A WHEELCHAIR, YOU REALLY NEED TO HAVE STRONG FEELINGS FOR THEM.
I DO FEEL IT'S DIFFERENT THAN OTHER RELATIONSHIPS.
...
I WONDER IF YOU CAN TRULY...
...FORGET...

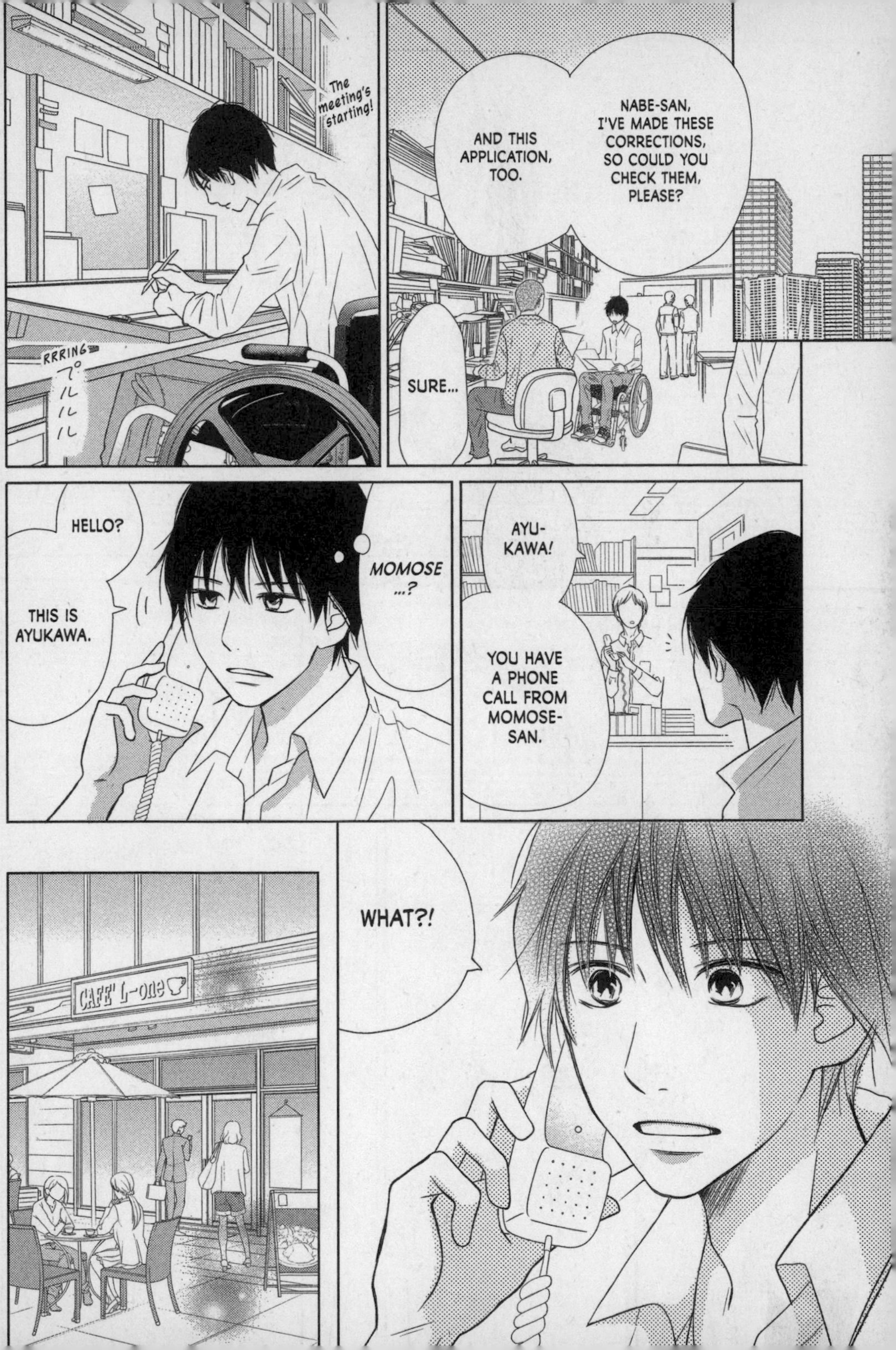
NABE-SAN, I'VE MADE THESE CORRECTIONS, SO COULD YOU CHECK THEM, PLEASE?
AND THIS APPLICATION, TOO.
SURE...
The meeting's starting!
RRRING
プルルル
AYU-KAWA!
YOU HAVE A PHONE CALL FROM MOMOSE-SAN.
MOMOSE ...?
HELLO?
THIS IS AYUKAWA.
WHAT?!
CAFE' L-one

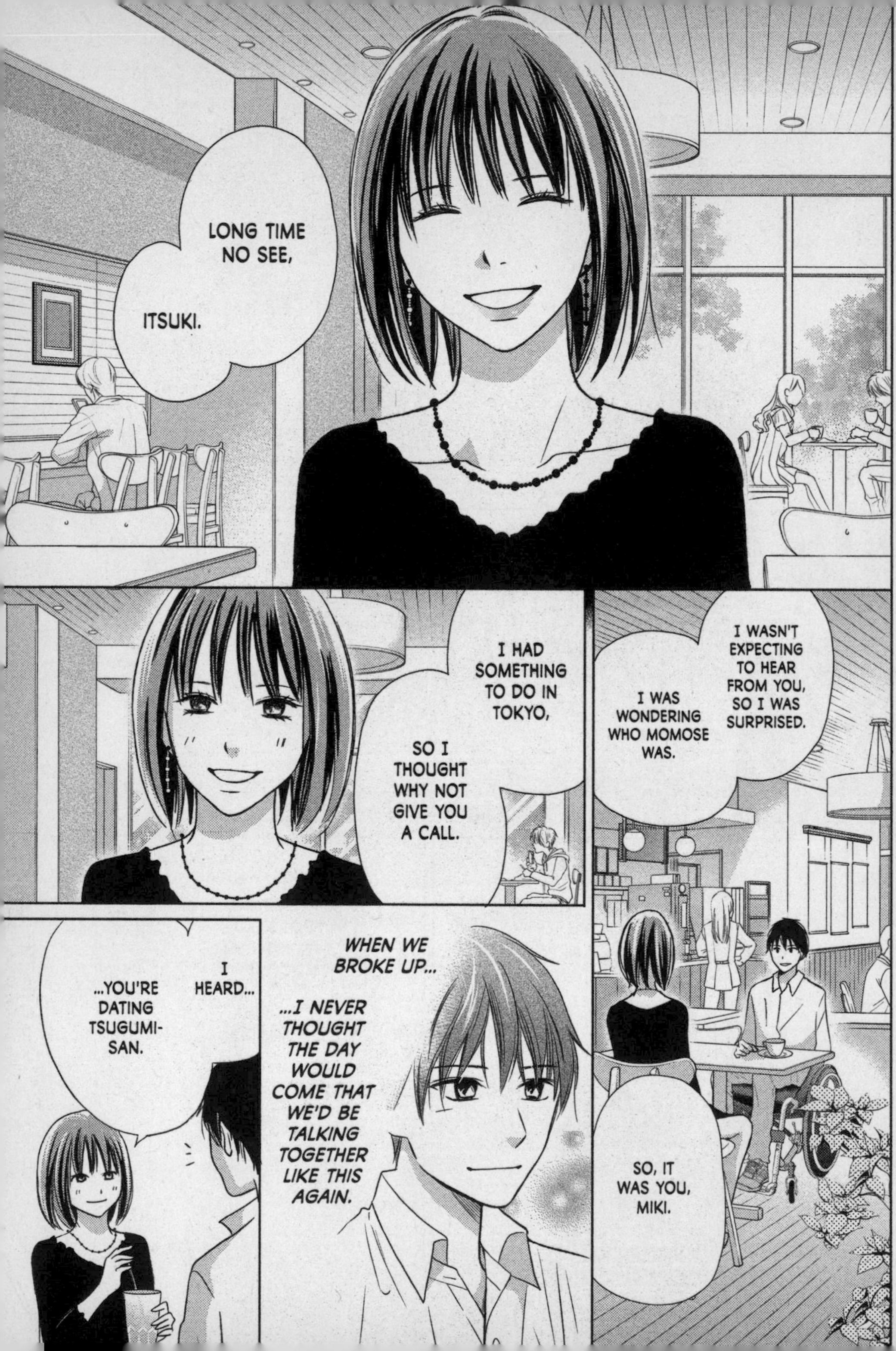

LONG TIME NO SEE,
ITSUKI.
I WASN'T EXPECTING TO HEAR FROM YOU, SO I WAS SURPRISED.
I WAS WONDERING WHO MOMOSE WAS.
SO, IT WAS YOU, MIKI.
I HAD SOMETHING TO DO IN TOKYO,
SO I THOUGHT WHY NOT GIVE YOU A CALL.
WHEN WE BROKE UP...
...I NEVER THOUGHT THE DAY WOULD COME THAT WE'D BE TALKING TOGETHER LIKE THIS AGAIN.
I HEARD...
...YOU'RE DATING TSUGUMI-SAN.

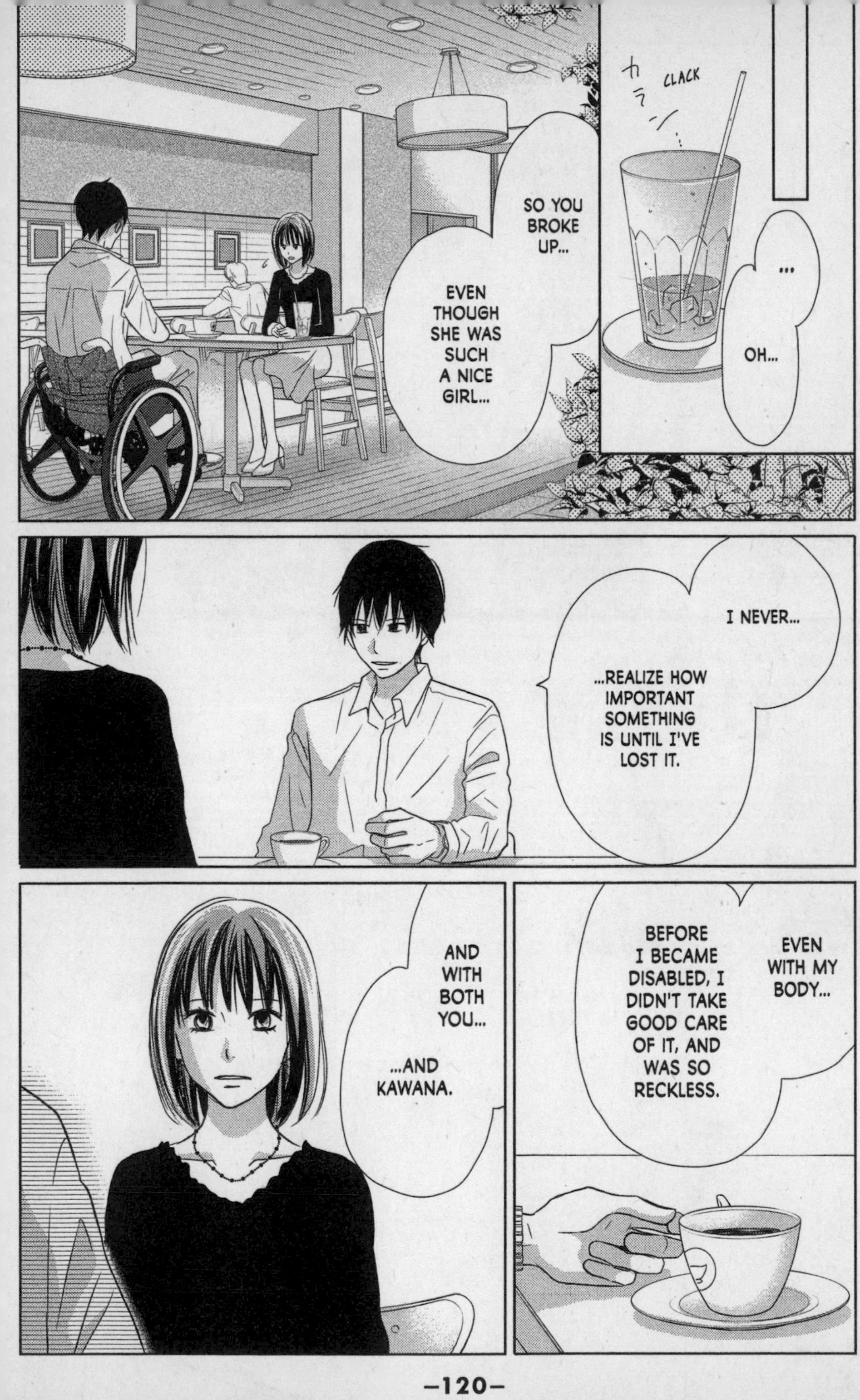
CLACK
...
OH...
SO YOU BROKE UP...
EVEN THOUGH SHE WAS SUCH A NICE GIRL...
I NEVER...
...REALIZE HOW IMPORTANT SOMETHING IS UNTIL I'VE LOST IT.
EVEN WITH MY BODY...
BEFORE I BECAME DISABLED, I DIDN'T TAKE GOOD CARE OF IT, AND WAS SO RECKLESS.
AND WITH BOTH YOU...
...AND KAWANA.

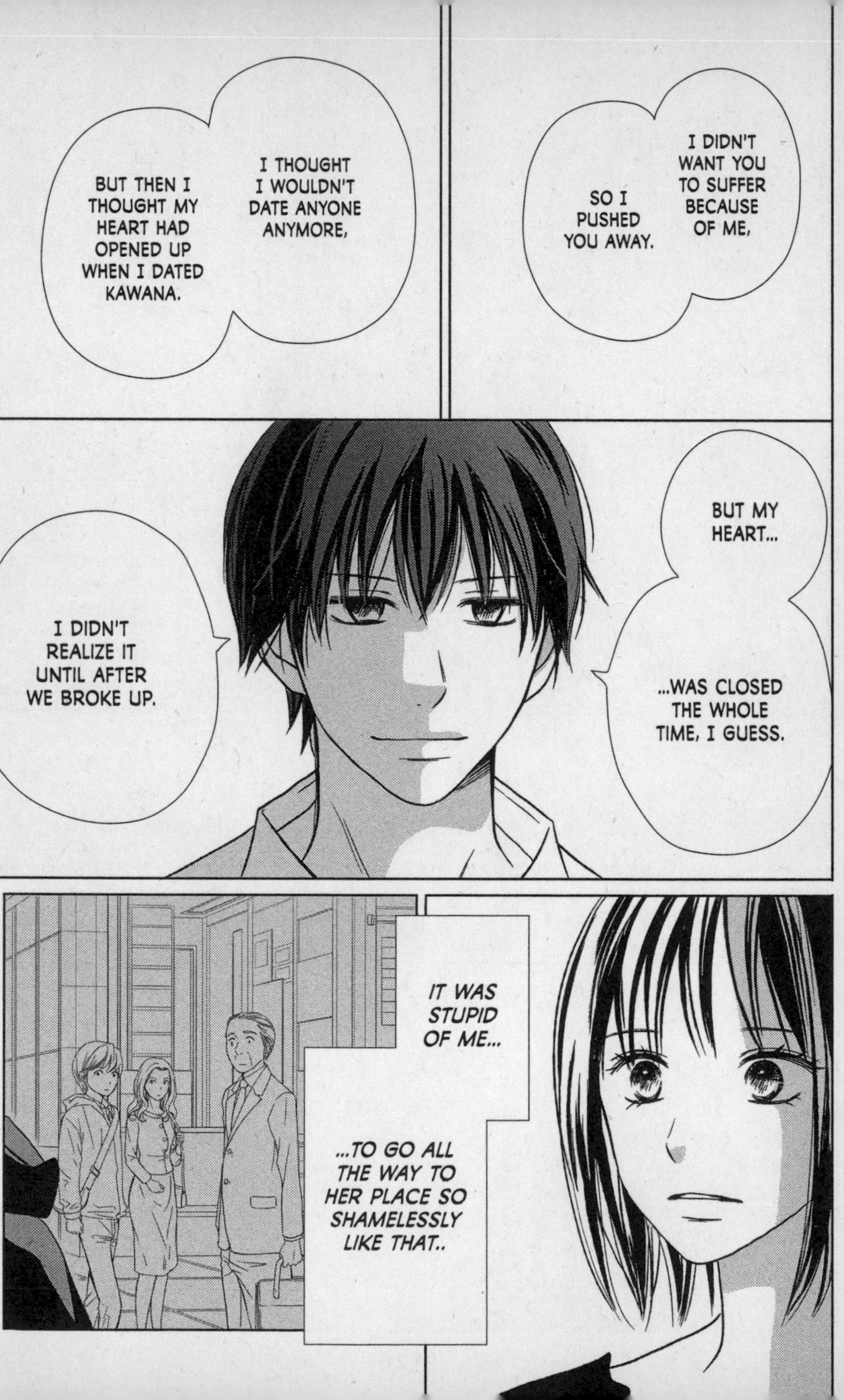
I DIDN'T WANT YOU TO SUFFER BECAUSE OF ME,
SO I PUSHED YOU AWAY.
I THOUGHT I WOULDN'T DATE ANYONE ANYMORE,
BUT THEN I THOUGHT MY HEART HAD OPENED UP WHEN I DATED KAWANA.
BUT MY HEART...
...WAS CLOSED THE WHOLE TIME, I GUESS.
I DIDN'T REALIZE IT UNTIL AFTER WE BROKE UP.
IT WAS STUPID OF ME...
...TO GO ALL THE WAY TO HER PLACE SO SHAMELESSLY LIKE THAT..

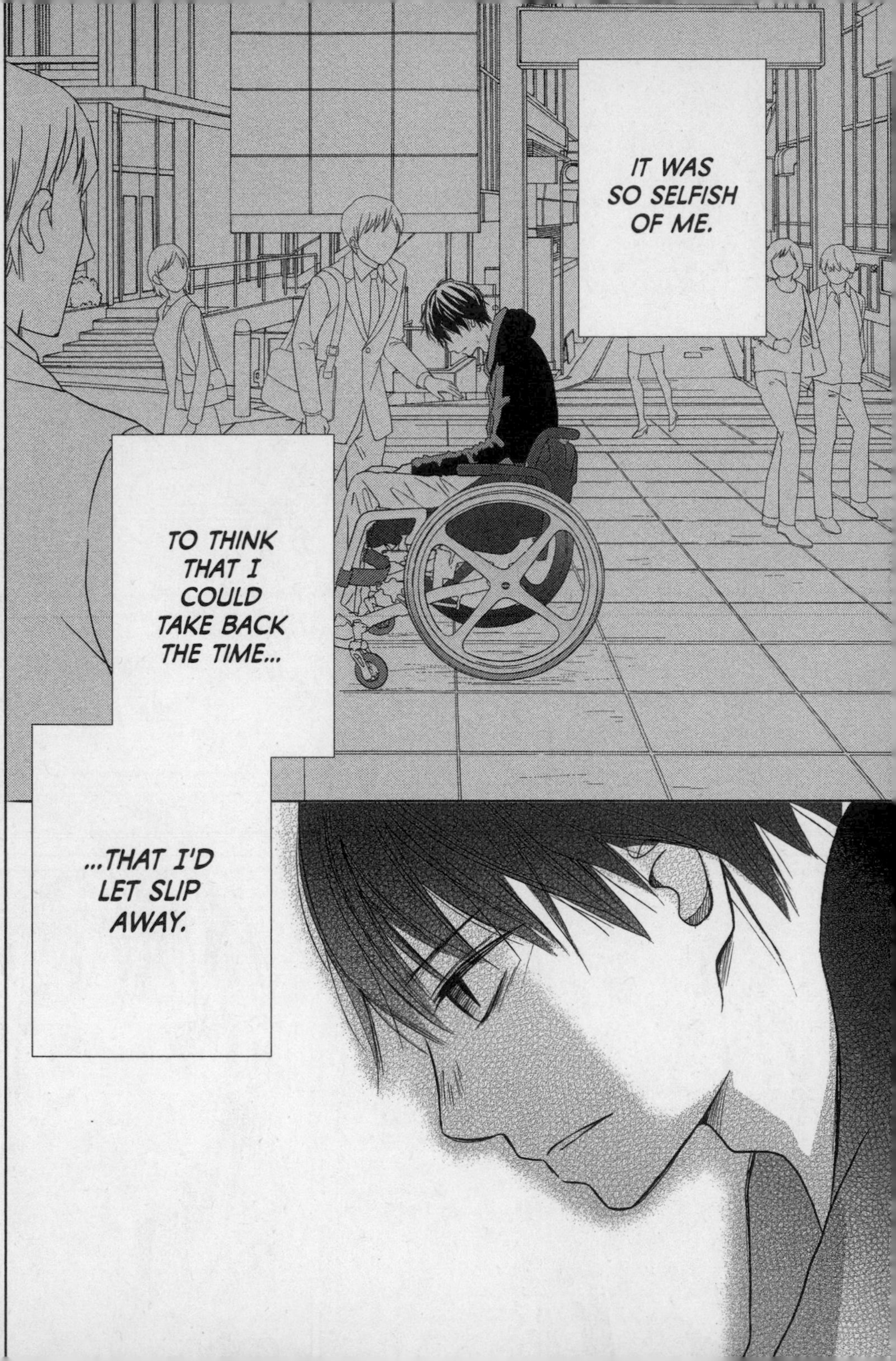
IT WAS SO SELFISH OF ME.
TO THINK THAT I COULD TAKE BACK THE TIME...
...THAT I'D LET SLIP AWAY.

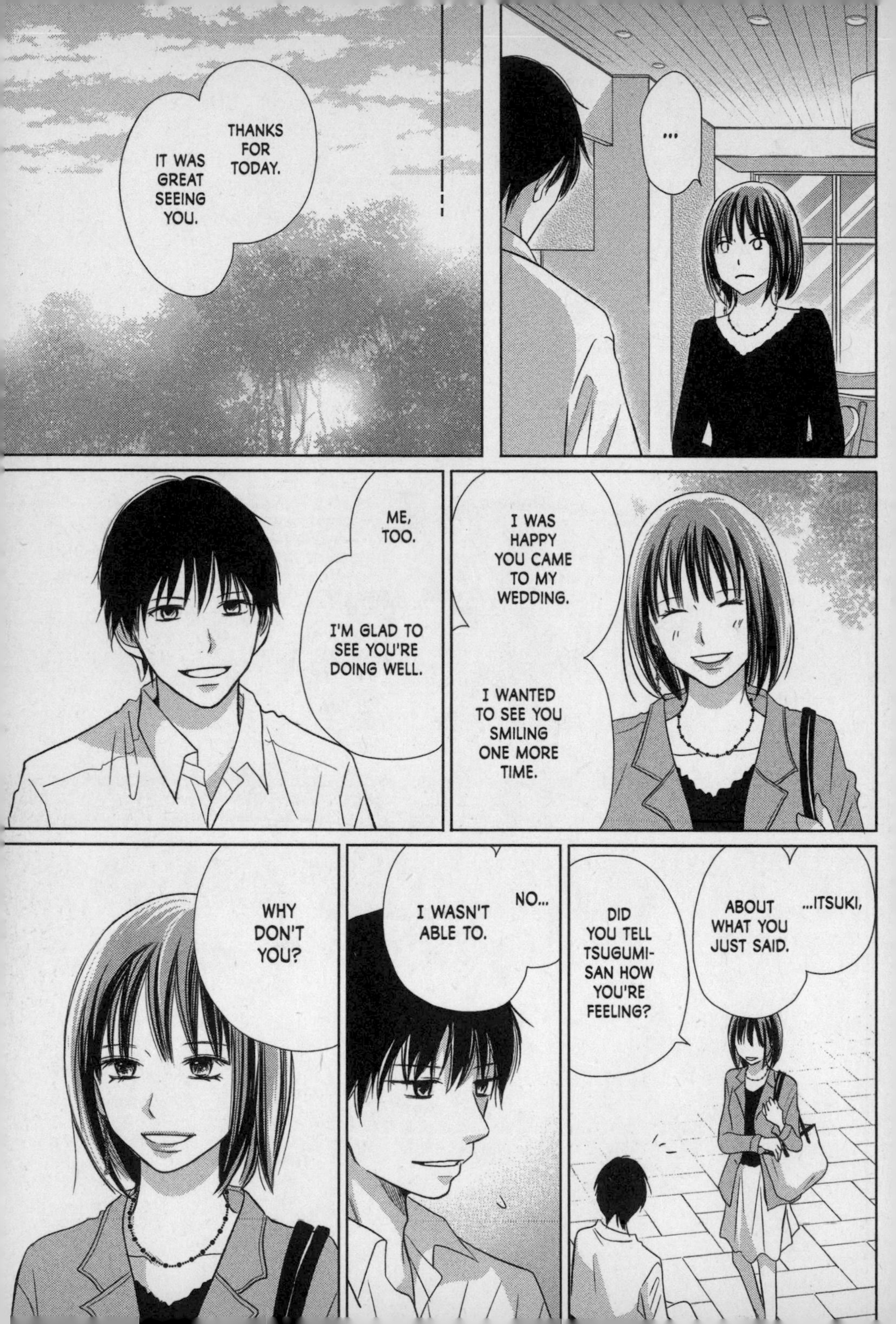
...
THANKS FOR TODAY.
IT WAS GREAT SEEING YOU.
I WAS HAPPY YOU CAME TO MY WEDDING.
I WANTED TO SEE YOU SMILING ONE MORE TIME.
ME, TOO.
I'M GLAD TO SEE YOU'RE DOING WELL.
...ITSUKI,
ABOUT WHAT YOU JUST SAID.
DID YOU TELL TSUGUMI-SAN HOW YOU'RE FEELING?
NO...
I WASN'T ABLE TO.
WHY DON'T YOU?

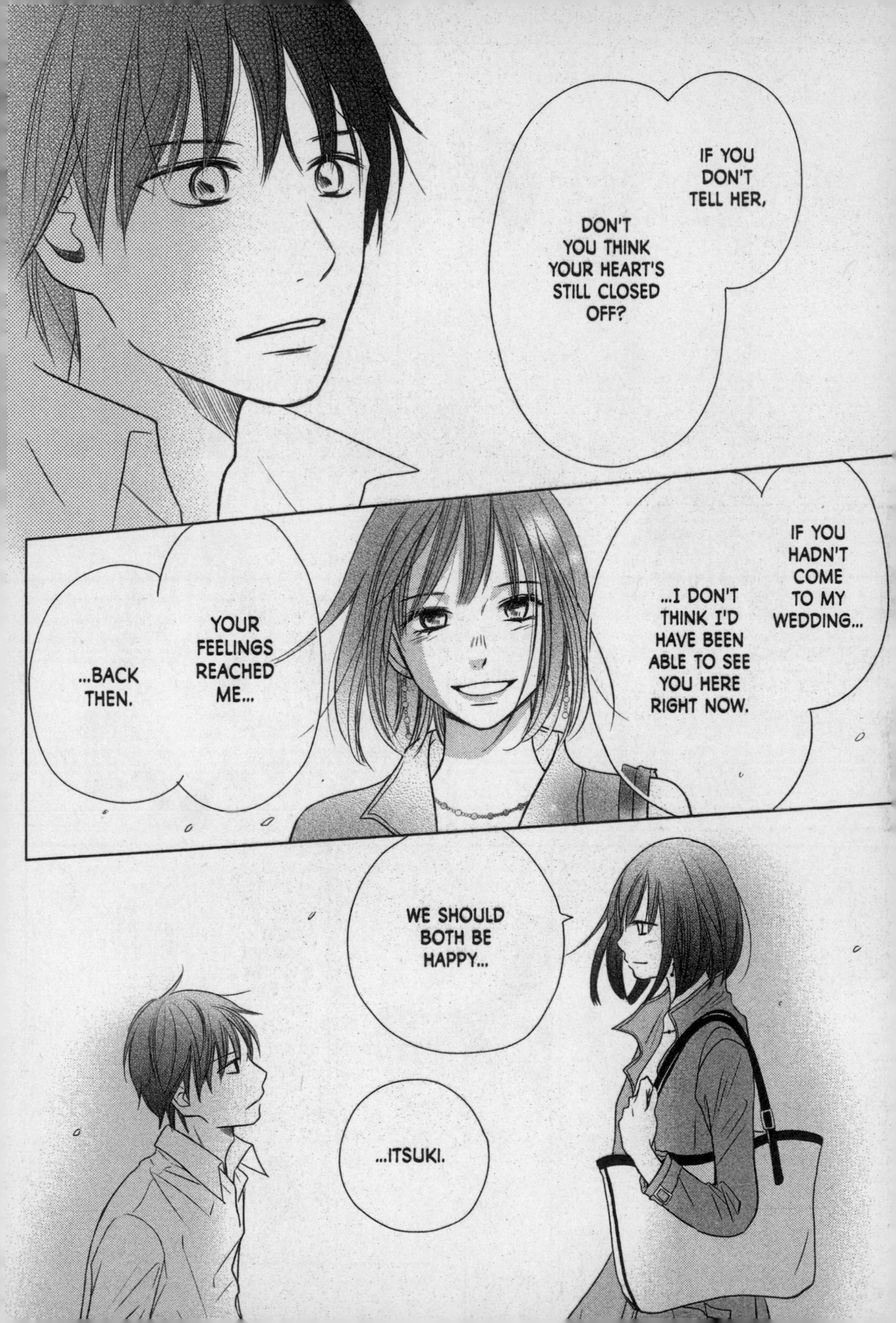
IF YOU DON'T TELL HER,
DON'T YOU THINK YOUR HEART'S STILL CLOSED OFF?
IF YOU HADN'T COME TO MY WEDDING...
...I DON'T THINK I'D HAVE BEEN ABLE TO SEE YOU HERE RIGHT NOW.
YOUR FEELINGS REACHED ME...
...BACK THEN.
WE SHOULD BOTH BE HAPPY...
...ITSUKI.

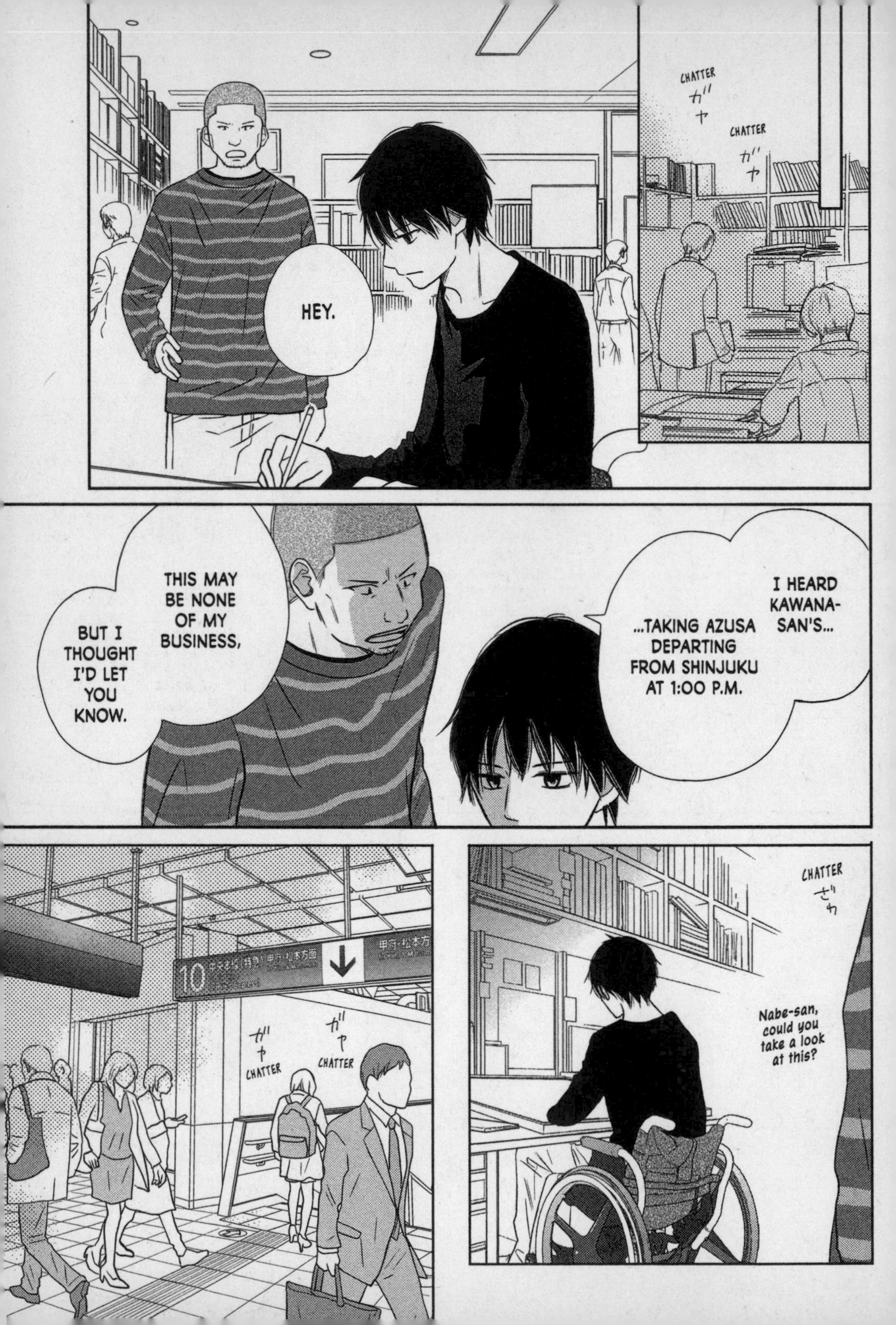
CHATTER
ガヤ
CHATTER
ガヤ
HEY.
I HEARD KAWANA-SAN'S...
...TAKING AZUSA DEPARTING FROM SHINJUKU AT 1:00 P.M.
THIS MAY BE NONE OF MY BUSINESS,
BUT I THOUGHT I'D LET YOU KNOW.
CHATTER
ざわ
Nabe-san, could you take a look at this?
10
甲府・松本方面
ガヤ
CHATTER
ガヤ
CHATTER

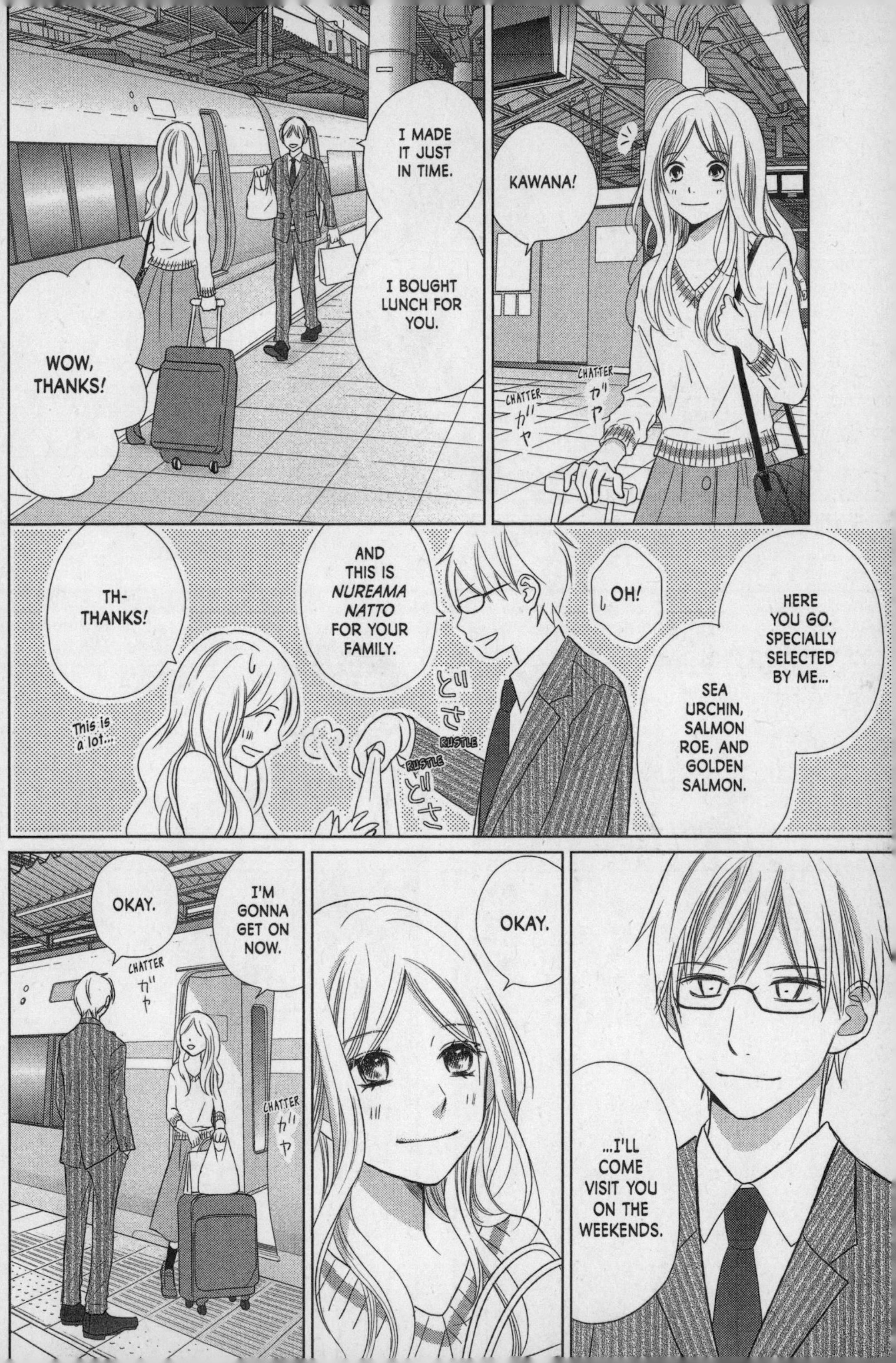
KAWANA!
CHATTER ガヤ
CHATTER ガヤ
I MADE IT JUST IN TIME.
I BOUGHT LUNCH FOR YOU.
WOW, THANKS!
HERE YOU GO. SPECIALLY SELECTED BY ME...
SEA URCHIN, SALMON ROE, AND GOLDEN SALMON.
OH!
AND THIS IS *NUREAMA NATTO* FOR YOUR FAMILY.
RUSTLE どさ
RUSTLE どさ
TH- THANKS!
This is a lot...
...I'LL COME VISIT YOU ON THE WEEKENDS.
OKAY.
I'M GONNA GET ON NOW.
OKAY.
CHATTER ガヤ
CHATTER ガヤ

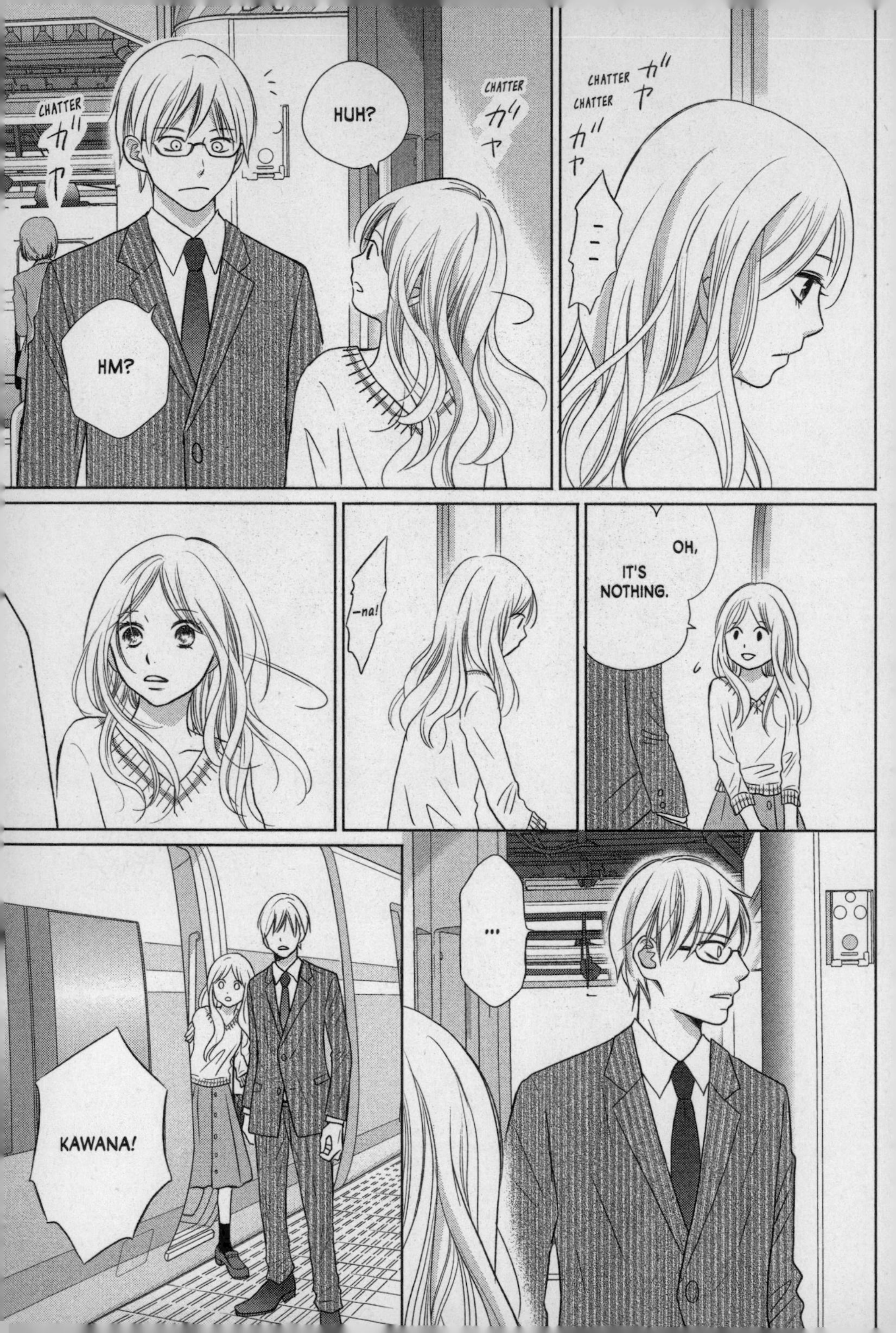
CHATTER ガヤ
CHATTER ガヤ
...
CHATTER ガヤ
HUH?
CHATTER ガヤ
HM?
OH, IT'S NOTHING.
—na!
...
KAWANA!

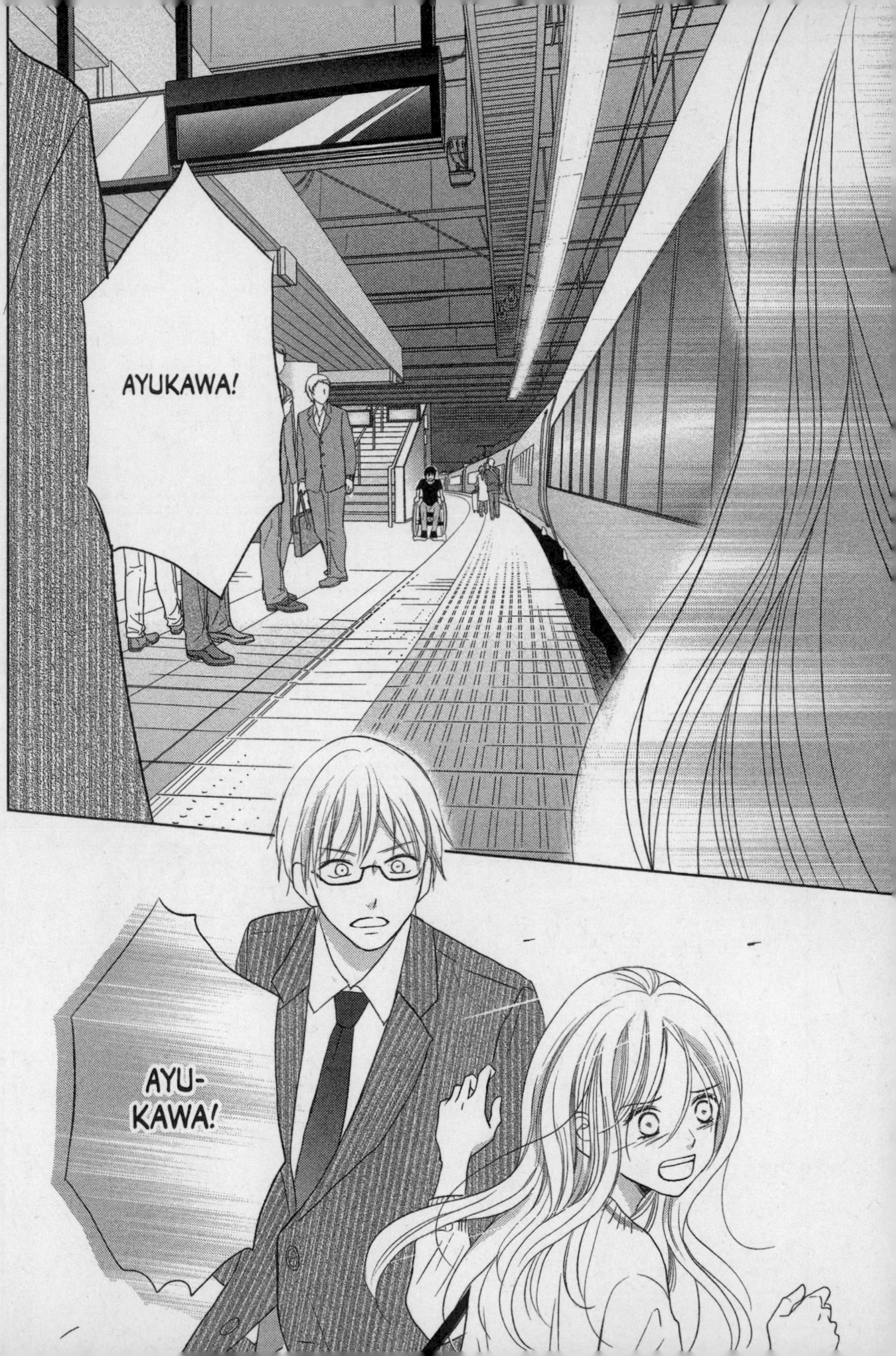
AYUKAWA!
AYU-
KAWA!

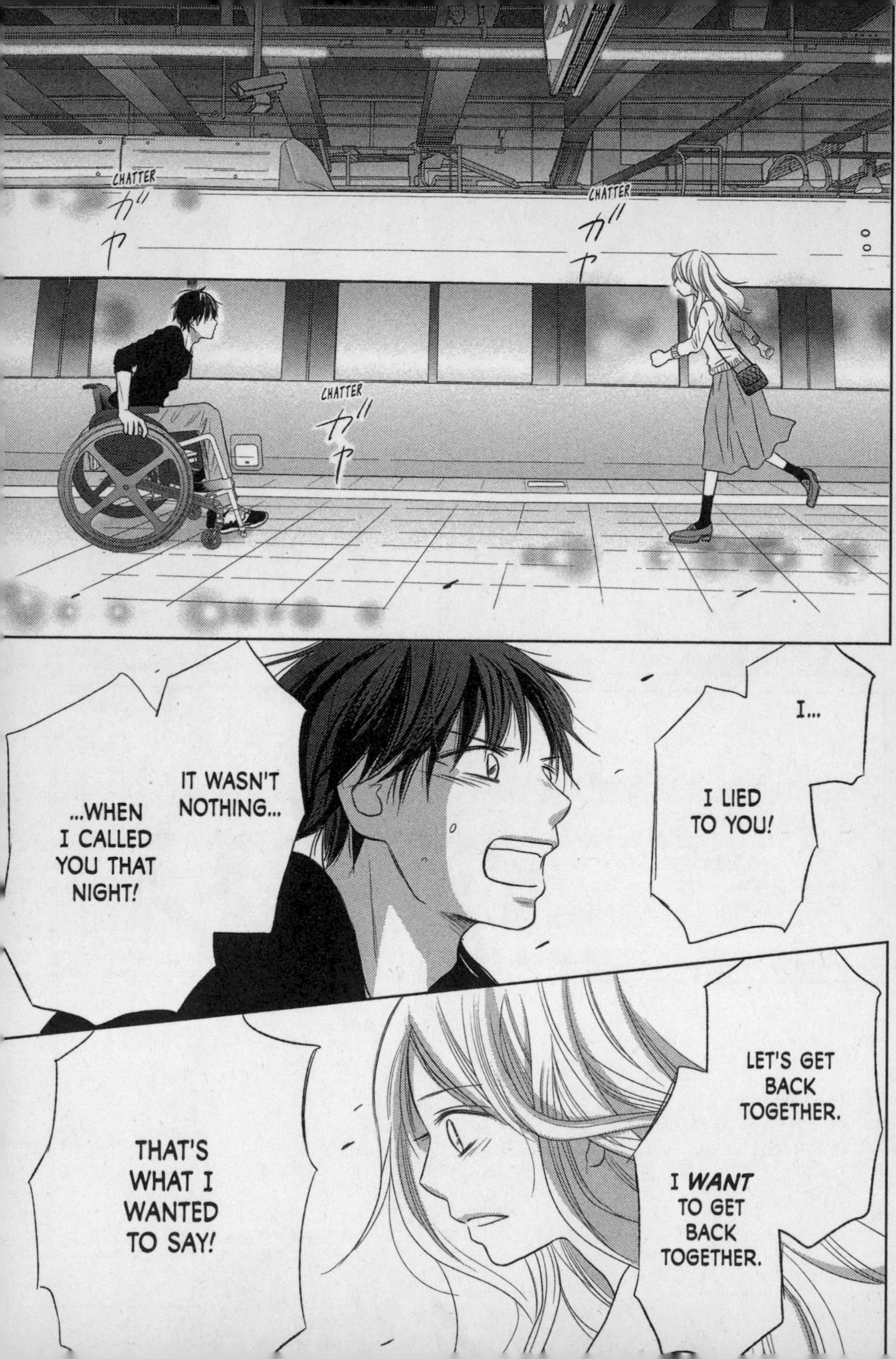
CHATTER
ガヤ
CHATTER
ガヤ
CHATTER
ガヤ
I...
I LIED TO YOU!
IT WASN'T NOTHING...
...WHEN I CALLED YOU THAT NIGHT!
LET'S GET BACK TOGETHER.
I *WANT* TO GET BACK TOGETHER.
THAT'S WHAT I WANTED TO SAY!

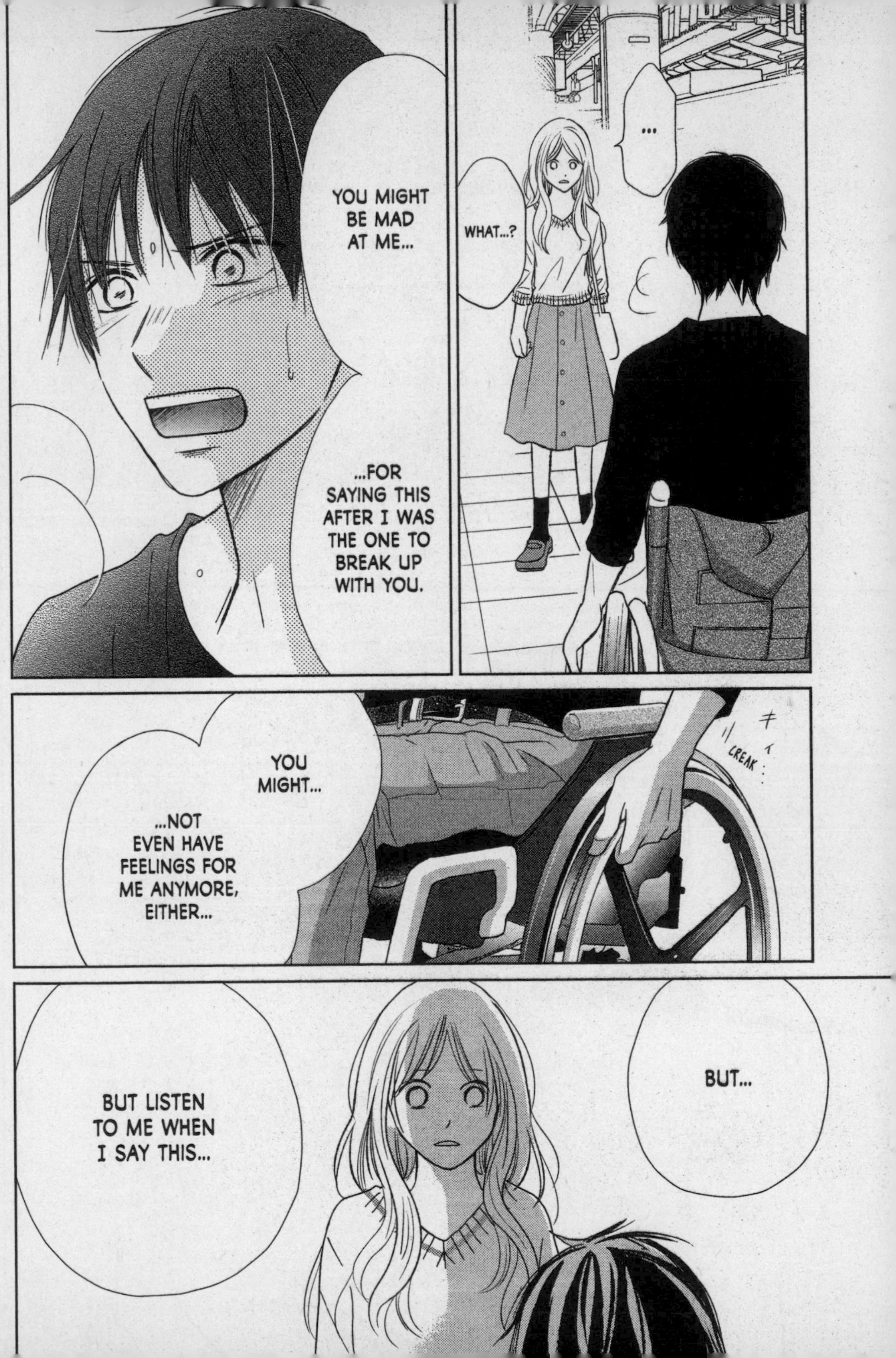
...
WHAT...?
YOU MIGHT BE MAD AT ME...
...FOR SAYING THIS AFTER I WAS THE ONE TO BREAK UP WITH YOU.
CREAK
YOU MIGHT...
...NOT EVEN HAVE FEELINGS FOR ME ANYMORE, EITHER...
BUT...
BUT LISTEN TO ME WHEN I SAY THIS...

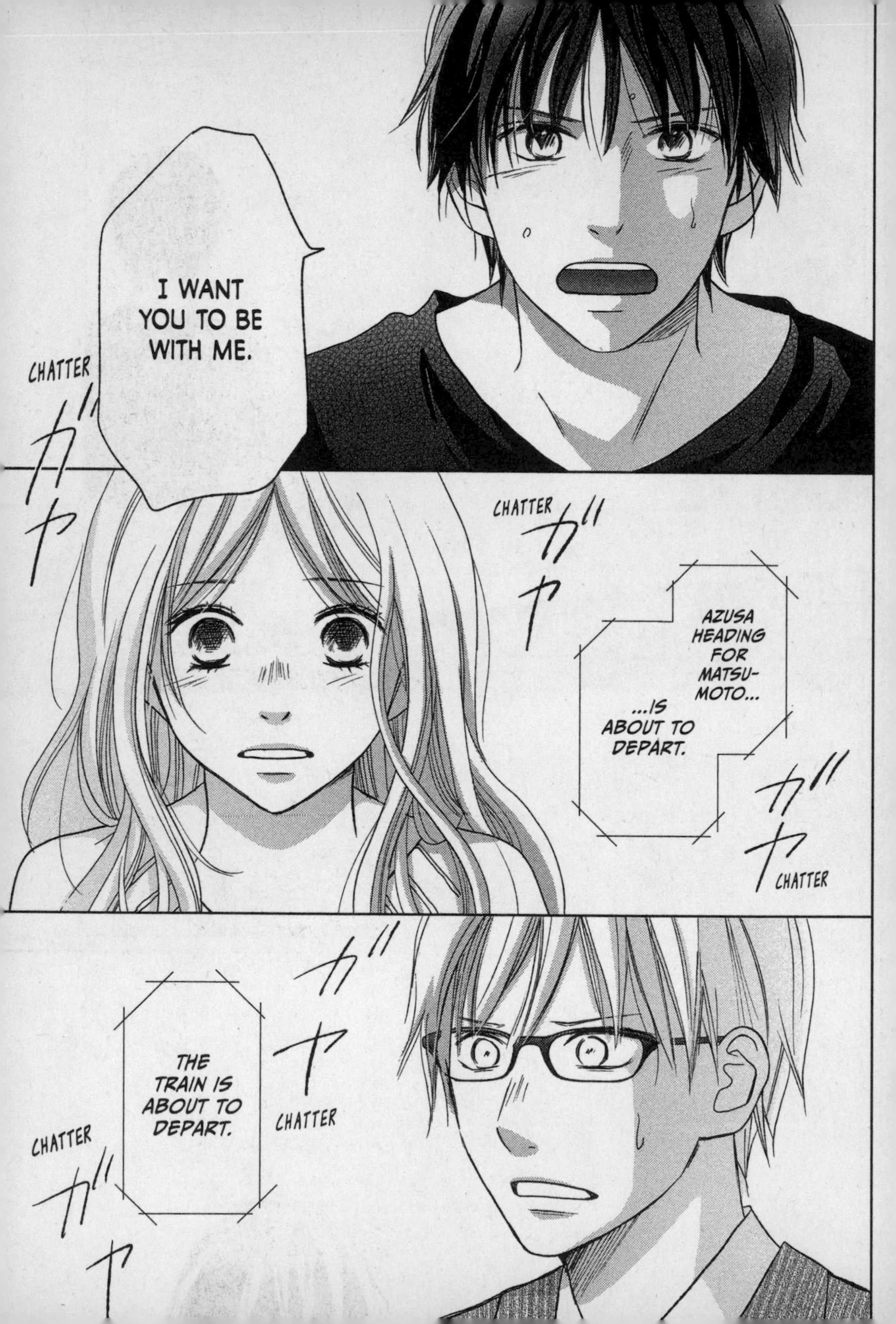
I WANT YOU TO BE WITH ME.
CHATTER
CHATTER
AZUSA HEADING FOR MATSU-MOTO...
...IS ABOUT TO DEPART.
CHATTER
CHATTER
THE TRAIN IS ABOUT TO DEPART.
CHATTER

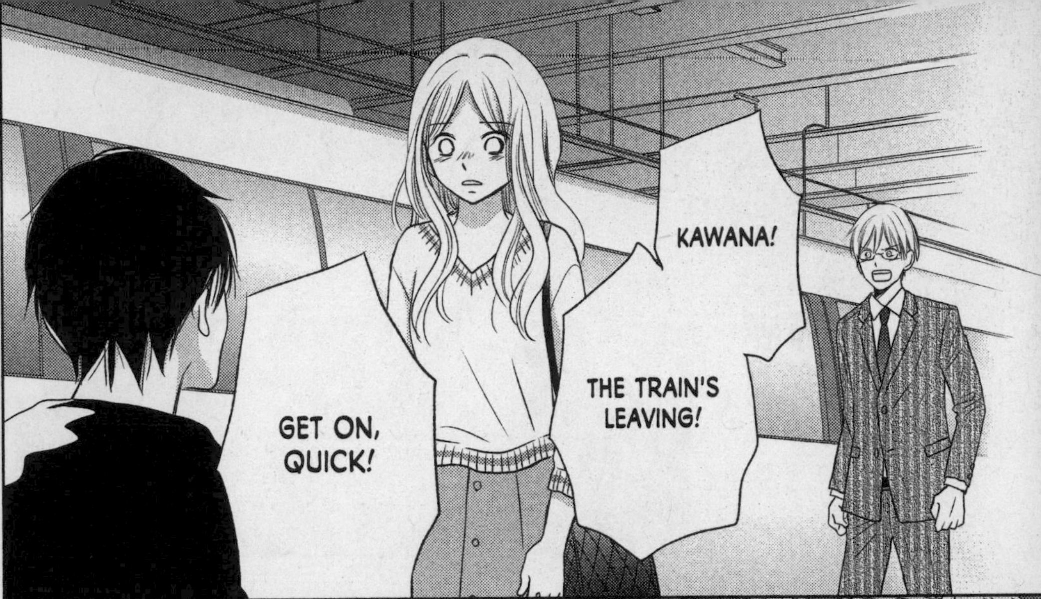
KAWANA!
THE TRAIN'S LEAVING!
GET ON, QUICK!

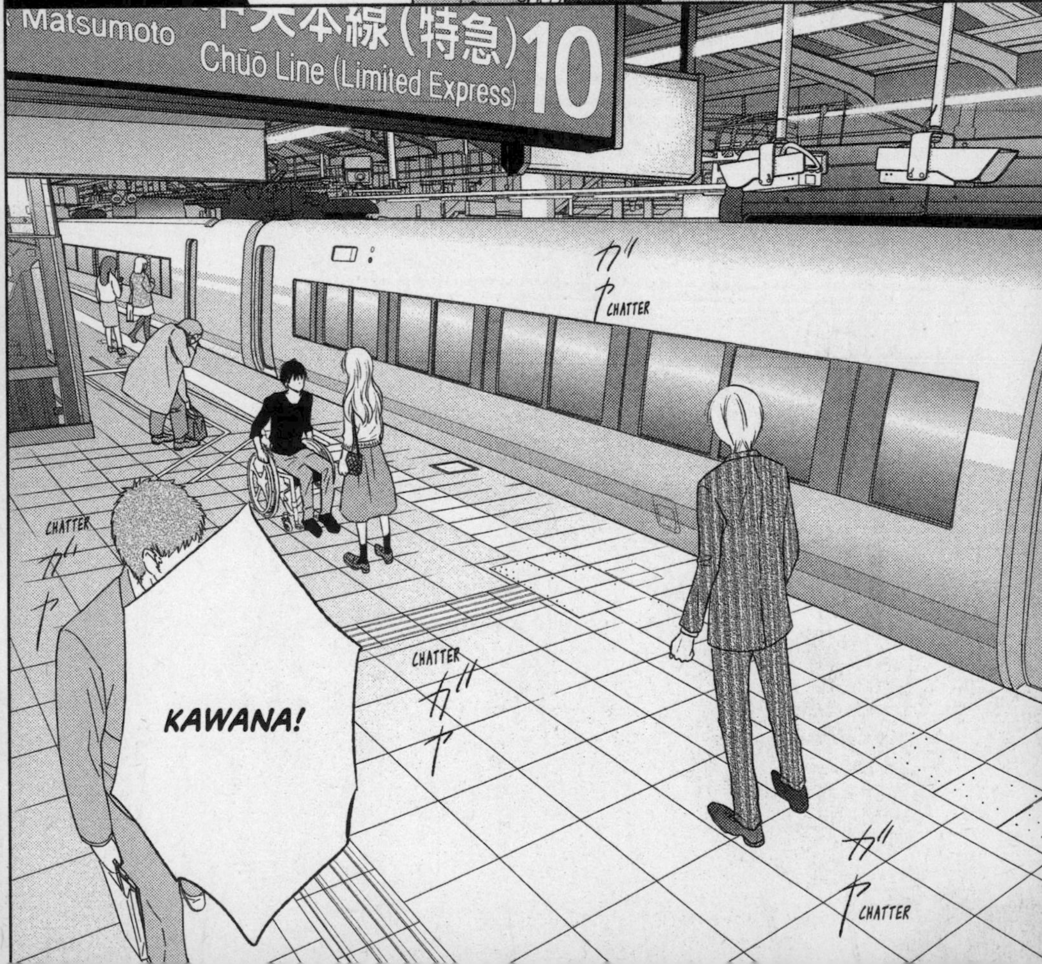
Matsumoto
Chūō Line (Limited Express)
10
ガヤ CHATTER
ガヤ CHATTER
ガヤ CHATTER
KAWANA!
ガヤ CHATTER

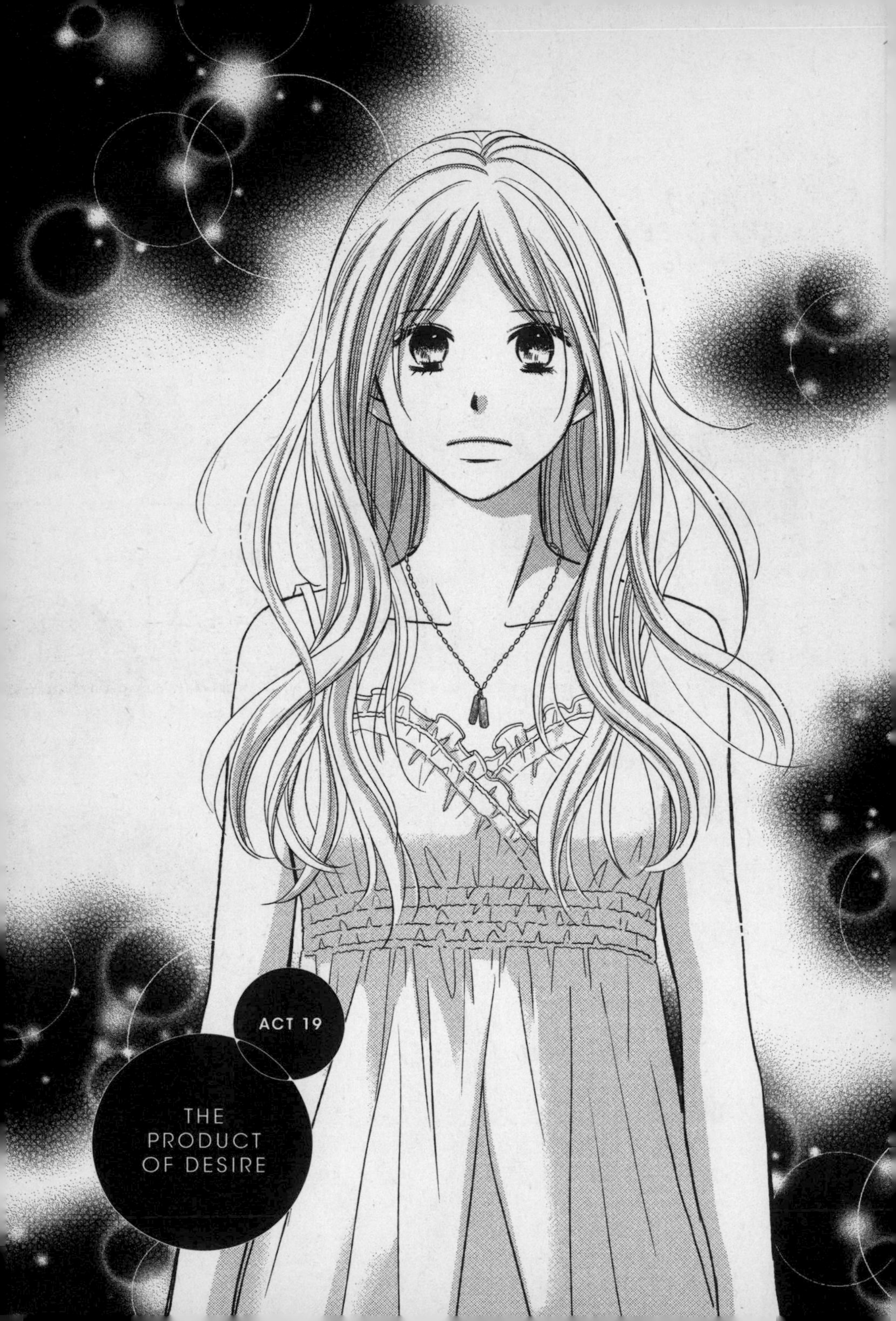
ACT 19
THE PRODUCT OF DESIRE

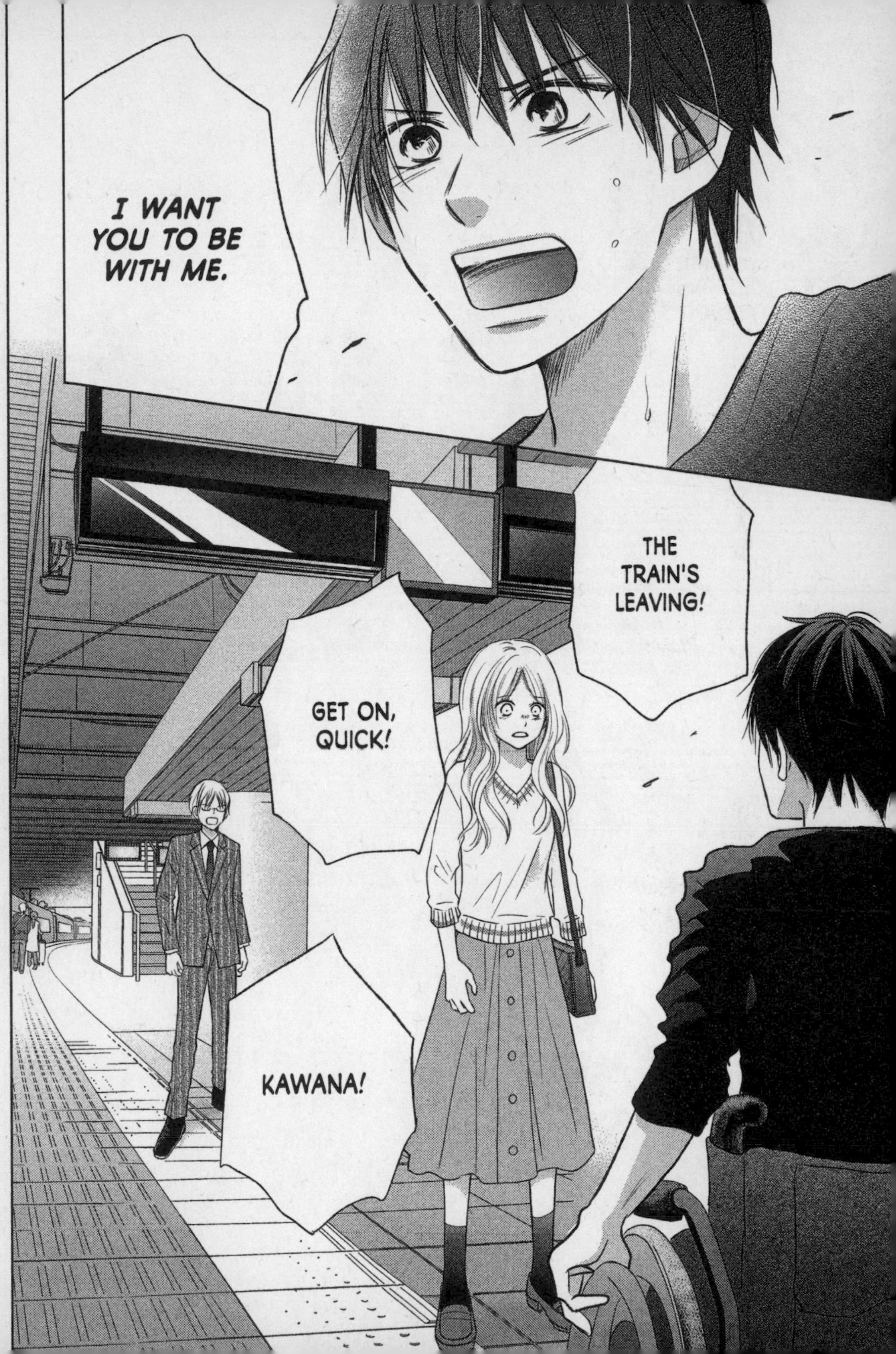
I WANT YOU TO BE WITH ME.
THE TRAIN'S LEAVING!
GET ON, QUICK!
KAWANA!

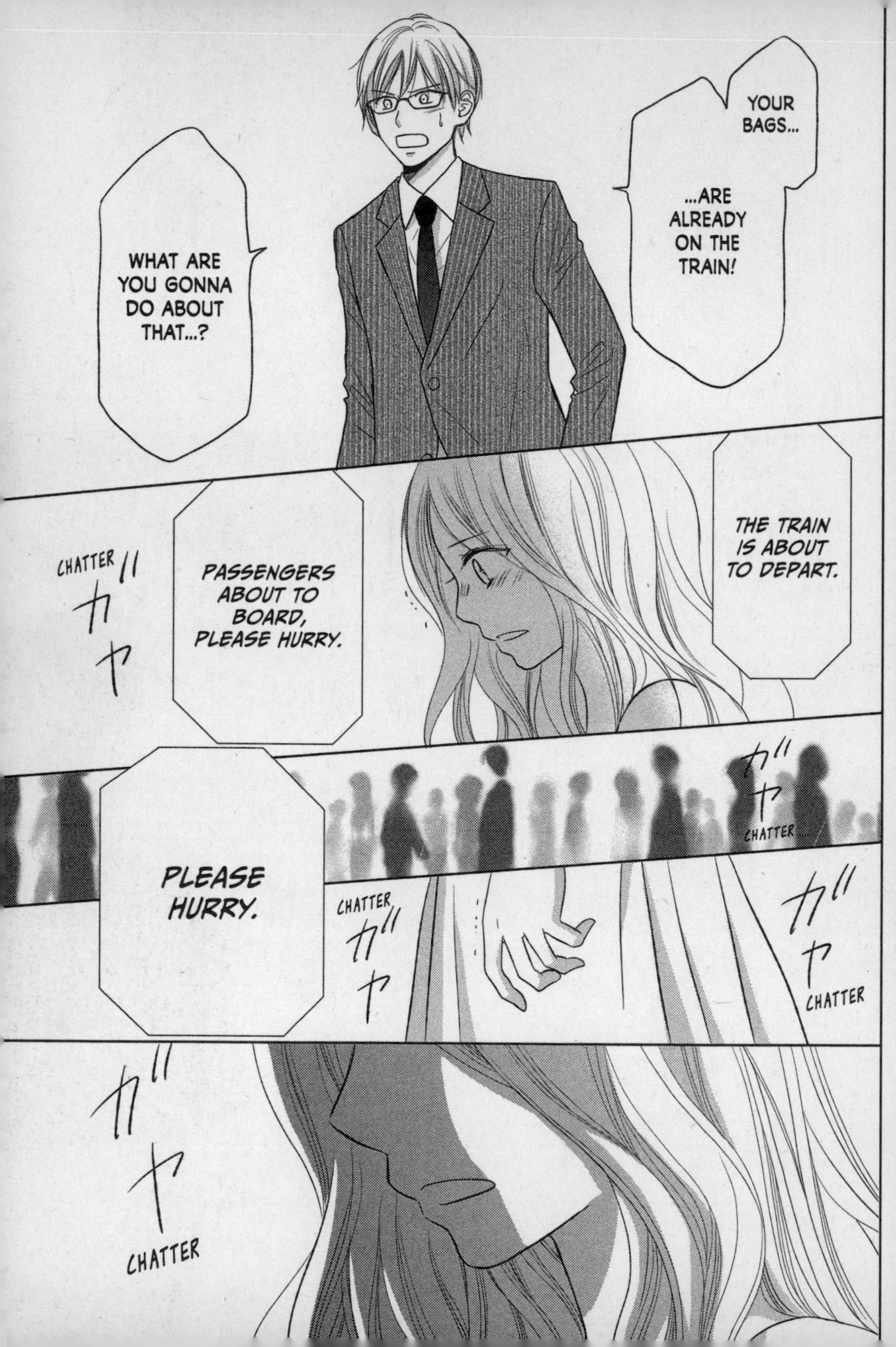
YOUR BAGS...
...ARE ALREADY ON THE TRAIN!
WHAT ARE YOU GONNA DO ABOUT THAT...?
THE TRAIN IS ABOUT TO DEPART.
PASSENGERS ABOUT TO BOARD, PLEASE HURRY.
ガヤ
CHATTER
ガヤ
CHATTER...
ガヤ
CHATTER
PLEASE HURRY.
ガヤ
CHATTER
ガヤ
CHATTER

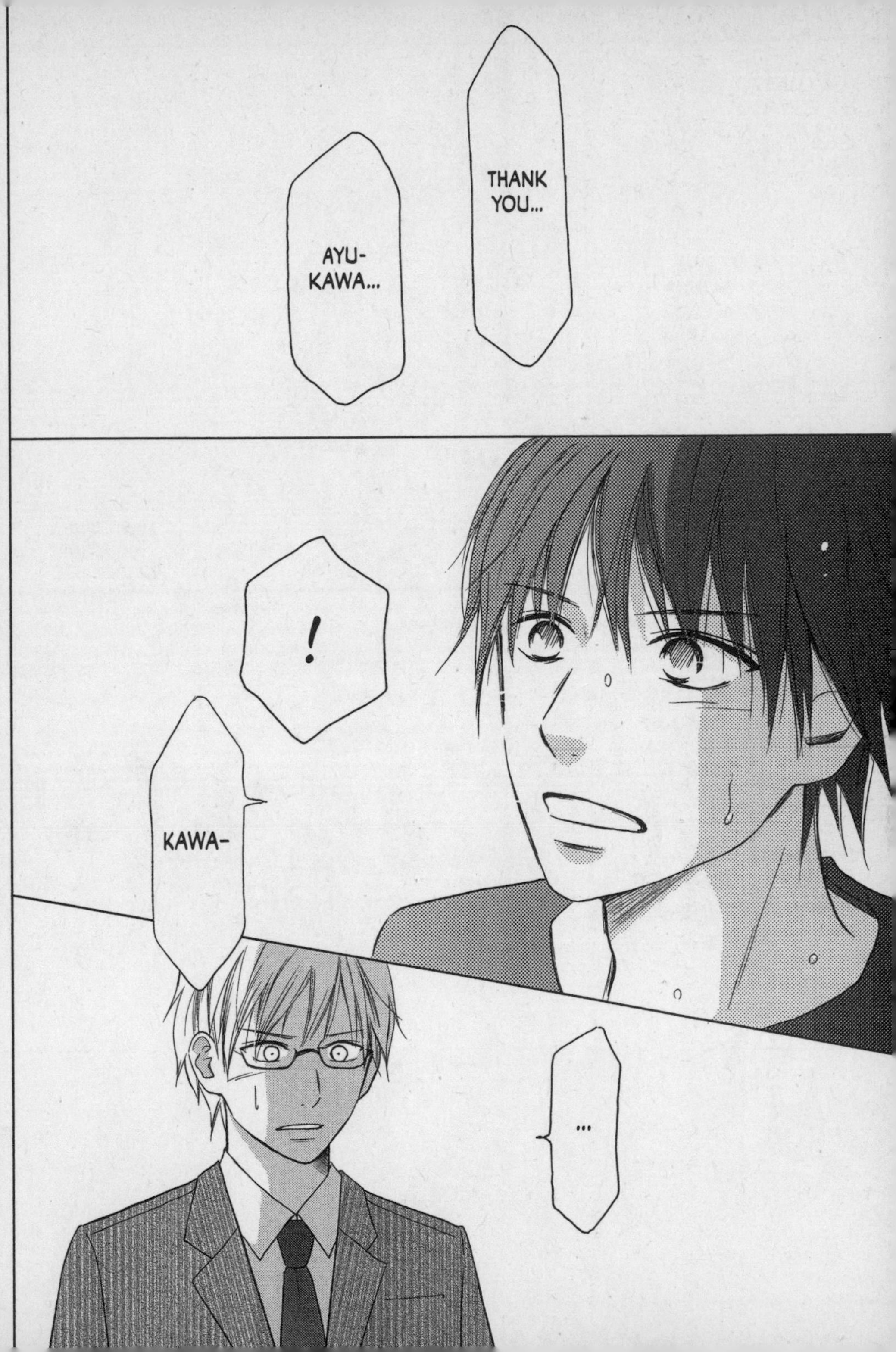
THANK YOU...
AYU-KAWA...
!
KAWA-
...

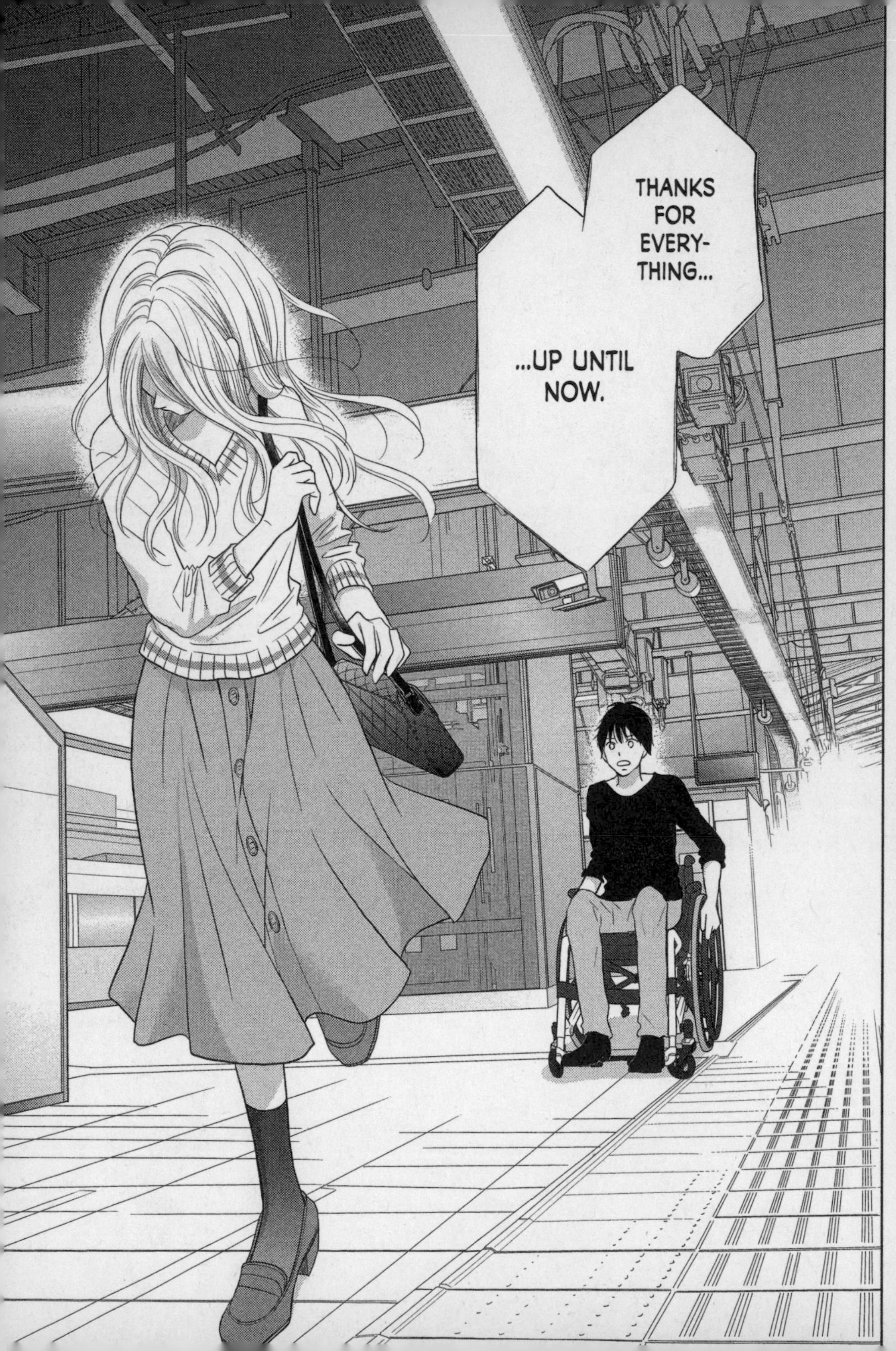
THANKS FOR EVERY-THING...
...UP UNTIL NOW.

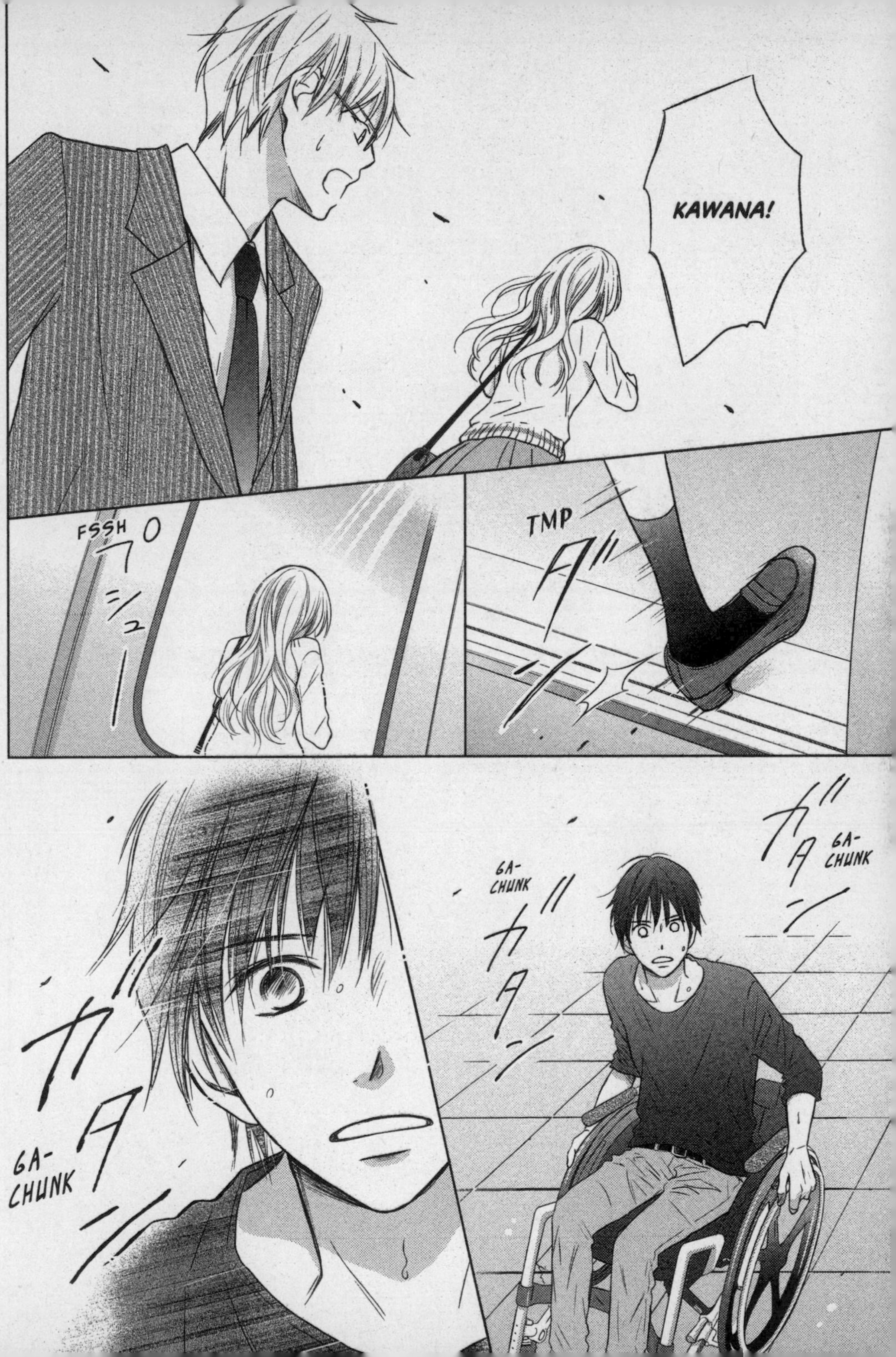
KAWANA!
TMP
FSSH
GA-CHUNK
GA-CHUNK
GA-CHUNK

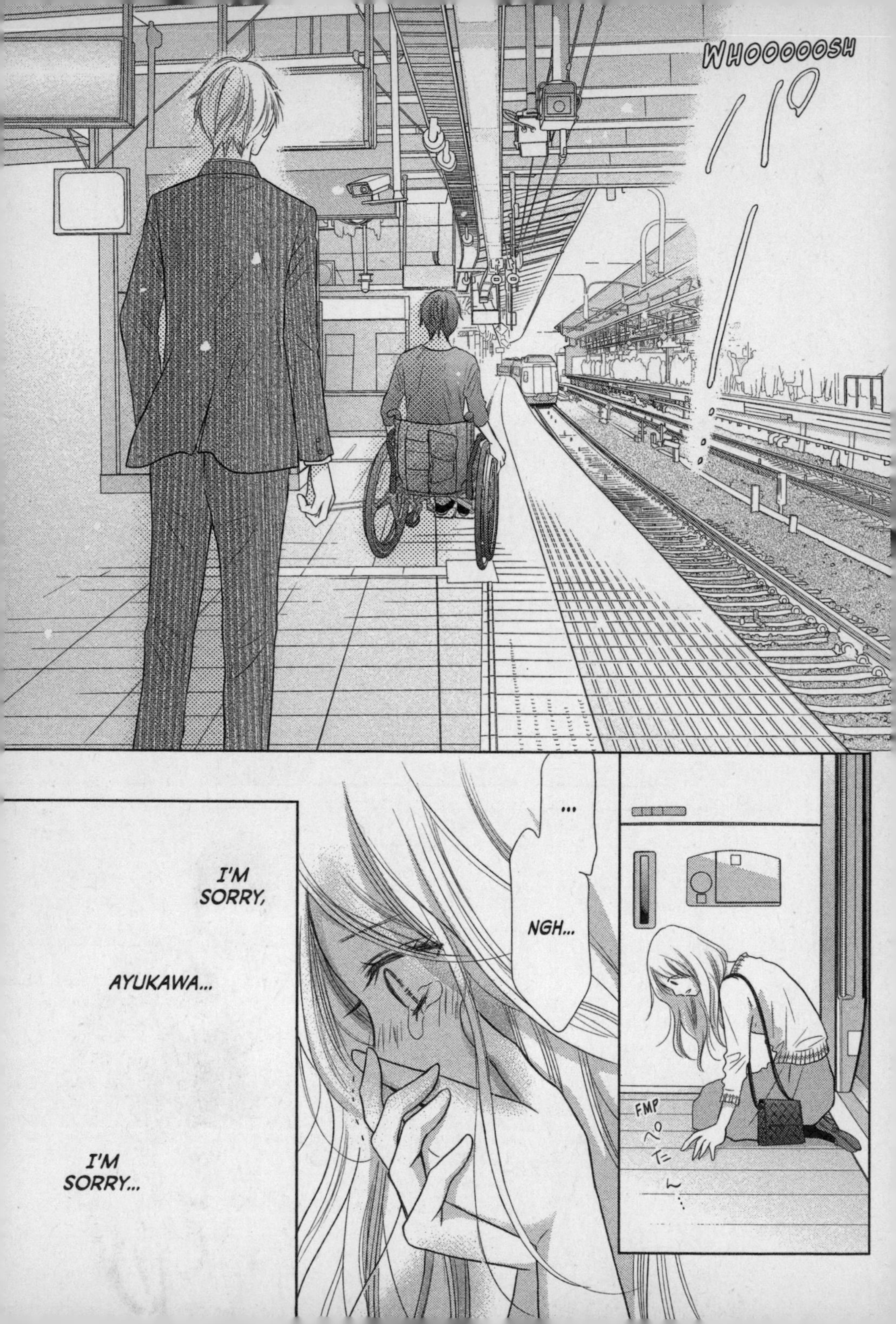
WHOOOOOOSH
FMP
ぺたん
...
NGH...
I'M SORRY,
AYUKAWA...
I'M SORRY...

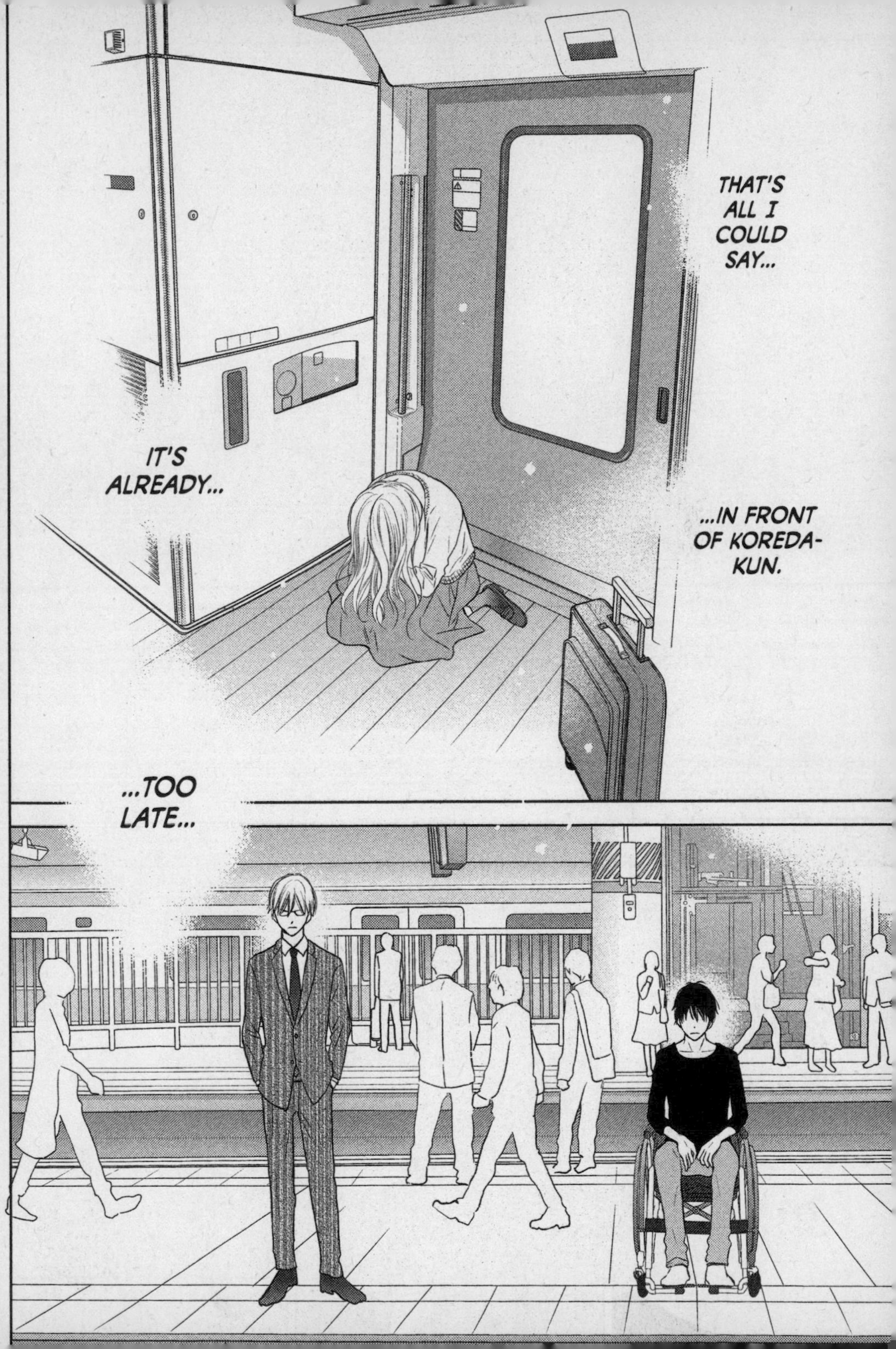
THAT'S ALL I COULD SAY...
...IN FRONT OF KOREDA-KUN.
IT'S ALREADY...
...TOO LATE...

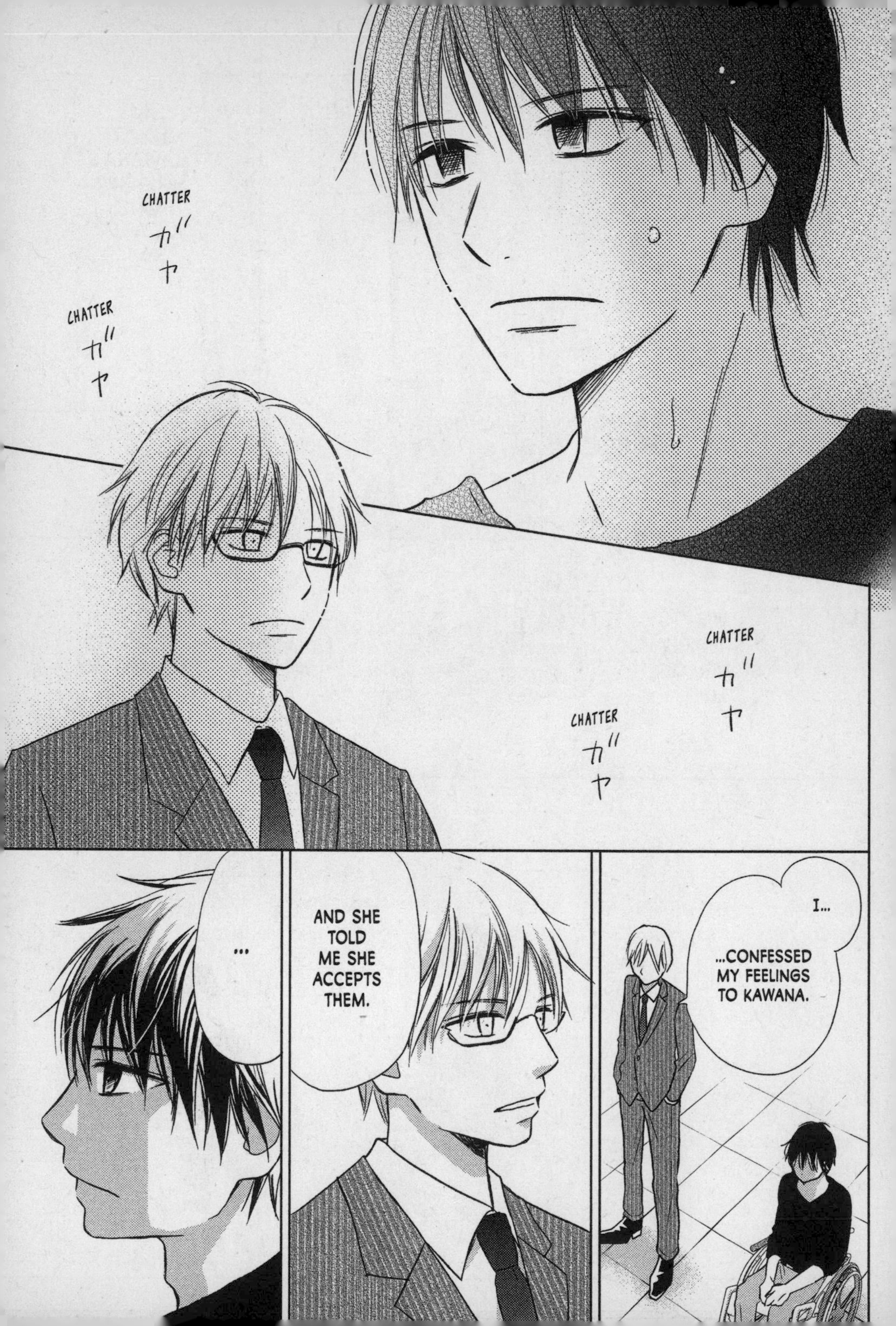
CHATTER
ガヤ
CHATTER
ガヤ
CHATTER
ガヤ
CHATTER
ガヤ
I...
...CONFESSED MY FEELINGS TO KAWANA.
AND SHE TOLD ME SHE ACCEPTS THEM.
...

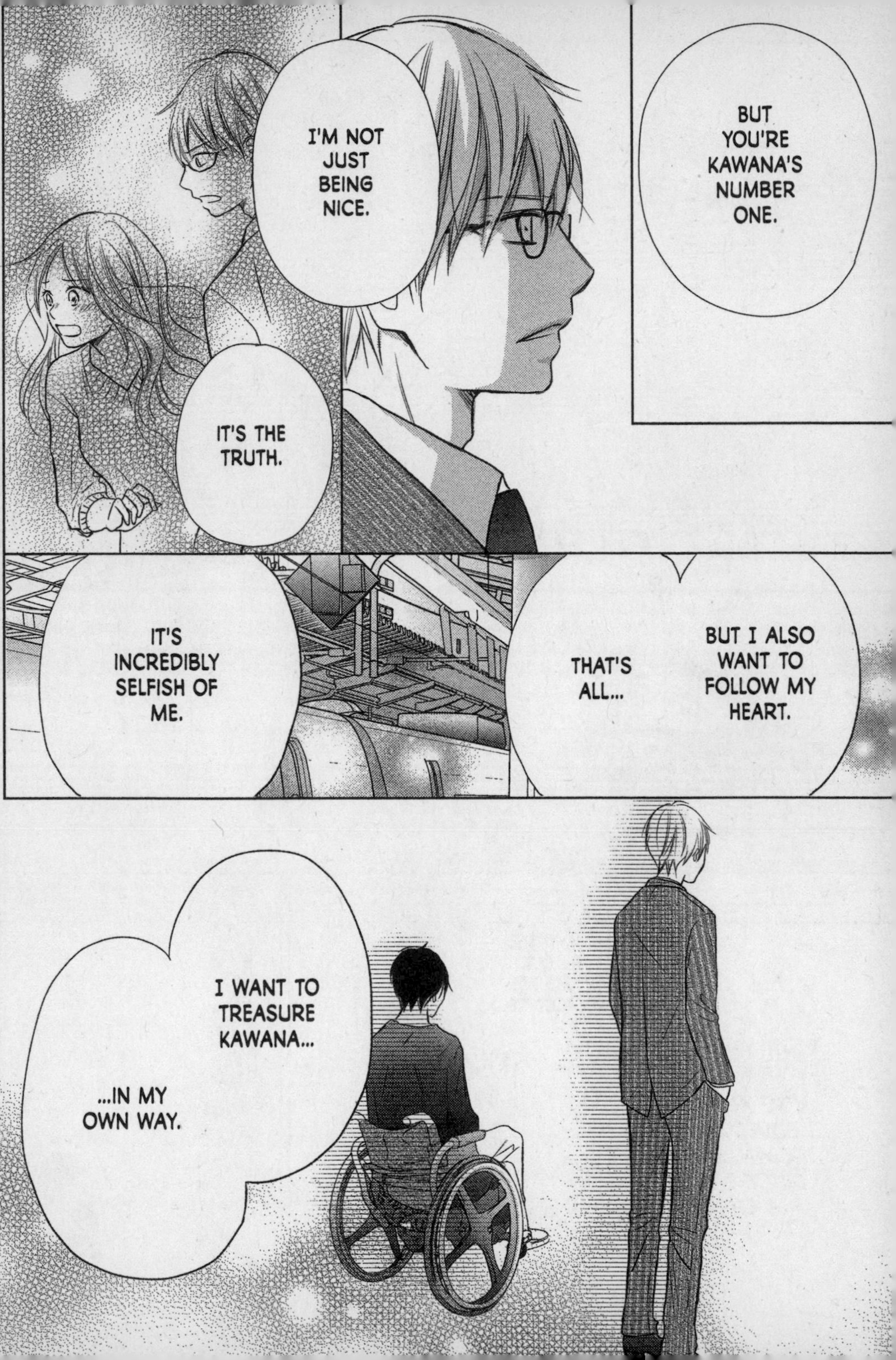
BUT YOU'RE KAWANA'S NUMBER ONE.
I'M NOT JUST BEING NICE.
IT'S THE TRUTH.
BUT I ALSO WANT TO FOLLOW MY HEART.
THAT'S ALL...
IT'S INCREDIBLY SELFISH OF ME.
I WANT TO TREASURE KAWANA...
...IN MY OWN WAY.

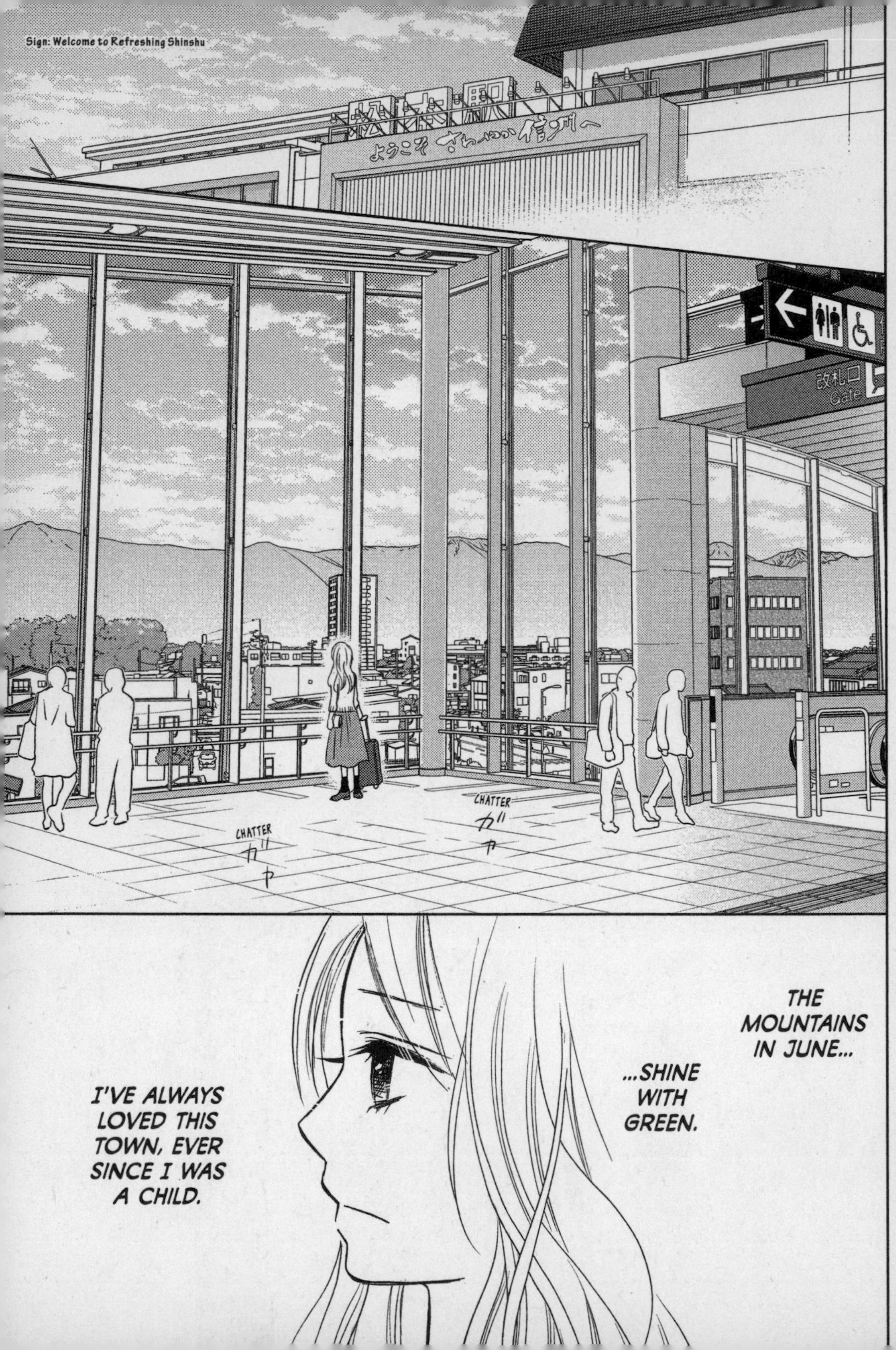
Sign: Welcome to Refreshing Shinshu
ようこそ さわやか信州へ
改札口
Gate
CHATTER
ガヤ
CHATTER
ガヤ
THE MOUNTAINS IN JUNE...
...SHINE WITH GREEN.
I'VE ALWAYS LOVED THIS TOWN, EVER SINCE I WAS A CHILD.

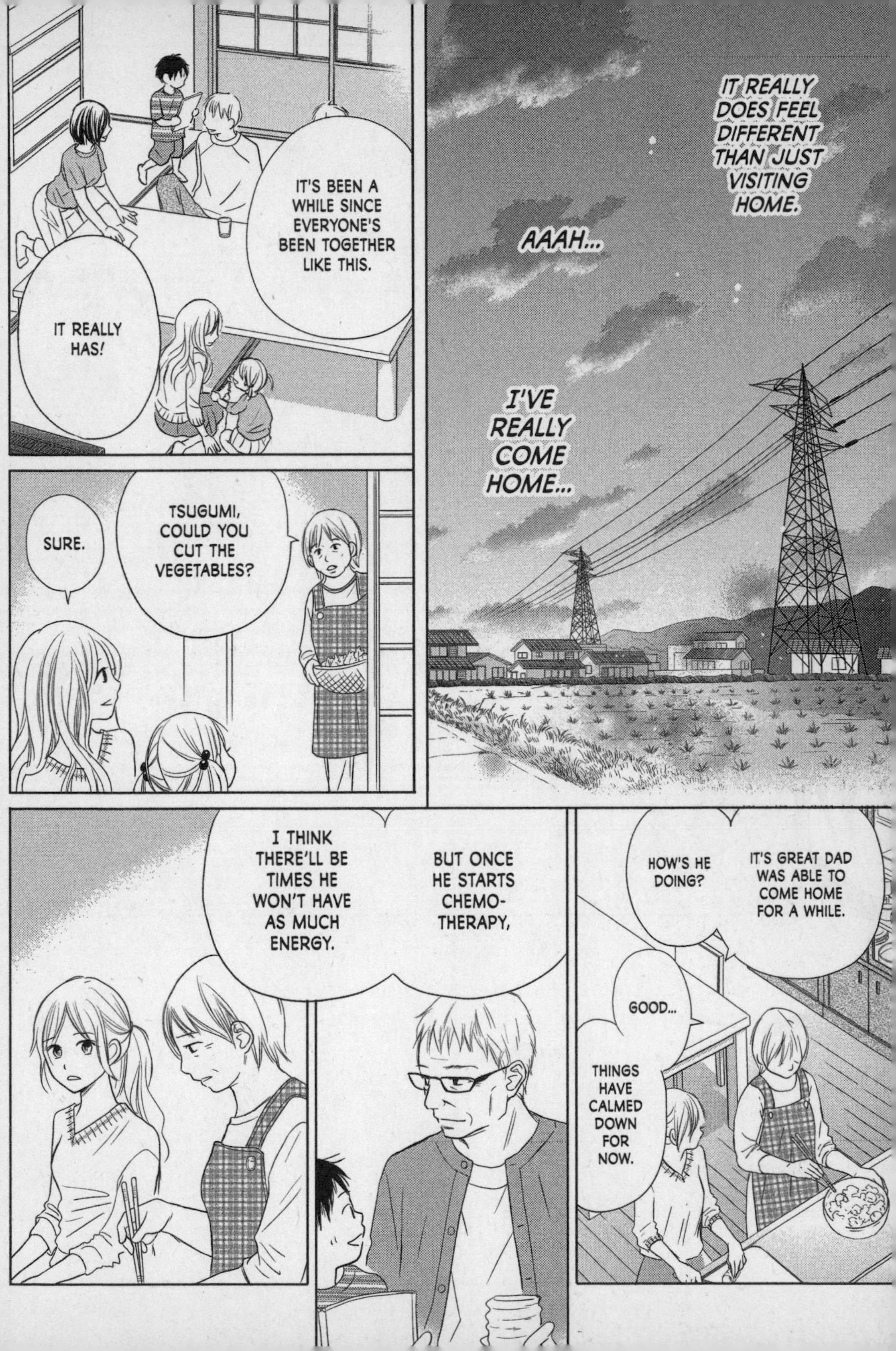
IT REALLY DOES FEEL DIFFERENT THAN JUST VISITING HOME.
AAAH...
I'VE REALLY COME HOME...
IT'S BEEN A WHILE SINCE EVERYONE'S BEEN TOGETHER LIKE THIS.
IT REALLY HAS!
TSUGUMI, COULD YOU CUT THE VEGETABLES?
SURE.
IT'S GREAT DAD WAS ABLE TO COME HOME FOR A WHILE.
HOW'S HE DOING?
GOOD...
THINGS HAVE CALMED DOWN FOR NOW.
BUT ONCE HE STARTS CHEMO-THERAPY,
I THINK THERE'LL BE TIMES HE WON'T HAVE AS MUCH ENERGY.

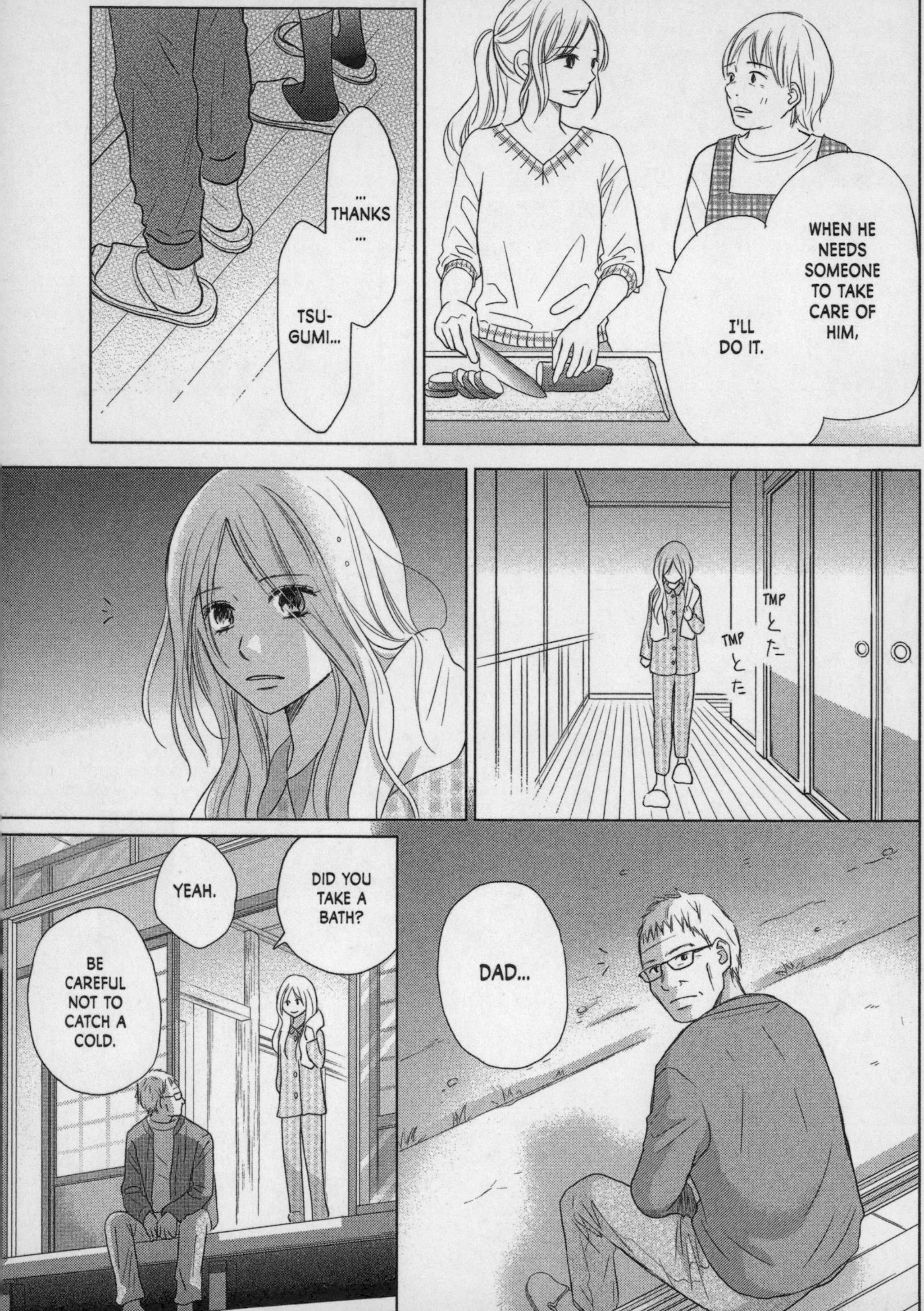
WHEN HE NEEDS SOMEONE TO TAKE CARE OF HIM,
I'LL DO IT.
... THANKS ...
TSU-GUMI...
TMP とた
TMP とた
DAD...
DID YOU TAKE A BATH?
YEAH.
BE CAREFUL NOT TO CATCH A COLD.

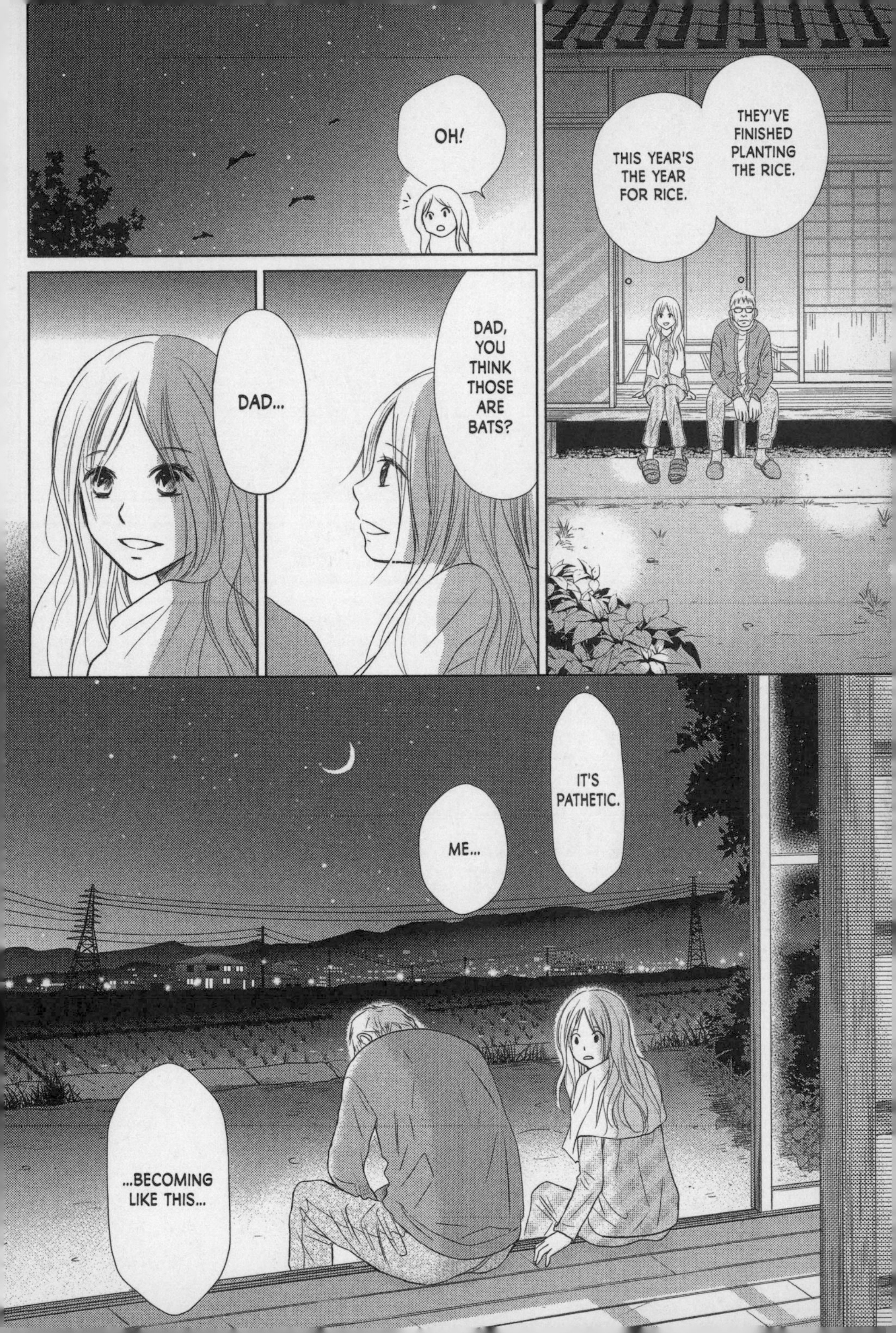
THEY'VE FINISHED PLANTING THE RICE.
THIS YEAR'S THE YEAR FOR RICE.
OH!
DAD, YOU THINK THOSE ARE BATS?
DAD...
IT'S PATHETIC.
ME...
...BECOMING LIKE THIS...

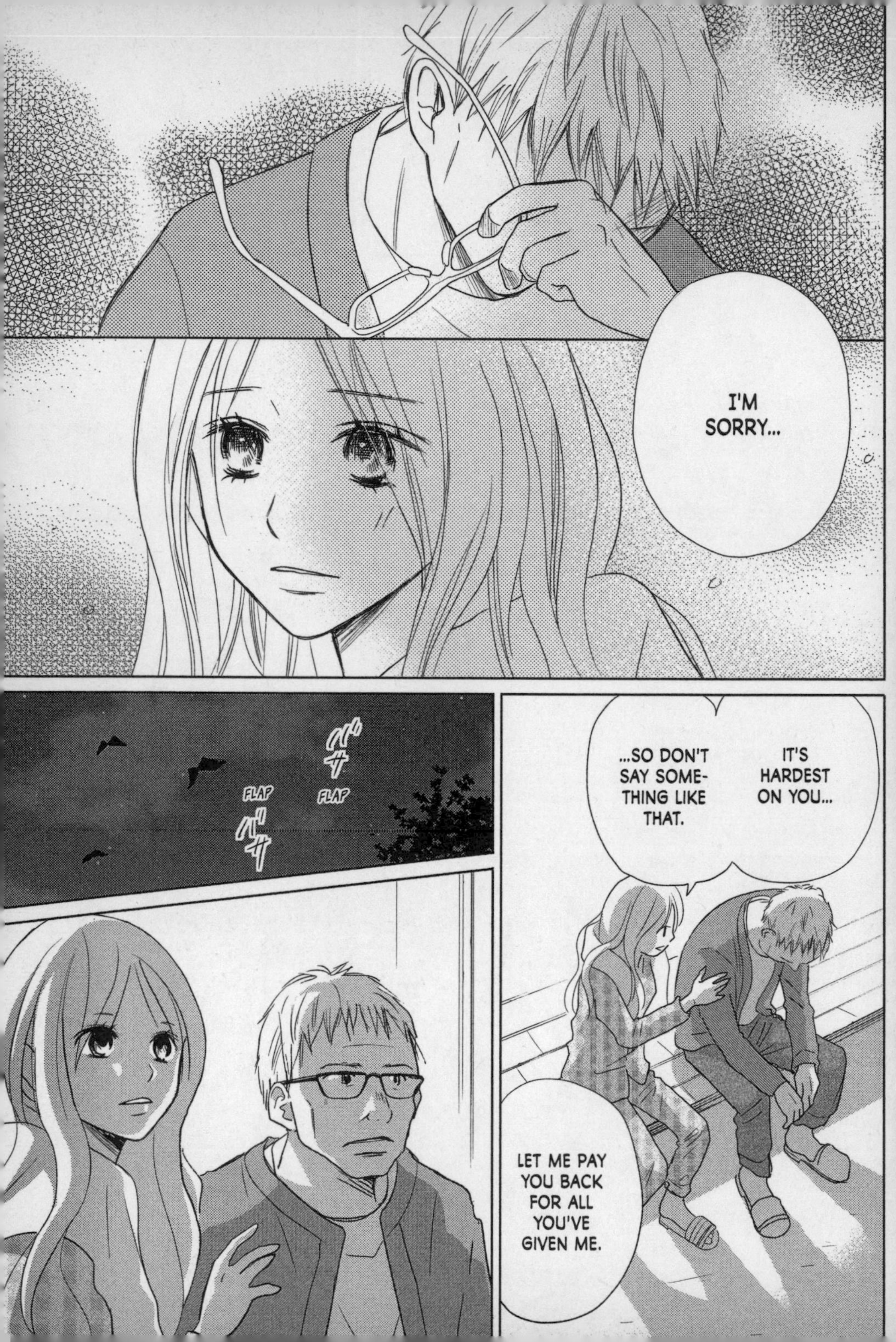
I'M SORRY...
IT'S HARDEST ON YOU...
...SO DON'T SAY SOME-THING LIKE THAT.
LET ME PAY YOU BACK FOR ALL YOU'VE GIVEN ME.
FLAP
FLAP

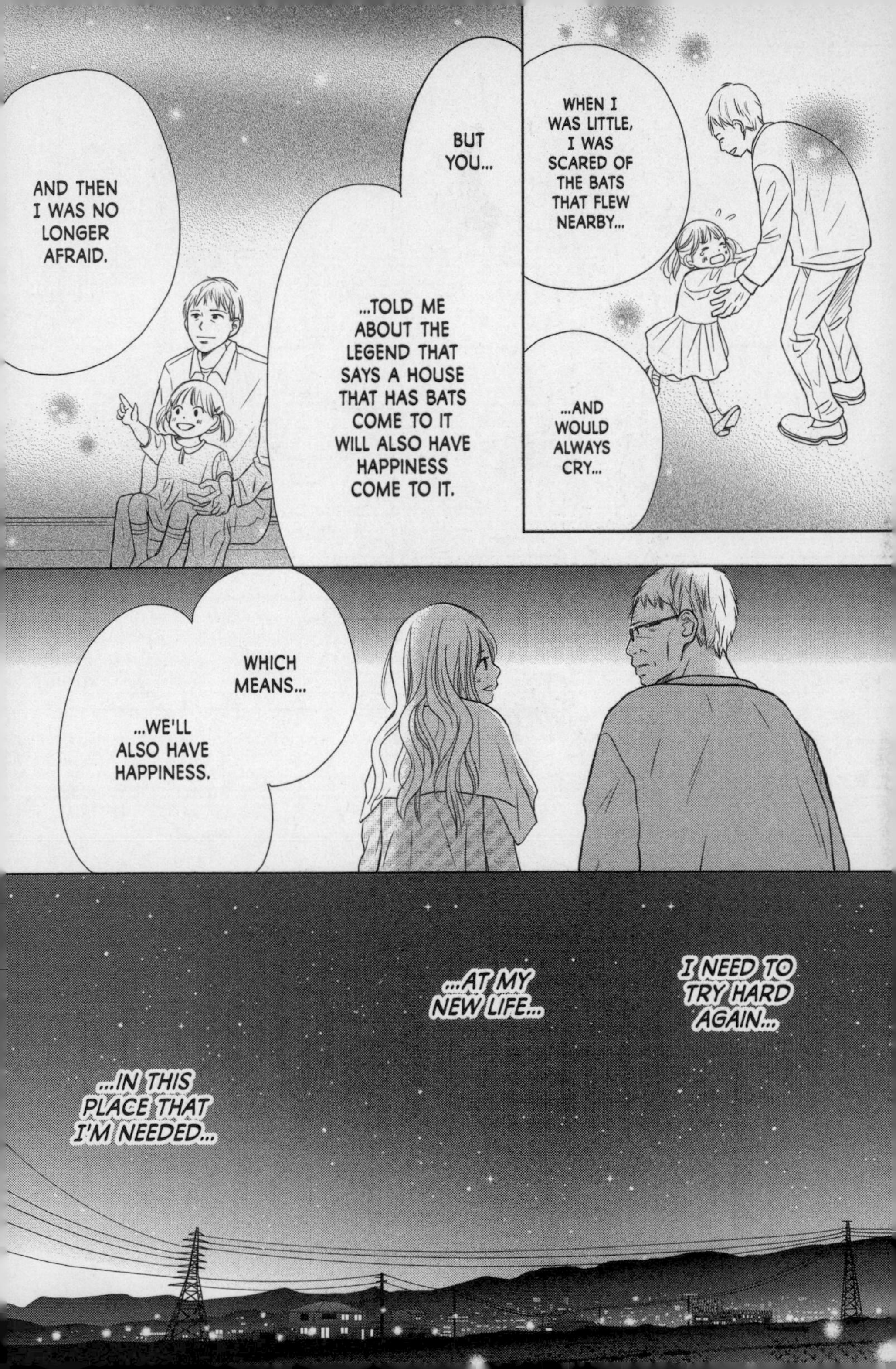
WHEN I WAS LITTLE, I WAS SCARED OF THE BATS THAT FLEW NEARBY...
...AND WOULD ALWAYS CRY...
BUT YOU...
...TOLD ME ABOUT THE LEGEND THAT SAYS A HOUSE THAT HAS BATS COME TO IT WILL ALSO HAVE HAPPINESS COME TO IT.
AND THEN I WAS NO LONGER AFRAID.
WHICH MEANS...
...WE'LL ALSO HAVE HAPPINESS.
I NEED TO TRY HARD AGAIN...
...AT MY NEW LIFE...
...IN THIS PLACE THAT I'M NEEDED...

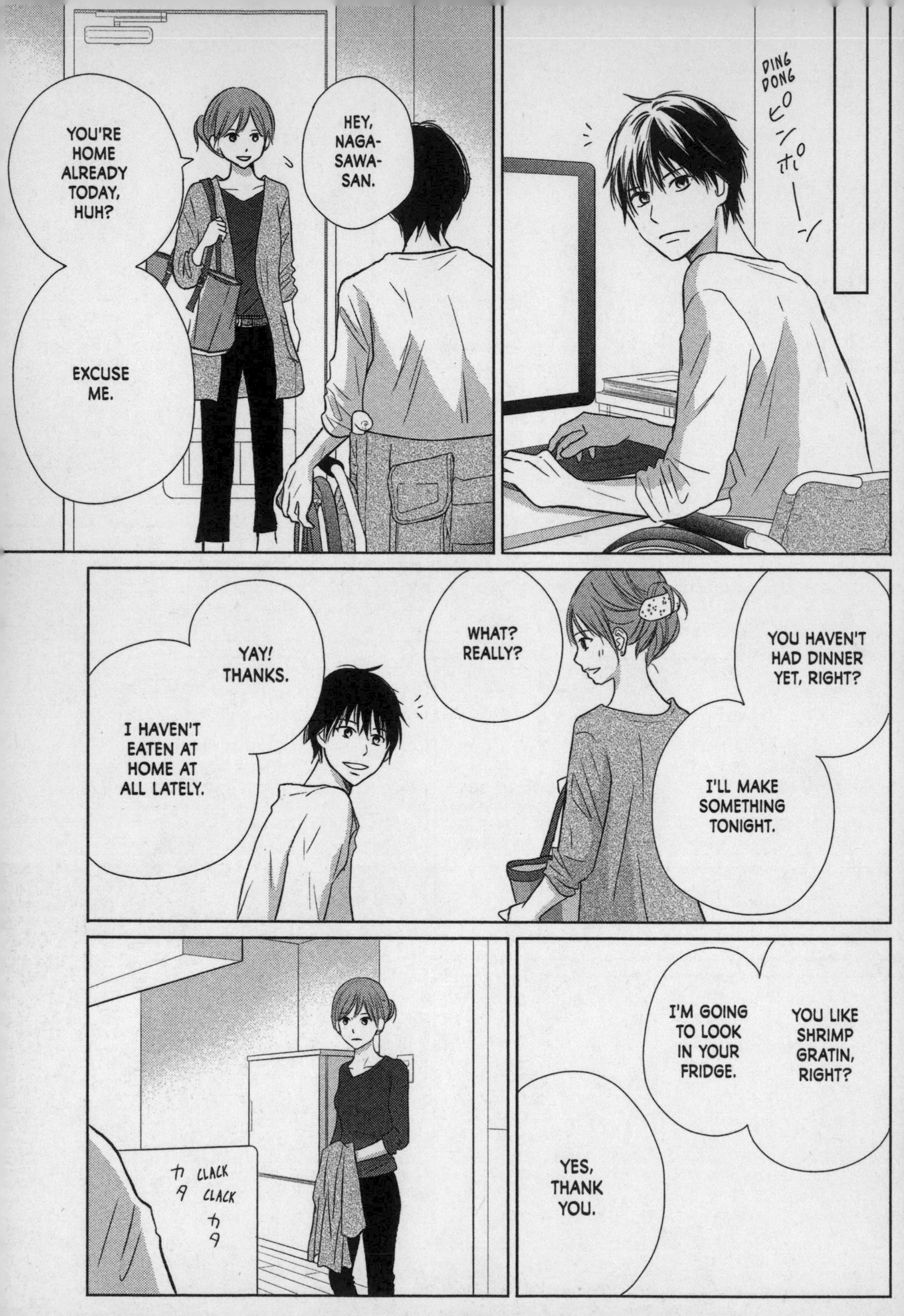
DING DONG
ピンポーン
HEY, NAGA-SAWA-SAN.
YOU'RE HOME ALREADY TODAY, HUH?
EXCUSE ME.
YOU HAVEN'T HAD DINNER YET, RIGHT?
I'LL MAKE SOMETHING TONIGHT.
WHAT? REALLY?
YAY! THANKS.
I HAVEN'T EATEN AT HOME AT ALL LATELY.
YOU LIKE SHRIMP GRATIN, RIGHT?
I'M GOING TO LOOK IN YOUR FRIDGE.
YES, THANK YOU.
カタ CLACK
カタ CLACK

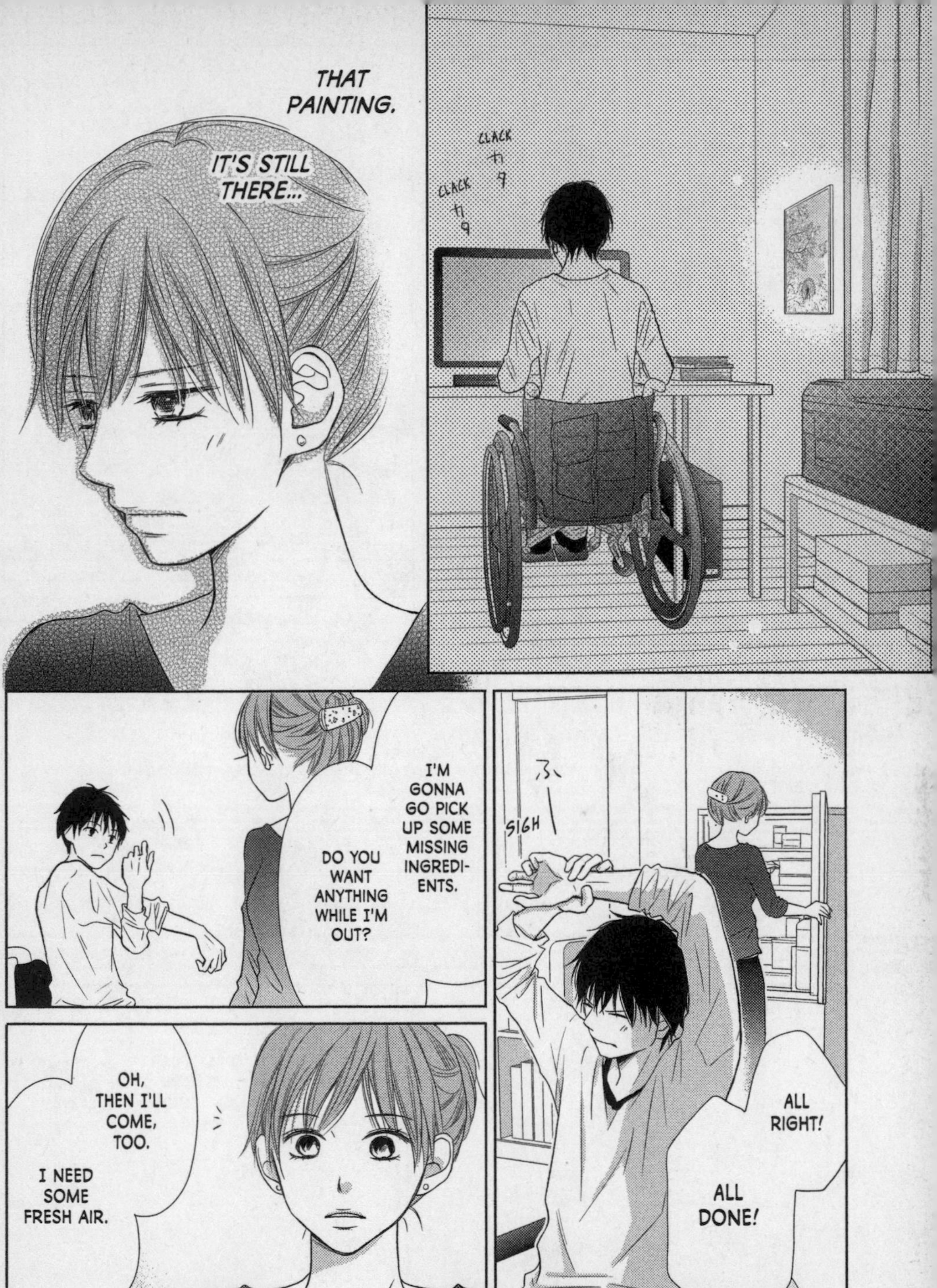
CLACK
CLACK
THAT PAINTING.
IT'S STILL THERE...
SIGH
ALL RIGHT!
ALL DONE!
I'M GONNA GO PICK UP SOME MISSING INGREDI- ENTS.
DO YOU WANT ANYTHING WHILE I'M OUT?
OH, THEN I'LL COME, TOO.
I NEED SOME FRESH AIR.

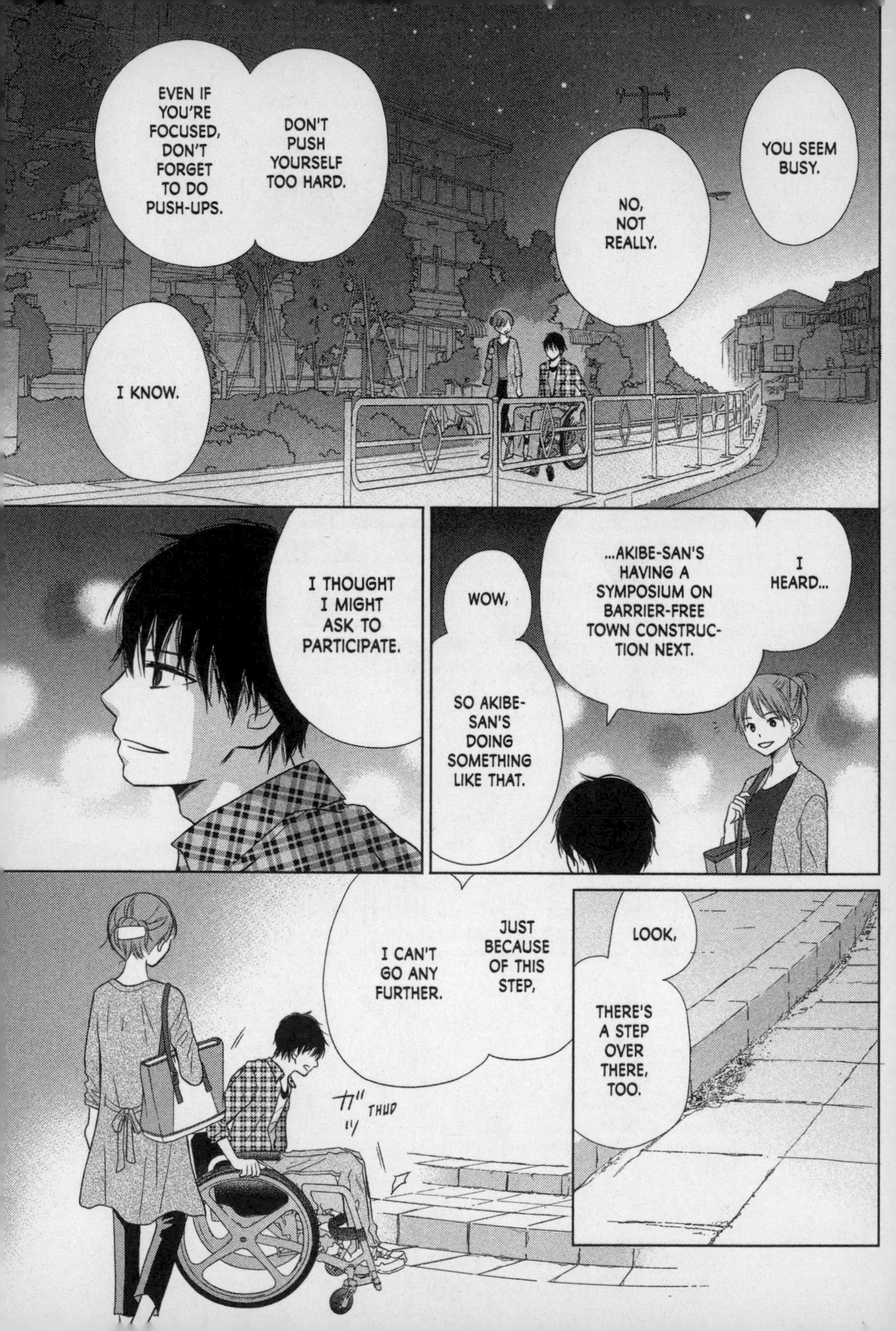
YOU SEEM BUSY.
NO, NOT REALLY.
DON'T PUSH YOURSELF TOO HARD.
EVEN IF YOU'RE FOCUSED, DON'T FORGET TO DO PUSH-UPS.
I KNOW.
I HEARD...
...AKIBE-SAN'S HAVING A SYMPOSIUM ON BARRIER-FREE TOWN CONSTRUC-TION NEXT.
WOW,
SO AKIBE-SAN'S DOING SOMETHING LIKE THAT.
I THOUGHT I MIGHT ASK TO PARTICIPATE.
LOOK,
THERE'S A STEP OVER THERE, TOO.
JUST BECAUSE OF THIS STEP,
I CAN'T GO ANY FURTHER.
ガッ THUD

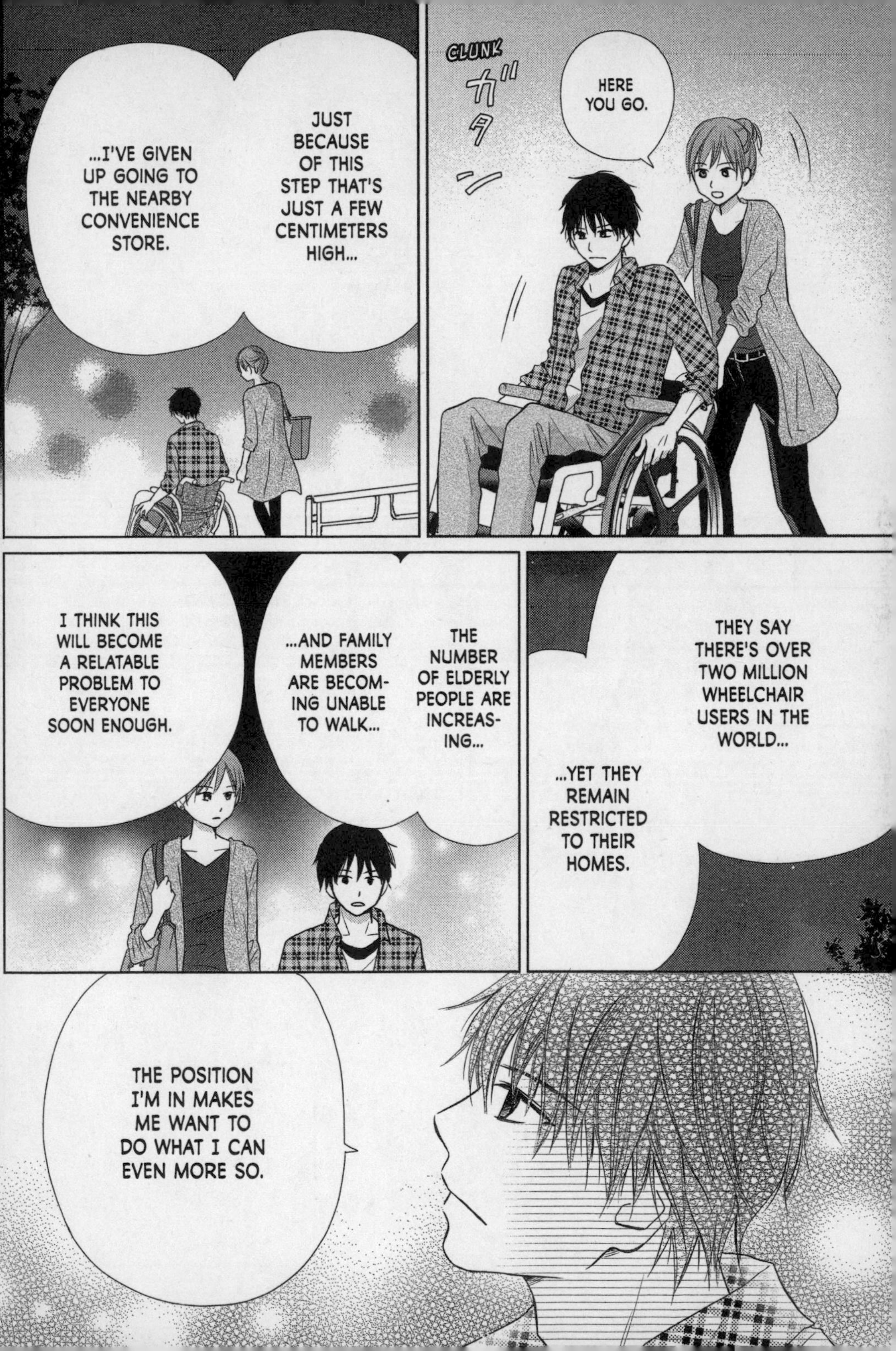

CLUNK
ガタン
HERE YOU GO.
JUST BECAUSE OF THIS STEP THAT'S JUST A FEW CENTIMETERS HIGH...
...I'VE GIVEN UP GOING TO THE NEARBY CONVENIENCE STORE.
THEY SAY THERE'S OVER TWO MILLION WHEELCHAIR USERS IN THE WORLD...
...YET THEY REMAIN RESTRICTED TO THEIR HOMES.
THE NUMBER OF ELDERLY PEOPLE ARE INCREAS-ING...
...AND FAMILY MEMBERS ARE BECOM-ING UNABLE TO WALK...
I THINK THIS WILL BECOME A RELATABLE PROBLEM TO EVERYONE SOON ENOUGH.
THE POSITION I'M IN MAKES ME WANT TO DO WHAT I CAN EVEN MORE SO.

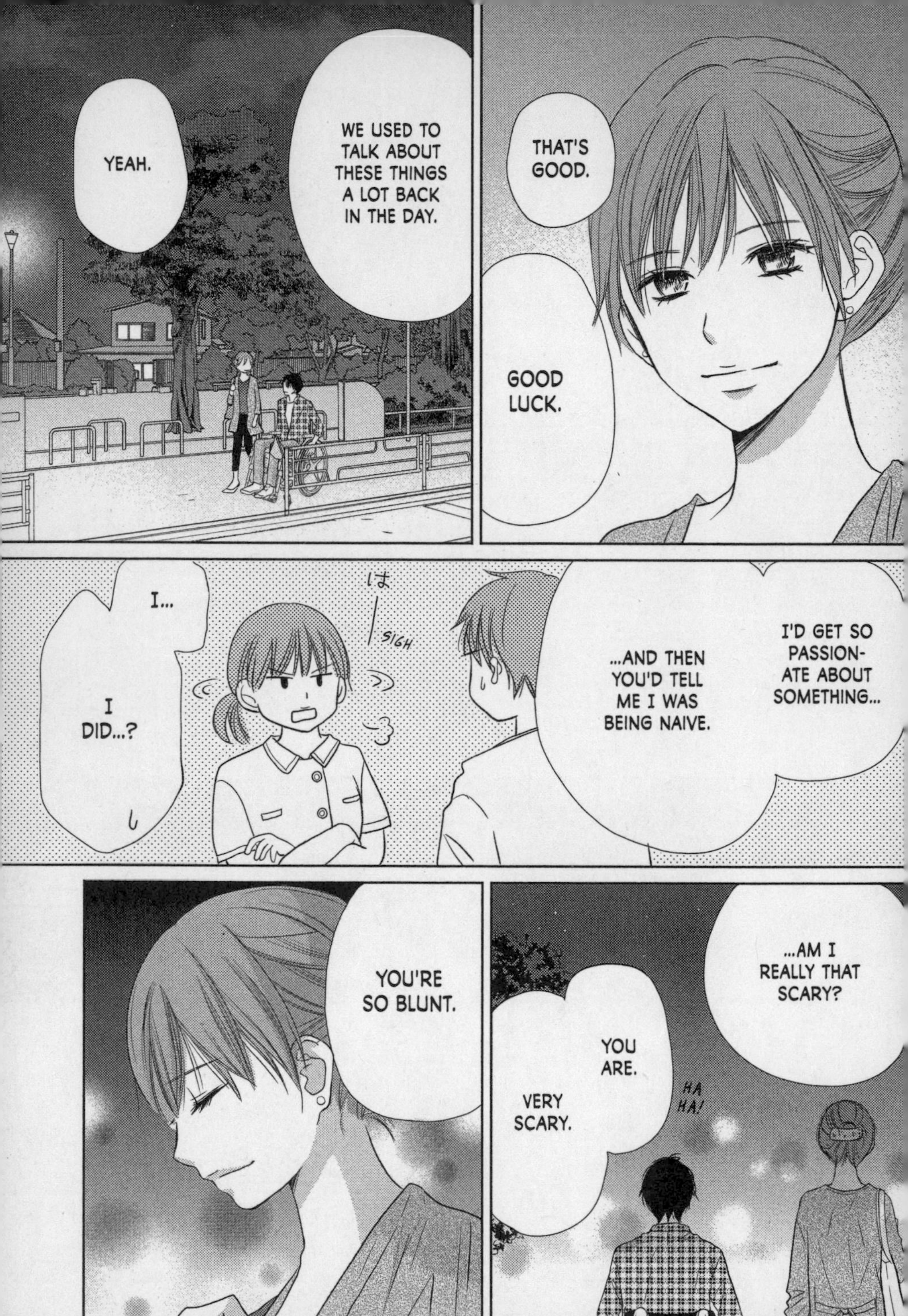
THAT'S GOOD.
GOOD LUCK.
WE USED TO TALK ABOUT THESE THINGS A LOT BACK IN THE DAY.
YEAH.
I'D GET SO PASSION-ATE ABOUT SOMETHING...
...AND THEN YOU'D TELL ME I WAS BEING NAIVE.
は
SIGH
I...
I DID...?
...AM I REALLY THAT SCARY?
YOU ARE.
HA HA!
VERY SCARY.
YOU'RE SO BLUNT.

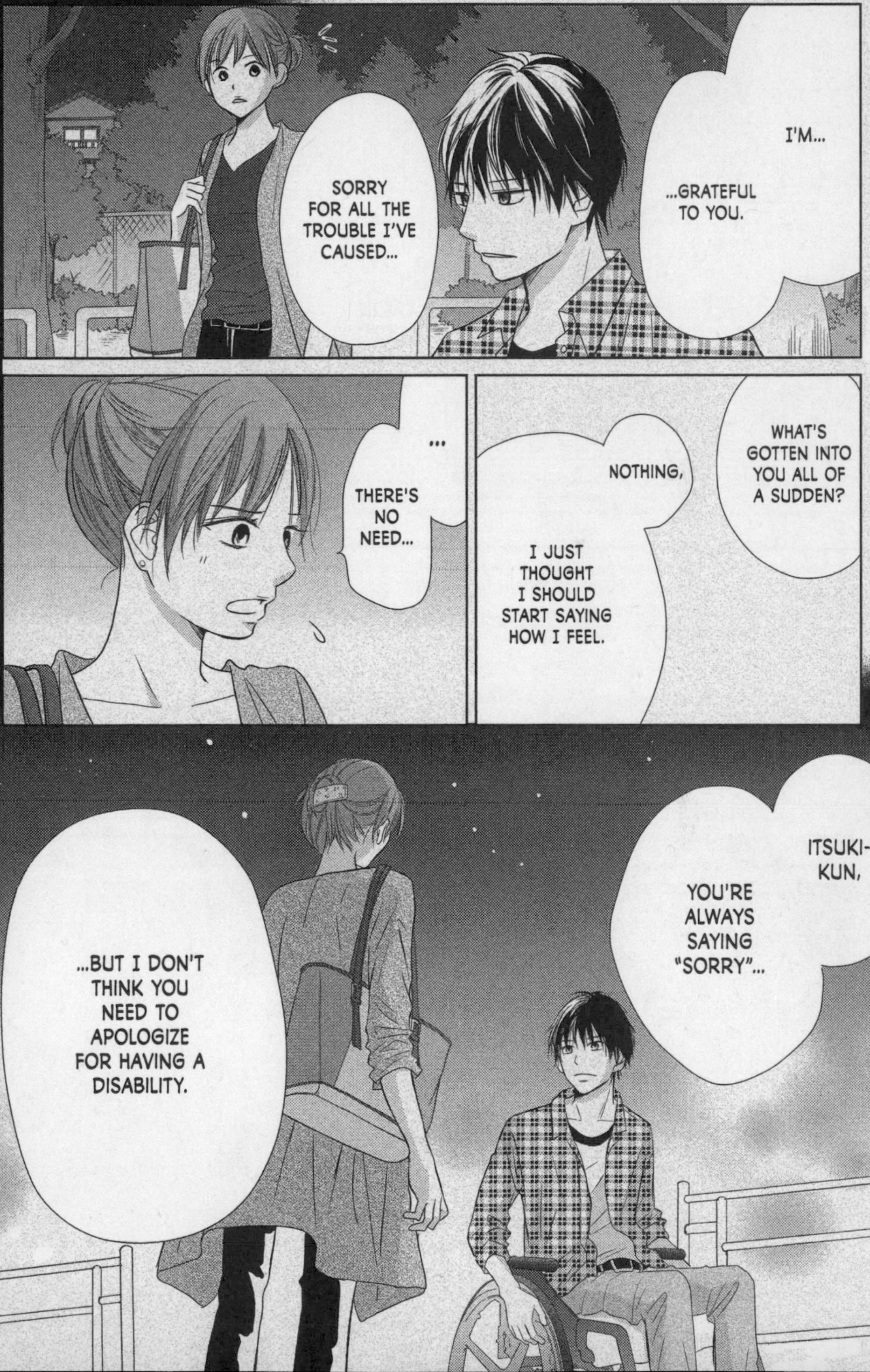
I'M...
...GRATEFUL TO YOU.
SORRY FOR ALL THE TROUBLE I'VE CAUSED...
WHAT'S GOTTEN INTO YOU ALL OF A SUDDEN?
NOTHING,
I JUST THOUGHT I SHOULD START SAYING HOW I FEEL.
...
THERE'S NO NEED...
ITSUKI-KUN,
YOU'RE ALWAYS SAYING "SORRY"...
...BUT I DON'T THINK YOU NEED TO APOLOGIZE FOR HAVING A DISABILITY.

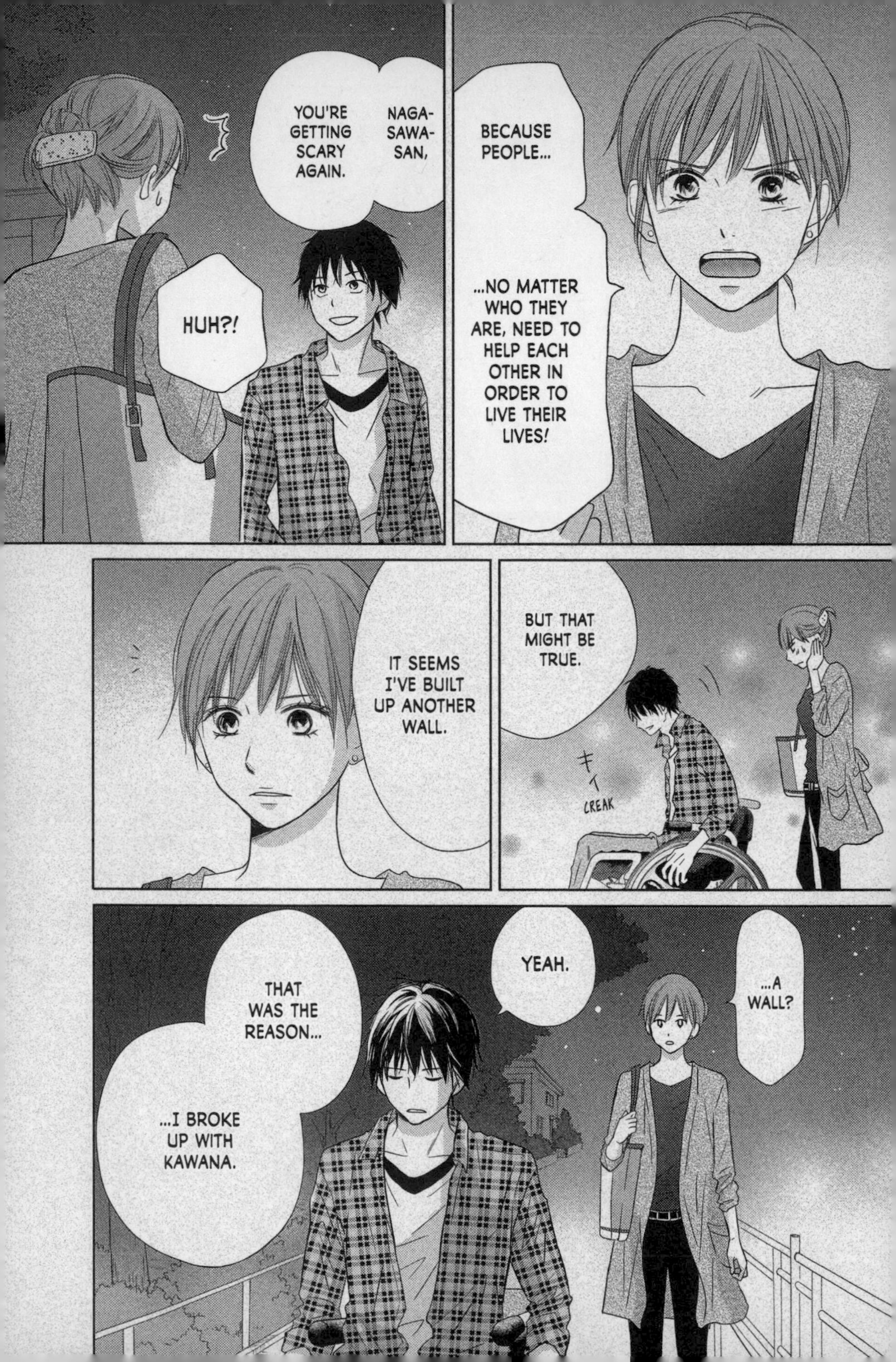
BECAUSE PEOPLE...
...NO MATTER WHO THEY ARE, NEED TO HELP EACH OTHER IN ORDER TO LIVE THEIR LIVES!
NAGA-SAWA-SAN,
YOU'RE GETTING SCARY AGAIN.
HUH?!
BUT THAT MIGHT BE TRUE.
キィ
CREAK
IT SEEMS I'VE BUILT UP ANOTHER WALL.
...A WALL?
YEAH.
THAT WAS THE REASON...
...I BROKE UP WITH KAWANA.

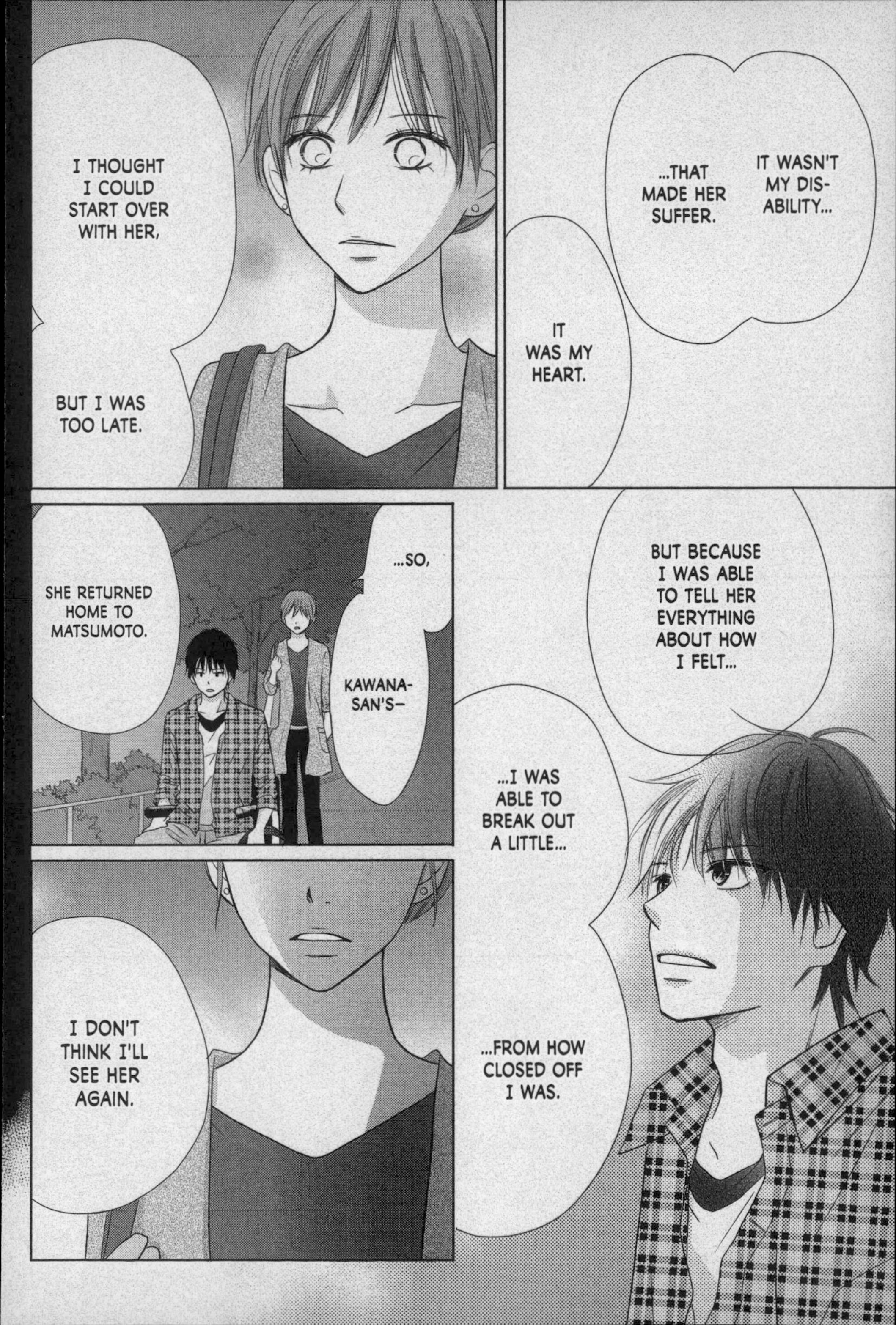
IT WASN'T MY DIS-ABILITY...
...THAT MADE HER SUFFER.
IT WAS MY HEART.
I THOUGHT I COULD START OVER WITH HER,
BUT I WAS TOO LATE.
BUT BECAUSE I WAS ABLE TO TELL HER EVERYTHING ABOUT HOW I FELT...
...I WAS ABLE TO BREAK OUT A LITTLE...
...FROM HOW CLOSED OFF I WAS.
...SO,
KAWANA-SAN'S—
SHE RETURNED HOME TO MATSUMOTO.
I DON'T THINK I'LL SEE HER AGAIN.

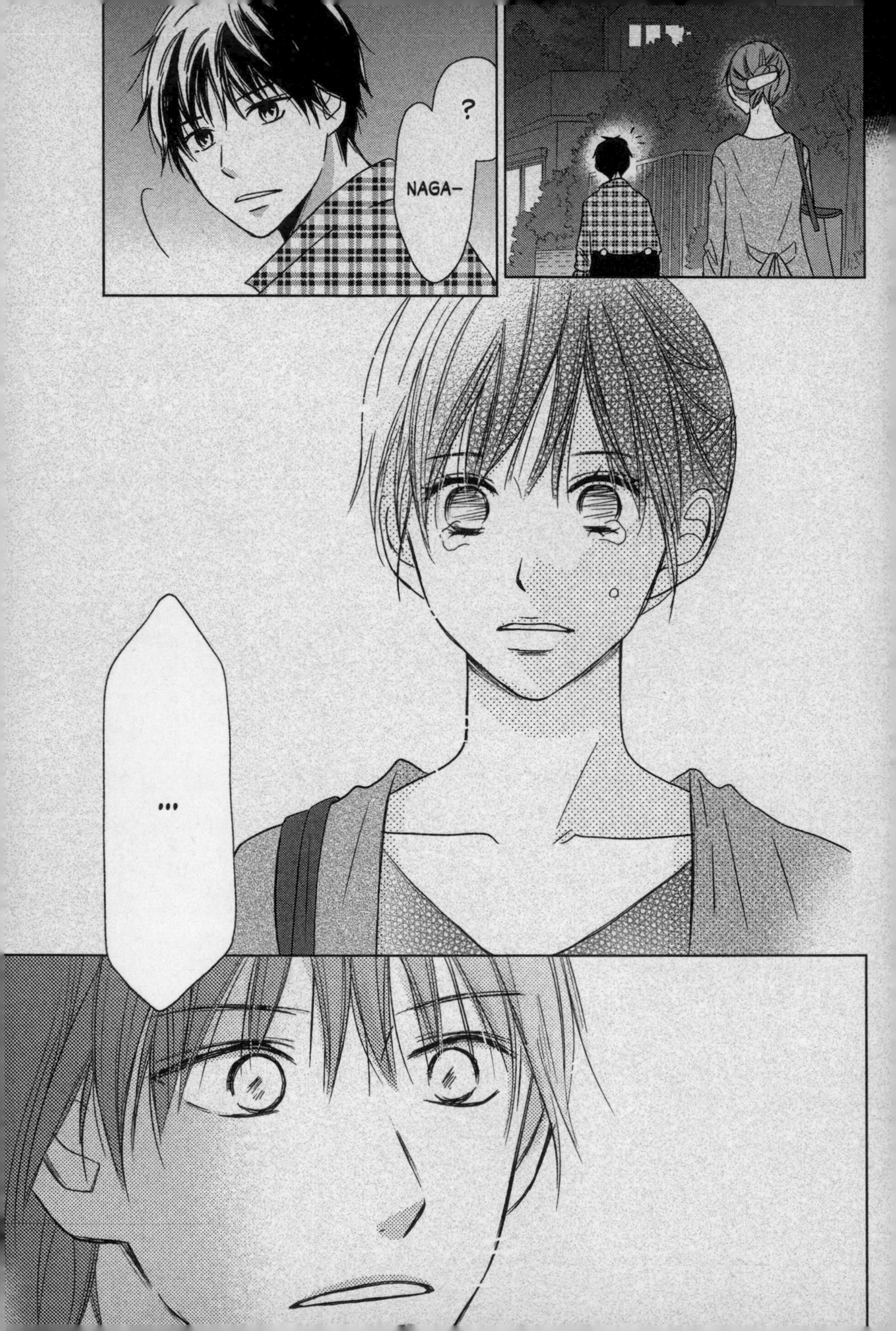
?
NAGA–
...

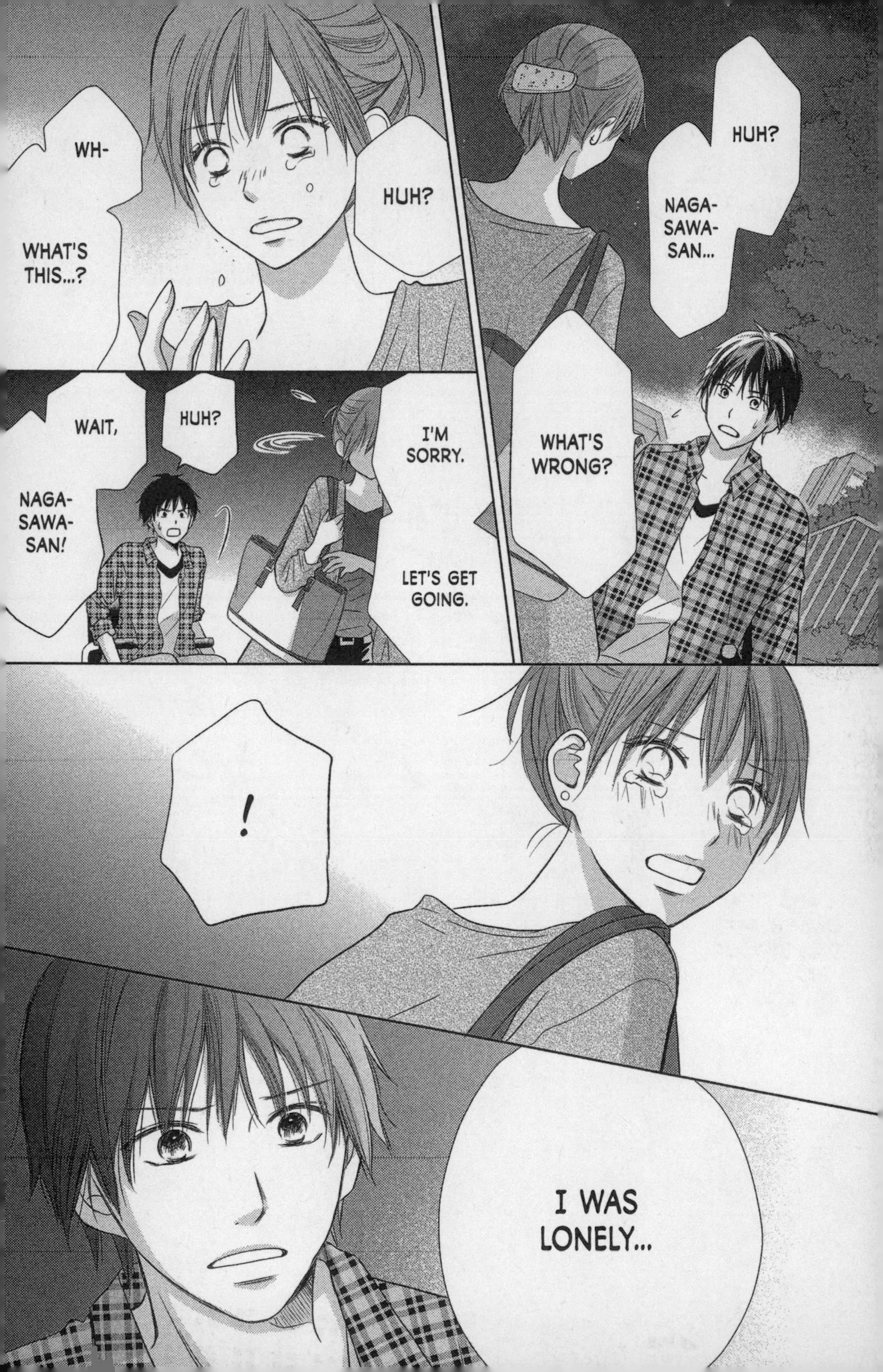
HUH?
NAGA-SAWA-SAN...
WHAT'S WRONG?
HUH?
WH-
WHAT'S THIS...?
I'M SORRY.
LET'S GET GOING.
HUH?
WAIT,
NAGA-SAWA-SAN!
!
I WAS LONELY...

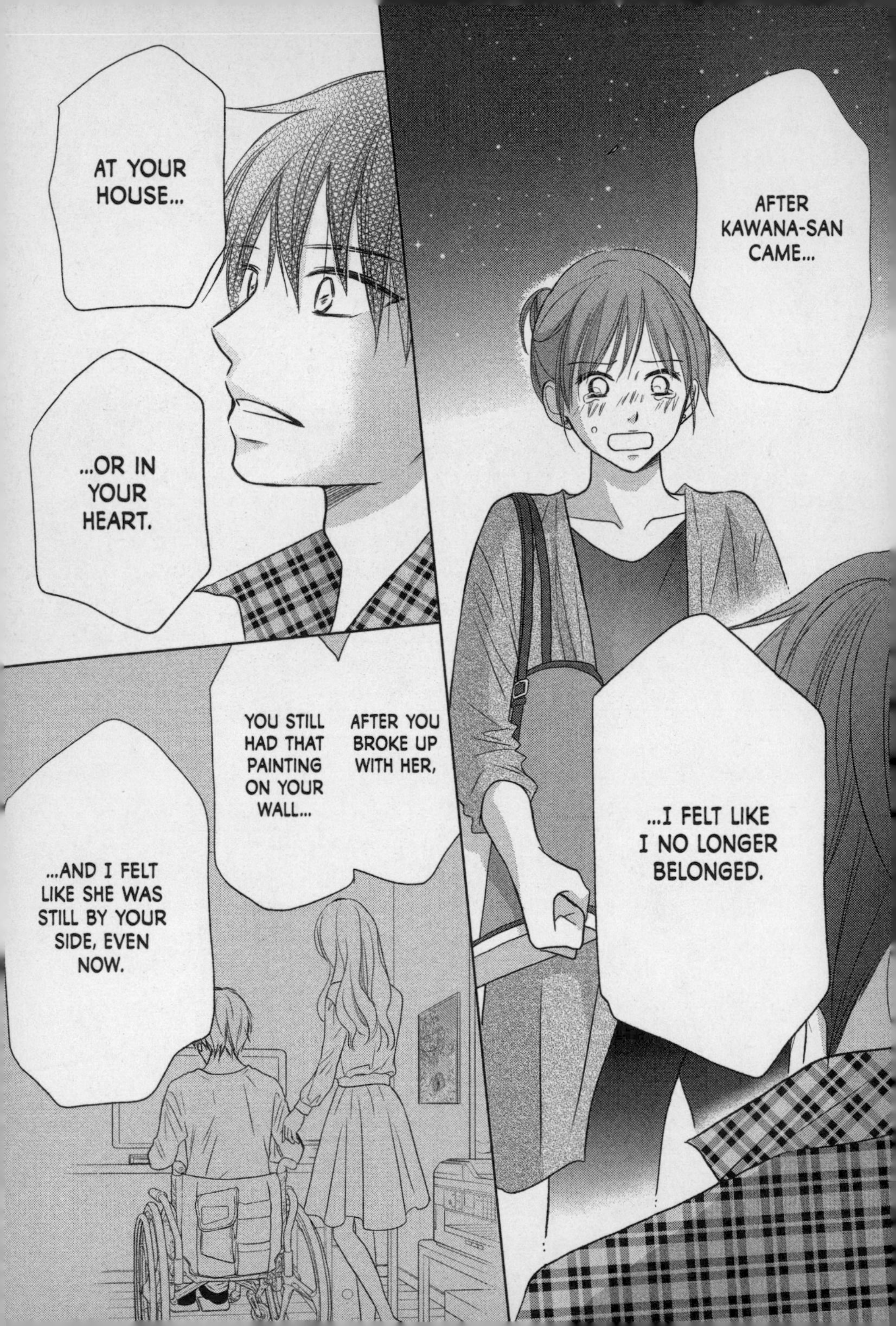
AFTER KAWANA-SAN CAME...
...I FELT LIKE I NO LONGER BELONGED.
AT YOUR HOUSE...
...OR IN YOUR HEART.
AFTER YOU BROKE UP WITH HER,
YOU STILL HAD THAT PAINTING ON YOUR WALL...
...AND I FELT LIKE SHE WAS STILL BY YOUR SIDE, EVEN NOW.

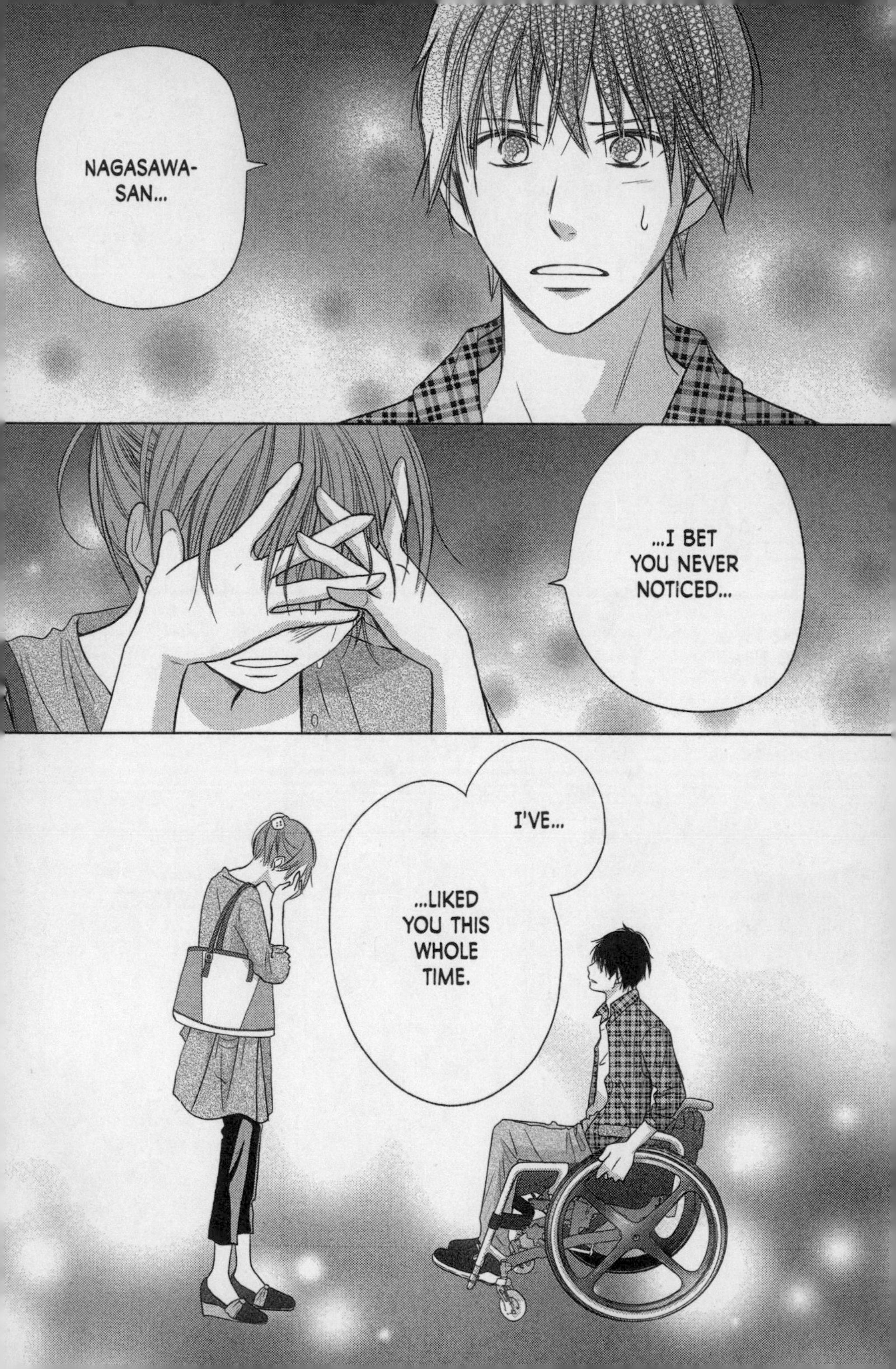
NAGASAWA-SAN...
...I BET YOU NEVER NOTICED...
I'VE...
...LIKED YOU THIS WHOLE TIME.

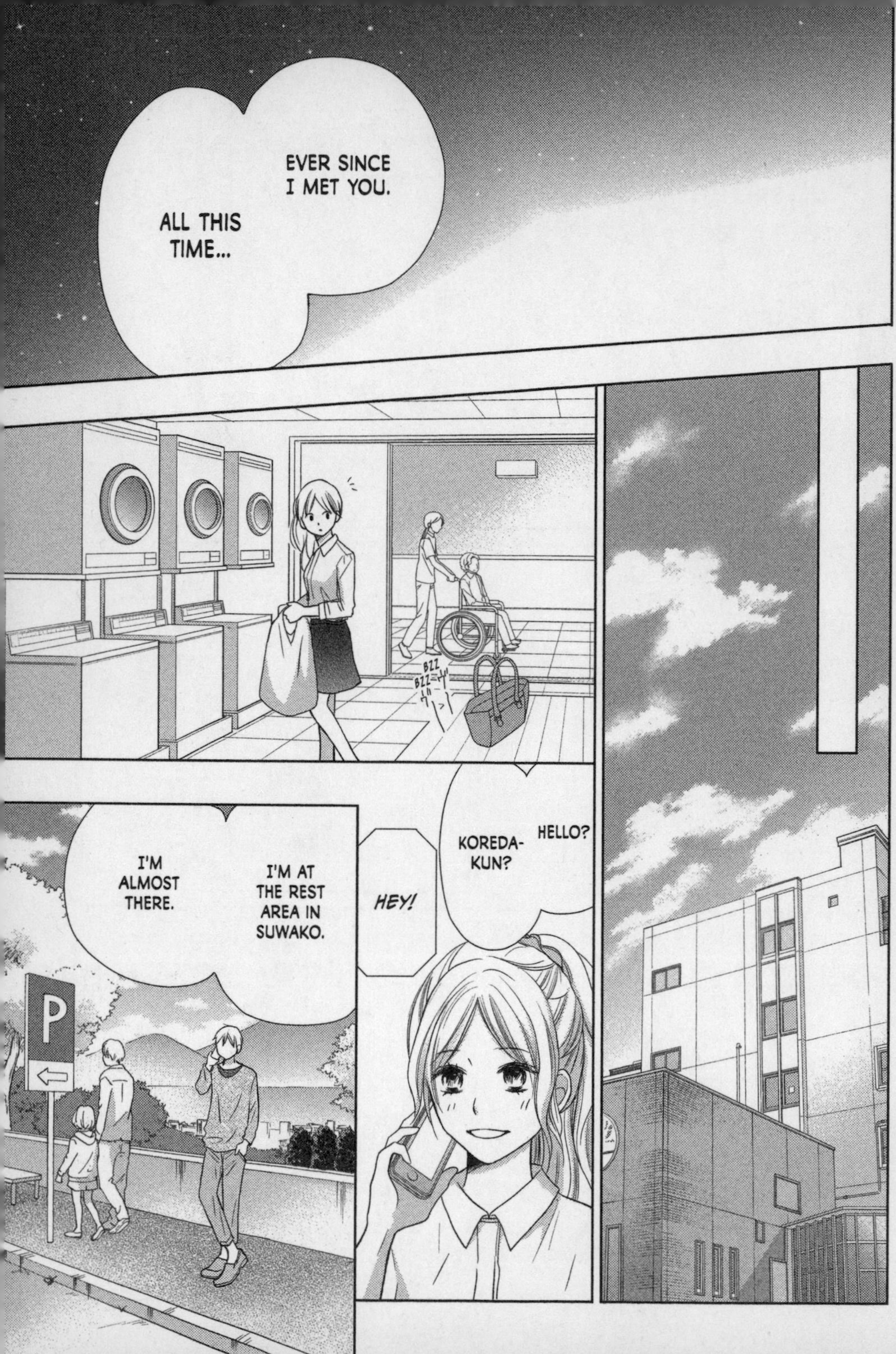
EVER SINCE I MET YOU.
ALL THIS TIME...
BZZ BZZ
HELLO?
KOREDA-KUN?
HEY!
I'M AT THE REST AREA IN SUWAKO.
I'M ALMOST THERE.

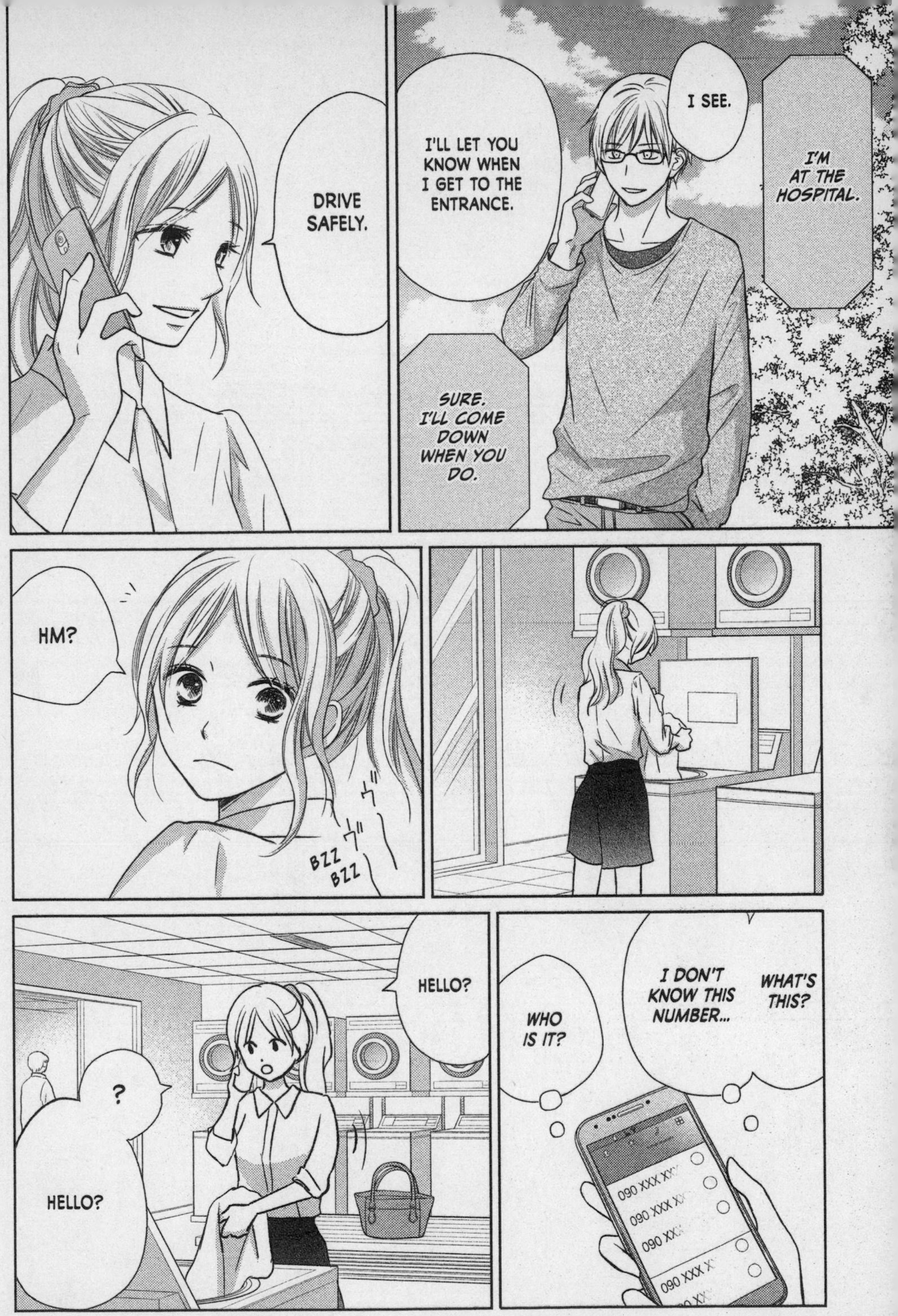
I'M AT THE HOSPITAL.
I SEE.
I'LL LET YOU KNOW WHEN I GET TO THE ENTRANCE.
SURE. I'LL COME DOWN WHEN YOU DO.
DRIVE SAFELY.
HM?
ヴ ヴ
BZZ BZZ
WHAT'S THIS?
I DON'T KNOW THIS NUMBER...
WHO IS IT?
HELLO?
?
HELLO?

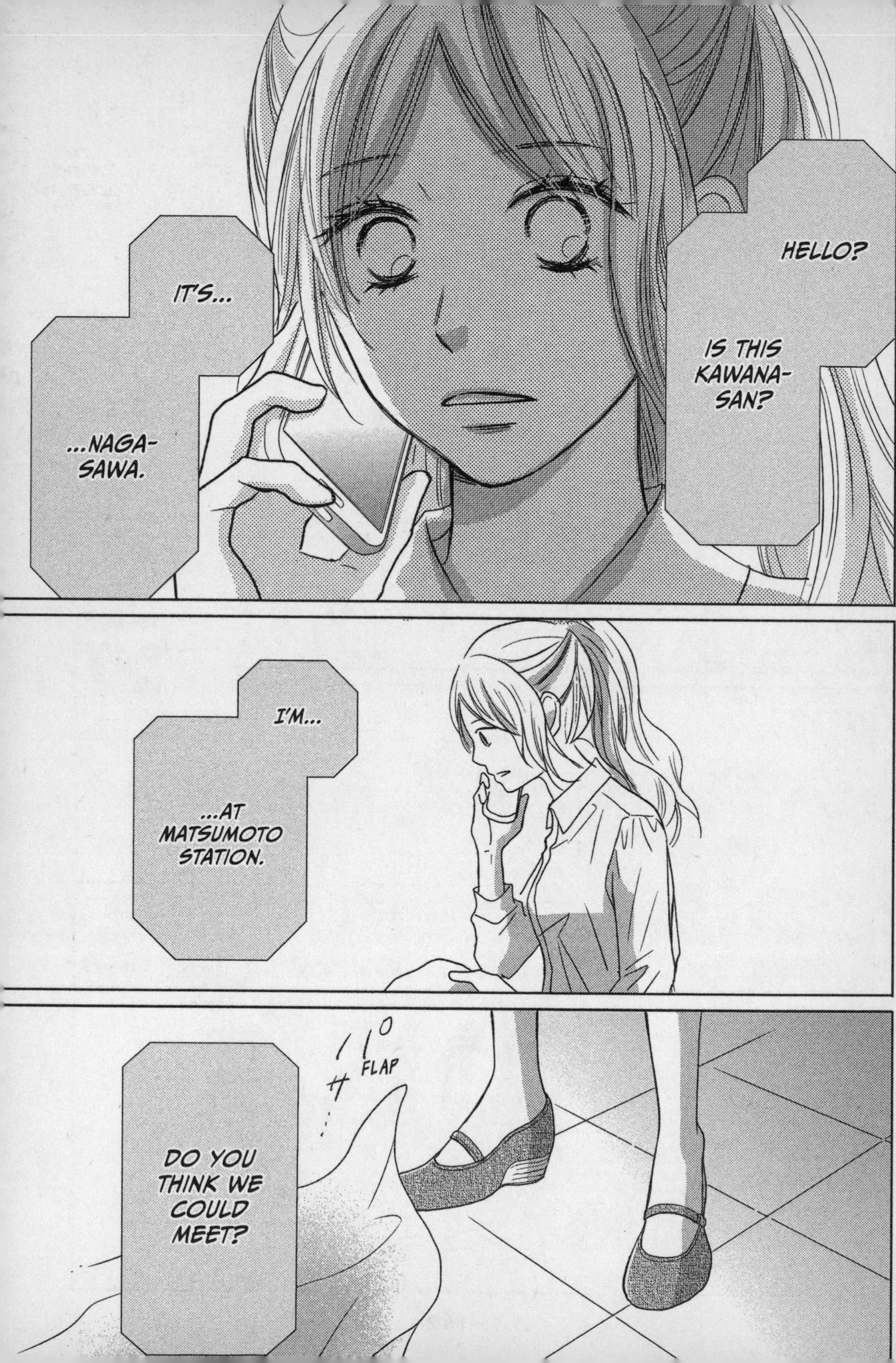
HELLO?
IS THIS KAWANA-SAN?
IT'S...
...NAGA-SAWA.
I'M...
...AT MATSUMOTO STATION.
FLAP
DO YOU THINK WE COULD MEET?

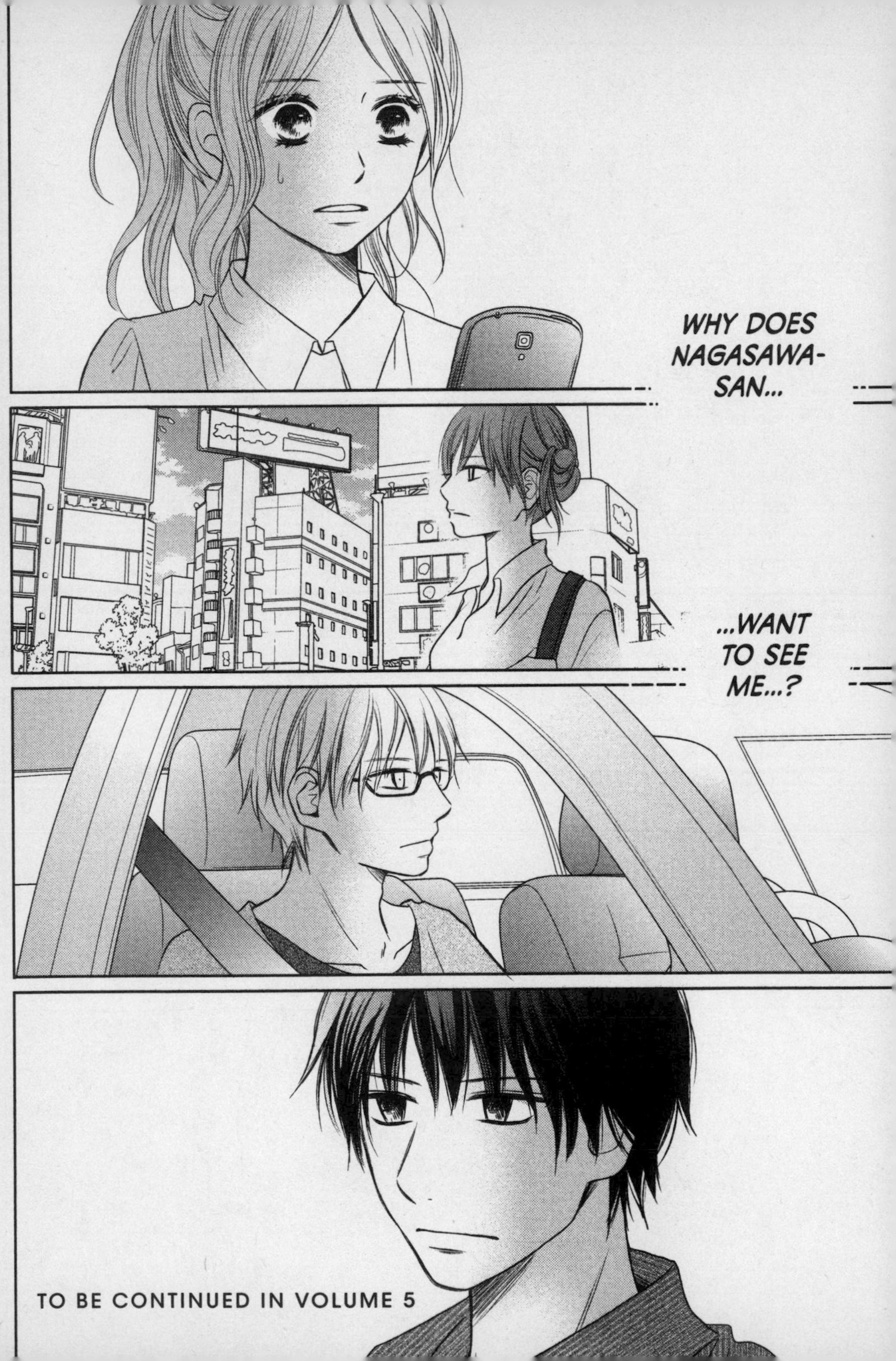
WHY DOES NAGASAWA-SAN...
...WANT TO SEE ME...?
TO BE CONTINUED IN VOLUME 5

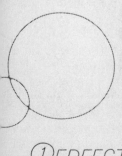

PERFECT WORLD.

Thank you for reading *Perfect World* volume four!

With everyone's encouragement keeping me going, I'm hard at work!

I've often heard comic artists around the world say, it's tough being serialized because the story ends up going in an unexpected direction, but now I'm finally experiencing that myself.

Even so, I'd like to at least try hard to make sure the ending stays the same as what I had originally planned.

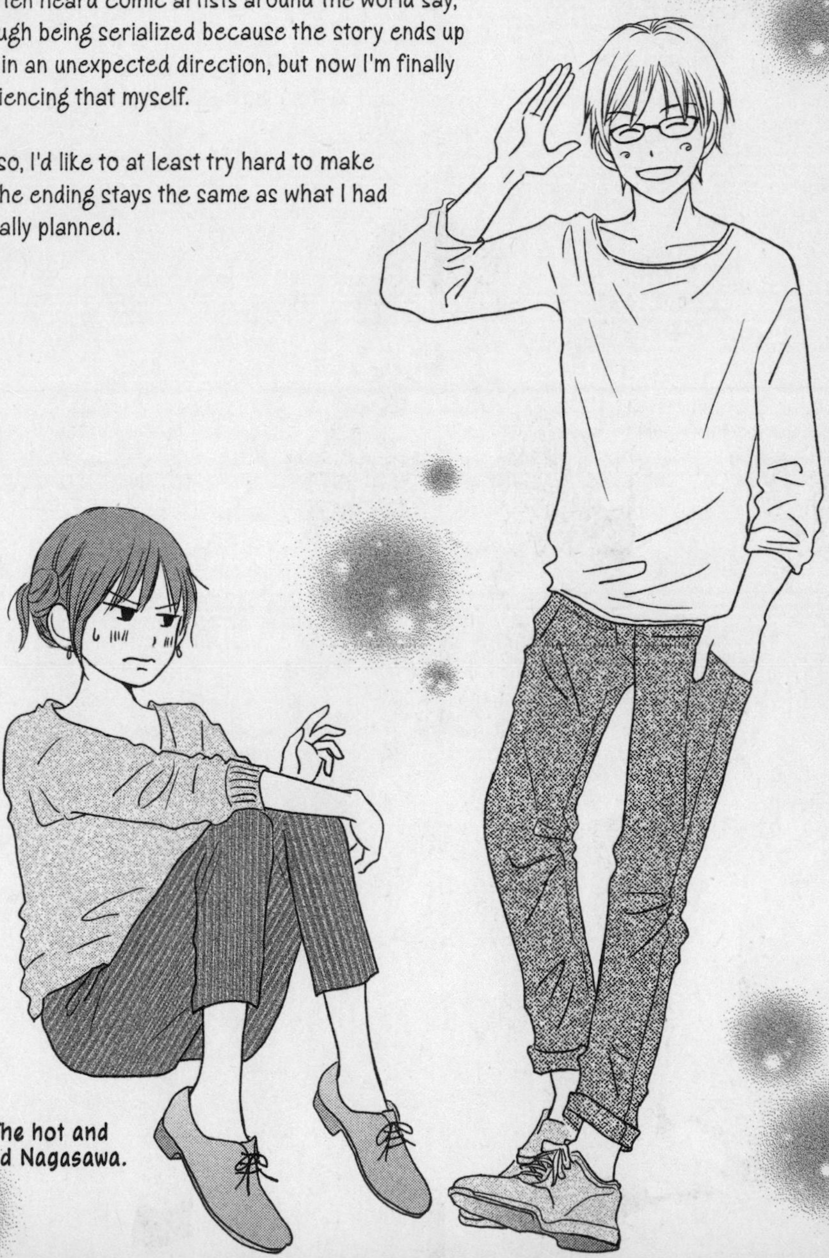

The hot and cold Nagasawa.

— From the bottom of my heart, thank you to all of those who helped me. —

* Kazuo Abe-sama from Abe Kensetsu Inc.
* Ouchi-sama * Yaguchi-sama * Those at OX Kanto ViVit
* My editor, Ito-sama * Everyone from the editorial department at *Kiss*
* The designer, Kusume-sama
* My assistants, T-sama, K-sama, and TN-sama
* Those who I met on Twitter who are in the medical/nursing field
* Everyone involved in getting this sold
* My family, friends, and also my readers

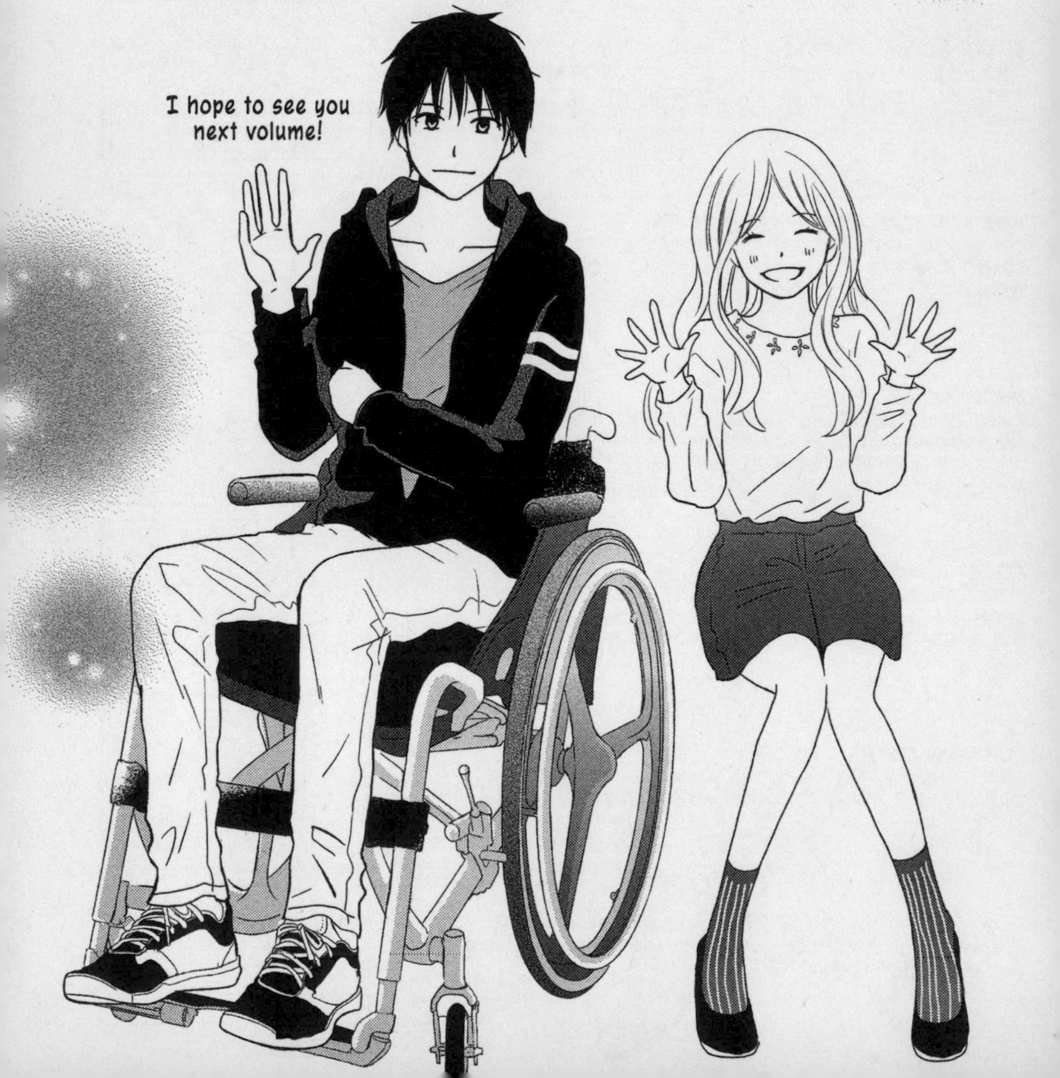
I hope to see you next volume!

TRANSLATION NOTES

GROUNDBREAKING CEREMONY, **PAGE 44**
A GROUNDBREAKING CEREMONY IS IS A PURIFICATION RITUAL THAT CELEBRATES THE CONSTRUCTION OF A BUILDING, AND INVOLVES BREAKING THE GROUND OF LAND OF THE BUILDING SITE FOR THE FIRST TIME.

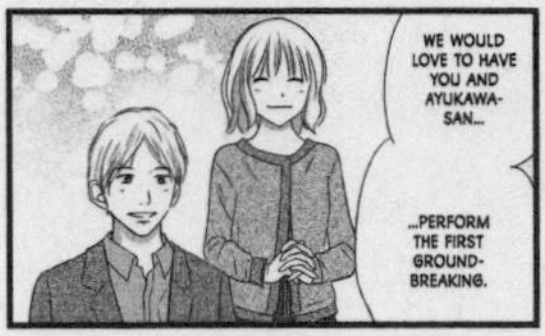
WE WOULD LOVE TO HAVE YOU AND AYUKAWA-SAN...
...PERFORM THE FIRST GROUND-BREAKING.

-SAMA, **PAGE 45**
-SAMA IS A GENDER-NEUTRAL SUFFIX USED TO ADDRESS SOMEONE IN A HIGHLY RESPECTFUL MANNER.

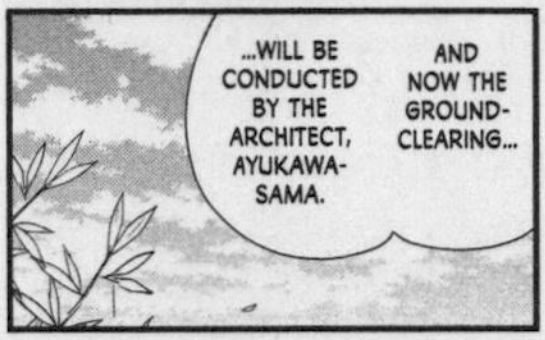
AND NOW THE GROUND-CLEARING...
...WILL BE CONDUCTED BY THE ARCHITECT, AYUKAWA-SAMA.

SHICHI-GO-SAN, **PAGE 62**
SHICHI-GO-SAN IS A JAPANESE HOLIDAY THAT CELEBRATES THE GROWTH OF CHILDREN AGED SEVEN (*SHICHI*), FIVE (*GO*), AND THREE (*SAN*).

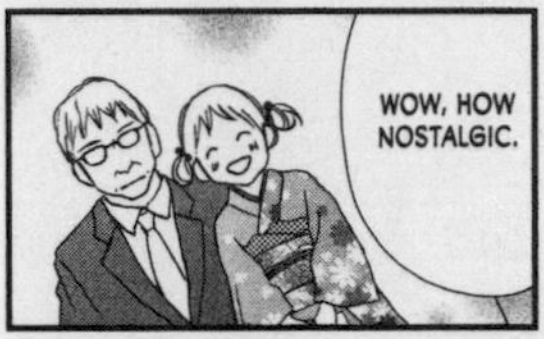
WOW, HOW NOSTALGIC.

FINE FEATHERS MAKE FINE BIRDS, **PAGE 64**
THIS IS A PROVERB THAT MEANS BEAUTIFUL CLOTHES WILL MAKE SOMEONE APPEAR JUST AS BEAUTIFUL AS THE CLOTHES THEY ARE WEARING.

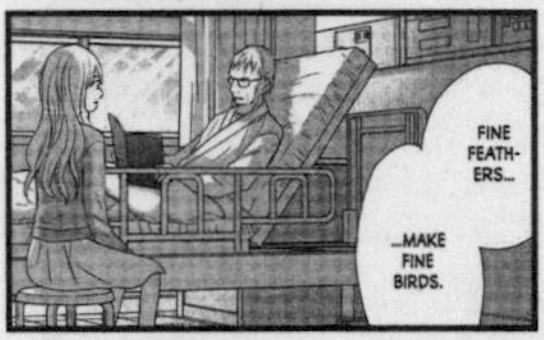
FINE FEATHERS...
...MAKE FINE BIRDS.

SNOW APPLES, **PAGE 69**
SNOW APPLES ARE FRESHLY PICKED APPLES THAT ARE BURIED IN THE SNOW INSIDE CRATES FOR MONTHS TO ENHANCE THEIR TASTE, AND THEN ARE TAKEN OUT IN THE SPRING TO BE EATEN.

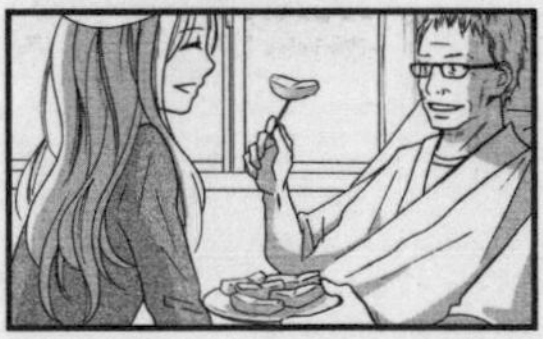

POCARI, **PAGE 108**
POCARI, OR POCARI SWEAT, IS A POPULAR JAPANESE SPORTS DRINK, SUPPOSEDLY FORMULATED TO REPLENISH ALL OF THE NUTRIENTS, IONS, AND ELECTROLYTES LOST FROM SWEATING.

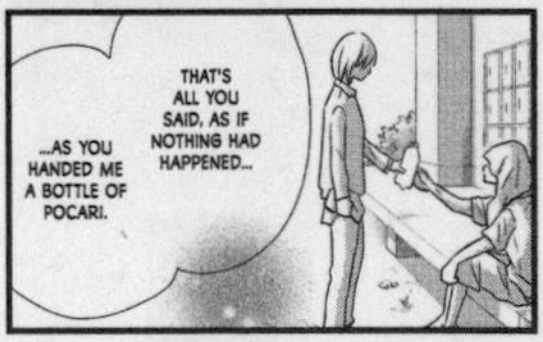
THAT'S ALL YOU SAID, AS IF NOTHING HAD HAPPENED...
...AS YOU HANDED ME A BOTTLE OF POCARI.

NUREAMA NATTO, **PAGE 126**
NUREAMA NATTO ARE FERMENTED SOYBEANS THAT HAVE BEEN SOAKED IN SYRUP AND POWDERED WITH SUGAR.

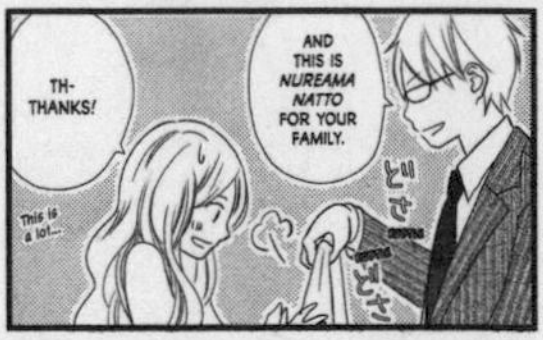
AND THIS IS NUREAMA NATTO FOR YOUR FAMILY.
TH-THANKS!
This is a lot...

"I'M GOING TO LOOK IN YOUR FRIDGE," **PAGE 149**
IN JAPAN, IT IS CONSIDERED IMPOLITE TO LOOK IN SOMEONE ELSE'S FRIDGE WITHOUT ASKING.

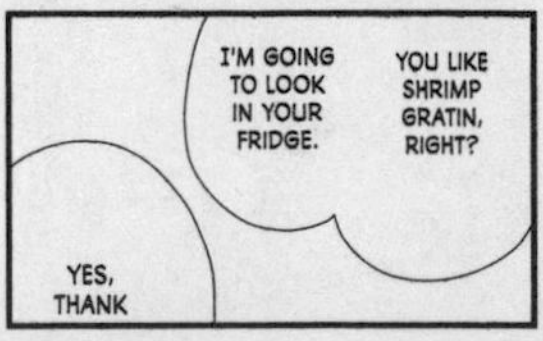
YOU LIKE SHRIMP GRATIN, RIGHT?
I'M GOING TO LOOK IN YOUR FRIDGE.
YES, THANK

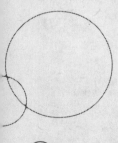

PERFECT WORLD

A SMART, NEW ROMANTIC COMEDY FOR FANS OF *SHORTCAKE CAKE* AND *TERRACE HOUSE*!

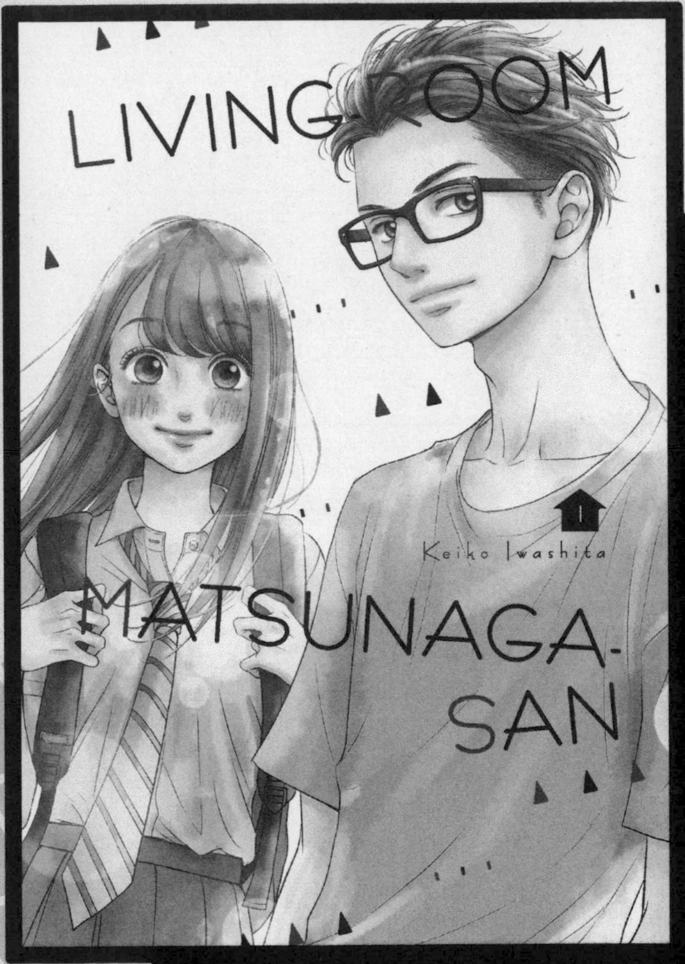
LIVING-ROOM
1
Keiko Iwashita
MATSUNAGA-SAN

A romance manga starring high school girl Meeko, who learns to live on her own in a boarding house whose living room is home to the odd (but handsome) Matsunaga-san. She begins to adjust to her new life away from her parents, but Meeko soon learns that no matter how far away from home she is, she's still a young girl at heart — especially when she finds herself falling for Matsunaga-san.

KC KODANSHA COMICS

Knight of the Ice ©Yayoi Ogawa/Kodansha Ltd.

SKATING THRILLS AND ICY CHILLS WITH THIS NEW TINGLY ROMANCE SERIES!

A rom-com on ice, perfect for fans of *Princess Jellyfish* and *Wotakoi*. Kokoro is the talk of the figure-skating world, winning trophies and hearts. But little do they know... he's actually a huge nerd! From the beloved creator of *You're My Pet* (*Tramps Like Us*).

Chitose is a serious young woman, working for the health magazine *SASSO*. Or at least, she would be, if she wasn't constantly getting distracted by her childhood friend, international figure skating star Kokoro Kijinami! In the public eye and on the ice, Kokoro is a gallant, flawless knight, but behind his glittery costumes and breathtaking spins lies a secret: He's actually a hopelessly romantic otaku, who can only land his quad jumps when Chitose is on hand to recite a spell from his favorite magical girl anime!

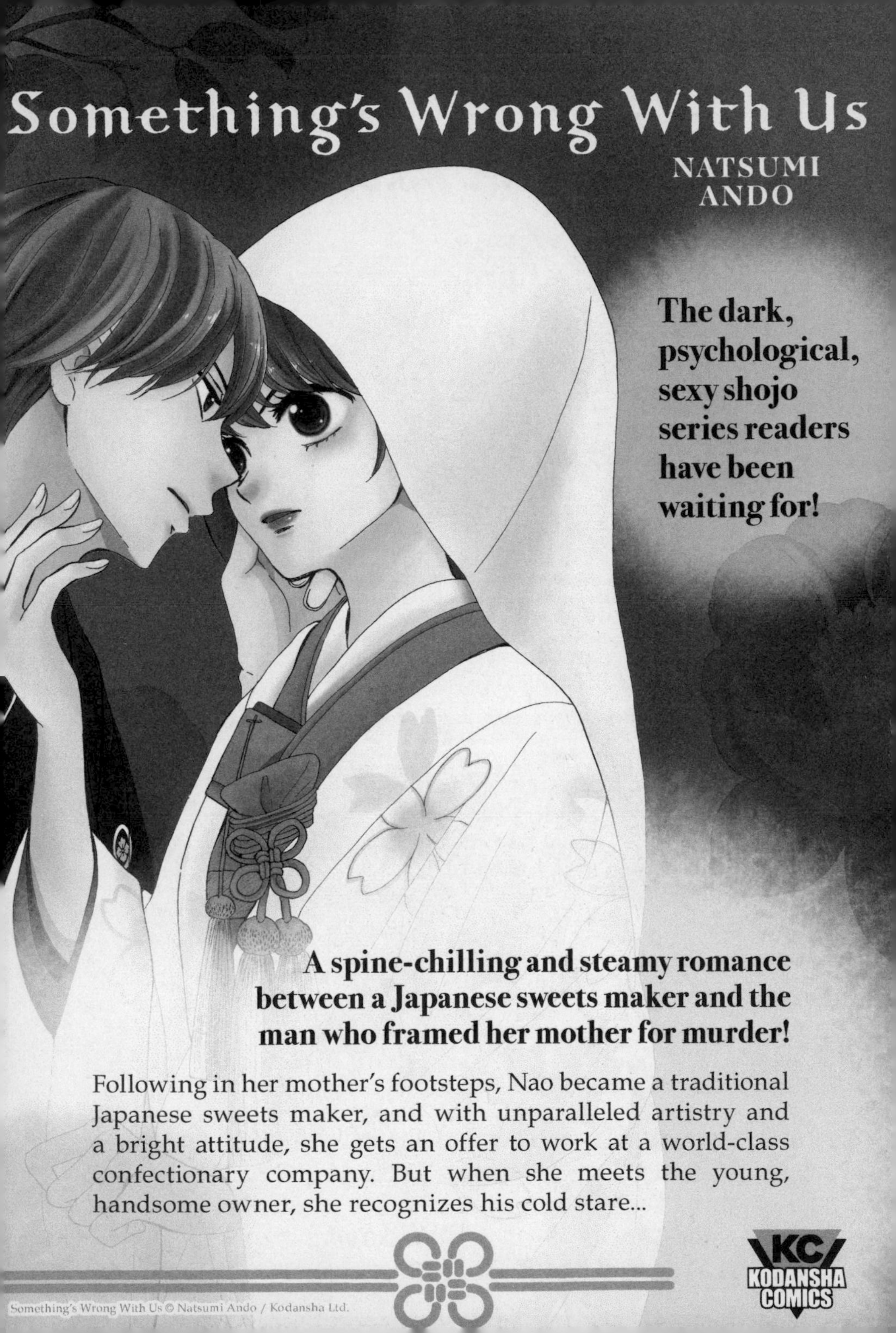
Something's Wrong With Us
NATSUMI ANDO
The dark, psychological, sexy shojo series readers have been waiting for!
A spine-chilling and steamy romance between a Japanese sweets maker and the man who framed her mother for murder!
Following in her mother's footsteps, Nao became a traditional Japanese sweets maker, and with unparalleled artistry and a bright attitude, she gets an offer to work at a world-class confectionary company. But when she meets the young, handsome owner, she recognizes his cold stare...
KC KODANSHA COMICS
Something's Wrong With Us © Natsumi Ando / Kodansha Ltd.

THE SWEET SCENT OF LOVE IS IN THE AIR! FOR FANS OF OFFBEAT ROMANCES LIKE *WOTAKOI*

Sweat and Soap © Kintetsu Yamada / Kodansha Ltd.

In an office romance, there's a fine line between sexy and awkward... and that line is where Asako — a woman who sweats copiously — meets Koutarou — a perfume developer who can't get enough of Asako's, er, scent. Don't miss a romcom manga like no other!

One of CLAMP's biggest hits returns in this definitive, premium, hardcover 20th anniversary collector's edition!

CLAMP

Chobits 1

20TH ANNIVERSARY EDITION

"A wonderfully entertaining story that would be a great installment in anybody's manga collection."
— Anime News Network

"CLAMP is an all-female manga-creating team whose feminine touch shows in this entertaining, sci-fi soap opera."
— Publishers Weekly

Chobits © CLAMP·ShigatsuTsuitachi CO.,LTD./Kodansha Ltd.

Poor college student Hideki is down on his luck. All he wants is a good job, a girlfriend, and his very own "persocom"—the latest and greatest in humanoid computer technology. Hideki's luck changes one night when he finds Chi—a persocom thrown out in a pile of trash. But Hideki soon discovers that there's much more to his cute new persocom than meets the eye.

KC
KODANSHA
COMICS

CUTE ANIMALS AND LIFE LESSONS, PERFECT FOR ASPIRING PET VETS OF ALL AGES!

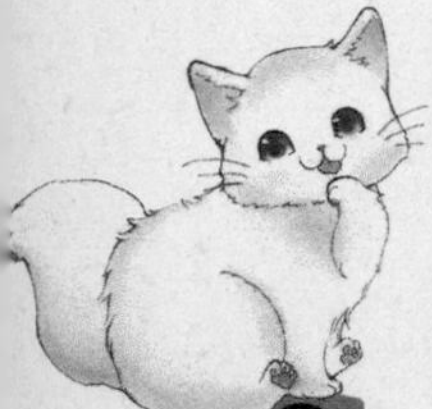

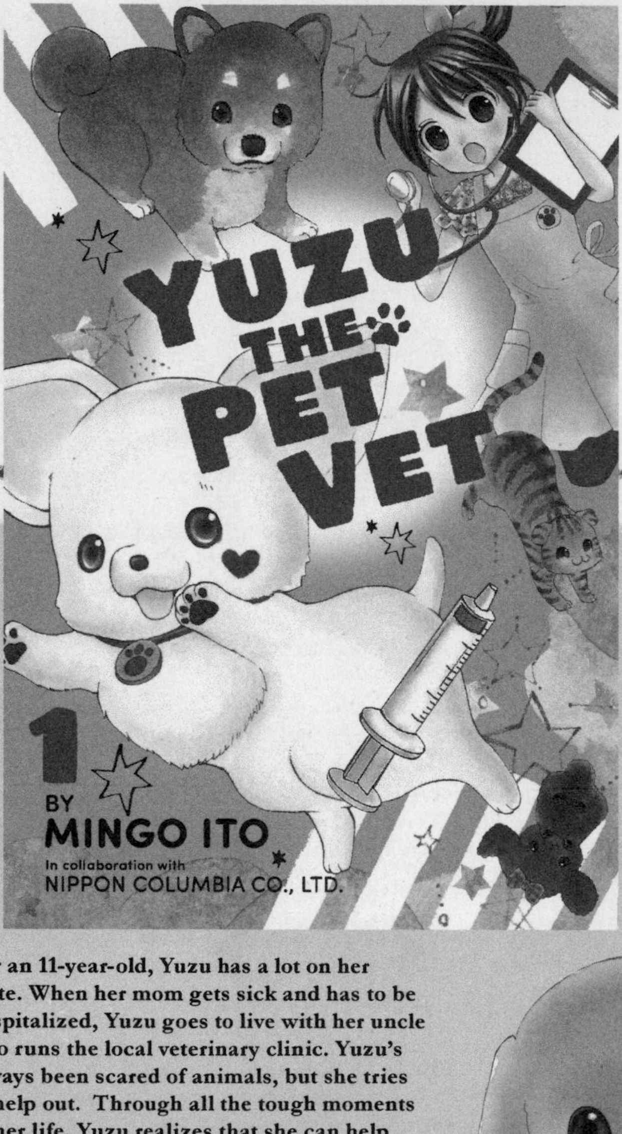
YUZU THE PET VET
1
BY
MINGO ITO
In collaboration with
NIPPON COLUMBIA CO., LTD.

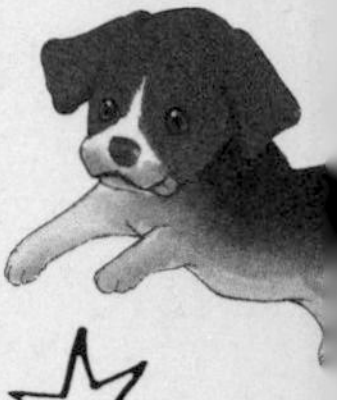

For an 11-year-old, Yuzu has a lot on her plate. When her mom gets sick and has to be hospitalized, Yuzu goes to live with her uncle who runs the local veterinary clinic. Yuzu's always been scared of animals, but she tries to help out. Through all the tough moments in her life, Yuzu realizes that she can help make things all right with a little help from her animal pals, peers, and kind grown-ups.

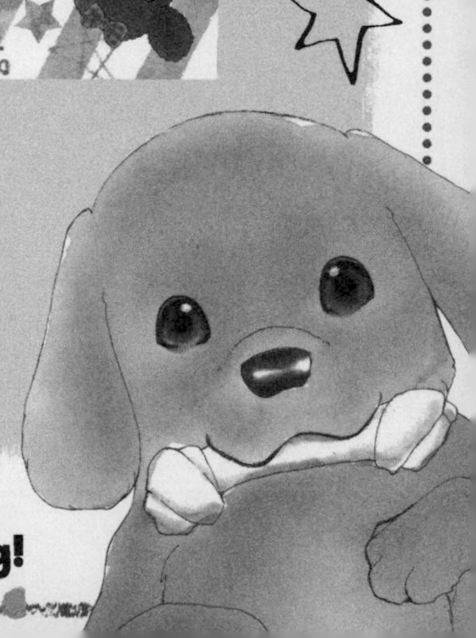

Every new patient is a furry friend in the making!

Perfect World 4 is a work of fiction. Names, characters, places, and incidents are the products of the author's imagination or are used fictitiously. Any resemblance to actual events, locales, or persons, living or dead, is entirely coincidental.

Published in the United States by Kodansha Comics, an imprint of Kodansha USA Publishing, LLC, New York.

Publication rights for this English edition arranged through Kodansha Ltd., Tokyo.

First published in Japan in 2016 by Kodansha Ltd., Tokyo as *Perfect World*, volume 4.

ISBN 978-1-64651-058-0

Original cover design by Tomohiro Kusume and Maiko Mori (arcoinc)

Printed in the United States of America.

www.kodanshacomics.com

9 8 7 6 5 4 3 2 1
Translation: Rachel Murakawa
Lettering: Thea Willis
Additional lettering: Sara Linsley
Editing: Jesika Brooks and Tiff Ferentini
Kodansha Comics edition cover design by Phil Balsman

KC
KODANSHA COMICS

Publisher: Kiichiro Sugawara

Director of publishing services: Ben Applegate
Associate director of operations: Stephen Pakula
Publishing services managing editor: Noelle Webster
Assistant production manager: Emi Lotto, Angela Zurlo